Classic Hikes
IN THE
Canadian Rockies

Graeme Pole

Mountain Vision Publishing
Hazelton, British Columbia, Canada

Researched and written by Graeme Pole.
Additional fieldwork and material by Marnie Pole
Editor: Marnie Pole
Design and maps: Scott Manktelow Design, Canmore, Alberta
Photo scanning and processing: Graeme Pole
Printed and bound in Canada by Friesens, Altona, Manitoba, on FSC paper using vegetable-based inks.

FSC
MIX
Paper from responsible sources
www.fsc.org   FSC® C016245

The author has taken the greatest care to ensure that the information in this book was accurate at the time of publication. Neither the author or publisher can be held responsible for any consequences arising from your use of this information.

Mountain Vision Publishing will donate one percent of the net proceeds from this book to Trees for the Future:
  🖥 www.treesftf.org

Library and Archives Canada Cataloguing in Publication

Pole, Graeme, 1956-
    Classic hikes in the Canadian Rockies / Graeme Pole. -- 3rd ed.

Includes bibliographical references and index.
ISBN 978-0-9697249-4-0

1. Rocky Mountains, Canadian (B.C. and Alta.)--Guidebooks.
2. Hiking--Rocky Mountains, Canadian (B.C. and Alta.)--Guidebooks. I. Title.

FC219.P643 2011   917.1104'4
C2010-907636-2

Distributed by Alpine Book Peddlers
140 - 105 Bow Meadows Crescent, Canmore, Alberta, T1W 2W8
) 403-678-2280, 866-478-2280
) Fax: 403-978-2280, 866-978-2840
  🖥 www.alpinebookpeddlers.com
  ✉ info@alpinebookpeddlers.ca

Please support your local, independent bookseller.

Mountain Vision Publishing
Hazelton, British Columbia, Canada
  🖥 www.mountainvision.ca
  ✉ Graeme@mountainvision.ca

9 8 7 6 5 4 3 2 1

> *As tangible results of the journey we had explored and mapped a snowfield of 30 square miles and 2 valleys not before travelled by white men; but the real gain was the filling of our lungs with mountain air, besides renewing our acquaintance with mountain trails, those capricious, tantalizing, exasperating and yet wholly seductive pathways, leading through bogs and fallen timber nowhere, and yet opening out the sublime things of the world and giving many an unforeseen glimpse of Nature hard at work constructing a world.*
>
> A.P. Coleman; *The Canadian Rockies, New and Old Trails*

Front cover: *Near Boulder Pass, Skoki trail, Banff National Park*

Back cover:
Main image: *Greater "Lake in the Sky," Iceline, Yoho National Park*
Lower images, l-r: *Athabasca River, Jasper National Park; Hoary marmot; On Badger Pass, Banff National Park; Glacier lily; Saskatchewan Glacier, Parker Ridge, Banff National Park*

Spine: *Twin Falls, Yoho Valley, Yoho National Park*

Title page: *Angel and Cavell glaciers, Cavell Meadows trail, Jasper National Park*

Page 4: *Iceline, Yoho National Park*

Page 5: *Mt. Louis, Cory Pass trail, Banff National Park*

Contents

The Classic Hikes

Acknowledgements

This book will soon be into its third decade of providing information to hikers in the Canadian Rockies. No one person could keep a handle on the many minor changes and the few major changes that have, during that interval, directly and indirectly affected the trails described. Updating the information has been enjoyable because of the willing assistance offered by many knowledgeable people.

Don Gorrie, Backcountry Facilities Manager, reviewed text for Banff National Park. Kim Baines, Backcountry Facilities Manager, and Jenny Klafki, External Relations Manager, reviewed text for Yoho, Kootenay, and northern Banff national parks. Roger Hostins, Visitor Centres Manager, provided additional information. A willing team vetted the Jasper material: Gord Antoniuk, Karen Beyers, Shawn Cardiff, Kim Forster, Ben Gadd, Cia Gadd, Greg Horne, Wayne Kennedy, Loni Klettle, Wendy Niven, Jim Suttill, Bert Wade, Vicki Wallace, and Kim Weir. Brad Romaniuk, Backcountry Coordinator, provided additional information. Edwin Knox, Bill Thorpe, and Locke Marshall, Visitor Experience Manager, reviewed text for Waterton Lakes National Park. Wayne Van Velzen commented on the Mt. Robson text. Wayne Sobool, Senior Park Ranger, reviewed the text for Mt. Assiniboine Provincial Park. Kim Winter, Senior Park Ranger, and Edwin Knox reviewed the Forum Lake – Wall Lake hike. Duane Fizor, Information Services Coordinator for Kananaskis Country, reviewed the K-Country hikes. Randy Axani, Kananaskis District Conservation Officer, provided additional information.

When I couldn't find an answer in his *Handbook of the Canadian Rockies* or *Canadian Rockies Geology Road Tours*, I tagged Ben Gadd with questions. Ben kindly provided answers and proofed passages on geology. Roger McQueen, retired geologist with the Geological Survey of Canada, provided detailed information on the naming of the McConnell Thrust. Text describing emergency preparedness and first-aid was reviewed by Dr. Jeff Boyd, Medical Director, Emergency Department, Banff Mineral Springs Hospital, and by Tim Auger, former Public Safety Supervisor for Banff National Park. Mike Gibeau, Carnivore Specialist for Parks Canada, reviewed text describing bears and bear safety. Dr. Desmond Collins, Curator in Charge of Invertebrate Paleontology at the Royal Ontario Museum, reviewed the text on the Burgess Shale. Mindy Brugman reviewed passages that describe glacial processes and climate change. Wildlife biologists, George Mercer and Jesse Whittington reviewed material on the mountain caribou. Andy MacKinnon reviewed portions of the text that describe vegetation. Jim Pojar added comments. Ian Pengelly, Vegetation Specialist, reviewed relevant text for Banff National Park. Park staff, Derek Petersen, Alan Dibb, Terry Damm, and John Niddrie fielded questions for Kootenay and Yoho. Rick Collier provided forensic help with some mountain identifications. Diane and Mike McIvor brought decades of experience as naturalists to bear on a few passages of text. Donna Nelson helped with maps. Lena Goon and D.L. Cameron at the Whyte Museum assisted with photos. David Richard Boyd provided an expert opinion on environmental legislation in Canada. Professor Dave Cruden, Department of Civil Engineering, University of Alberta, ferreted out a paper that describes the Palliser Slide, and proofed my subsequent attempt to paraphrase it. Dr. David Schindler, Killiam Memorial Professor of Ecology, Department of Biological Sciences at the University of Alberta, explained the process behind atmospheric pollution of glacial lakes. I am grateful to the late Eleanor Romp for her assistance, and to my parents, Grace and Ernie Pole. Peggy Muir and Phil Muir provided working space in Hazelton, frequently allowing me to plop my mobile office on their dining room table at all hours.

With all this expert help, I should have everything right, but…. When you see an error, please visit mountainvision.ca and send me an e-mail.

I was blessed with the generosity and the company of friends who opened their homes during the fieldwork for the second and third editions of this book: Cia and Ben Gadd, Diane and Mike McIvor, Nadine Delorme and Mike Henderson, Ann and John Henderson, Alice Wagenaar and Edwin Knox, Nadine Fletcher and Joel Hagan, Samantha and Doug McConnery, Jill and Basil Seaton, and Alex Taylor.

I am grateful to Robert Bateman for writing the Foreword to this edition, and to Alex Fischer and Kate Brotchie for their assistance in this regard.

SPECIAL ACKNOWLEDGEMENT

Throughout the three editions of this book, Marnie Pole has been a champion of the project. Since we began "work" with a hike to Aylmer Pass in May 1992, Marnie has logged thousands of kilometres on trail and hundreds of hours proofing text and vetting photographs. She has contributed countless ideas for the written and visual material, and has been a great force behind getting required work done in the time available, and in keeping our family on the trail as children came along. I am certain that having two focused minds at work on this project has more than doubled the richness and the quality of the book that you now hold in your hands. Thank you, Marnie.

Foreword

By Robert Bateman

A Parks Canada official in Jasper National Park recently told me a troubling fact. When many families drive the Icefields Parkway – which ranks as one of the more beautiful highways in the world – it is often the case that the kids in the back seat do not even look out the window. They are too busy staring at electronic screens while they watch movies or play games.

A juggernaut is rolling over our younger generation. It has bleak implications for the future of our species and the futures of other species on this planet. The typical 14-year old North American spends more than 7 hours a day staring at electronic screens. If their world is not the real world but has become one of fantasy and entertainment, what kinds of parents and voters will they be ... what kinds of stewards for the planet?

Hiking, in its fundamental form, offers a great antidote to this malaise. It can stimulate mind, body, and spirit. On the other hand, there exists a certain segment among the outdoor-minded that promotes more of an ego-relationship with nature than an eco-relationship. A conquest complex can develop, which brings a self-centered obliviousness to the wonder of wild places. I would hope that hikers do not rush heedlessly along the trails, but move mindfully through the varied worlds made possible by them. This book helps to create that reality by describing pathways that provide points of contact with, and appreciation for, resident species and natural processes.

A well-trodden trail causes some deterioration of nature but much less than if we were to each crash helter-skelter through the bush. There is no doubt in my mind that the future of the planet and the human race will be better served by the collective experience of those who hike on established paths in the mountains and elsewhere, especially if they allow the resulting wonder to help shape their lives.

NOTICE OF ASSUMPTION OF RISK

Hiking, backpacking, backcountry travel, and backcountry camping may expose you to dangers. These include, but are not limited to: getting lost, black bears and grizzly bears, aggressive wildlife, insect bites and diseases, rough trails, unbridged streams, unfenced canyons, exposed cliff edges, slippery footing, log bridges, suspension bridges, hunting, inclement weather, lightning, forest fires, falling trees, contaminated drinking water, avalanches, late-lying snow, rockfalls, mudslides, and flash-floods. There are places on some of these hikes where if you slip and fall, you will probably die. But perhaps the greatest danger – more so because it is the least considered – is travelling on the highway to and from trailheads. Summer traffic in the Canadian Rockies is often heavy and chaotic. Drive with caution.

I have hiked every trail in this book at least once. Some I have travelled more than 40 times. My aim has been to render trail descriptions with clarity, accuracy, and safety in mind. However, conditions in the backcountry are not static.

Nature rules. Bridges and trail signs may or may not be present as described in the text, and the locations of stream crossings, avalanche deposits, snow patches, and ice-cored moraines may change from year to year. Park regulations may differ from those described. Trail closures may be in effect.

Although this book contains ample information to assist you in preparing for safe backcountry travel, you alone are responsible for your welfare while on the trail, while camping, and while otherwise travelling in the Rockies. Neither the author or the publisher can be held responsible for any difficulties, injuries, disabilities, misfortune, or loss of property or income that arises from using the information presented.

In this book, "backpacking" means to hike and to camp self-sufficiently in the backcountry. It does not imply that any of the services associated with low-budget travel (also called "backpacking" in Europe and Australasia) will be present.

Opabin Plateau, Yoho National Park

Preface

When I first came to the Rockies, the landscape held secrets and kept secrets. I was hard-pressed to find someone who had been where I wanted to go in the backcountry. There was one trail guide – an atlas of sorts. I chose an outing and went discovering. Surprises came at almost every turn.

Thirty years later, the landscape harbours few secrets. The backcountry of the Rockies has been given away in a glut of guidebooks and on a myriad websites. About the only surprises left are sudden changes in the weather and encounters with wildlife. I realize that I have played a role in this, but the three editions of this book have not included, as a principal trail, any outing that was not already an established route. While encouraging active and respectful appreciation of the backcountry of the Rockies, I have attempted to keep a finger in the dyke.

The argument that we must send more people into wild places so that they can come back and speak for wilderness preservation is a fallacious, often self-serving axiom. Quite obviously, a wild place no longer is, when it becomes peopled in any significant way. The value in going somewhere special in the natural world is not in turning it into a commodity, but in honouring it; in holding its essence in our heart and our soul when we return. We, as a culture, are losing our ability to honour most things. Hiking can help to retrain us in this most fundamental and necessary of human traits.

Respect for the land is an early casualty when every nook and cranny is opened up to experience. Wild species and wild processes soon follow. Whether it be a new logging road that offers easy access to a formerly inaccessible place, or a new guidebook description that sets a parade of boots to untrammeled mountain heather or ancient ridgetop screes, the effect is the same. The land soon becomes devoid of secrets, and is consumed by our culture as are most other things. Time to head over the next ridge, partner. But in a curious parallel, the insatiable wilderness-seeker becomes akin to the wild species being displaced by incursions of people – always in quest of profitable habitat where little remains.

What wilderness requires of us, and what we as a culture correspondingly lack, are the collective willingness and discipline to leave some places alone. We must, in our hearts and minds, be able to come to peace with the concept that beautiful, wild places exist and, perhaps, abound, but that we as a culture, individually and collectively, do not have to experience every one of them.

The outings in this book describe established routes into a variety of landscapes that are the essence of the Canadian Rockies. This is a place unlike any other. Many of those who know it well consider it sacred. Let us not run roughshod in the cathedral.

> There is told, in the Northwest, the story of an old prospector of whom, returning home after many years, it was asked what he had to show as the equivalent of so much lost time; and he answered only, "I have seen the Rocky Mountains."
>
> James Monroe Thorington; *The Glittering Mountains of Canada*

Carthew Summit, Waterton Lakes National Park

A Mountain Marvel

The Canadian Rockies are part of one of the world's great mountain regions – the Western Cordillera (core-dee-YAIR-ah) – which includes all of the mountains of western North America. The Rocky Mountains are the backbone of this region and of the continent, extending from New Mexico to Alaska. The Canadian Rockies proper are the subset range of mountains stretching from Marias Pass in Glacier National Park, Montana in the south, to near the Liard River in northern British Columbia (BC). In the southern part of the range, which is the focus of this book, the Rockies are oriented southeast to northwest along the continental divide. This height of land is the boundary between the provinces of Alberta and BC, and separates rivers that flow to the Atlantic Ocean or the Arctic Ocean, from rivers that flow to the Pacific Ocean.

The Canadian Rockies appear different from other mountain ranges. The reasons for their distinctive appearance are not unique – they are sedimentary mountains in a northern climate, shaped by recent and present-day glaciation. However, the arrangement of these details has created a mountain biome whose features *are* unique. The details are also remarkably consistent throughout the range, from north to south, from east to west.

During mountain creation, the peaks were thrust skyward, when huge slabs of rock piled up, moving from southwest to northeast. You see this best in the front ranges of Banff, Jasper, and Kananaskis

Country – where parallel ranges of steeply dipping, gray limestone peaks stand like waves made of stone. Along the continental divide in Banff and Jasper, the thrust sheets were not tipped as steeply. The rock formations lie more typically in horizontal layers, which have been eroded to create castle-like peaks.

Hiking puts you boots to rubble with this geology, and usually, you are following a path carved by a glacier. Moving ice has chunked away at these mountains. Again and again as you hike, you will encounter variations on the glacial blueprint: you approach along a broad, U-shaped valley; you climb steeply to a waterfall-graced, hanging valley; then hike through meadows and boulderfields to the destination lake or pass at its head, perhaps with a relict glacier in view. Because most of the glaciation has taken place relatively recently in geologic terms (within the past 30,000 years), the mountains are still raw, with sharp edges and many abrupt points of transition – the Wow! places.

The geology also affects what grows where and what lives where. As you become familiar with these mountains, you will find yourself sensing the transitions in the forest and in the ground cover that will take place at the top of a headwall, over the crest of a ridge, or where the trail draws alongside a glacier. You will begin to learn where to look for certain wildlife and plant species. You will become hooked, as so many other hikers have been, into the boundless fascination of the many intricacies of this mountain marvel.

Getting to the Rockies and Getting Around

Calgary and Edmonton are the principal entry points to the Canadian Rockies. It's easy getting that far but regional public transportation is, alas, something of an endangered species in the mountains. If you will be visiting for a week or more and can afford to, rent a car. All of the major agencies are represented in Calgary, Edmonton, Canmore, Banff, and Jasper. Greyhound Canada provides inter-city bus transportation on Highways 1 and 93 South, and on the Highway 16 through Jasper. Brewster Transportation provides bus service between Calgary airport, Kananaskis Village, Canmore, Banff, Lake Louise, and Jasper. For other transportation contacts, see pp. 280-81.

If you don't have wheels, you can sometimes find a ride by talking to people in campgrounds and hostels, or in town. If you hitchhike (not recommended), make a cardboard sign that shows your destination. For trails that begin and end at locations greatly distant from each other, make transportation arrangements for the end of your hike in advance. Otherwise, plan to arrive at trail's end early enough in the day to avoid being benighted in a parking lot. Most roads are not well travelled after dark.

On the Trail

When you hike in the Rockies, you need to be prepared and self-reliant. Help is seldom close at hand.

No matter how experienced, every hiker from time to time encounters difficult situations. In the Rockies, these could include a bear encounter, a squirrel or jay eating your food, a lost or broken backpack, a fall into a river, a fall on a patch of late-lying snow, a mid-summer blizzard, and injury or illness. In addition, there are the hazards that you might create by attempting an outing that is beyond your ability, or by venturing off-trail into hazardous terrain.

SOLITUDE, PLEASE

While travelling in the backcountry, we should recognize the intangible spiritual value of the Canadian Rockies, and act in a manner that does not tarnish that value or the safety of others.

- Respect the right of others to solitude. Hike and camp in small groups. Do not use cell-phones except for emergency calls. Use portable music devices only with ear-gear, and only while at camp.
- Share the facilities provided.
- Those hiking downhill have the right of way. Yield to them.
- Step to the downhill side of the trail to allow horse parties to pass. Do not speak or make any movement that might startle the horses.
- Fish odors attract bears. Do not fish on overnight trips. Anglers should dispose of fish viscera properly.

A HOME BETWEEN HIKES

You can choose from hundreds of hotels, motels, and B&Bs in Canmore, Banff, Lake Louise, Field, Jasper, Hinton, Mt. Robson, Valemount, Tete Jaune Cache, Golden, Radium, Invermere, and Waterton. Make reservations well in advance (see p. 281) or check at a park information centre for assistance. If you are on a budget, your choices are hostels and frontcountry campgrounds. Again, check at a park information centre. Some of the campgrounds have showers; all have cook shelters, but none has dorms, cabins or kitchens.

If you are travelling on foot or by bicycle, the following summarizes the Classic Hikes that are reasonably close to frontcountry campgrounds or hostels. "CG" means campground.

Hike	Accommodation/Campground
Aylmer Pass, C-Level Cirque	Two Jack Main and Lakeside CGs
Rockbound Lake, Castle Lookout	Castle Mountain CG and hostel
The Beehives, Saddleback Pass, Paradise Valley, Skoki	Lake Louise CG and hostel
Mosquito Creek, Dolomite Pass	Mosquito Creek CG and hostel
Brazeau, Wilcox Pass	Columbia Icefield CG, Wilcox Creek CG, Hilda Creek hostel
Fryatt Valley	Athabasca Falls hostel, Mt. Kerkeslin CG
Cavell Meadows, Tonquin Valley	Mt. Edith Cavell hostel
Maligne Canyon	Maligne Canyon hostel
Berg Lake	Robson River CG, Robson Meadows CG
Iceline, Yoho – Little Yoho	Takakkaw Falls CG, Whiskey Jack hostel
Mt. Allan	Kananaskis Wilderness hostel
South Kananaskis Pass, North Kananaskis Pass	Interlakes CG, Mt. Sarrail CG
Bertha Lake, Crypt Lake	Waterton CG

Big wolf, little wolf

The principal wildlife hazards are bears, elk, moose, and wood ticks. You will find a thorough discussion of bear safety on pp. 275-78. Please read it before you hike. Avoid elk, moose, and other deer family members during the autumn rut and in spring when calves are born. Keep at least 30 m away from any large mammal, especially if it is with young. The bite of the wood tick can cause complications. Check yourself for ticks and tick bites after hiking in May and June. Wolves may take a curious look at you or your camp but, at press time, they had not attacked people in the Rockies. However, please note that wolves in the Rockies are becoming less wary. Coyotes and cougars have attacked people, and encounters are becoming more common. Be especially cautious of these animals if you encounter them when you are hiking with children. If any large mammal other than a bear approaches, group together and scare it off by making loud noises and by waving your arms over your head. Do not hike while wearing earphones or buds – you need to hear what is going on around you to ensure your safety.

Porcupines, red squirrels, ground squirrels, chipmunks, marmots, martens, wolverines, jays, and ravens can raid your food supply and damage unattended equipment around camp. There are no poisonous spiders, venomous snakes or scorpions in the Rockies. Bees, wasps, and hornets are a concern only to those prone to systemic allergic reactions.

In an emergency, preparedness will be your best ally. Keep calm and think your predicament through. In general, your first option in the face of backcountry calamity should be to consider retreat. If you must spend another night out, pitch camp quickly in order to stay warm and dry. Don't worry about using a designated campground in a true emergency. Carry reliable, lightweight equipment. Ensure that each person in the party knows how to operate the stove and set up the tent, and is aware of the hiking route, potential exit routes, and the locations of campgrounds and park patrol cabins. Although there is no guarantee of finding help at these locations, they are the best initial destinations in an emergency when you are more than a day's hike from the trailhead. Your party should carry a first-aid kit. Skills you should practise

BLACK OR GRIZZLY?

	Black	Grizzly
Colour	Typically black, but can be any shade of brown	Typically brown with silver highlights to fur
Muzzle	Long and conical	Short, face is "dish-shaped," nose is upturned
Shoulder hump	None	Prominent
Ears	Pointed	Rounded
Claws	Short	Long

Black bear
rounded back
no shoulder hump
uniform sheen to coat
ears flat
narrow face
straight muzzle
shorter claws

Grizzly bear
prominent shoulder hump
larger ears
broad face
dished muzzle
"grizzled" highlights on fur
long claws

are treatment for ck, management of fractures and sprains using in provised splints, and hemorrhage control. See pp. 271-72.

It would be nice to set off into the backcountry on your own terms, to make your own rules or to go without them. But practice has shown that an "anything goes" approach soon results in a ruined wilderness. For a list of regulations that govern hiking and backcountry use, please see pp. 259-60.

Leaving Word

Whether you are going on a day-hike or a multiday backpacking trip, write down your itinerary and leave it with a responsible person. Specify the number in your party, your route, where you intend to camp, and when you will be completing your trip. Describe your vehicle, its licence plate number, and where it will be parked. Tell your contact person when to report you as overdue, and where to make the report.

If you don't live in the Rockies, and you are hiking in a national park, you may use the voluntary registration system to ensure that someone will be looking for you if you are overdue. (Provincial parks do not offer this service.) Contact a park information centre for details.

Whichever of these two safety plans you choose, always carry an extra night's rations with you in the event that your trip takes longer than planned. Even on a day-hike close to the highway you should be equipped for extremes of weather and for the possibility of having to stay out overnight. You don't have to carry sleeping gear on day-hikes. However,

HIGH-COUPS

High: far above ground or sea level
Coup: a notable or successful stroke or move
  Canadian Oxford Dictionary

The haiku is a traditional form of Japanese poetry. It is brief, incorporating three phrases. English translations of classical haiku run about 12 syllables, although modern English writers who imitate the haiku style often stretch things out to 17 syllables, with the three phrases counted thus: 5/7/5. The haiku's brevity is its beauty. Thoughts cannot be fully described; only their essence can be suggested. Traditional haiku incorporated a word or a figure of speech that referred to the season being described. Over the centuries this requirement has broadened but it is still generally true that a haiku is used to describe the natural world and the experience of the writer in it. What better place than on a trail in the Canadian Rockies to go poetic in this style?

Here are a couple of haiku-like pieces:

Limestone, water, cliff:
I walk; I listen.
Rock music.

Reaching,
I touch a falling raindrop.
This is where the sky begins.

Have a go. If you would like to share your creations, e-mail them to me, and I will post them on the Mountain Vision website.

YOUR TIME IN THE CANADIAN ROCKIES

Nature is never boring. Being outdoors in nature is never a waste of time. But, of course, almost everyone's schedule dictates some degree of urgency. You probably want to cram in as much experience as possible. If you are from afar and have only a week or two to spend, you may strike gold and have your visit coincide with a monster high-pressure ridge. Every day will be stellar. After a week, you will be craving for a cloud or two to bring some shade each mid-afternoon. You will be staggered by awe; close to bursting with the ice-wrought, tumbling stream, meadow-decked, chiselled-stone beauty of this place. Your memory cards – built-in and outboard – will be full.

The more typical experience will be a mix of weather. Capitalizing on it will require some flexibility on your part. Aim long and high on the beauty days, around about treeline on the fickle ones, and take rest on the days when the weather shuts you down. The hikes chosen for this book present options that will make this possible.

The mountains run the show. You can't "do" the Rockies in a day. Given the fortunes of decades spent trying, with a body that held out and better than average luck with the weather, you couldn't "do" the Rockies in a lifetime. There will always be another valley to ascend, another ridge to top, another pass to cross. The unknown will always beckon. What you *can* do is come to know this place in your own way, at your own pace, in whatever time you have available. Slow down, let the mountains work their way into your bones through the soles of your boots, through the very fabric of your being. Treasure the moments along a nondescript, wooded stream, ten minutes from the car at the beginning of an outing, as much as the mind-opening vista from the destination pass, half a day's hike into the sky. Stop for each of them and let some time go by. In the greater picture, wooded glade and craggy pass are equal pieces of the same beautiful, never-quite-complete journey. Keep travelling.

warm clothing, rain gear, extra food, a space blanket, and any essential daily medications should be in your pack.

Weathering the Heights

Hiking trails in the Rockies are generally clear of snow from late-May to early-October at low elevations, and from mid-June to mid-September higher up. At treeline, the average annual temperature is -4°C, and more than 75 percent of the precipitation falls as snow. In the high country you will frequently encounter snow, whether freshly fallen or lingering from last winter. After a few outings you may agree with some locals, who describe the climate of the Rockies as "nine months of winter, and three months of poor skiing." In summer, you can count on rain about one day in three.

GRIDLOCK AND RUSH HOURS

Solitude is hard to find on some of the day-hikes. The hectic hours are between 10:00 a.m. and 3:00 p.m., with fair weather days being the busiest. Parking lots at Moraine Lake, Lake Louise, and Mt. Edith Cavell will be jammed during these times. Avoid nearby trails. The other trails that experience a mid-day crush are Bow Glacier Falls, Parker Ridge, Wilcox Pass, Maligne Canyon, Bald Hills, Chester Lake, and Ptarmigan Cirque.

The prevailing weather systems arrive from the southwest. The trend is for more precipitation on the western side of the continental divide – Yoho, northern Kootenay, and Mt. Robson. In May and June, "upslope" storms – which arrive from the east – can plague Banff and Jasper. During these times, the weather may improve if you travel west to Yoho, Kootenay or Mt. Robson. On days when the weather is mixed, marked changes often occur a short distance away. For example, if it is raining at Lake Louise, it might be partly cloudy with the odd shower north of Bow Summit, or in Yoho or Kootenay.

To obtain Environment Canada's online forecasts:
💻 www.weatheroffice.ec.gc.ca

Select the Alberta or BC page and navigate to the forecasts for Banff, Jasper, Waterton Park, Yoho Park, Kootenay Park, or Valemount (for Mt. Robson). You can also access satellite imagery and other weather resources. To obtain free recorded forecasts any time:
- 403-762-2088 (Banff, Canmore, Kananaskis)
- 780-852-3185 (Jasper, Mt. Robson)

Reading the Hike Descriptions

Each hike begins with a snapshot that tells you:
- if it is a day-hike or an overnight excursion
- the best time of day (when relevant) for viewing the destination(s)
- how to get to the trailhead
- any quotas, access restrictions, and special considerations that may apply

MINIMUM IMPACT TRAVEL

When backpacking became popular in the 1970s, "no-trace" camping and hiking was the buzz. The idealism was short-lived, butting against the harsh edge of clumsy human reality. It is not possible for most mortals to move without leaving a trace in the landscape but, with a concerted effort, it is possible to minimize impacts. The "how-to" is easily listed; putting the bits and pieces into practice is a challenge. Read the following before each hike. At trail's end, review these items to see if you can make improvements on your next outing.

- Inform yourself about where you are going and what to expect. Plan ahead; prepare and equip yourself appropriately.
- Keep to maintained trails.
- Concentrate your impacts in high use areas.
- Spread your impacts in pristine areas.
- Avoid places where human impacts are beginning to show, and places which are recovering from impacts.
- Walk through snow, muck, and puddles to stay on the trail.
- Keep off sections of trail that are closed for rehabilitation.
- Keep to the trail on switchbacks.
- Pack out all your trash, and pick up any left by others. Make the effort to recycle what you can.

- Cigarette butts and spent matches are litter, too. Pack them out.
- Protect freshwater. Be responsible with human waste and dishwashing. Use the facilities provided.
- Use a campstove for cooking.
- Use fires responsibly, only where permitted, and only when necessary. Gather firewood carefully.
- Do not remove or disturb natural objects.
- Respect wildlife. Do not feed them. Keep at least 30 m away from large mammals, especially when they are with young. Leave your dog at home.

- the landmarks along the route, and accompanying distances
- the NTS and Gem Trek map(s)
- possible variations.

If you are a competent day-hiker, you can complete some of the shorter overnight trips in a day. You can turn some of the longer day-hikes into overnight hikes by using campgrounds along the route.

Distances are given between the trailhead and landmarks – passes, lakes, bridges, trail junctions, ridgecrests, and campgrounds (CG) – and their elevations are shown. By comparing elevations, you can estimate the elevation gain or loss for different sections of the hike. When a parking lot is not immediately adjacent to a trailhead, I have included the intervening distance to more accurately represent the total for the outing. On some of the longer

backpacking trips, you can use campgrounds that are a short distance from the described route, on adjoining trails. These campgrounds appear in the route information summary with a "+" in the distance column. Add that distance to and from the main trail if you camp there. I use the same method for indicating the distances to sidetrail destinations. If, while on one of the longer backpack outings, the weather deteriorates or you are beset by an emergency, you can sometimes curtail your trip by exiting along an adjoining trail from junctions indicated.

In the descriptions, "trail" refers to designated and maintained trails. You will find that maintenance standards vary between parks, and between heavily used and remote areas within each park. "Path" and "track" refer to unmaintained routes where travel will likely be slower and more difficult. "Rooted" means that a trail

AVERAGE DAYTIME TEMPERATURE IN °C

STATION	MAY High	MAY Low	JUNE High	JUNE Low	JULY High	JULY Low	AUGUST High	AUGUST Low	SEPTEMBER High	SEPTEMBER Low	OCTOBER High	OCTOBER Low
Banff 1384 m	14.5	1.7	18.5	5.4	22.9	7.4	21.3	6.9	16.3	2.7	10.1	-1.3
Lake Louise 1524 m	12.8	-1.6	16.7	2.2	20.1	3.9	19.9	3.2	14.5	-0.9	7.7	-5.6
Columbia Icefield 1965 m	9.1	-3.5	12.1	0.2	15.2	2.9	14.3	2.7	10.3	-0.5	3.5	-5.9
Jasper 1062 m	15.8	2.4	19.3	6.2	21.9	8.1	21.6	7.4	16.4	3.3	10.1	-1.2
Yoho 1219 m	14.8	1.7	19.0	5.3	21.8	7.3	21.3	6.8	15.9	2.6	8.2	-1.8
Kootenay Crossing 1170 m	16.4	0.2	19.6	3.5	23.1	5.3	22.8	4.2	17.1	0.1	9.0	-3.9
Waterton Park 1281 m	15.0	2.0	19.0	6.0	23.0	7.0	22.0	7.0	17.0	3.0	12.0	0.0

AVERAGE PRECIPITATION: RAIN IN MM; SNOW IN CM

STATION	MAY Rain	MAY Snow	JUNE Rain	JUNE Snow	JULY Rain	JULY Snow	AUGUST Rain	AUGUST Snow	SEPTEMBER Rain	SEPTEMBER Snow	OCTOBER Rain	OCTOBER Snow
Banff 1384 m	44.3	17.0	59.8	1.8	54.1	0	60.0	0.2	37.0	5.7	13.8	19.8
Lake Louise 1524 m	34.9	6.4	53.5	0.3	57.3	0	54.3	0	39.4	3.2	15.2	20.0
Columbia Icefield 1965 m	7.1	35.0	58.5	10.0	49.9	1.4	55.4	2.1	39.5	13.8	17.8	64.1
Jasper 1062 m	30.3	3.1	54.8	trace	49.7	0	48.4	0.1	36.8	1.1	24.2	5.4
Yoho 1219 m	55.3	1.4	69.4	0.1	81.2	0	66.6	0	45.2	1.5	27.2	11.5
Kootenay Crossing 1170 m	55.2	1.7	65.8	0.2	55.6	0	54.6	0	40.9	1.0	26.2	6.5
Waterton Park 1281 m	79.0	15.6	80.8	0	70.8	0	65.6	3.0	53.7	7.1	29.5	36.6

Sulphur Skyline squall

contains many tree roots. All river, creek, and stream crossings should be bridged unless stated.

Read the entire text for a hike before you decide if it is appropriate for your ability, fitness, the trail conditions, and the time of year. Before each hike consult a park information centre for current conditions, warnings, restrictions, and closure information. You can obtain a weather forecast, purchase maps, and participate in the voluntary safety registration program. You will also be able to purchase your camping permit, vehicle permit, and pay any other necessary park use fees.

Those familiar with the Rockies may note that some mountains have "grown" and some have "shrunk" in this edition. In an attempt to help bring consistency to the dog's breakfast that has developed from using multiple sources for elevations, I have revised the elevations of mountains and passes using the Canadian Mountain Encyclopedia, available at www.bivouac.com

A consequence of this, for example, is that Mt. Assiniboine is now the 8th-highest mountain in the Rockies, not the 7th-highest.

RAINED OUT?

There are summers and then there are those that masquerade. If you find yourself in the Rockies during a not-so summer, or otherwise beset by a stretch of inclement weather, here are some diversions to having squeegee feet.

- Public libraries: Banff, Canmore, Jasper, Hinton, Golden, Invermere, Waterton
- Museums and archives: Banff (2), Canmore, Jasper, Golden, Waterton
- Indoor swimming: The Banff Centre, Canmore, Jasper, Golden, Waterton
- Hot springs: Banff, Radium, Miette
- Park information centres: Banff, Lake Louise, Field, Columbia Icefield, Jasper, Waterton.
- The Canadian Rockies Companion Guide, *Walks and Easy Hikes in the Canadian Rockies* is packed with shorter outings, ideal for capitalizing on fickle weather.

SEASON OPENERS AND LAST GASPS

These Classic Hikes are usually the first to become snow-free and the last to become snowbound. In most years, you can attempt these outings as early as the third week of May and as late as the third week of October. To prevent erosion and damage to surrounding vegetation, please make every effort to stay on the trail. If your chosen trail is snowbound or is too wet, please select another outing.

- Aylmer Pass #1
- C-Level Cirque #2
- Elk Pass #5
- Castle Lookout #12
- Sarbach Lookout #23
- Glacier Lake #24
- Saskatchewan Glacier #26
- Maligne Canyon #34
- Sulphur Skyline #38
- Ha Ling Peak #51
- Prairie View #52

GET HIGH

These are the 25 highest points reached on the Classic Hikes. The day-hikes that get you the highest for most of the day are Centennial Ridge (#53) and the Lake O'Hara Alpine Circuit (#42.) The backpacking trips with the most distance up high are Brazeau (#28) and the Skyline (#37.)

1. 2819 m, Mt. Allan summit (#53)
2. 2744 m, Fairview Mountain summit (#14)
3. 2635 m, Windy Ridge (#7)
4. 2612 m, Sentinel Pass (#16)
5. 2604 m, Wenkchemna Pass (#17)
6. 2590 m, North Molar Pass (#19)
7. 2560 m, Lineham Ridge (#62)
8. 2539 m, Badger Pass (#6)
9. 2530 m, Wiwaxy Gap (#42)
10. 2530 m, Skyline trail summit (#37)
11. 2510 m, The Notch (#37)
12. 2500 m Dolomite Pass trail summit (#20)
13. 2490 m, Jonas Shoulder (#28)
14. 2475 m, Deception Pass (#18)
15. 2469 m, Kiwetinok Pass (#45)
16. 2469 m, Harvey Pass (#10)
17. 2457 m, "Olympic Summit" (#53)
18. 2454 m, Poboktan Pass (#28)
19. 2435 m, All Soul's Prospect (#42)
20. 2430 m, Snowbird Pass (#39)
21. 2408 m, Ptarmigan Cirque (#58)
22. 2408 m, Ha Ling Peak (#51)
23. 2395 m, Dolomite Pass (#20)
24. 2393 m, Kindersley Summit (#50)
25. 2390 m, Nub Ridge (#7)

Before you hike, please visit www.mountainvision.ca, where I will endeavour to post any important changes that permanently affect these outings.

Distances and Times

Trail distances are metric (SI). A minimum and a maximum number of days are suggested for each overnight trip. The minimum infers that you will make no sidetrips, and that you will spend longer days backpacking. The maximum infers that you will make all the sidetrips, and that you will spend shorter days backpacking. The distance for an overnight trip does not include any sidetrips. Adjust your estimated time and the food and fuel that you carry according to your plans.

Most trailheads and junctions have signs. I refer to those without as "unsigned." The trail distances given in the text are usually those provided by the parks. These have been checked against the Gem Trek maps, on which trails were plotted from GPS waypoints. If you find a distance in the book that is at variance with a sign or a map, it is because I corrected an error after field-checking. Trail sign vandalism is a problem in all parks. Please report damaged or missing signs.

This book describes a traditional, boots and pack approach to backcountry trail use. Mountain runners, mountain bikers, and mega-athletes will make short work of most of these outings. How fast you travel will depend on your experience, ability, and your energy and the conditions of the day. As a rule, if you are accustomed to backpacking in mountains you will average 2.5 km per hour, including stops. Novices will average 1.5 km per hour. Those of intermediate ability will cover somewhere between these two figures. On day-hikes, strong hikers with light packs can cover 4-5 km per hour. However, most people average 2.5-3.5 km per hour. You will enjoy your hiking experience more if you focus on the landscape, not on your pace.

Take note of trails that you share with horses and with mountain bikers. Some trails have horse barriers, designed to keep horses from sections of trail intended only for use by hikers.

VARIATIONS

Variations include:
- day-hiking the first leg or the last leg of a longer outing
- using a backcountry campground as a basecamp to explore adjacent trails
- linking trails
- alternate beginnings and endings for longer outings
- hiking a longer outing in reverse
- alternate loop hikes.

Maps

The maps in this book should suffice for getting you to the trailhead and to your destination and back, but most of us are curious about the surrounding landscape. Although they do a good job with landscape features, the 1:50,000 map sheets of the National Topographic Survey show most trails in the Canadian Rockies inaccurately, incompletely or not at all. You can download free versions, but these are not as good as the printed versions, which are pricey. Gem Trek makes the best maps for hikers. A selection of ten Gem Trek maps covers most of the Classic Hikes. Chrismar Mapping markets two products under the brand name, The Adventure Map: Lake O'Hara, 1:20,000; and The Rockwall, 1:50,000. When you see the name of a landscape feature in quotation marks, it means that the name is unofficial. When more than one NTS sheet is listed, you will require all of them to cover the relevant area.

Natural Resources Canada
- http://maps.nrcan.gc.ca/

Gem Trek
- http://gemtrek.com/

Chrismar Mapping Services
- http://www.chrismar.com/

SIDETRIPS

This symbol indicates convenient sidetrips that you can make from the route of overnight trips. Except for loop hikes, the sidetrip distances are one-way. The overall distance of an outing does not include any sidetrips. Add accordingly.

NOVICE BACKPACKS

These campgrounds are a short distance from their respective trailheads. You may camp at any of these, and day-hike beyond with lighter packs.
- Aylmer Pass Junction (#1)
- Healy Creek (#8)
- Paradise Valley (#15)
- Hidden Lake (#18)
- Mosquito Creek (#19)
- Norman Lake (#25)
- Evelyn Creek (#37)
- Kinney Lake (#39)
- Yoho Lake (#44, #45, #46)
- Laughing Falls (#45)
- Twin Falls (#45)
- Forks (#56, #57)
- Akamina Creek (#63)

Ptarmigan Lake and Boulder Pass

Banff National Park

Established in November 1885, Banff is Canada's oldest national park. It includes 6641 km^2 of the front ranges and eastern main ranges, and features many of the trademark Rocky Mountain views. Banff has approximately 1500 km of maintained hiking trails. Some are among the more heavily used in the country; others are remote outings completed by only a few hundred backpackers a year.

Banff town (129 km west of Calgary) and Lake Louise village (187 km west of Calgary) are the major centres. Access is by car or by passenger bus along Highway 1. You will find a full range of services, supplies, and accommodation at these places, and at Canmore 22 km east of Banff. You can purchase basic groceries and fuel at Castle Mountain Village and at Saskatchewan River Crossing. The park information centres are in Banff town and at Lake Louise village.

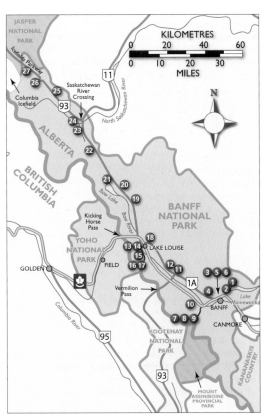

1. Aylmer Pass – Aylmer Lookout

Aylmer Pass

TRAIL THUMBNAIL

Day-hike or overnight

Route	Elev. (m)	Dist. (km)
Trailhead gate	1480	0
Trailhead sign	1480	0.5
Stewart Canyon	1486	1.7
Aylmer Pass jct and CG	1488	7.8
Aylmer Lookout jct	1982	10.1
Aylmer Lookout	2134	+1.7
Aylmer Pass	2301	13.5

Trailhead
Follow Banff Avenue 3 km from Banff town to the Highway 1 interchange. Keep straight ahead (northeast) on the Lake Minnewanka Road for 5.9 km to the Lake Minnewanka parking area. Park on the north side of the road. Walk east from the parking area to the gate. The trail begins as a road through the picnic area.

Special considerations
Sections of this trail, and the campground, may be closed to reduce the potential for conflicts with grizzly bears. A mandatory hiking group size may be in effect. Check at the Banff park information centre. Cougars and wolves frequent the area.

Maps
NTS: 82 O/3, 82 O/6
Gem Trek: *Banff and Mt. Assiniboine*

The Aylmer Pass trail takes you from shoreline to timberline in a landscape typical of Banff's front ranges. The outing features views of the largest body of water in Banff National Park. You walk through a patchwork of burned and unburned forest – a result of the park's prescribed burn program. Bighorn sheep frequent the pass and the slopes of Mt. Aylmer. Because the front ranges are in a snow shadow and this trail traverses south-facing slopes, Aylmer Pass is often Banff's first high-country destination to become snow-free. For the same reasons, it is also prime early season grizzly bear habitat. You share the trail with mountain bikers as far as Aylmer Pass junction.

Trailhead to Aylmer Pass Junction

The trail skirts the shore of Lake Minnewanka for 1.7 km to Stewart Canyon. Here, the Cascade River flows along a fault in bedrock of the Etherington Formation. The axis of the canyon is along the strike of the Rockies, southeast to northwest. The canyon commemorates George Stewart, the first Superintendent of Banff National Park. Cross the bridge and take the trail angling uphill to the north (left). Turn east (right) at the next junction.

The steep, south-facing slope traversed by the trail is typical of the montane life zone in the front ranges. The principal trees in the forest are lodgepole pine, trembling aspen, Douglas-fir, and limber pine. Colourful wildflowers grace these dry soils in late spring. Among them are the striking blooms of blue clematis, northern blue columbine, and scorpionweed. The blue and purple pigmentations assist in blocking harsh ultraviolet radiation, enabling the plants to better survive on these sun-baked slopes. Prescribed burns in 1994 and 2003 burned the forest nearby.

After the trail crosses a series of flash-flood stream courses, a bridge takes you across the stream that drains Aylmer Pass. Apart from the lake, this is the only water source on the hike. You reach the Aylmer Pass junction 100 m later. The campground is 200 m to the south (right). Aylmer Pass and Aylmer Lookout are to the north (left).

> *After leaving timber line we entered a beautiful alpine valley which continued to the divide and which was bright with flowers. We started many coveys of ptarmigan and saw a number of marmots.*
>
> Surveyor J.J. McArthur; *Report of the Department of the Interior 1891*

Aylmer Lookout

Constructed in 1948, Aylmer Lookout was one of seven fire lookouts in Banff. It saw use until 1978. Parks Canada removed the buildings in 1985. The site provides an excellent view of Lake Minnewanka, 654 m below. Bighorn sheep frequent the site; the lookout knoll reeks of their urine. One of the lookout keepers used to put out salt blocks to attract sheep. If you park it here, check yourself for ticks afterward. The 1990 prescribed burn consumed most of the trees nearby – an irony that underscores the change in outlook toward forest fires.

Aylmer Lookout Junction to Aylmer Pass

Back on the trail to Aylmer Pass, the forest soon becomes upper subalpine in character. The trail crosses several avalanche slopes, where crimson coloured paintbrush, white globe-flower, and western springbeauty thrive. Keep alert – this is grizzly country. The trail cuts through a shale ravine and drops to the creek just before the pass. Rock-hop to the west side. From here, the track is sometimes sketchy as it crosses the tundra of scree, rockslide, sedges, and snow patches for the remaining 700 m to the pass.

Aylmer Pass marks the boundary between Banff National Park and the Ghost River Wilderness, a 153 km^2 provincial wilderness area. Self-reliant backpackers, competent at route finding, may explore north. Random camping is allowed; permits are not required. Looking south, Mt. Inglismaldie (2964 m) forms the backdrop to Lake Minnewanka. Inglismaldie castle was the Scottish home of the Earl of Kintore, who visited Banff in 1887. Mt. Aylmer (3162 m), the highest mountain in this part of Banff National Park, towers above the east side of the pass. The mountain, first climbed in 1889 by surveyor J.J. McArthur, remains a popular ascent today. Aylmer was McArthur's hometown in Quebec.

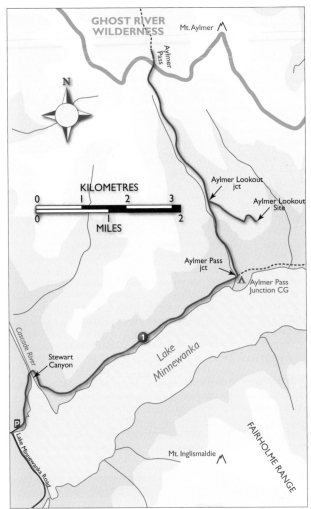

Aylmer Pass Junction to Aylmer Lookout Junction

You have gained little elevation so far. Ahead, the trail climbs 800 m in the 5.7 km to Aylmer Pass. You reach the Aylmer Lookout junction in 2.3 km, from where a 1.7 km sidetrail leads southeast to the former site of Aylmer Lookout.

VARIATIONS

- Day-hike to Aylmer Lookout; 23.6 km return.
- Day-hike to Aylmer Pass; 27.0 km return.
- Day-hike to both destinations; 30.4 km return.
- Camp at Aylmer Pass Junction and day-hike to the pass and lookout; 2-3 days.

WORKING WITH FIRE

Fire helps to regulate the vitality of forest and grassland ecosystems. Park managers suppressed forest fires in the mountain national parks until the late 1980s. Their efforts were so effective, in the 1960s and 1970s wildfires burned less than 6 km2 of Banff National Park.

With the aim of restoring a more natural fire regime, park managers have inventoried the forests – mapping tree stands and determining the locations, dates, frequency, extent, and intensity of past fires. It is principally the frequency and the intensity of fires that control vegetation patterns. Research determined that, near Lake Minnewanka, large, moderately intense fires should occur every 20 to 50 years. The most recent significant wildfires had taken place in 1884. So in the late 1980s, park managers decided to "prescribe" a series of burns.

After preparing fire guards in the autumn of 1987, fire techs ignited the forest on April 17, 1988. This first burn affected 750 ha. Park staff studied the burn to appraise its success in terms of duplicating a natural fire. More burning was needed, so the forest was re-ignited in September 1990, affecting another 400 ha. In total, 36 percent of the forested area was burned with an intensity that killed all vegetation. The area just east of Stewart Canyon was burned in 1994.

As you hike through the area, notice the patchwork that resulted from the prescribed burns. You will see some trees that candled or "crowned." The thick bark of many older Douglas-fir trees enabled them to survive, while the fires consumed some smaller trees nearby. The resulting mosaic of new and old growth has enhanced the forest's vitality. Elk, which were absent before the burns, rediscovered the area, attracted by the new growth of aspens.

From a public relations point of view, the prescribed burn program has been an uphill effort. Some critics see fire as destructive and as a source of pollution. Occasionally, prescribed fires get out of hand or rekindle, creating wildfires in high profile locations. This happened twice in 2003, just across Lake Minnewanka on the slopes of the Fairholme Range, and in the Rocky River valley in Jasper. However, what the critics fail to acknowledge is that, because of a relative absence of fires in the past century, many forest stands in the Rockies offer poor habitat for most species. These forests also beg the possibility of Yellowstone-scale conflagrations. By using prescribed burns and by letting wildfires burn in remote areas, park managers may be able to simulate the vital, natural process of forest succession.

WATER AND SPIRITS

Lake Minnewanka is the largest of the 480 mapped lakes and ponds in Banff National Park. The lake we see today is a hydro-electric reservoir, the only one in a Canadian national park. The lake's outlet has been dammed three times, raising the water level a total of 25 m and lengthening the body of water 8 km. The most recent dam was constructed in 1941 under the War Measures Act. The lake now has an area of just over 2217 ha, and is slightly more than 97 m deep.

George Simpson, Governor of the Hudson's Bay Company, and his entourage were probably the first Europeans to see the lake. Simpson followed its north shore in 1841 on his way across Canada and around the world. First Peoples knew of the lake long before Simpson's visit. It fills a massive breach in the eastern wall of the Rockies, and offers an obvious travel route. Archaeologists have excavated a campsite on the north shore near the mouth of the Cascade River, where they found a 10,400 year-old spear point.

The Stoney name for the lake was *Minnee-wah-kah*: "lake where spirits dwell." The Cree knew it as *Much-Manitou-sa-gi-agun*: "the devil's lake." A Stoney legend tells of a creature – half fish, half human – that could move the lake waters at will. The Stoneys would not canoe or swim in the lake.

Lake Minnewanka is in the montane life zone, which comprises only 2.95 percent of Banff National Park. Highways, roads, towns, and the railway have severely impacted this life zone, disrupting wildlife habitat and severing travel corridors. Banff's montane life zone would be significantly larger today if Lake Minnewanka's area had not been doubled by the dams.

To help fill the reservoir in 1941, engineers diverted the upper Ghost River at the east end of the lake. The reservoir inundated the village of Minnewanka Landing. Today, scuba divers explore the submerged ruins. Adding to Lake Minnewanka's unusual character: it is the only lake in Banff where you can launch a power boat.

2. C-Level Cirque

C-Level Cirque

TRAIL THUMBNAIL

Day-hike

Route	Elev. (m)	Dist. (km)
Trailhead	1461	0
C-Level buildings	1646	1.0
C-Level Cirque	1920	4.0

Trailhead
Follow Banff Avenue 3 km east from town to Highway 1. Keep straight ahead (northeast) on the Lake Minnewanka Road for 3.7 km. Turn north (left) into the Upper Bankhead picnic area. There are two trailheads here; the one for C-Level Cirque is on the west (left) side of the parking area.

Maps
NTS: 82 O/4
Gem Trek: *Banff and Mt. Assiniboine* or *Banff Up-Close*

Best lighting: morning

In the short outing to C-Level Cirque, you climb from aspen parkland in the montane life zone to avalanche swept alpine slopes beneath the east face of Cascade Mountain (2998 m). This coupling of ecological diversity with interesting human history makes the trail one of the more popular excursions near Banff town. It's also a stiff climb, offering a solid piece of exercise. Although the cirque itself is snowbound well into summer, the trail is often clear early in the hiking season – when a post-hike tick-check will be mandatory.

> There are indications of coal along the cutbanks, and upon the slopes of Cascade Mountain. Anthracite [coal] of an excellent quality has been discovered.
>
> Surveyor J.J. McArthur; *Report of the Department of the Interior 1890*

Trailhead to Mine Ruins

The trail climbs steadily for 1 km through montane forest to the remains of two mine buildings. This was the uppermost of the three workings of the Bankhead claim – the "C-Level" mine. Fenced-off ventilation shafts are nearby. You can walk east from the buildings onto a coal tailings pile, which grants fine views – east to Lake Minnewanka, south into the Bow Valley, and north into the Cascade Valley.

Bankhead

The Canadian Pacific Railway (CPR) developed the Bankhead coal mine in 1903 to supply coal for its locomotives. However, the coal shortage of 1906-07 created a national demand for coal. The CPR quickly expanded its mining operations and built a town nearby.

Mine production peaked in 1911, when more than 250,000 tonnes were extracted. The population of Bankhead reached its peak the same year, with estimates varying from 900-2000 people. Most of the miners were immigrants from Europe and China. The mine featured a coal-burning power plant that also supplied electricity to Banff.

Miners extracted Bankhead's semi-anthracite coal in an unusual fashion. Instead of removing the coal through vertical shafts, miners excavated tunnels, known as raises, that angled slightly upward into the mountainside. They knocked the coal down into railcars that gravity propelled back to the portals. In all, miners excavated more than 300 km of tunnels for mining, transportation, and ventilation in the flanks of Cascade Mountain.

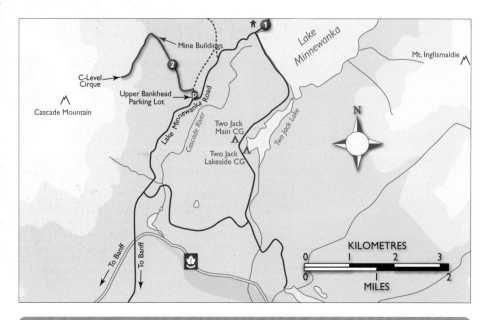

NOISY LEAF

The trailhead is in a stand of trembling aspen, the most common and widely distributed tree species in North America. A member of the willow family, aspen is abundant in the montane life zone of the front ranges, where it grows on the calcium-rich soils of glacial and alluvial rubble, often close to streams. Aspens propagate principally by root suckering. They form dense clonal stands of uniform age, in which each tree leafs-out at the same time in the spring, and sheds its leaves at the same time in late summer. Some aspen stands may have originated at the end of the Late Wisconsin Glaciation, making them among the older and larger organisms on earth.

The whitish-green trunks of mature aspens are often scarred to several metres in height, where elk or deer have stripped the protective outer bark to gain access to the sugary cambium layer beneath. These animals may also use small aspens as "rub trees," to remove the velvet from their antlers before the autumn rut. Where aspens grow near wetlands there will be beavers – the tree is the animal's staple food and building material. From the point of view of birdlife, aspen forests are the most productive in Canada. Look and listen for woodpeckers, vireos, and warblers.

Fire is essential to the regeneration of aspen forests. In the absence of forest fires, browsing by ungulates has put severe pressure on the aspen stands of the Bow Valley. New suckers don't have a chance to become established, while the older trees are dying as they reach their maximum age – approximately 120 years. In the late 1990s, Banff undertook an elk reduction program in the Bow Valley, in part to help regenerate aspen forests.

Some First Peoples knew the aspen as "noisy leaf" – an appropriate name when a breeze is blowing. The flat leaf stems readily catch the slightest wind, causing the leaves to flutter. The tree bark is coated in a silvery dust that helps block UV radiation. First Peoples reportedly used the dust as a sunscreen and as a cure for headaches – ASA, the medicinal compound in Aspirin, comes from the willow family.

Bankhead

Rillenkarren

Labour unrest and failing economics put an end to the Bankhead mine in 1922. Total production was 2.6 million tonnes. Most of the buildings were soon demolished or moved – many went to Banff; the church went to Calgary. Bankhead became a ghost town. New mining claims in national parks have not been allowed since the National Parks Act was proclaimed in 1930. However, a few mining titles – including some held by Canadian Pacific – are yet to be surrendered.

CLIFF BUILDER

The cliffs that flank C-Level cirque display a sequence of sedimentary rock formations common in the front ranges. The lower cliffs are Palliser Formation limestone, the middle ledge is Banff Formation shale, and the cliffs above are Rundle Formation limestone. This vertical world is home to mountain goats and bighorn sheep, and offers nesting sites for ravens.

To C-Level Cirque

About 500 m beyond the mine buildings, the trail narrows and angles sharply west (left). The forest at trailside becomes subalpine in character. Between here and the entrance to the cirque, the trail cuts through several coal seams.

If you are hiking in June, displays of glacier lilies and calypso orchids will line the last few hundred metres of trail. Although the elevation here is 300 m below "normal" for treeline in this area, the cirque is a treeless, alpine environment. The northeast-facing slope, with its rocky soils and perennial snow patches, is avalanche-swept each winter. Many of the trees along the eastern edge of the cirque are in krup-pelholz form; stunted by the cold, and damaged by avalanches.

C-Level Cirque

C-Level Cirque is not a classic, deeply eroded gla-cial cirque. Much of this cirque's shape is the result of frost shattering, erosion by water, and avalanches. The hummock at the end of the maintained trail is moraine debris known as a kame; the lakelet is a kettle pond – double proof that a glacier was once at work here. You may see pikas, hoary marmots, and golden-mantled ground squirrels on the hummock. The reddish tinge in snowpatches is watermelon snow – coloured by algae with a red pigment.

An unmaintained path heads north along the eastern edge of the cirque to a larch covered knoll, from where you may enjoy a fine prospect south over the Bow Valley. The limestone boulders on the knoll exhibit *rillenkarren* – furrows eroded over centuries by naturally acidic rainwater and by snowmelt, in a process called solution.

3. Cascade Amphitheatre

Cascade Amphitheatre

A Banff landmark, Cascade Mountain forms the northern skyline in the view from town. The Cascade Amphitheatre trail ascends into a steeply walled cirque on the southwest flank of the mountain. The approach trail is generally snow-free by mid-May. You share the trail with horses as far as the Amphitheatre junction.

Trailhead to Forty Mile Creek

Walk on asphalt between the ski area ticket office and the day lodge to pick up the trail, which begins as a bulldozed track. Just past the Mystic chairlift, the trail begins a steady descent north through open lodgepole pine forest. (Yes, it's nice to start a hike with a downhill, but remember, this will be an uphill poke at the end of the day.) Keep straight ahead at the Mystic Pass-Forty Mile Summit junction at 0.8 km. At km 3.0, you reach a "T" junction on the banks of Forty Mile Creek. Turn east (right). Cross Forty Mile Creek in 150 m on a bridge.

Forty Mile Creek to Cascade Amphitheatre

Across the bridge, the uphill begins in earnest – 640 m of gain in the remaining 4.6 km. The dogtooth spire of Mt. Louis (LOO-eee) (2680 m) in the Sawback Range dominates the views west. At the

> *Day after day the Cascade gazed in steadfast calm upon the changing scenes of the valley below. The old gray face rudely scarred from its age-long conflict with the elements, looked down in silent challenge upon the... village at its feet.*
>
> Ralph Connor; "How We Climbed Cascade," *Canadian Alpine Journal 1907*

TRAIL THUMBNAIL

Day-hike

Route	Elev. (m)	Dist. (km)
Trailhead	1701	0
Forty Mile Creek jct	1680	0.8
Forty Mile Creek bridge	1560	3.1
Cascade Amphitheatre jct	1799	4.3
Cascade Amphitheatre	2195	7.7

Trailhead
Follow Gopher Street north from Banff. Cross Highway 1. Follow the Mt. Norquay Road 6 km to the first parking area on the north (right) at the ski area. The trailhead kiosk is at the north (far) end of the parking area.

Maps
NTS: 82/04
Gem Trek: *Banff and Mt. Assiniboine* or *Banff Up-Close*

Best lighting: afternoon

FORTY MILES FROM SOMEWHERE

The first Europeans in the Rockies often named a feature for its distance from a known location. Forty Mile Creek is not forty miles long, so it was probably named because it is forty miles distant from somewhere. The creek crossed the route of the Canadian Pacific Railway approximately forty miles from two points: the old railway siding of Padmore to the east, which was a major resupply point during the railway survey of 1881-82; and the crest of Kicking Horse Pass to the west.

For most of a century Banff town took its drinking water from Forty Mile Creek. In the spring and summer of 1982, Banff endured an outbreak of "beaver fever" (giardiasis), caused by contamination of drinking water with the parasite, *Giardia lamblia*. Beavers living in the town water reservoir on lower Forty Mile Creek were deemed the carriers. They were trapped and destroyed as a short-term solution to the problem. In July 1983, Banff completed the switch to three groundwater wells. This was good news for townsfolk and for the ensuing generations of beavers, for whom the meanders of Forty Mile Creek provide excellent habitat.

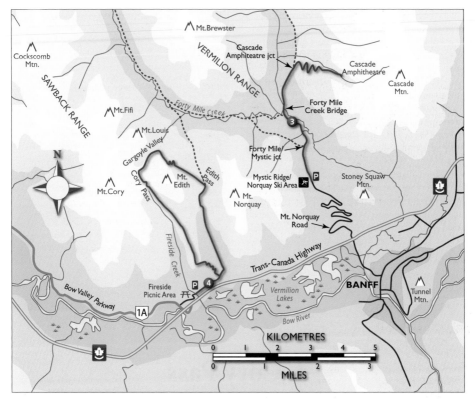

CASCADE MOUNTAIN

The summit of Cascade Mountain (2998 m) rises east of trail's end. James Hector named the peak in 1858 with a translation of the Stoney word *Minnehappa* – "the mountain where the water falls." Cascade is a miniature mountain range – a massif – 12.5 km long, with half a dozen summits. The most northerly summit is slightly higher than the one you see here.

Cascade is a dip-slope mountain. Its tilted, southwest-facing slope (the ridge south of the amphitheatre), ends on a northeast-facing cliff (seen from C-Level Cirque). Approximately 75 million-years-ago, huge stacks of the sedimentary rock layers that comprise the mountain became fractured along faults, and were then thrust upward and northeastward over underlying layers.

The rock layers of Cascade Mountain exhibit great folding. When deep within the earth's crust, heat made the layers pliable. They were subsequently warped into folds by the forces of mountain building. U-shaped folds are called synclines (SIN-clines). Arch-shaped folds are called anticlines. You can see a prominent syncline from the end of trail. From the Lake Minnewanka Road you can see a tremendous assortment of folds in Cascade Mountain's eastern flank, along with the mountain's namesake waterfall. The upper slopes of the peak are Rundle Formation limestone and dolomite. Although it appears inhospitable, this terrain is excellent habitat for bighorn sheep.

Cascade Amphitheatre junction, turn east (right) to continue the steady ascent to the cirque.

During the climb from Forty Mile Creek, you pass from the montane life zone into the subalpine life zone, although the forest of lodgepole pines changes little. These trees seeded after a large forest fire in 1894. The trail levels at the entrance to the amphitheatre, where there is a marked transition from pine forest to a mix of Engelmann spruce and subalpine fir, typical of the upper subalpine life zone. The paths that branch south (right) join the approach to the regular mountaineering route on Cascade Mountain. Keep straight ahead.

Cascade Amphitheatre

Cirque valleys, such as Cascade Amphitheatre, were created by glaciers during the various ice ages of the last 2.6 million years. Glaciologists currently think that there have been at least seven significant glaciations – each lasting tens of thousands of years – in the Rockies during the last 800,000 years. The trail undulates over a series of low recessional moraines as it enters the amphitheatre. These moraines mark places of brief pause during the most recent glacial retreat.

Although the glacial ice is now gone from the slopes of Cascade Mountain, a chill remains on the floor of the amphitheatre. Cold air flows downhill and collects in depressions, creating frost hollows where full-sized trees cannot develop. The many small mounds are earth hummocks, relict formations produced when the soil was permanently frozen. (See p. 220.) The meadows support a typical array of moisture-loving, alpine wildflowers, along with sedges and willows.

The trail is vague in places but keeps to the western edge of the meadows. You cross rockslides from which several springs issue. About 1 km after entering the amphitheatre, you climb through a small stand of trees to trail's end on a knoll of rockslide debris. You may see white-tailed ptarmigan, pikas, and hoary marmots nearby.

Cascade Falls

4. Cory Pass

Gargoyle Valley

TRAIL THUMBNAIL

Day-hike; see map, p. 25

Route	Elev. (m)	Dist. (km)
Trailhead	1415	0
Cory Pass jct	1470	1.1
Cory Pass	2377	5.8
Mouth of Gargoyle Valley	2134	7.4
Edith Pass jct	1860	9.6
Cory Pass jct	1470	12.5
Trailhead	1415	13.6

Trailhead
Follow Highway 1 west from the Mt. Norquay (Banff) interchange for 5.6 km to the Bow Valley Parkway exit (Highway 1A). Follow the Bow Valley Parkway 500 m west and turn east (right) onto the Fireside picnic area access road. Follow this narrow road 600 m to its end.

Maps
NTS: 82 O/4
Gem Trek: *Banff and Mt. Assiniboine* or *Banff Up-Close*

Best lighting: early afternoon in the Gargoyle Valley

The Cory Pass outing is, hands-down, the most spectacular and strenuous day-hike near Banff town. Set among the rugged limestone peaks of the Sawback Range, the trail displays tremendous ecological diversity as it ventures from montane valley bottom to well above treeline. You may see bighorn sheep, white-tailed deer, mule deer, and elk.

Locals are split on the preferred direction for hiking this loop, but the direction described has at least three advantages.

1. You ascend the steepest parts of the trail – although you may huff and puff, your knees won't take such a pounding on the way down.
2. From Cory Pass, you can assess the snow cover before descending northeast. If it still looks

like winter in the Gargoyle Valley, you can turn around and go home.

3. The homestretch is in shaded forest – perfect on a hot afternoon.

Trailhead to Cory Pass

From the trailhead, cross the footbridge over "Fireside Creek" and turn south (right) onto a broad trail. At the junction in 200 m, turn north (left). This part of the trail is in a forest typical of south-facing slopes in the montane life zone of the front ranges. Although lodgepole pine is the most common tree, there are homogenous stands of trembling aspen, and a few ancient specimens of Douglas-fir. The understory contains buffaloberry, prickly wild rose, common juniper, paintbrush, showy aster, and groundsel. I have seen a pileated woodpecker here.

You reach the Cory Pass junction at km 1.1. Turn north (left), and get ready to burn up your breakfast as you climb 350 m in the next 1.5 km. The

VARIATIONS

- Hike to Cory Pass; 11.6 km return.
- Hike the loop in reverse.

initial part of the grind is on a grassy, flower-filled slope, dotted with aspens and frequented by elk, deer, and bighorn sheep. Pause at the knoll about halfway into the climb; the really steep part is just ahead. The grade backs off as you gain the thinly-forested south ridge of Mt. Edith at km 2.6. About 1 km along the ridge, you encounter a short step. Ignore the path that heads east (right). Descend northish (left). It's not really downclimbing, but take care. After this awkward bit, the trail breaks through treeline to traverse a steep sideslope as it completes the climb to the pass. Use caution if snow lingers in the gullies – you could take a tumble here. The open slopes feature wildflowers with yellow blooms: stonecrop, alpine bladder pod, golden fleabane, yellow beardtongue, alpine cinquefoil, and yellow mountain saxifrage. Look back for fine views of distant Mt. Assiniboine (3616 m) and the many meanders of the Bow River.

Cory Pass

Cory Pass is a narrow, rocky, and often windswept breach. Set in the alpine life zone, the thin soils of the pass support only scattered mats of hardy wildflowers. Views south include the Bow Valley, Mt. Rundle, Sulphur Mountain, and the Sundance Range. West of this range, the Fatigue Thrust separates the gray

DOUGLAS-FIR

A few Douglas-fir trees grace the grassy slopes near the trailhead. The Douglas-fir is the climax tree species of the montane life zone. It is not a true fir; it is in the pine family. The Latin genus name, *Pseudotsuga*, means "false hemlock." The thick, grooved, corky bark of the mature tree allows it to withstand moderate ground fires and infestation by many insects, although in places in the Rockies, entire stands are succumbing to beetles. Forest fires remove competing vegetation in older Douglas-fir forests, creating open parkland dotted with stately trees. Douglas-firs in such settings in the Rockies may live 600 years. The last wildfire on these slopes was in 1910, although prescribed burns in the 1990s touched spots nearby. The oldest known Douglas-fir in Alberta, estimated at about 700+ years, grows just east of Banff on a terrace above the Bow River.

There are two varieties of Douglas-fir: coastal and interior. Although they hybridize, the interior or "blue Douglas-fir" is the variety in the Rockies. Large specimens are 30 m to 40 m tall, and 1 m in diameter, often with a gracefully curving trunk. In Pacific rainforests, the coastal variety commonly attains heights of 80 m (record approximately 100 m), diameters in excess of 4 m, and ages of more than 1000 years (record: 2000 years).

The common name of the tree commemorates David Douglas, a Scottish botanist who collected in the Rockies in 1826 and 1827. The species name, *menziesia*, celebrates another Scot – Archibald Menzies (MINN-giss), surgeon and naturalist on George Vancouver's 1792 voyage. Menzies was the first botanist to describe the huge conifer species of the North American Pacific coast.

limestone peaks of the front ranges from the eastern main ranges. The "gargoyles" flanking Cory Pass are shattered pinnacles of Eldon Formation limestone. The weathering of the ages has eroded an opening, or "window" into one of them. Cory Pass and Mt. Cory (2802 m) commemorate William Cory, Deputy Minister of the Interior, from 1905-1930.

Gargoyle Valley

Mt. Louis (LOO-eee) (2680 m) beckons you to take the plunge northeast into the Gargoyle Valley. Use care if portions of the route are snow-covered. After the initial drop, veer right (northeast) to begin a side-hill descent on the south flank of the valley, in the shade of Mt. Edith (2554 m). Edith Cox accompanied Prime Minister John A. Macdonald when he visited Banff in 1886. The mountain has three summits; the most northerly is the highest. But it won't be Mt. Edith's shaded slabs that grab your attention – your eyes will be glued to Mt. Louis. Its dogtooth spire of vertically thrust, Palliser Formation limestone is one of the more striking pillars in the Canadian Rockies. First climbed in 1916, the south ridge is popular with rock climbers today. Louis Stewart was a Dominion Land Surveyor and a companion of explorer, A.P. Coleman, on two of his travels to the Rockies, in 1892 and 1903.

Don't become so rapt with the view that you miss an important turn in the trail, 1.6 km from the pass. Here, the trail heads sharply southeast (right). More than a few hikers have inadvertently plodded straight ahead and followed the drainage (no trail) all the way down to Forty Mile Creek. Depending on snow cover, you can choose between any of half a dozen paths beaten into the scree as you sidehill across. Try to keep elevation. You are aiming for the obvious point where the trail re-enters the forest – sometimes marked by a painted metal target.

Having turned the north end of Mt. Edith, you then make a descending traverse to the southwest, with fine views into Forty Mile Creek and onto the forested saddle of Edith Pass. Mt. Norquay (NOR-kway) (2523 m) is east across the pass. John Norquay was Premier of Manitoba when he reportedly climbed this peak in 1888. The mountain to the

The Gargoyles

north, across Forty Mile Creek, is Mt. Brewster (2859 m), named for Jim Brewster, trail guide, outfitter, and Banff businessman. A huge limestone block sits on its southwest slope. After about 1.5 km, the trail descends steeply on an avalanche slope to gain the Edith Pass trail. Turn south (right).

Edith Pass Trail to Trailhead

The trail drops into the shady ravine that drains Edith Pass. The forest here is markedly different from any other on this hike – a mix of lodgepole pine, Douglas-fir, and a few white spruce. Fire studies show that this forest has not seen a wildfire since 1850. The rocky soils are home to feathermosses and shade-tolerant wildflowers, including several species of orchids. To complete the loop, keep straight ahead at the Cory Pass junction – you don't want to go up that hill again!

BLOWOUT!

In July 1999, a debris flow – or blowout – transformed seemingly innocuous "Fireside Creek" into a torrent. The deluge destroyed part of the picnic area and piled debris – including a picnic table – on Highway 1, forcing its closure for two days. Debris flows occur when a heavy rain or a sudden snowmelt mixes with the surface layer of soil and rock on a steep slope, transforming that material into a slurry. In this case, 50 mm of rain fell in one evening. Debris flows are common in the front ranges of the Rockies, and have created many of the alluvial fans that spread into valley bottoms – the places where we have built towns, campsites, and picnic areas. A lesser flow occurred along the creek in 2000. Parks Canada subsequently built berms in the creek bed to divert far-reaching flows out of the main channel, dispersing them on the lower mountain slope. The agency hopes that this will help to protect the highway and the railway while also sustaining some of the natural process of the alluvial fan formation.

We stopped and looked back at our mountain, which towered up magnificently in the dusk, and Conrad [Kain] spoke volumes when he said, "Ye Gods Mr. MacCarthy; just look at that; they never will believe we climbed it."

A.H. MacCarthy; *Canadian Alpine Journal* *1917*

5. Elk Pass

Elk Lake

TRAIL THUMBNAIL

Day-hike or overnight

Route	Elev. (m)	Dist. (km)
Trailhead	1701	0
Forty Mile Creek jct	1680	0.8
Forty Mile Creek bridge	1560	3.1
Cascade Amphitheatre jct	1799	4.3
Elk Pass CG	2055	11.5
Elk Lake jct	2055	11.6
Elk Pass	2060	12.8
Cascade River bridge	1631	20.2
Stony Creek bridge	1631	20.4
Stony Creek CG	1635	+0.3
Cascade trail jct	1640	21.0
Cascade River Bridge CG	1545	29.2
Upper Bankhead parking area	1461	35.8

Trailhead
Follow Gopher Street north from Banff. Cross Highway 1. Follow the Mt. Norquay Road 6 km to the first parking area on the north (right) at the ski area. The trailhead kiosk is at the north (far) end of the parking area.

Maps
NTS: 82 O/4, 82 O/5
Gem Trek: *Banff and Mt. Assiniboine*

Best lighting: morning at Elk Lake

Although close to town, the loop over Elk Pass provides a taste of Banff's front range hinterland of rugged limestone peaks; an area that is home to grizzly bears, wolves, coyotes, cougars, elk, deer, mountain goats, and bighorn sheep. You share the loop with commercial horse parties. Mountain bikes are allowed on the Cascade fireroad.

Trailhead to Elk Pass

Walk on asphalt between the ski area ticket office and the day lodge to pick up the trail, which begins as a bulldozed track. Just past the Mystic chairlift, the trail begins a steady descent north through open lodgepole pine forest. Keep straight ahead at the Mystic Pass-Forty Mile Summit junction at 0.8 km. At km 3.0, you reach a "T" junction on the banks of Forty Mile Creek. Turn east (right). Cross Forty Mile Creek in 150 m on a bridge.

The trail ascends for 1.2 km through lodgepole pine forest to the Cascade Amphitheatre junction.

VARIATIONS

- Day-hike to Elk Lake and back in a long day; 27.4 km return.
- For an easy two-day backpack, camp at Elk Pass, day-hike to the lake, return the same way; 27.4 km return.
- Hike the loop in reverse.

Most of the pines here seeded after a large forest fire in 1894. The resin-sealed cone of the lodgepole cracks open at 45°C, scattering the seeds and producing a doghair forest of pines. At this elevation, most of the pines would normally have been replaced within 60 years by Engelmann spruce and subalpine fir – the climax species of the subalpine forest. However, these steep, well-drained, sun-exposed slopes offer a perfect niche for pines. A few small spruces are taking hold beneath the canopy, where buffaloberry, bearberry, and wolf willow also grow. Views west through the forest feature the dogtooth spire of Mt. Louis (LOO-eee) (2680 m) in the Sawback Range.

Keep straight ahead at the Cascade Amphitheatre junction. The wide and sometimes rocky horse trail continues north, crossing several flash-flood stream courses. As you climb toward Elk Pass, note the subtle transition to upper subalpine forest. From openings in the trees you have views south to Cascade Mountain (2998 m), Mt. Norquay 2523 m), Sulphur Mountain (2438 m), and the Sundance Range. The purple bloom of silky scorpionweed graces some of the shale banks at trailside. Open glades of willow mark the final approach to the pass. The slopes to the east are covered in silver spar trees from a 1914 forest fire.

At km 11.5, follow a trail 100 m northwest (left) from the main trail to Elk Pass campground, a pleasant camping place set in a grove of spruce. The water source is questionable – a small stream rich with organic material and frequented by deer, elk, and horses. Boil, filter or treat the water before consumption.

While we were camped here, a mule deer doe and buck approached within 5 m. While drifting off to sleep, I was awakened by the unmistakable snarl of a big cat near the tent – probably a cougar. In the morning, we woke to the yelping and commotion from a coyote den on the opposite side of the valley. We found the skin of a goat in the willow meadows near the campground junction. The goat may have been killed by a cougar or by wolves.

Elk Pass to Cascade Fireroad

The willow meadow stretches for 1.5 km across Elk Pass. This is ideal habitat for snowshoe hares, mice, voles, least chipmunks, and Columbian ground squirrels. You may see tracks and scats of wolves, coyotes, lynx, martens, and cougars at trailside. From the north edge of the pass, the trail descends parallel to the stream course.

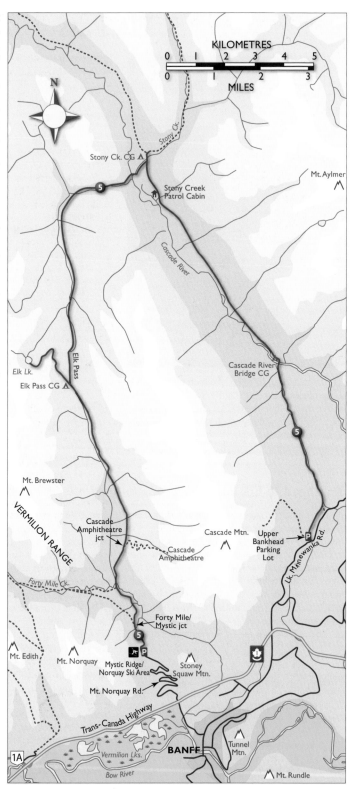

Scorpionweed

During wet weather, there is some awful muck here, churned by horse traffic. However, fine views west to Mt. Brewster compensate.

Roughly 5 km north of Elk Pass, the trail crosses the stream to its north bank on a bridge, and turns east toward the Cascade Valley. The final 2.2 km to the Cascade River is through a montane valley typical of the front ranges. Bright and attractive wildflowers dot the slopes: common dandelion – transported here in horse feed and dung – orange-flowered false dandelion, goatsbeard, yellow columbine, prairie

ELK LAKE, 2.2 KM

An early morning visit to Elk Lake is the highlight of this outing. From the junction on the main trail just north of the campground, a wide and sometimes muddy trail climbs northwest (left) into treeline forest. After crossing a spur of Mt. Brewster, the trail descends west to Elk Lake. Lyall's larch is common in the forest. If you are hiking in early summer you will see white globeflowers and glacier lilies among the tufts of heather at trailside. On the north side of the trail, you may see moose and elk in a nearby slough. The trail fades at the lakeshore, which is buggy, boggy, and fringed with alpine buttercup.

Elk Lake is a classic cirque lake, nestled in a glacial depression beneath Mt. Brewster (2859 m). The mountain's cliffs are the leading edge of the Sulphur Mountain Thrust. They display a common cliff-building sequence of the front ranges: Palliser Formation limestone, Banff Formation shale, with a topping of Rundle Formation limestone.

Cutthroat trout inhabit the lake. As there is no record of stocking at Elk Lake, these fish may be endemic – a rarity among accessible lakes in the Rockies.

groundsel, paintbrush, yellow penstemon, blue penstemon, and yellow hedysarum.

The steep, grassy slopes to the north of the trail are ideal habitat for mountain goats and bighorn sheep. The shaded avalanche slopes to the south offer good food sources for bears. Toward the mouth of the creek, the trail passes through several groves of trembling aspen. Visibility is limited and the creek is noisy. Make lots of noise in this area to alert any bears to your presence.

The trail cuts through a limestone bluff that marks the Rundle Mountain Thrust, and emerges onto the west bank of the Cascade River near its junction with Stony Creek. Cross the river on two footbridges located 50 m to the south (right). Turn north (left) 20 m beyond the second bridge, and follow this trail for 30 m. Angle northeast (right) onto a well-beaten trail that parallels the north bank of Stony Creek. Cross this creek on a series of split-log bridges. There is a maze of horse trails, paths, and fireroads leading away from the south bank of the creek. Disregard them. Follow Stony Creek upstream for 600 m to the concrete bridge on the Cascade fireroad. If you want to camp nearby, cross this bridge to the campground on the north bank.

Stony Creek to Upper Bankhead Parking Lot

The outing concludes with an enjoyable walk south along the Cascade fireroad. Keep your head up. You are more likely to see a grizzly bear here than anywhere else in Banff National Park. The Stony Creek patrol cabin is on a sidetrail to the west, approximately 1.3 km south of Stony Creek. The Cascade River Bridge campground is on the west side of the fireroad, just before it crosses the Cascade River. Beyond the bridge, the trail climbs into lower subalpine forest that features a number of sloughs created by beavers. With views of the Bow Valley ahead, the trail descends to the Upper Bankhead parking area on the Lake Minnewanka Road. If you have not prearranged transportation, plan to arrive early enough to sort out how to get home. The 6.7 km of pavement into town is a heel-burner. I've done it in the dark.

> *Several years ago, two gentlemen decided to ascend Cascade Mountain, one of the highest peaks in the neighbourhood... They started out with the intention of returning within twenty-four hours, but instead mysteriously disappeared for three days....*
>
> Walter Wilcox; *The Rockies of Canada*

The headwaters of the Cascade River are the wilderness heartland of Banff National Park; an area vital to wolves and grizzly bears. The existence of the Cascade fireroad epitomizes the change in attitudes toward resource management in the mountain national parks.

The most extensive wildfires in Banff National Park took place in 1936, when three major burns consumed about 70 km2 of park forests. Almost 90 percent of this total resulted from a single fire at Flints Park in the upper Cascade Valley. Park managers of the day were obsessed with protecting timber. They quickly mobilized to extinguish the fire.

As part of the firefighting effort, crews bulldozed a road north to Flints Park. In the years following the fire, crews upgraded and lengthened the road, north over Wigmore and Snow Creek summits to the Red Deer River, and then east to the park boundary – a distance of almost 70 km.

By the 1950s, fireroads ran the lengths of most major backcountry valleys in the mountain national parks. Warden cabins sprang up along the roads. Park maintenance crews and wardens routinely drove into the heart of prime wildlife habitat. In 1971, Parks Canada announced plans to pave many of the fireroads and open them to public traffic. Fortunately, public reaction was so negative, the agency dropped the idea.

When Parks Canada began using helicopters for smoke patrols and initial attack on fires in the 1980s, the fireroads became obsolete. Road deactivation has been achieved by installing "tank traps" near trailheads, by removing bridges, or by downscaling bridges to pedestrian width. Park managers now refer to the Cascade fireroad as a "trail," but it will be decades before vegetation reclaims the tread to trail width.

6. Sawback

Mystic Pass

The Sawback trail connects a series of spectacular passes as it winds from Banff to Lake Louise over the crest of its namesake range. The spacing of campgrounds allows for short days on the trail and time for exploration. You share the tread with horse traffic.

Trailhead to Mystic Valley Campground

Walk on asphalt between the ski area ticket office and the day lodge to pick up the trail, which begins as a bulldozed track. At the junction in 0.8 km, just past the Spirit chairlift, branch left, following signs for Mystic Pass. The trail ascends over a spur of Mt. Norquay, gaining 70 m of elevation, before descending to a bridge over Forty Mile Creek at km 4.0.

For the next 12 km, the trail climbs gradually through open coniferous forest along the east bank of Forty Mile Creek. In places, the tread has been hardened with gravel to withstand the impacts of horse traffic. Views are limited, except where the trail crosses avalanche paths or draws alongside the creek. The dogtooth spires of Mt. Louis (LOO-eee) (2680 m) and Mt. Fifi (2621 m) rise above the west

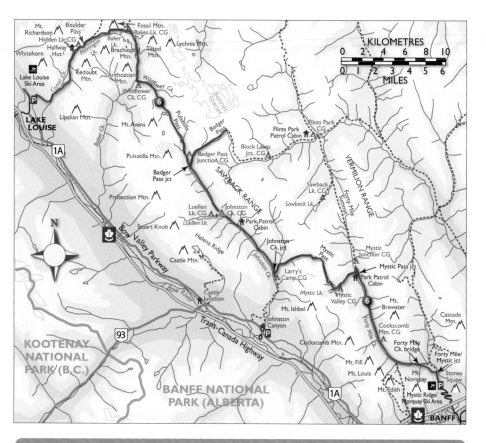

TRAIL THUMBNAIL

Overnight, 4-7 days

Route	Elev. (m)	Dist. (km)
Trailhead	1701	0
Forty Mile-Mystic jct	1707	0.8
Forty Mile Creek bridge	1631	4.0
Cockscomb Mountain CG	1723	8.2
Mystic Pass jct	1838	15.9
Mystic Junction CG	1840	+0.5
Mystic Valley CG	1921	18.6
Mystic Lake jct	1951	19.1
Mystic Pass	2270	22.7
Johnston Creek jct	1692	29.3
Larry's Camp CG	1692	+0.1
Luellen Lake jct	1890	37.8
Luellen Lake CG	1970	+0.8
Johnston Creek CG	1875	38.0
Badger Pass jct	2027	43.7
Badger Pass Junction CG	2043	44.2
Pulsatilla Pass	2355	47.6
Baker Creek jct	1814	54.0
Wildflower Creek CG	1814	54.0
Red Deer Lakes jct	2133	59.2

Trail Thumbnail (cont.)	Elev. (m)	Dist. (km)
Baker Lake CG	2210	60.0
Boulder Pass	2340	64.9
Hidden Lake CG jct	2195	7.2
Hidden Lake CG	2198	+0.1
Fish Creek parking area	1698	73.5

Trailhead

Follow Gopher Street north from Banff. Cross Highway 1. Follow the Mt. Norquay Road 6 km to the first parking area on the north (right) at the ski area. The trailhead kiosk is at the north (far) end of the parking area.

Special consideration

Parks Canada is considering restricting access in the Skoki area at trail's end. Check at a park information centre.

Maps

NTS: 82 O/4, 82 O/5, 82 N/8
Gem Trek: *Banff and Mt. Assiniboine*

side of the valley. You reach the Edith Pass junction 6.0 km from the trailhead. Keep straight ahead. The Cockscomb Mountain campground at km 8.2.

The unmarked trails that branch west prior to the Mystic Pass junction lead to a horse outfitter's camp. Keep straight ahead until the junction. The trail can be very poor in this area. Turn west (left) at the Mystic Pass junction, and descend to a bridge over Forty Mile Creek. (If you want to camp at Mystic Junction campground, hike north – straight ahead – from the Mystic Pass junction for 500 m. When you leave camp, take the cutoff trail that heads southwest from the campground, to rejoin the Mystic Pass trail in 800 m.)

The trail skirts the north side of the Mystic patrol cabin. Keep straight ahead (west) at the junction just beyond, where the cutoff trail from Mystic Junction campground joins. After climbing and traversing a forested sideslope for 2 km, the trail descends avalanche paths to a bridge across Mystic Creek. The Mystic Valley campground is just beyond, situated on a bench between the creeks that drain Mystic Pass and Mystic Lake. Upstream, horses ford both creeks. Treat all drinking water.

Mystic Valley Campground to Johnston Creek

At the junction 500 m west of the campground, turn north (right). The trail climbs moderately, with one bridged stream crossing and one rock-hop, to reach treeline at the southern entrance to Mystic Pass.

Mystic Pass is a narrow cleft between two parallel ridges of the Sawback Range. Larches dot the pass, adding to the allure in late summer. The axis of the pass lies on the Sawback Thrust, which separates the drab, gray Devonian-aged, Palliser limestone on the east side of the pass, from the more varied and older

> *Our next trip was up Forty Mile Creek. To avoid the canyon, we entered by the pass to the east of Mt. Edith. It is about 5 miles across on a good trail... to the valley which runs in a northwest direction parallel to the Sawback Range. About 7 miles from the crossing, a good sized creek comes in from the west, and along this a trail leads across the Sawback Range to Johnston Creek.... We made a trip to the lake [Mystic Lake] and caught two dozen trout.*
>
> Surveyor J.J. McArthur; *Report of the Department of the Interior 1891*

Mystic Lake

MYSTIC LAKE (2015 M), 1.1 KM

Mystic Lake is nestled in a glacial cirque under the eastern ramparts of Mt. Ishbel (2908 m). The trail to the lake heads west from Mystic Valley campground, crosses the lake's outlet stream and ascends to a junction in 500 m. Keep straight ahead. The muddy and rocky trail improves dramatically after the horse-hiker barrier about 300 m beyond the junction.

Mystic Lake has an area of 8 ha and is 15 m deep. It is fringed by an ancient forest of spruce and fir that last burned in 1645. Arnica, fleabane, and leather-leaved saxifrage grow on the damp shoreline, along with the sedge, cottongrass. Cutthroat trout and bull trout inhabit the lake.

The first recorded visits to Mystic Lake took place in 1891, when William Twin led Jim Brewster here, and when surveyor J.J. McArthur stopped by. Ishbel was the daughter of Ramsay MacDonald, a British prime minister in the 1920s and 1930s. Although you can make a rough circuit of this enchanting body of water, most visitors are content to gaze at the lake and Mt. Ishbel from near trail's end on the east shore.

Luellen Lake

LUELLEN LAKE, 750 M

The route to Luellen Lake crosses Johnston Creek and climbs a rough track for 750 m to the campground. Luellen Lake is an attractive ribbon of water, 1.75 km long, with an area of 47 ha. The peculiar, blocky summit to the west is Stuart Knob (2850 m), named for Benjamin Stuart Walcott, son of Charles Walcott, the man who discovered the Burgess Shale. The 500 m high quartzite cliffs of Helena Ridge form the backdrop for the lake. Walcott climbed the ridge in 1910, and named it for his second wife.

You may hear the calls of common loons at Luellen Lake. Many backcountry lakes in the Rockies are home to a pair of loons. Loons eat fish and aquatic insects. They nest near water and are unable to take off from land. Loons in the Rockies migrate to the Pacific coast during winter.

VARIATIONS

- Traverse Mystic Pass, with exit or approach along Johnston Creek; 37.2 km, 2-4 days.
- Add portions of the Skoki loop. See Classic Hike #18.
- Begin the hike at Lake Louise. An alternate exit, bypassing Mystic Pass, is along Johnston Creek; 51.8 km.
- Backpack to Mystic Valley campground; day-hike to Mystic Lake and Mystic Pass.
- See *Heart of the Sawback*, p. 37.

Cambrian-aged rocks to the west. These include the purple shales of the Arctomys (ARK-toe-miss) Formation at trailside. Bighorn sheep and mountain goats frequent the kilometre-long tundra of the pass. Their trails criss-cross the surrounding slopes. The name of this pass seems fitting but is, alas, grammatically incorrect. "Mystic" is a noun and, as it is not a proper name in this case, the pass should either be named Mystical Pass or Mystic's Pass.

Leaving Mystic Pass, the trail swings west and plunges toward Johnston Creek. This sidevalley can be a scorcher on a hot afternoon. Sedimentary formations in the unnamed mountain to the north display extensive folding and small solution caves. As it levels, the trail alternates between rockslides and willow plains. Some sections are routed along a flash-flood stream course. Look for cairns that mark the way where the trail becomes faint.

The stream that drains Mystic Pass emerges from the base of a rockslide about 2.5 km below the pass. This rockslide may be the pika capital of the Rockies. In dry weather, this will be your last water source for 3 km. Cross another flash-flood stream course and rock-hop the creek to its north bank. Continue the descent on a delightful section of trail. You cross an unnamed tributary stream about 1 km before the Johnston Creek junction. A multitude of colourful montane wildflowers blooms in July on the steep, dry slopes north of the trail. You have views south along Johnston Creek to Copper Mountain (2795 m). Johnston Creek commemorates a prospector who frequented the area near Silver City, nearby in the Bow Valley, in 1882.

Johnston Creek to Luellen Lake

At the Johnston Creek junction, turn south (left) if you would like to stay at nearby Larry's Camp campground. You can also exit from this point to the Bow Valley Parkway, 7.9 km south.

The Sawback trail continues northwest (right) from the junction, as a mucky, rooted horse trail along Johnston Creek. Views south include the spire-like summit of Mt. Ishbel. In places, ancient spruce forest encloses the trail. Listen for golden-crowned kinglets and for the drumming of woodpeckers. Look for trout in the creek at undercut banks. A wooden fence and gate mark the horse pasture at the Johnston Creek patrol cabin. Please close the gate behind you.

Horsetails grow at trailside in this area. The genus they belong to – *Equisetum* – is one of the more primitive and ancient groups of vascular plants. When dinosaurs roamed, tree-sized horsetails dominated many forests. Nine horsetail species occur in the Rockies. Those with prominent side-branches are known as horsetails; those without are called scouring rushes. Most people know these plants as "snake

Badger Pass

grass" because of their segmented, hollow stems. Horsetails reproduce by shedding spores. They prefer damp habitats and are a favourite early summer food of bears.

The upper Johnston Creek valley is oriented along the Castle Mountain Thrust. Bedrock in the lower slopes on the west side of the valley is purple and brown Miette Formation (mee-YETT) gritstone and shale. Miette rocks underlie much of the eastern main ranges, and are the oldest rocks visible in this part of the Rockies. Miette sediments accumulated to a maximum thickness of 8 km.

You have two camping options near the Luellen Lake junction. Johnston Creek campground is 200 m west (left) from the junction, on the near bank of the creek. This pleasant campground is an excellent choice for those wishing more solitude and fewer bugs than at nearby Luellen Lake campground.

Luellen Lake to Badger Pass Junction

The Sawback trail continues northwest (straight ahead) from the Luellen Lake junction, along the east bank of Johnston Creek. This section of trail is narrower and much less travelled. The trail soon crosses to the west bank. The forest becomes more open and views improve. The trail descends to the creek and crosses it again. For the next 3 km, the route is through willow and shrub thickets near the creek. Keep to the hiker trail at the horse-hiker barrier or

---

FISHING

Luellen Lake is one of the more popular backcountry fishing destinations in Banff National Park. Cutthroat trout are native; rainbow trout and brook trout have been introduced. Park staff formerly stocked Luellen Lake and many other lakes with non-native species to promote angling – this lake was named for the daughter of a fish hatchery superintendent. As a result, few backcountry lakes in the Rockies now host a natural complement of species.

Park managers are contemplating various measures to re-establish natural regimes in backcountry lakes. These may include increasing catch limits for introduced species until they are "fished out," and then closing the lakes to angling; or managing the lakes as "catch and release" fisheries only. Stocking of fish is now only considered to assist the recovery of native species.

BADGER PASS (2539 M), 5.0 KM

You are fortunate indeed if you can visit the exquisite alpine realms of Badger Pass and Pulsatilla Pass on successive days. I suggest adding an extra day to your outing to make this possible. The trail to Badger Pass follows an idyllic stream through forest and meadows to the craggy divide between Johnston Creek and the upper Cascade River. The prospect east into the headwaters of the Cascade River is one of the wilder ones in Banff National Park. Ridge upon ridge of sawtooth mountains rear up like rocky waves in an ocean of sky. Badger Pass is the 8th-highest point on the Classic Hikes, and can be snowbound until mid-July. The horn mountains northwest of the pass feature extensive grassy slopes that are excellent habitat for bighorn sheep, grizzly bears, and mountain goats. I have twice encountered grizzly bears in this valley.

you may be obliged to ford and re-ford numerous braids of the creek. Cross Badger Creek to the Badger Pass trail junction. The Sawback trail heads north, reaching the Badger Pass Junction campground in 500 m. In late summer, the water source at this campground may dry up, requiring a 500 m walk to Johnston Creek. Bring a water billy.

Badger Pass Junction to Baker Creek

For 2 km beyond Badger Pass Junction campground, the Sawback trail works through shrub thickets in the valley bottom. Boulder-hop or ford Johnston Creek to its west bank. Wet meadows here feature an

NO BADGERS HERE

Badger Pass is named for the American badger, a nocturnal member of the weasel family. The alpine terrain of Badger Pass is not badger habitat – not by a long stretch – the animal prefers low elevation grasslands and shrub meadows where it seeks the small rodents that comprise most of its diet. Southeast of the pass in the Cascade River valley, badgers are sighted more frequently than in any other watershed in Banff National Park – which is still to say, not very often. Some people think that the name of the pass records a case of mistaken identity, that the namesake "badger" was really a hoary marmot.

astounding array of wildflowers, including elephant-head, fleabane, bracted lousewort, yellow hedysarum, and yellow paintbrush.

Pulsatilla Mountain (3035 m) forms the west wall of the valley. The east face of the mountain is a cliff, 6 km long, riddled with cirques. One of these cirques is still home to a sizeable glacier, which formed part of the mountain's first ascent route in 1930. From bottom to top, the cliffs display the main range, "castle-building" sequence: Cathedral Formation limestone, Stephen Formation shale, and Eldon Formation limestone, best known at Castle Mountain, 10 km to the south.

The shrub thickets give way to larch forest as the trail nears Pulsatilla Pass. Look for a Z-shaped cascade in the creek. Rock-hop the creek to its east bank, take the northwest (left) trail fork, and begin the final climb to the pass, which is steeper going and farther away than it looks. Impressive wildflower displays make the climb enjoyable. "Pulsatilla" is an old genus name for the western anemone (*Anemone occidentalis*). This showy member of the buttercup family grows here in profusion. Anemone means "wind flower." Along with other typical upper sub-alpine wildflowers, these meadows contain two species normally found at lower elevations – mountain death-camas and cow parsnip. Contorted lousewort is also abundant.

Look back for a fine view of the upper Johnston Creek valley. The unnamed peak on the east side of the valley, just south of Badger Creek, features a formation known as a *klippe*. The horn-like, summit

HEART OF THE SAWBACK

Competent backpackers can make a superb loop variation at this point on the Sawback trail. From Badger Pass junction, cross Badger Pass to the upper Cascade River – one of the better days that you can spend in the high country of the Rockies. It's 5 km to the pass, and 7 km from there to the Block Lakes Junction campground. Heading east on a fireroad through forest that burned in 1936, you reach Flints Park campground in another 5.5 km. From Flints Park, head south along Sawback Creek. You reach the Sawback Lake junction in 4.4 km. A 1.4 km sidetrail leads to Sawback Lake campground, from which a rough, 800 m track leads to the lake. If you stay at Sawback Lake campground, you do not have to backtrack to the Sawback Lake junction, a trail angles southeast from the campground to rejoin the main trail just before it climbs to the next destination, Forty Mile Summit (photo, 2149 m). This pass is a spectacular, 2 km-long meadow, *below* treeline – a great place to see elk, deer, coyotes, wolves, and bears. From the south end of Forty Mile Summit, you

begin a steady descent into Forty Mile Creek valley (keep left, on the hiker trail), reaching the Mystic Junction campground in 5.7 km, and the Mystic Pass junction in another 300 m. Continue south along familiar ground to the Mt. Norquay trailhead. The base distance for this loop is 84.5 km. Add accordingly if you will be camping at Badger Pass Junction, day-hiking to Pulsatilla Pass, and visiting Sawback Lake. Allow 6-8 days.

formation stands alone atop the bedding plane of a less-resistant, underlying formation. The final slopes leading to Pulsatilla Pass will be snow-covered well into July, most years.

The view north from Pulsatilla Pass reveals one of the more exquisite alpine landscapes in Banff National Park. The centrepiece is Pulsatilla Lake, framed perfectly between the wild crags that border upper Wildflower Creek. In the distance, with its perennial snowpatch, Fossil Mountain (2946 m) keeps watch over the scene. While you stop to take in the view, keep an eye on your packs. Bold hoary marmots inhabit the pass – high country highwaymen who will quickly depart with any loose object they find. I've heard tell of one that stole a T-shirt here and took it down its burrow.

On Pulsatilla Pass

Dropping north from the pass, the trail hugs the east side of the valley to avoid wet meadows. About 500 m from the pass, the trail forks. The left-hand path descends to the shore of Pulsatilla Lake. The right-hand path traverses the steep sideslope above the lake, with one awkward step at a gully. Take your pick; the routes converge 1 km north.

Pulsatilla Lake is a sink lake. It has no visible outlet, indicating subterranean drainage (known as karst) in the limestone bedrock. An upturned edge of glacier-worn rock dams it. The front ranges of Banff feature many sink lakes impounded in a similar fashion, but few are as large as Pulsatilla Lake.

From the cliff edge beyond the lake, you begin a steep descent into the valley of Wildflower Creek. The trail passes an unnamed pond, dammed by rockslide debris. It was near this pond that Mary Vaux Walcott, third wife of Charles Walcott, and a gifted botanist and artist, collected 82 species of flora during a visit in July 1921. In his diary, Charles recorded that Mary found, "50 species in bloom within 200 feet of our tent." Accordingly, Mary called the valley "Wild Flower Canyon," the origin of today's name. The pond is often dry by late summer.

The valley bottom forest contains ancient Engelmann spruce and lodgepole pine. Some of the spruces are 45 m tall. The trail is vague where you rock-hop a tributary stream that comes in from the east. About 5.5 km from Pulsatilla Pass, ford Wildflower Creek to its west bank. The steep descent continues to the Wildflower Creek campground, skirting ancient moraines on the way.

Wildflower Creek to Baker Lake

From the campground, cross Wildflower Creek on a bridge and turn west (left) as far as Baker Creek; then turn north (right). As you climb beside Baker Creek, you cross several avalanche slopes that offer views southwest to the Wenkchemna Peaks. Vegetation here is incredibly lush. The trail drops into a clearing where you will probably lose the route – a taste of things to come. There is an outfitter's camp at the north edge of this meadow. The trail descends to an extensive wet meadow along Baker Creek. Don't get suckered toward the creek. Keep to the east of this boggy area, and do the best you can to keep your feet dry.

North of the wet meadow, the trail crosses the alluvial rubble of a flash-flood stream course – the handiwork of Lychnis Creek. Flash-floods here often knock out the bridge. *Lychnis* is an old genus name for various species of campion – showy wildflowers of the upper subalpine and alpine – now classified in the genus, *Silene*. If you lose the trail here, don't look for it in the forest; it keeps to the open willow plain. On the west side of the valley, two waterfalls on Anthozoan Mountain (2697 m) emerge from underground. They drain a series of lakes concealed on the bench above. *Anthozoans* are fossilized, reeflike deposits of coral found in the dolomite bedrock of this peak and on other mountains nearby.

The steep ascent to the meadows south of Baker Lake may try your patience. It is braded and mucky, with many churned rocks – a product of horse use. This section lasts but a kilometre. Delightful upper

---

THE SAWBACK RANGE

James Hector merely commented on the obvious when he named the "Saw-back" Range in 1858. The limestone slabs, capped by weak shales, were thrust vertically during mountain building. This created steep, southwest-facing slopes that just happen to be oriented perpendicular to the prevailing weather systems. Mechanical weathering, solution, and abrasion have readily eroded the shales atop the slabs, creating the sawtooth ridges and hourglass-shaped gullies in the slopes below. The gullies collect runoff and debris from vast areas near the ridgetops, funneling the water through slots between "flatirons" of resistant limestone onto the lower slopes. Not surprisingly, flash-floods are common.

Baker Lake

subalpine meadows greet you at the top of the climb, silencing any curses that may have been about to spring forth.

Rock-hop Baker Creek to its west side just above a colourful shale canyon. You reach an important junction 800 m beyond. Turn northwest (left) for the final 800 m to Baker Lake campground, a welcome sight if you have come all the way from Badger Pass Junction. The series of upturned rock benches that impound the lake mark the edge of the Castle Mountain Thrust. The outlet stream has eroded an interesting channel through these formations. Look for dippers here.

Baker Lake is another popular backcountry fishing destination; home to rainbow trout and cutthroat trout. Besides a multitude of campers, you will probably share this campground with mosquitoes, porcupines, and snowshoe hares. Oh, and did I mention the mosquitoes?

Baker Lake to Fish Creek

The Sawback trail concludes by heading west along the north shore of Baker Lake before climbing to Ptarmigan Lake and Boulder Pass. On the pass, the mountains of the Slate Range are close at hand. Mt. Temple (3544 m) looms to the southwest, across the Bow Valley. Halfway Hut and Hidden Lake campground are 1.5 km beyond the pass, set in glades of larch forest. The hut, built as a stopover for packers supplying Skoki Lodge, is located halfway between the Lake Louise train station and the lodge. See Classic Hike #18 for more information on this area.

Beyond the hut, the trail re-enters subalpine forest. After 3 km, the trail emerges onto a ski run at the Lake Louise ski area. It is 3.5 km of steady downhill on a gravel road to the Fish Creek parking area, with occasional views of Mt. Victoria en route. Keep your head up – grizzly bears frequent this area. (You can also walk on the ski-out, downslope from the road.) If you need a telephone to arrange transportation, follow a track north from the parking area for 1 km to Whiskeyjack Lodge at the Lake Louise ski area. Otherwise, it's a downhill walk on gravel for 1 km to Whitehorn Drive, where you turn left for another 2 km on pavement (ouch!) to Lake Louise village. Ah, civilization.

FINDING FAULTS

Although the ragged peaks of the front ranges seem chaotic, there is geologic order in this landscape. Pulsatilla Pass, Wildflower Creek, and upper Johnston Creek lie on the Castle Mountain Thrust. As with most faults in the front ranges, this one is oriented along the strike of the Rockies – southeast to northwest. This creates a symmetrical landscape – each strike valley is walled by parallel mountain ranges that are composed of the leading edges of a thrust sheets.

On the crest of Pulsatilla Pass, you can see the contact surfaces of the Castle Mountain Thrust. The trail follows the dividing line between whitish Gog Formation quartzite (Early Cambrian) to the west, and Survey Peak Formation shale (Late Cambrian) to the east. The quartzite is the leading edge of the thrust sheet, brought from near the sedimentary basement of the Rockies to rest atop the younger shales. This rocky seam also separates two of the geological provinces of the Rockies – the main ranges to the west, from the younger front ranges to the east.

7. Mt. Assiniboine

Mt. Assiniboine

S traddling the continental divide, "The Matterhorn of the Rockies," Mt. Assiniboine (a-SIN-ni-boyne) (3616 m), is the 8th-highest peak in the Canadian Rockies. It is also the 2nd-highest peak in Banff National Park. First noted by missionary Pierre-Jean De Smet in 1845, the mountain was named in 1883 by surveyor G.M. Dawson. *Assiniboine* means "those who cook by placing hot rocks in water." Dawson was referring to a tribe of the Sioux Confederation. Known elsewhere as the Nakoda or Dakota peoples, they were known locally as the Stoneys.

Half a dozen backpacking routes lead to Lake Magog at the base of Mt. Assiniboine. This outing describes a traverse of Mt. Assiniboine Provincial Park using Citadel Pass and Wonder Pass. This traverse, combined with the day-hiking options, provides you with a complete experience of Mt. Assiniboine's spectacular scenery. Do not expect solitude. You will be sharing the area with hikers, mountain bikers, helicopters, and horse traffic. The Lake Magog campground is frequently crowded, and

VARIATIONS

- Hike the described route in the opposite direction.
- Backpack from Sunshine to Lake Magog campground and return the same way; 71.0 km.
- Exit from Lake Magog jct via Assiniboine Pass, to reach the Bryant Creek trail at the Wonder Pass jct. Carry on to Mt. Shark trailhead; 58.6 km.
- Make a loop using Bryant Creek. Approach from Mt. Shark trailhead over Assiniboine Pass to Lake Magog (24.7 km). Exit via Wonder Pass (25.6 km); 3-5 days.
- Camp at Howard Douglas Lake (12.3 km) and explore Citadel Pass and Sunshine Meadows.
- Day-hike Citadel Pass; 31.8 km return.

Trailhead
Follow Highway 1, 8.3 km west from Banff to the Sunshine Interchange. Follow the Sunshine road 9 km to its end at the ski hill parking area. The trailhead kiosk is west of (behind) the gondola terminal. If you want to skip the 6.2 km hike along the Sunshine access road, contact White Mountain Adventures to book a seat on the bus; 403-760-4403, 800-408-0005.

Special consideration
You require a wilderness pass to camp at Howard Douglas Lake, Marvel Lake, Big Springs, and the Bryant Creek shelter in Banff; and separate camping permits for Porcupine, Og Lake, and Lake Magog campgrounds in Mt. Assiniboine Provincial Park. See contacts, p. 280.

Maps
NTS: 82 O/4, 82 J/13, 82 J/14
Gem Trek: *Banff and Mt. Assiniboine*

BANFF NATIONAL PARK

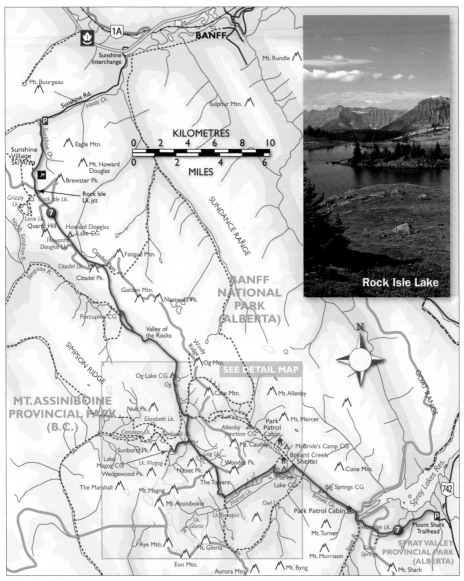

Rock Isle Lake

the Naiset cabins are overrun during poor weather. To reserve space at either, phone Mt. Assiniboine Lodge, 403-678-4877.

Trailhead to Sunshine Meadows

If you want to hike with a crowd, book a seat on the bus that runs from the ski hill parking area to Sunshine Meadows. If you want to avoid schedules and the general crush of humanity, hike the road. Yes, it will take you longer – perhaps two hours – and it will burn up your breakfast. You gain the road at the trail junction at 0.9 km. Take the left-hand fork and switchback away on gravel for the next 5.3 km.

The Sunshine ski area originated with a cabin built by the Canadian Pacific Railway in 1928. Between 1929 and 1932, several ski parties from Banff visited the area. They were delighted with the winter snow. Jim Brewster, then owner of Brewster Transportation, was one of those skiers. In 1934, he leased the cabin for the winter, buying it outright in 1936. Brewster hired mountain guides to teach skiing, and the area's popularity grew rapidly.

Development at Sunshine has long been a thorny issue. As with most commercial enterprises in the national parks, the various owners of Sunshine Village have sought to expand their facilities and their lease area. Environmentalists have questioned the appropriateness of private, commercial enterprise on national park land, due to the negative effects caused by such incessant incremental expansion. Skiers and Banff business people note that the area has excellent snow. Many of them desire that Sunshine should be allowed to expand further to cater to a larger market. By increments, they have been successful – new ski runs, new lifts, new buildings, a bigger parking area – the "footprint" of the ski area is forever expanding.

Sunshine Village is at road's end. Follow the crushed stone path south, through the sprawl of buildings. Fifteen metres past the avalanche station turn east (left) onto a gravelled trail and ascend south through larch forest to the Sunshine Meadows – a spectacular hiking environment. Open vistas fill all directions. The towering horn of Mt. Assiniboine beckons from the south. After 1.1 km, the trail crests the continental divide and crosses from Banff National Park, Alberta, into Mt. Assiniboine Provincial Park, BC. The trail forks. The wider, right-hand trail leads to Rock Isle Lake. If you do not want to make this sidetrip, continue on the left-hand trail.

Sunshine Meadows to Citadel Pass

For 2.5 km beyond the Rock Isle Lake junction, the Assiniboine trail rambles through Sunshine Meadows and re-enters Banff National Park. Limestone erratics dot the meadows; these boulders were deposited by retreating glaciers. After descending into a hollow northeast of Quartz Hill, the trail climbs over Quartz Ridge, with unimpeded views south to Mt. Assiniboine. Here, the trail improvements end, and a heavily braided, slippery trail descends to the campground on the east shore of Howard Douglas Lake (incorrectly named "Sundown Lake" on older topographic maps). Howard Douglas was the second superintendent of Banff National Park. Mountaineers may readily ascend Quartz Hill (2566 m) from either the campground or from the trail's high point on Quartz Ridge (easier). Eastern brook trout inhabit Howard Douglas Lake.

A classic alpland dotted with lakelets lies beyond Howard Douglas Lake. Near here, in August 1933, three hikers watched two wolves attack and kill a grizzly bear. After crossing Citadel Pass, you re-enter Mt. Assiniboine Provincial Park. You may see a sign that optimistically informs you that Lake Magog is 17 km and 5.5 hours distant. As it is 18 km to the Magog Lake junction on a tough trail, most mortals with backpacks should count on adding three hours to the suggested hiking time.

> *The majestic mountain, which is a noble pyramid of rock towering above snow fields, was clearly reflected in the water surface. Such a picture so suddenly revealed aroused the utmost enthusiasm of all our party, and unconsciously everyone paused in admiration...*
>
> Walter Wilcox; *The Rockies of Canada*

SUNSHINE AND SNOW

The Sunshine Meadows occupy a 14 km arc along the continental divide, at an average elevation of 2225 m. Together with the meadows at Simpson Pass, Healy Pass, and above Lost Horse Creek, they form a vast heath tundra. Mountain heather, woolly everlasting, fleabane, valerian, arctic willow, western anemone, and sedges are the characteristic plants. In addition, 340 other plants have been recorded. This represents more than one third of the plant species of Banff and Jasper national parks. Some of the species are rare, and many are at either the extreme northern or southern limits of their ranges.

The average temperature on the meadows is -4°C, and more than 7 m of snow falls each year. Snowbanks linger well into July. Vegetation is specially adapted, storing nutrients from summer's sunshine to release in a burst that promotes rapid growth the following year. Still, with a growing season so short, it may take decades before some plants mature enough to carry blooms – 20 years is typical for moss campion. Snowmelt saturates the thin soils for much of the summer. Travel off-trail can cause long-lasting damage to the ground cover. Please keep to maintained trails.

Mt. Assiniboine, Lake Magog

Citadel Pass to Og Lake

A kilometre south of the pass, the trail drops below treeline into larch forest, contours beside a small tarn – the last water source for 13 km – and then begins a steep, switchbacking descent through avalanche paths. This is excellent bear habitat. After traversing south onto a sideslope, you reach the Porcupine campground junction. If you make the steep descent to this campground, you don't have to climb back up to continue next day. Follow a faint track south from the campground for 2.1 km to rejoin the main trail at the Simpson River junction.

From the Porcupine campground junction, the high trail continues its southward traverse of the sideslope of Golden Mountain (2933 m). I have counted more than 25 species of wildflowers in bloom here in early July. At the south end of this traverse, the trail contours around a rockslide that heralds the entrance to the Valley of the Rocks.

The Valley of the Rocks is not a valley, but a depression in the debris of an enormous landslide that originated from the mountains to the east. This landslide is estimated to contain more than a billion

ROCK ISLE-GRIZZLY LAKE-LARIX LAKE, 5.7 KM LOOP

This loop visits three lakes in the northern part of Mt. Assiniboine Provincial Park. Some of the BC Parks trail signs refer to this outing as The Garden Path. You reach the Rock Isle Lake viewpoint in 500 m. Turn southwest (left) at the next junction in 200 m. The trail descends through a flower-filled larch forest. Turn southwest (right) at the next junction to pass along the east shore of Grizzly Lake. The trail curves south to a viewpoint that overlooks the upper Simpson Valley. After circling around Larix Lake, with impressive views west to The Monarch (2895 m), the trail climbs back to the loop junction below Rock Isle Lake.

An upturned lip of Outram Formation limestone dams Rock Isle Lake. Another bedrock exposure creates the "isle." The lake drains underground. Grizzly Lake is shallow and is being filled with vegetation. Larix Lake is deeper, with underwater ledges visible. *Larix* is the genus name of the Lyall's larch. You must carry your backpacks on this loop hike, as there is no place to cache them.

"THE CANADIAN MATTERHORN"

Mt. Assiniboine was the object of several mountaineering attempts in the 1890s. Its remote location and difficult approach thwarted all comers, but competition was keen. In 1901, Edward Whymper, of Matterhorn fame, visited the Rockies at the behest of the Canadian Pacific Railway, whose executives hoped that he would make Mt. Assiniboine's first ascent. However, Whymper was past his mountaineering prime and could not even be enticed to make the approach. The first ascent was made in September that year by James Outram (OOTrum) and guides. They ascended the southwest face, and descended the northeast arête, toward Lake Magog. This arête is the "regular" ascent route today. Although the climb is not difficult by contemporary standards, unpredictable weather, poor rock, and the presence of snow or ice make any attempt on Mt. Assiniboine a serious undertaking.

cubic metres of material, making it by far the largest known rockslide in the Rockies, and among the twenty-largest in the world. The winding trail through the Valley of the Rocks seems double its 6 km length, and is virtually devoid of water. At the Simpson River junction, turn southeast (left). The small rockslide depression lake nearby is the only source of water before Og Lake. You should treat this water before consumption.

You will know that the travail through the Valley of the Rocks is over when Mt. Assiniboine again becomes visible. The trail descends to Og Lake and its campground. Og Lake is a sink lake; its waters drain underground. Many of the lakes near Mt. Assiniboine empty in a similar fashion. Although the karst system fed by the lakes is unstudied, more than a century ago Walter Wilcox speculated that the disappearing water emerges as the source of the Simpson River, 6 km northwest.

Og Lake to Lake Magog

From Og Lake, it is 5.9 km to the Lake Magog campground junction. Half of this distance is across a flat subalpine meadow, the probable location of an ancient lake. Trails proliferate as you approach Lake Magog. Any attempt to describe the lefts and rights will only confuse. If you are destined for the campground or for the Naiset Cabins, follow trail signs accordingly. The campground is set on a glacial terrace on the

Cerulean Lake

THE NUB, 6.7 KM LOOP

Follow the trail north past Sunburst Lake to Cerulean Lake. At the junction on the far shore of Cerulean Lake, turn northeast (right) for Elizabeth Lake. After a short climb, you reach The Nub junction. Turn east (right) and climb steadily to Nub Ridge (2390 m). If you would like to ascend higher onto Nub Peak, watch for a faint track that angles sharply to the north where the trail levels. By following this rough path to the prominent high point, you obtain superb views of the soaring fang of Mt. Assiniboine. You can see six lakes – Gog, Magog, Sunburst, Cerulean, Elizabeth, and Wedgewood. For those inclined, an unmaintained track leads north for 2 km along a shattered limestone ridge to the summit slopes of Nub Peak (2746 m). The view from this modest peak is without equal in the vicinity.

From Nub Ridge you can return to the campground via your route of ascent (more direct), or make a loop by following the trail south from the end of the ridge to the Assiniboine Pass trail. At this junction, turn southwest (right) to reach the campground in 1.5 km.

SUNBURST CIRCUIT-CHUCK'S RIDGE, 9.1 KM LOOP

Follow the trail north past Sunburst Lake to Cerulean (seh-ROO-lee-an) Lake. *Cerulean* means "resembling the blue colour of the sky." At the junction on the far side of the lake, turn west (left) and follow the north shore. There are fine views of Sunburst Peak (2849 m) across the lake. At the west end of the lake, the trail descends to the north (right). After 200 m, angle east (right) at a junction, and climb 1.4 km to Elizabeth Lake. The aquamarine lake commemorates Lizzie Rummel, who operated Sunburst cabin as a tourist lodge from 1951 to 1970. The cabin has since been moved from its original location. I have seen a bald eagle here.

At the outlet of Elizabeth Lake, the 800 m sidetrail to Chuck's Ridge veers north. Chuck's Ridge (2347 m) provides an excellent overview of this area, and of the meadows and lakes at the head of Nestor Creek. The glacier-draped form of The Marshall (3180 m) dominates the view southwest. You can also see Wedgewood Lake. The ridge was a favourite haunt of Chuck Millar, a packer for Mt. Assiniboine Lodge.

Return to Elizabeth Lake and follow the trail along the west shore to a junction in 400 m. If you would like to ascend to The Nub, turn east (left). Otherwise, continue straight ahead and descend to Cerulean Lake. Return via Sunburst Lake to the campground.

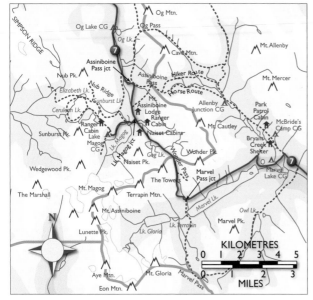

Many people who visit Mt. Assiniboine – 64 percent in summer – fly to the area by helicopter. BC Parks allows helicopters to land near the ranger station three days a week. The Mt. Assiniboine area is also a highlight of "flightseeing" trips which originate at Canmore. Although the flightseeing helicopters do not land, they are frequently overhead. On a typical fly-in day, there may be 40 round-trip flights from Canmore, and as many flightseeing flights.

Helicopters create an exceptional aesthetic disturbance in the backcountry. Some backpackers take advantage of helicopter access; others plug their ears and begrudgingly tolerate their presence. Imagine what your overall experience of the Rockies would be like if all the parks permitted helicopter access to this degree.

The negative effects of helicopter traffic go beyond aesthetics. Most helicopters that visit Mt. Assiniboine have flown over areas of Banff National Park – and sometimes, Kananaskis Country and Kootenay National Park – zoned as wilderness, where protection of wildlife and habitat is the prime intent. Recreational helicopter landings are prohibited in these areas, however national parks cannot control the airspace above. Helicopter traffic subjects wildlife to stress. Particularly vulnerable are mountain goats, bighorn sheep, elk, and caribou, especially when with young. Thus, the helicopter policy of BC Parks thwarts the wildlife protection objectives of Banff and Kootenay national parks, not to mention the protection of wildlife within Mt. Assiniboine Park.

northwest shore of Lake Magog. It offers a commanding view of Mt. Assiniboine, whose graceful summit towers more than 1400 m above. As with most isolated and lofty peaks, Mt. Assiniboine creates local weather. Clouds frequently adorn the summit, and precipitation is common nearby – meaning on your tent.

After the energy you've invested in reaching Mt. Assiniboine, you will probably want to spend several days in the area. The best day-hiking options are described below. All distances are measured from Lake Magog campground.

Mt. Assiniboine Lodge and Naiset Cabins

Mt. Assiniboine's popularity assures that you will have lots of company during your visit. Many stay at the Naiset Cabins or at Mt. Assiniboine Lodge. The five original Naiset Cabins were built in 1925 by A.O. Wheeler, founder of the Alpine Club of Canada. The cabins accommodated clients on "Wheeler's Walking Tours" of the Rockies. The enterprise soon went bankrupt, and the cabins were leased to various interests until 1944, when the ACC took them over. In 1971, ownership of the decrepit cabins passed to BC Parks, which refurbished them for use by hikers. The capacity is 31. Mt. Assiniboine Lodge now operates the cabins. *Naiset* is a word from the Sioux language; it means "sunset."

The Canadian Pacific Railway built Mt. Assiniboine Lodge in the summer of 1928, at the behest of Italian sportsman, Marquis delgi Albizzi, and Norwegian skier, Erling Strom. The two had visited Assiniboine the previous spring and were delighted with the skiing terrain. Strom subsequently operated the lodge for more than four decades. The lodge is now owned by the BC government, and is operated privately under lease. The park ranger station is located southeast of the lodge and cabins.

Lake Magog to Marvel Lake

Because it is difficult to arrange transportation at the Mt. Shark trailhead at trail's end, some backpackers exit from Mt. Assiniboine via Sunshine. If you choose to backtrack, include Wonder Pass (4.4 km) as a half-day-hike before you go.

The trail to Wonder Pass skirts the shore of Lake Magog to Naiset Cabins. Half a kilometre south of the cabins, the trail crosses the outlet of Gog Lake. Great blue herons nested at this lake in 1983 – the highest nesting elevation yet recorded for this species. The names Gog, Og, and Magog refer to legendary giants of Biblical times. The cliffs south and west of Gog Lake are the "type locality" for the Gog group of sedimentary formations. This is where these rocks – quartzite, sandstone, and siltstone – were first studied in detail. Gog Formation quartzite – a metamorphic, quartz-rich sandstone – is the hardest rock exposed in the central Rockies.

Continuing south from Gog Lake, the trail climbs through wildflower meadows and larch forest to a viewpoint that overlooks a small waterfall and canyon. This canyon is cut in Miette (mee-YETT) Formation shale. You reach treeline about 500 m before Wonder Pass. From the crest of the pass, located on the Banff National Park boundary, you have inspiring views south to the dip-slope, limestone peaks of the Blue Range. On a clear day, the view north will include the mountains that flank Sunshine Meadows. Look for mountain goats on the cliffs of The Towers (2842 m), west of the pass.

Cross Wonder Pass. After 700 m, a faint track branches southeast (left) for 600 m to a viewpoint that overlooks Marvel Lake. This is an excellent extension for day-hikers. Dropping south to treeline, the main trail cuts southwest across a gully. From this sideslope you have a spectacular vista of Marvel Lake, 550 m below. The lake is the 6th-largest in Banff National Park, and is 67 m deep.

The next 1.8 km involves a steady descent. Initially the trail heads west, providing views of the extensive glacier beneath Mt. Gloria (2889 m), Mt. Eon (3305 m), and Aye Mountain (3236 m). You can now see two more lakes in the valley above Marvel Lake – Lake Gloria and Lake Terrapin. The colours of these lakes are caused by concentrations of glacial rock flour in their waters. These lakes act as settling ponds, preventing much of the rock flour from entering Marvel Lake. Hence the water of Marvel Lake is a deeper blue in colour. A waterfall marks the outflow of Lake Terrapin.

WINDY RIDGE (2635 M), 8.7 KM

Follow the Assiniboine Pass trail northeast from the campground. At all junctions follow signs for Og Pass-Windy Ridge. The trail climbs toward Og Pass, and levels in meadows at a final junction at km 6.5. Og Pass is 300 m east. The Windy Ridge trail veers north (left) from the junction, and climbs 2.2 km to the 3rd-highest point reached on the Classic Hikes – the barren ridgecrest north of Og Mountain. The vistas are splendid; especially alluring is an unnamed lake to the northeast, in the upper reaches of Brewster Creek.

Keep straight ahead (southeast) at the Marvel Pass junction. Although the trail ahead is well travelled, the Marvel Lake valley is a wild corner of Banff National Park. As you begin the 4.5 km-long traverse above the north shore of the lake, watch for grizzly bears. A variety of wildflowers decorates the south-facing avalanche slopes.

Marvel Lake to Mt. Shark Trailhead

The trail re-enters forest at the east end of Marvel Lake. Keep straight ahead at the first junction. At the second junction, turn south (right) to reach the outlet of Marvel Lake in 500 m. Head east from the outlet to Marvel Lake campground in 1.1 km. From the campground, it is 600 m to the Bryant Creek trail. Turn southeast (right), and follow this rolling backcountry artery through lodgepole pine forest, 6.2 km to the mouth of the Bryant Creek valley, passing the Big Springs campground in 3.3 km. The trail is fireroad width. You share it with horses, and with the odd four-wheeler who is off route. The valley was named for Henry Bryant, who joined Walter Wilcox in the first attempt to climb Mt. Assiniboine in 1899.

The trail junction at the Banff National Park boundary is known as Trail Centre. Take the south (right) trail for the Mt. Shark trailhead. Cross Bryant Creek on a footbridge and continue south for 500 m. This is part of the historic trail travelled by the Palliser Expedition in 1858. The Spray Lakes Reservoir is to the north. The Spray Lakes area was removed from Banff National Park in 1930 for a hydroelectric development, completed in 1951.

Turn east (left) at the Palliser Pass junction, and cross the Spray River at a small canyon. The remaining 5.8 km to the Mt. Shark trailhead is along old logging roads. Watridge Lake and the nearby Karst Spring – one of the larger by volume in North America – make interesting sidetrips.

The hike to the Mt. Shark trailhead is a very long day from Lake Magog campground. Many backpackers use Marvel Lake or Big Springs campgrounds to break the journey into two days. If you do not have transportation prearranged, plan to arrive at the Mt. Shark trailhead early. There is no telephone service here. The trailhead is 4.6 km along a gravel road from the Spray Lakes Road (Alberta Route 742). The junction of these two roads is 37 km south of Canmore. Traffic is light in the evening. Bears frequent the parking area – it's not a good place to sleep.

8. Simpson Pass – Healy Pass

Healy Meadows

In the deep forest along Healy Creek and on the meadows above, you may find, as many do, backcountry bliss. Keep this in mind as you assemble your pack in the parking area. No other departure point in the Rockies so readily prompts me to put on my boots and my pack and to get away. It's a busy place, almost all of it designed for commerce. Don't worry; twenty minutes down the trail, all that will literally be behind you.

Trailhead to Simpson Pass Junction

The trail to Healy Pass from Banff was one of the earlier recreational trails built in the park. Outfitter Jim Boyce cut the route in 1909. The road-width trail climbs gradually on the bank between Healy Creek and the Sunshine access road. At 0.9 km, the trail forks and narrows. Take the right-hand trail and begin a short descent to Sunshine Creek, whose course is eroded into Palliser Formation limestone. Karst fissures upstream capture much of the water, often leaving the lower reach of the stream dry.

Across Sunshine Creek, the climb resumes through a wonderful subalpine forest of Engelmann spruce, subalpine fir, and a few lodgepole pines. The delicate blooms of pink wintergreen and the tiny red fruits of grouseberry add colour to the forest floor. The list of plants that typify the subalpine forest floor is nearly complete here. Listen for the songs of golden-crowned kinglets, winter wrens, black-

TRAIL THUMBNAIL

Day-hike or overnight

Route	Elev. (m)	Dist. (km)
Parking area	1690	0
Trailhead	1692	0.2
Healy Pass jct	1706	0.9
Healy Creek CG	1973	5.7
Simpson Pass jct	1981	6.1
Simpson Pass	2107	7.7
Healy Meadows jct	2095	10.3
Healy Pass	2340	11.8
Healy Meadows jct	2095	13.3
Trailhead	1692	21.0
Parking area	1690	21.2

Trailhead
Follow Highway 1, 8.3 km west from Banff to the Sunshine Interchange. Follow the Sunshine road 9 km to its end at the ski hill parking area. The trailhead kiosk is west of (behind) the gondola terminal, 200 m from the parking area.

Maps
NTS: 82 O/4

Gem Trek: *Banff and Mt. Assiniboine* or *Kootenay National Park*

capped chickadees, red-breasted nuthatches, pine siskins, Tennessee warblers, boreal chickadees, and varied thrushes; for the trilling of dark-eyed juncos; for the rasping calls of Clark's nutcrackers; and for the tapping of three-toed woodpeckers. The middens of red squirrels dot the forest floor; their chattering greets you from the trees.

If you have hit the trail late, the bridged creek crossing at km 3.3 makes a pleasant lunch stop. Here, Healy Creek has eroded a shallow canyon into the upturned edges of fossil-rich dolomite of the Cairn Formation.

For the next 2.4 km, the trail follows the north bank of Healy Creek, crossing three avalanche slopes before Healy Creek campground. Pressure-treated wood structures span sidestreams that are but trickles. This overkill was part of the clean-up of the trail in the late 1980s. At that time, horse-use was banished, sections of trail were re-routed, and stone and gravel were incorporated into the tread in wet areas. In the upper valley, there are sections of inlaid natural stone that are both attractive and highly effective. Look for low larkspur, white camas, and meadow

VARIATIONS

- Day-hike Healy Pass; 18.8 km return.
- Day-hike Simpson Pass; 15.2 km return.
- Camp at Healy Creek CG and day-hike to the either or both passes.
- An optional exit for backpackers from Healy Creek CG is to Simpson Pass, Wawa Ridge, and the Sunshine Road; 13.3 km.

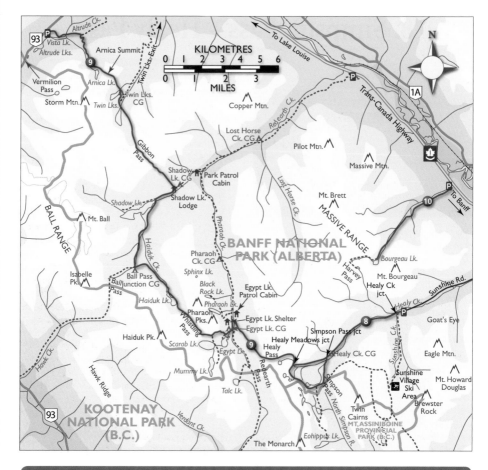

A LUNKER OF A CALLING CARD

George Simpson was Banff's first tourist. If he were alive today, he might be a CEO who played squash before jogging to the office, worked out at lunch, "down-sized" half his staff in the afternoon, and fitted in a 100 km bike ride before dinner. In the 1820s and 1830s he trooped relentlessly through Prince Rupert's Land, and was said to have met every employee of the Hudson's Bay Company. He had his own corporate jet – an 8-seater express canoe. One seat was allotted to a piper, who would herald his lordship's arrival at far-flung forts and trading posts. In 1841, freshly knighted for his services to the British Empire and to commerce in general, and then Governor of the HBC, Simpson set out to make the first circuit of the globe by essentially a terrestrial route. He did it in just under 20 months, a feat achieved in no small

part by the pace he kept across the Rockies – sometimes covering 80 km a day. His mean and uncompromising behaviour earned him the tag, The Little Emperor. He wrote: "It is strange that all my ailments vanish as soon as I seat myself in a canoe." Presumably, this was because someone else was paddling the breakneck pace. Dip, dip, and swing.

Simpson's party, led by a Cree guide, Alexis Piché, crossed what is now known as Simpson Pass in 1858. (Simpson had called it Shuswap Pass.) Sir George left a calling card of sorts. In 1904 a party of Banffites camped on the pass found Simpson's initials and those of companion, John Rowland, and the date 1841 carved in a fallen tree. The relevant portion of the tree, now known as the Simpson Register, is preserved at the Whyte Museum in Banff.

buttercup in the avalanche clearings. The ruin of a cabin foundation lies about 30 m south of the trail, on the far side of the last avalanche slope. I've seen a pair of pine grosbeaks here.

You reach the campground – a fine destination for novice backpackers – 200 m beyond the third avalanche slope. Just past the campground, the presence of white mountain heather in the understory indicates the transition to the upper subalpine life zone. The Simpson Pass junction is 400 m beyond the campground. If you want to make a loop hike in the upper valley – including Simpson Pass, Healy Meadows, and Healy Pass – turn south (left) to cross the bridge over Healy Creek. If you want to hike directly to Healy Pass, head west (straight ahead), climbing 1.9 km to the Healy Meadows junction. Skip ahead in this description to that point.

GLACIER LILY

Healy Pass and the surrounding meadows are renowned for their early summer displays of glacier lilies. The nodding, yellow flower is the first to appear in the upper subalpine life zone, growing through receding snowbanks. Its bloom is testimony to nature's remarkable means for ensuring that plants survive in harsh climates. Here, the growing season is less than two months, and the average annual temperature is -4°C. The glacier lily stores nutrients synthesized from last year's sunshine, releasing them in a burst in late spring, promoting rapid growth. Grizzly bears relish the protein-rich corm, and will excavate entire meadows in quest for this food.

Simpson Pass Junction to Simpson Pass

The trail climbs away from Healy Creek as a narrow track. During wet weather, water often runs down the tread. Seeps abound near trailside. Look for moose tracks in the mud. Wildflowers decorate the trail edges. Halfway to the pass, the trail breaks in and out of glades that feature the first larches. After 1.4 km, the trail swings south and descends slightly over the last 200 m to Simpson Pass, with views ahead of The Monarch (2895 m).

Simpson Pass is a narrow breach in the forest, well below treeline – a frost meadow where cold air stunts the growth of trees. Larches dot the glade, along with the blooms of wildflowers, and the diggings of a colony of Columbian ground squirrels. The ancient stumps of axe-felled trees suggest the handiwork of a former occasional resident of the area – Bill Peyto – trail guide, park warden, prospector, and Banff legend. It is a curiosity that this pass, something of a highway to travellers in the early and mid-1800s, now features no through-trail to the Simpson River valley.

If you are hiking the optional backpacking exit, head northeast (left) from the junction on Simpson Pass. The trail climbs into the forest and makes an undulating traverse beneath a limestone cliff for roughly 2 km, before trending southeast and climbing to the Monarch viewpoint on Wawa Ridge (2362 m) at km 3.3. Carry on east for 300 m to the Twin Cairns-Meadow Park junction. Keep straight ahead (east) to descend a ski run of the Sunshine Village ski area in 1.7 km. From the base of the ski run, make your way to the access road and turn north (left), from where it is 6.0 km of steady downhill to the parking area.

Simpson Pass to Healy Meadows Junction

To continue to Healy Meadows and Healy Pass, head west (right) from the junction in Simpson Pass. The trail angles north as it climbs steeply into the forest alongside a stream. The bedrock here is Cathedral Formation limestone but the scrunching under your feet is quartz grit of the Miette and Gog formations, eroded from above and carried here in runoff. Early season hikers will be treated to astounding displays of glacier lilies from this point onward.

You reach the Eohippus Lake junction in 400 m. Keep straight ahead. The trail soon levels and emerges from forest at the southern end of the Healy Meadows. These meadows loosely connect with those of Healy Pass, Lost Horse Creek, Harvey Pass, Citadel Pass, and Sunshine to form an extensive alpland – known as Sunshine Meadows – that covers approximately 40 km². Twenty-two rare plants have been recorded. Cotton-grass (which is a sedge, not a grass) graces the shores of the lakes. I've seen spotted sandpipers at the first lake. The meadows are bug heaven in July.

For the next 2 km, the sometimes spongy trail undulates north, winding through draws and cutting through stream courses, with the Monarch Ramparts off to the west. Vibrantly coloured, pink and scarlet paintbrush highlight the wildflower displays. In the last basin before the Healy Meadows junction, an ocean of glacier lilies rings a wet meadow. Mountain marsh marigold, western anemone, red-stemmed saxifrage, mountain sorrel, and sticky false-asphodel grow beside the inlet streams. The trailside boulders here are quartz-veined gritstone of the Miette Group – the oldest rock exposed in this part of the Rockies. The view downvalley includes the distant Fairholme Range, and Mt. Bourgeau (2931 m). A short climb brings you to the Healy Meadows junction, with its quartzite "couch" nearby – a wonderful place to lounge on a pleasant day.

Healy Meadows Junction to Healy Pass

You can exit from this junction by turning northeast (right) to descend 7.9 km to the parking area.

For Healy Pass, turn northwest (left). You soon leave the forest behind as you climb along the stream that drains the basin beneath the pass. The wildflower meadows here are on every experienced hiker's short-list of "best wildflower gardens in the Rockies." For many locals, a trip here is an annual ritual. Look for the blooms of low larkspur and blue columbine. And look up every now and then. This is a great place to spot raptors on the wing. I have seen a prairie falcon here.

Healy Pass provides a wonderful prospect over the southern Rockies. The quartzite bluff of the

> *About seven hours of hard work brought us to the height of land, the hinge, as it were, between the eastern and the western waters. We breakfasted on the level isthmus, which did not exceed fourteen paces in width, filling our kettles for this our lonely meal at once from the crystal sources of the Columbia and the Saskatchewan.*
>
> George Simpson; *Narrative of an Overland Journey Round the World in the Years 1841 and 1842*

BILL'S PLACE

Bill's place in 1913...

...and in 2002

The environs of Simpson Pass were a favourite haunt of Bill Peyto (PEE-toe), who began his association with the Rockies in 1893 or 1894 as a trail guide working for Tom Wilson. Peyto set up his own company in 1901, when he achieved fame by guiding mountaineer James Outram to the base of Mt. Assiniboine and back on the occasion of its first ascent. After serving in the Boer War, Peyto became a Banff park warden in 1913. During his trail guiding years, Peyto trapped and prospected near Simpson Pass in the off-season. He built a cabin in the meadows – a palace by backcountry standards – which served as his base. The cabin still stands.

Peyto's best known prospecting claim – staked in 1917 – was at Talc Lake, a short distance away

in what is now Kootenay National Park. The government of the day denied Peyto permission to develop the talc claim, citing that the would-be mine was located in a national park. The bureaucrats were, as is still often the case, a mineshaft shy on knowledge about the land in their care. The claim was outside of Banff. Kootenay National Park was not established until 1920. By that time, Peyto had given up hassling with the feds. Ironically, the National Talc Company took over the claim and was granted permission to mine it.

Although it is popular to characterize Peyto as a wild man and as a gruff recluse, archival photos show a gentler side – with wife and children in later years, near his Simpson Pass hideaway.

Monarch Ramparts extends southeast from the pass, bordering Healy Meadows. Mt. Assiniboine (3616 m), highest in the southern Rockies, soars skyward 30 km to the south. From Mt. Assiniboine to Crowfoot Mountain in the north, the view encompasses a 110 km length of the continental divide.

To the west, the cluster of exquisite lakes in the vicinity of Egypt Lake will catch your eye. The arrangement of the three largest – Mummy, Scarab, and Egypt – is known as a cirque staircase. Glacial ice that flowed from the south created the three basins, each at a progressively lower elevation. Today, only a remnant glacier remains at the western end of Scarab Lake. To the southwest, you can see the cliffs of the unnamed peak above Talc Lake. They feature a fossil-rich outcrop of the Stephen Formation – popularly known as the Burgess Shale.

Return

The way home is a steady downhill trundle. Return to the Healy Meadows junction (1.5 km). Keep straight ahead and follow the trail, steeply at first, through ancient forest down the Healy Creek valley to the Simpson Pass junction, from where you hike familiar ground to the parking area – total distance, 7.9 km.

9. Lakes and Larches

Egypt Lake

B ecause it is central to many short and wonderful day-hikes, Egypt Lake is the most popular backpacking destination in Banff National Park. The Lakes and Larches trail includes the Egypt Lake region, along with Healy Pass, and a series of passes farther north on the eastern flank of the continental divide. This is a spectacular terrain of cliff, meadow, glacier, and tarn – the hallmark scenery of the Canadian Rockies.

Trailhead to Healy Pass

The road-width trail climbs gradually on the bank between Healy Creek and the Sunshine access road. At 0.9 km, the trail forks and narrows. Take the right-hand trail to continue west, where you begin a short descent to Sunshine Creek. The ensuing climb in the Healy Creek valley is through an ancient subalpine forest. You cross the creek at km 3.3, reach the campground at km 5.7, and the Healy Meadows junction at km 7.9. From this junction, near which you see your first larches, it is a steady climb through marvelous meadows to Healy Pass at km 9.4. In most years, between early- and mid-July, the displays of glacier lilies and white globeflowers are likely to be a marvel. For more detailed information on the Healy Creek valley, see Classic Hike #8.

Healy Pass to Egypt Lake Campground

Healy Pass provides a wonderful prospect over the southern Rockies. The quartzite bluff of the Monarch Ramparts extends southeast from the pass, ringing the Healy Pass meadows. Mt. Assiniboine (3616 m), highest in the southern Rockies, soars skyward 30 km to the south. From Mt. Assiniboine to Crowfoot Mountain in the north, the view encompasses a 110 km length of the continental divide.

Whistling Pass

TRAIL THUMBNAIL

Overnight, 3-6 days; see map, p. 48

Route	Elev. (m)	Dist. (km)
Parking area	1690	0
Trailhead	1692	0.2
Healy Pass jct	1706	0.9
Healy Creek CG	1973	5.7
Simpson Pass jct	1981	6.1
Healy Meadows jct	2095	7.9
Healy Pass	2340	9.4
Pharaoh Creek jct	1992	12.4
Egypt Lake CG	1997	12.6
Whistling Pass	2295	15.9
Haiduk Lake	2067	18.1
Ball Pass jct and CG	1921	21.4
Shadow Lake	1851	25.7
Gibbon Pass jct	1814	26.6
Shadow Lake CG	1814	+0.1
Gibbon Pass	2300	29.7
Lower Twin Lake	2058	32.4
Twin Lakes jct	2058	32.6
Upper Twin Lake and CG	2088	33.4
Arnica Summit	2287	35.0
Arnica Lake	2149	35.8
Vista Lake	1570	39.4
Kootenay Parkway	1707	40.8

Trailhead
Follow Highway 1, 8.3 km west from Banff to the Sunshine Interchange. Follow the Sunshine road 9 km to its end at the ski area parking area. The trailhead kiosk is west of (behind) the gondola terminal, 200 m from the parking area.

Maps
NTS: 82 O/4, 82 N/1
Gem Trek: *Banff and Mt. Assiniboine* or *Kootenay National Park*

EGYPT LAKE-SCARAB LAKE-MUMMY LAKE, 3.5 KM

From the trail sign in front of the Egypt Lake shelter, head south through the campground on the Whistling Pass trail for 300 m to the Egypt Lake junction. Turn south (left) and follow a rough, undulating trail for 150 m to the north shore of Egypt Lake. The lake is 32 m deep and has an area of 16 ha. Cutthroat trout and eastern brook trout are present. A waterfall that drains Scarab Lake cascades over the colourful quartzite cliffs to the west.

The Egyptian motif for the names in this area originated with the Interprovincial Boundary Survey in 1922. It all started with a flight of fancy – a supposed resemblance (when viewed from above) of the outline of nearby Scarab Lake to that of a beetle. The scarab beetle was an Egyptian symbol of resurrection. With their minds thus Egyptified, the surveyors dropped the names Egypt, Mummy, and Pharaoh nearby.

Backtrack to the Whistling Pass trail. Turn west (left). The next 1.4 km involves a steep ascent of the headwall above Egypt Lake. The trail descends slightly from the top of the headwall through a stand of larches to reach the Scarab Lake junction in 200 m. Turn south (left). Descend to the outlet of Scarab Lake in 600 m.

Rock-hop the outlet of Scarab Lake to continue south on a rough track. After an initial climb, the trail drops into a meadowed basin. Follow cairns through rockslide debris, angling upward toward a break in the cliff that grants access to rocky slopes above the east shore of Mummy Lake. This large lake occupies an extremely barren setting, beautiful in its simplicity. Travel is difficult along the boulderfields on the lakeshore.

To the west, the cluster of exquisite lakes in the vicinity of Egypt Lake will catch your eye. The arrangement of the three largest – Mummy, Scarab, and Egypt – is known as a cirque staircase. Glacial ice that flowed from the south created the three basins, each at a progressively lower elevation. Only a remnant glacier remains at the western end of Scarab Lake.

Leaving Healy Pass, the trail dives, crossing wet subalpine meadows and glades of larch forest, losing 348 m of elevation to reach the Pharaoh Creek junction in 3 km, just south of the Egypt Lake patrol cabin. Turn south (left). Cross Pharaoh Creek on a bridge in 150 m. The trail ascends the creekbank to the Egypt Lake campground and shelter. You require a reservation and permit for overnight use of the shelter, available from the Banff park information centre. Even with a reservation, you may find the building overrun. Plan on spending a few days at Egypt Lake to enjoy the day-hiking options.

PHARAOH LAKE-BLACK ROCK LAKE, 2.4 KM

Northeast facing cirques riddle the mountain wall north of Egypt Lake. Pharaoh Lake, backed by the quartzite cliffs of the Pharaoh Peaks, occupies the largest cirque. Walk north from the campground on the west side of Pharaoh Creek for 500 m to a junction. Turn west (left) and ascend a steep, rough trail for 800 m to the lakeshore. To continue to Black Rock Lake, rock-hop the outlet of Pharaoh Lake, and follow a track northwest for 1.1 km. The last 100 m is alongside a delightful stream. There is a massive rockslide at the west end of the lake. "Black Rock" describes the lichen-covered cliff to the south.

VARIATIONS

- Camp at Egypt Lake and return over Healy Pass, 25.2 km; 2-3 days.
- Exit from Egypt Lake along Pharaoh Creek to Redearth Creek, 31.9 km; 2-3 days.
- Exit along Redearth Creek from Gibbon Pass junction, 40.0 km; 3-4 days.
- Exit at Twin Lakes junction, 40.4 km; 3-4 days.
- Hike the trail in reverse.
- Hike from the northern trailhead to Twin Lake CG, 7.4 km; an excellent novice backpack.
- By crossing Ball Pass and descending 9.7 km along Hawk Creek, you can link a portion of this outing with the Rockwall, making possible a trip of 88.8 km; 7-9 days.

Egypt Lake to Ball Pass Junction

From Egypt Lake campground, the Lakes and Larches trail tackles the headwall above Egypt Lake. The 1.4 km climb is steep. Persevere; scenic rewards lie just ahead.

From the top of the headwall, the trail descends slightly to contour around a rockslide at the base of the southern Pharaoh Peak (2711 m). Keep straight ahead (west) at the Scarab Lake junction. (If you haven't visited Scarab Lake as a day-hike, nip down the sidetrail as short distance for a view.) The trail swings northwest and works its way through rock benches and sparse forest, climbing to the rocky saddle of Whistling Pass – named for the whistle of the hoary marmot. You may see these large rodents in the quartzite boulderfields nearby.

The views from Whistling Pass include glacier-capped Mt. Ball (3294 m) to the north, the highest mountain on the 80 km length of the continental divide between Mt. Assiniboine and Moraine Lake. Haiduk (HAY-duck) Lake lies on the floor of the U-shaped valley north of the pass. Although the lake was named by the Interprovincial Boundary

TALC LAKE (NATALKO LAKE), 4.2 KM

From Egypt Lake campground, backtrack to the Pharaoh Creek bridge. Cross the bridge and turn south (right). Follow the east bank of Pharaoh Creek on a rough and often ill-defined trail, for 2.3 km to a junction. Turn west, cross the wet meadow, and pick up the trail that ascends the opposite bank. The trail between here and Talc Lake is an old cart track, constructed by the National Talc Company. Boulders line the trail edges. In this vicinity, you enter Kootenay National Park.

Talc Lake occupies an austere setting, walled by cliffs that feature the Cathedral-Stephen-Eldon sequence of sedimentary formations. The fossil-rich Stephen Formation is popularly known as the Burgess Shale. A 100 m-high waterfall cascades to the west shore. The presence of a small drift glacier harks back to colder climes and the glacial origin of the cirque that contains the lake. You can see the portals of the talc mine in the cliffs to the south. You can inspect the old foundations and refuse from the mine by hopping the outlet of Talc Lake and walking south.

Those capable of routefinding and travel on difficult boulder slopes can head north from Talc Lake to cross a rocky saddle ("Natalko Pass," 2303 m) that grants access to the valley east of Mummy Lake. Distance for this loop hike is 9.5 km return from Egypt Lake campground. Otherwise, return the way you came.

Survey, its name is not Egyptian. It seems that surveyor A.O. Wheeler named it with a Polish word, but the explanations given in various sources seem lame – everything from a saucy girl to a group of Hungarian mercenaries. The pass is a good place to see gray-crowned rosy finches. These alpine-dwelling birds often congregate on snow patches to eat insects, snow worms, seeds, and spiders, which are easy to see on the white background.

The steep descent to Haiduk Lake is on a trail beaten into screes and boulderfields. If hiking in early summer, you will encounter snow on this north-facing slope. Several easy rock-hops of the adjacent stream lead to a boggy area on the south shore of Haiduk Lake. Follow the east shore on a rough trail to another inlet at the north end. Spectacular views north to Mt. Ball and south to the waterfalls that drain the cirque below Haiduk Peak (2901 m), compete for your attention.

The trail parallels an extensive wet meadow for 300 m before crossing Haiduk Creek to its west bank. For the next 2 km, you descend gradually through subalpine forest before swinging west to plunge down forested moraines to the Ball Pass junction and campground.

Ball Pass Junction to Gibbon Pass Junction

The first section of the trail to Shadow Lake features open views as it skirts wet meadows along the west fork of Haiduk Creek. Cross the principal meltwater stream from Ball Glacier on a bridge, slightly west of where the horse trail fords the stream. After you cross to the east bank of Haiduk Creek, the trail may be wet, slowing your pace.

You will pick up your step just before the outlet of Shadow Lake, where the trail has been gravel-capped. The lake's outlet is the setting for one of the

THE NATIONAL TALC COMPANY

Talc is magnesium silicate, one of the softer minerals. It is used in talcum powder, explosives, and insulators. Bill Peyto (PEE-toe) staked the Talc Lake claim in 1917. He was thwarted in his attempt to develop the claim by the government's erroneous contention that it lay within Banff National Park. (Kootenay National Park did not exist at that time.) The National Talc Company took over the claim, and mined talc during the 1920s. The claim then passed to Western Talc Holdings, and finally to Wartime Metals, which mined it in 1943. The talc was shipped by horse and cart to Massive, a railway siding in the Bow Valley – an incredible enterprise in what was then a remote corner of the Rockies.

more inspiring scenes in the Rockies – the awesome, glacier-draped, northeast face of Mt. Ball. The lake is 25 m deep, has an area of 57 ha, and is home to cutthroat trout and eastern brook trout. Haiduk Creek has created a sizeable alluvial fan at the inlet on the south shore, almost dividing the lake in two. As its name suggests, the lake spends the latter part of each day in the shadow of Mt. Ball. The best lighting is in early morning. If you will be camping at the nearby campground, return to the outlet for sunrise. East of the outlet, you have an unusual view of Pilot Mountain (2954 m), a landmark in the Bow Valley.

The Shadow Lake campground is 1.2 km east of the lake, just east of Shadow Lake Lodge and the Gibbon Pass junction. There is a lot of horse traffic here. Treat your drinking water. You can exit the Lakes and Larches trail at this point by following the Redearth Creek trail 13.4 km northeast to Highway 1. The Lost Horse Creek campground is at km 6.2.

The Canadian Pacific Railway built the original Shadow Lake Rest House in 1928 as part of a system of backcountry shelters for its clientele. Brewster Transport purchased the building in 1938, and sold

BALL PASS (2205 M), 2.7 KM

This short sidetrip takes you to the crest of the continental divide, offering detailed views of the south face of Mt. Ball, and a panorama over the valley of Redearth Creek. The first 1.5 km climbs gently to the upper reaches of the west fork of Haiduk Creek. Rock-hop the stream and begin a steep ascent. The route ahead looks unlikely, as the trail aims straight toward the boulderfield and cliff beneath the pass. However, a well-conceived series of switchbacks breaks through the headwall to deliver you easily to the craggy north entrance of the pass. The red, iron-rich soil underfoot is a possible origin of the name, "Redearth."

Mt. Ball dominates the view. Its cascading glacier flies in the face of climate warming, clinging magnificently to the south slopes of the mountain. James Hector brought the name "Ball" to the Rockies to commemorate John Ball, a British public servant who rallied government support for the Palliser Expedition. Ball later became an accomplished mountaineer, and first president of the Alpine Club (of England). It is likely that Hector named the peak now known as Storm Mountain.

Walk 500 m south across the pass to obtain a view over the upper Hawk Creek valley in Kootenay National Park. Much of this valley burned in 2003. The source of Hawk Creek is a stream that discharges from the ground, southwest of the pass.

Shadow Lake

it to Bud Brewster in 1950. In 1991, the lodge was redeveloped, with six new cabins built. The lodge is now one of the larger backcountry facilities in the Rockies.

Gibbon Pass Junction to Arnica Lake

The steady climb to Gibbon Pass earns you the delights of another upper subalpine landscape. Numerous animal trails criss-cross the expansive, larch dotted alp of the pass. You may be fortunate to see mountain goats here. On the slope east of the pass, treeline is approximately 2400 m, well above the local norm of 2200 m. The slope is southwest facing and is in the lee of Storm Mountain. This may create an area with soils that are warmer and drier than normal. On the pass itself, young Lyall's larch trees are colonizing the tundra, transforming it – slowly – into upper subalpine forest. Gibbon Pass was named in 1929 for John Gibbon, public relations manager with the CPR and founder of the Trail Riders of the Canadian Rockies.

From Gibbon Pass, the trail makes a gradual, sideslope descent north along the eastern side of the valley. After about 2.5 km, it switchbacks down to the outlet of lower Twin Lake. This is the first of another series of lakes that occupy northeast facing cirques – this time beneath Storm Mountain (3158 m). The cirques are separated by arêtes – narrow rock ridges

that descend from the summit area. All of these arêtes, and many of the gullies between, have been climbed by mountaineers.

The trail is boggy in the vicinity of Lower Twin Lake. Cotton-grass grows in abundance. Cross the outlet on a bridge to an important trail junction. Ahead, the "up and down" nature of this hike continues, with two stiff climbs and two descents in the remaining 8.2 km to the Kootenay Parkway. If you have had enough at this point, make a direct, downhill exit by following the trail northeast (right) from this junction, for 7.8 km to Castle Junction on Highway 1.

Upper Twin Lake and the Twin Lakes campground are 800 m north of the junction. The campground is a popular overnight destination for backpackers travelling south from the Kootenay Parkway. Rock-hop the outlet and ascend steeply to Arnica Summit, a forested saddle on the northeast buttress of Storm Mountain. A steep descent brings you to Arnica Lake.

Arnica Lake to the Kootenay Parkway

Leaving Arnica Lake, the trail descends onto the north flank of Storm Mountain. After passing the east shore of a rockslide depression lake, the trail emerges onto the southern edge of the Vermilion Pass Burn. This lightning-caused forest fire consumed 2630 ha of subalpine forest in July 1968. The open area of the burn offers fine views east to Mt. Ishbel (2908 m), Castle Mountain (2850 m), and Protection Mountain (2972 m).

You reach the lowest elevation on this hike just 1.4 km from trail's end, at Vista Lake. This deep valley is a curious landscape feature. It was not eroded over eons by the tiny creek we see today, but by a meltwater surge from a detached block of glacial ice at the end of the Late Wisconsin Glaciation. This meltwater also eroded the canyon west of the lake. Altrude Creek drains Vista Lake. A surveying crew named the creek by combining the Latin words *altus* (high), and *pulchritude* (beautiful).

From the outlet of Vista Lake, a well-graded trail climbs to the Kootenay Parkway, bisecting a hoodoo-like formation en route. The final Bow Valley advance of the Late Wisconsin Glaciation ended near here. Irregular mounds of moraine dot the forest. This hoodoo may have been eroded from such a moraine. It is the only formation of its kind visible in the area.

Trail's end is at the Vista Lake-Twin Lakes trailhead on the Kootenay Parkway, 39 km by road from the starting point.

> On 16th September, I started up Healy's Creek... To the west of the Divide there is a beautiful piece of alpine park country, about one mile wide and several miles in length, dotted with emerald lakes and open groves of mountain larch...
>
> Surveyor J.J. McArthur; *Report of the Department of the Interior 1891*

10. Bourgeau Lake

Bourgeau Lake

Tucked away in a glacial cirque beneath Mt.
Bourgeau (boor-ZJOWE), Bourgeau Lake is a
gem of a destination. The elevation gain is considerable, but the well-graded trail makes for relatively
easy access to the upper subalpine environs at the
lake. Because it ascends a shaded valley, consider
hiking it in mid-July or later when the route will
probably be clear of lingering snow. This is among
the newer trails in Banff, cut in the late 1950s after
the completion of Highway 1.

Trailhead to Bourgeau Lake

For the first 2.5 km, the trail winds through forest on
the slopes above Wolverine Creek. There are subtle
changes in the vegetation at almost every turn. Most
noticeable is the "doghair" forest of lodgepole pines
and Douglas-firs, evidence of a 1904 forest fire. The
trail passes between two stately Douglas-firs, one of
which shows bark blackened by the fire. Beyond this
point, Engelmann spruce is the most common tree.
You may see spruce grouse here. About 1 km from
the trailhead there is a wonderful squirrel midden.
Although we tend to think of them as tree-dwelling
creatures, red squirrels nest on the ground in these
accumulations of seed shells shucked from conifer
cones.

The first avalanche slope features fine views
northeast to the Bow Valley and the Sawback Range,
on whose slopes you can see charred forest that
resulted from the 1998 Hillsdale fire, and from prescribed burns in 1991 and 1993. The meandering
course of the Bow River reveals oxbow lakes, including Muleshoe Lake. Hole-in-the-Wall, a solution cave
eroded by glacial meltwater, sits high and dry on the
southwest face of Mt. Cory (2802 m).

The cliffs across Wolverine Creek dip northeastward toward the Bow Valley. Look for mountain
goats on the terraces. The rock is limestone of the
Livingstone Formation. The dip reveals the eastern
arm of an anticline. The cliffs are an outlying ridge of
Mt. Brett (2984 m). Dr. R.G. Brett was a businessman
and politician, prominent in the affairs of Banff and
the province of Alberta from 1886 to 1925.

*Looking up the valley... we had before us a
truncated mountain, evidently composed of
massive horizontal strata, and which I named
Mount Bourgeau.*

James Hector, August 17, 1858; *Papers
Relative to the Exploration of British North
America*

Harvey Lake

A MODEST MAN, AN IMPOSING MOUNTAIN

James Hector named Mount Bourgeau for Eugene Bourgeau, botanist with the Palliser Expedition of 1857-60. Bourgeau was a likable man and a first-rate botanist. He was only in the Rockies for part of one season, but he collected 460 species – including 50 varieties gathered above 2560 m. He carted 60,000 specimens back to Kew Gardens. Surveyor J.J. McArthur and packer Tom Wilson made the first ascent of the 2930 m mountain in 1890. Although the mountain appears formidable, a "walk-up" route exists along the west slopes from Harvey Pass. The lake's name was made official in 1912.

Roughly a kilometre beyond the first avalanche slope, the trail crosses a tributary stream and curves gradually south. This stream, and the south fork of Wolverine Creek, crossed at km 5.5, are often choked with trees avalanched from the surrounding mountainsides. The first creek is bridged. However, any bridge across the second creek would be destroyed by avalanches, so gabion (gah-bee-ON) bags have been installed as stepping stones.

Gabion is French for "cage." Gabion bags are wire mesh baskets filled with rock, in this case, from the stream bed. By nature of their tremendous weight and low profile, gabions resist avalanching snow. They also dissipate the force of water by allowing most of the flow to pass between the rocks. Gabions are often successfully used for bridge footings and shoring in sites prone to erosion.

A waterfall tumbles from the hanging valley west of Wolverine Creek. After crossing the creek at km 5.5, you climb steadily on switchbacks to the

WHO MAINTAINS THE TRAILS?

Trail crews employed by each park maintain most of the hiking trails in the Rockies. The principal jobs are to keep the trails clear of fallen trees, avalanche debris, and rocks; and to insure that tread surfaces remain well-drained. The construction of bridges, boardwalks, and campground facilities, and the installation and maintenance of signs are also sometimes trail crew tasks. Workers pack most tools and materials to the worksites each day. However, they sometimes use a helicopter to reach remote worksites, or for projects involving heavy materials. Rewarding physical work in spectacular mountain scenery creates heavy interest in the few available trail crew positions.

subalpine wet meadow adjacent to Bourgeau Lake. The trail becomes muddy and indistinct. Do your best to keep to the beaten path. Cold air collects in the hollow of this meadow; the damp soils are subject to frequent frosts that stunt the growth of trees. On the slightly higher ground nearby, a dwarf forest of subalpine fir and a few Lyall's larches ekes out a chilly existence in the shade of Mt. Bourgeau.

A rockslide dams Bourgeau Lake; its waters drain beneath the debris. The lake sits in a pocket of Banff Formation limestone. The massive cliffs that ring the lake are also limestone, but of the slightly younger, Livingstone Formation. This rock consists principally of the fossilized remains of crinoids – marine animals related to the starfish of today.

Harvey Pass (2469 m), 2.4 km

When the slopes beyond Bourgeau Lake are free of snow, you can extend this outing by following any of several paths along the northwest shore to the west end of the lake. Look for low larkspur here. This member of the buttercup family has mauve

flowers. The leaves contain alkaloids that are poisonous. Ascend a rough track on the north side of the inlet stream, and follow cairns. A stiff climb brings you to a tarn set in a beautiful alpland. Keep straight ahead. Another, shorter climb leads to a large basin that features yet another tarn. You may be fortunate to see bighorn sheep here. A 1981 estimate gave a population of 120-130 sheep for the vicinity of Mt. Bourgeau. Sixty-five mountain goats were also reported to live in this area, but in recent decades, the numbers of both species have declined. Grizzly bears frequent the meadows and the slopes leading up to them.

A faint track swings south and climbs a compacted scree slope to the climax of this exceptionally scenic hike – Harvey Lake, nestled in the hollow of Harvey Pass. The pass commemorates Ralph Harvey, who accompanied Jim Brewster here in the 1920s. Mt. Assiniboine (3616 m) soars skyward in the view south. From the southern brink of the pass, you have a wonderful vista over the larch-filled forest of Healy Creek, Sunshine Meadows, and the lake-dotted terrain near Simpson Pass.

11. Rockbound Lake

Rockbound Lake

Nestled beneath the colossal ramparts of Castle Mountain, Rockbound Lake is part of an elemental landscape of water, rock and sky, inspiring in its simplicity. Wildflower displays, larches, intriguing geology, and human history add interest to this outing.

Trailhead to Tower Lake

The first 5 km of trail is fireroad width, and makes a steady climb through the lodgepole pine forest that cloaks the Bow Valley. This forest grew in the aftermath of an 1896 forest fire. At approximately km 2.4, the trail angles sharply east (right) at an unmarked junction. Straight ahead is an unmaintained path to the former site of the Castle Mountain fire lookout

TRAIL THUMBNAIL

Day-hike

Route	Elev. (m)	Dist. (km)
Trailhead	1450	0
Silverton Falls jct	1450	0.3
Silverton Falls	1515	+0.7
Tower Lake	2128	7.7
Rockbound Lake	2210	8.4

Trailhead
East side of the Bow Valley Parkway (Highway 1A), 29.5 km west of Banff; 200 m east of Castle Junction. You can access the Bow Valley Parkway from Castle Junction on Highway 1.

Maps
NTS: 82 O/5
Gem Trek: *Banff and Mt. Assiniboine* or *Kootenay National Park*

Best lighting: mid-morning to mid-afternoon

(see Classic Hike #12). Storm Mountain (3158 m) is prominent in the view west. The forested mounds on the floor of the Bow Valley are ancient moraines.

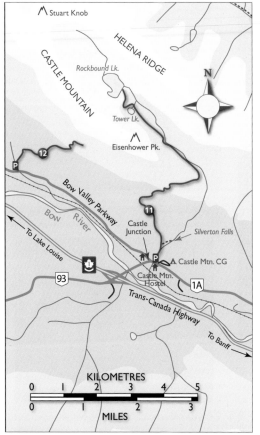

As the trail climbs over the treed ridge south of Castle Mountain, the forest becomes more subalpine in character. After it swings north behind the ridge, the trail narrows, the grade eases, and the tread surface becomes poor. If you are hiking early in the season, you may find it a challenge to stay on track. As a consolation to the mud underfoot, the moist glades at trailside feature stunning displays of white globeflowers – in some years, the best in the Rockies.

The trail undulates over a series of forested recessional moraines, then becomes vague as it crosses a wet meadow just before Tower Lake. This shallow lake mirrors the southern-most summit of Castle Mountain (2700 m) – "the tower" – first climbed in 1926. Rockslides near the lake are home to hoary marmots. The surrounding forest contains Lyall's larch. The needles of this deciduous conifer turn golden yellow in late summer.

Tower Lake to Rockbound Lake

Rock-hop the outlet of Tower Lake. The trail switchbacks steeply up the limestone headwall to Rockbound Lake, passing through an ancient stand of Engelmann spruce. Drummond's anemone and alpine springbeauty are common wildflowers here. The trail braids and becomes indistinct.

Rockbound Lake is a perfect glacial tarn. Cliffs of Eldon Formation limestone, up to 220 m high, provide a spectacular backdrop. Cutthroat trout, rainbow trout, and eastern brook trout in the lake attract osprey. You may see these raptors as they circle the lake before plunging to the water to catch fish. The osprey has an opposable outer talon that works much

White globeflower

Above the edge of the cliff, however, the going was easy, so that the highest part of the Castle (nine thousand feet) was not hard to reach, and the wonderful view of the valley of the Bow River, four thousand feet below, was quite worth seeing. The tower standing in front of the Castle to the south-east looked as unscalable as it was reported to be.

A.P. Coleman; *The Canadian Rockies, New and Old Trails*

A SHATTERED LANDSCAPE

Explorer A.P. Coleman – a geology professor by vocation – called the valley above Rockbound Lake, "Horseshoe Valley." This valley is known for its "clint and grike," karst landscape – extensive limestone pavement that has been shattered by millennia of frost action. The "clints" are limestone blocks and the "grikes" are the fissures that separate them. The words come from the dialect of Yorkshire, England, where this type of landscape is common. Karst topography accounts for 12 percent of the world's landmass. The front ranges and main ranges of the Rockies, being predominantly limestone on the surface, contribute their fare share.

Silverton Falls

Osprey

CASTLE AND CONTROVERSY

the same as a human thumb. One study found that osprey catch fish on 90 percent of their attempts.

Rockbound Lake marks the southernmost point of a syncline complex, a series of U-shaped folds in the bedrock that extends 260 km north to Mt. Kerkeslin in Jasper National Park. The Cathedral Formation limestone slab underlying the lake is tipped upward toward the south, damming the waters. You can walk east along this natural pavement to the high water outlet of the lake. Most of Rockbound Lake's outflow now drains underground through karst fissures eroded into the bedrock.

Silverton Falls

You can make the sidetrip to Silverton Falls on your return. (The falls are shaded in the morning.) Turn southeast (left) at the junction 300 m before you reach the trailhead. Follow the sidetrail to Silverton Creek and the beaten path to an unfenced viewpoint that overlooks the upper cataracts of the falls. Use caution.

"Silverton" refers to the railway and mining boom town of Silver City that flourished nearby from 1882-84. In its heyday, Silver City boasted a population of 2000 people, making it larger than Calgary. A round-trip visit to Silverton Falls adds 1.4 km to the outing.

Castle Mountain is one of the better known and better named landmarks in the Rockies. James Hector first described it in 1858, and called it a textbook example of a "castellated mountain." The lower cliff is Cathedral Formation dolomite and limestone, the middle terrace is Stephen Formation shale, and the upper cliff is Eldon Formation limestone. This sequence, known as the "Middle Cambrian sandwich," creates the castellated appearance of many mountains in the eastern main ranges.

In 1946, politicians decided to rename Castle Mountain in honour of Dwight D. Eisenhower, WWII commander of Allied forces in Europe, and later U.S. president. Canadians were generally unimpressed, but being polite folks, waited until a decade after Eisenhower's death to do something about it. The name, Castle Mountain, was reinstated in 1979. As a compromise, the tower is now called Eisenhower Peak. It is not the highest point on Castle's 6.5 km long ridge. The true summit (2850 m) is the one farthest north, hidden from view on this trail.

12. Castle Lookout

The Bow Valley from Castle Lookout

TRAIL THUMBNAIL

Day-hike; see map, p. 59

Route	Elev. (m)	Dist. (km)
Trailhead	1460	0
Castle Lookout Site	2010	3.8

Trailhead
On the Bow Valley Parkway (Highway 1A), 4.9 km west of Castle Junction; 34.6 km west of Banff; 20.1 km east of Lake Louise. You can access the Bow Valley Parkway from Castle Junction on Highway 1.

Maps
NTS: 820/5
Gem Trek: *Banff and Mt. Assiniboine* or *Kootenay National Park*

Best lighting: any time; afternoon and evening are especially good

The Canadian Rockies look the way that they do for three principal reasons: they are made from sedimentary rocks, the rock layers were thrust upward during mountain creation, and the landscape has since been heavily eroded – principally by glacial ice. Although you spend much of this short outing in pine forest, the destination delivers a "Wow!" view – the massive, glacially-carved trough of the Bow Valley. With its southwest aspect, this trail is a great prospect for a shoulder season hiking. If you go early in the year, check for wood ticks during and after the trip.

Trailhead to Lookout Site

The parking area buzzes with activity – it seems that many people, not intent on hiking, turn in here looking for something else. They make a U-turn and soon leave. But some of that business carries on into the hike – you will hear noise from the roads and the railway throughout.

Evidence on many mountainsides in the Bow Valley testifies to a short-lived mining industry of the late 1800s. The hopefuls were in quest of gold, but lead, zinc, and copper were the only minerals present, and even those – especially given the remoteness – were not in quantity to make mining profitable. For just over half the distance to the lookout site, this trail is road-width. It may originally have been cleared that way by miners, but it was certainly maintained that way by park staff from the 1940s to the 1970s, when the fire lookout was operational and park staff often drove as far as they could to deliver supplies. You head north from the parking area for a

> *Seeming to stand out in the centre of the valley is a very remarkable mountain, still at the distance of 12 miles, which looks exactly like a gigantic castle.*
>
> James Hector; August 17, 1858,
> *Papers Relative to the Exploration of British North America*

short distance, before the trail swings easterly for the duration of the hike.

Much of the Bow Valley between Banff and Lake Louise burned in a massive fire in 1896. The near-homogenous lodgepole pine forest that surrounds this trail dates to that event. As lodgepole forests go, this one is in decline. Periodic fires are required to break-up pine forests and maintain diversity. In the absence of fire, the pine forest of the Bow Valley now presents ideal habitat for mountain pine beetles. If you are hiking in late June or early July, a special treat awaits – the blooms of blue clematis. They grow here with an abundance I have not seen elsewhere. Look also for calypso orchids and arnica. You will see a few Engelmann spruce and the odd Douglas-fir at trailside.

At about km 1.5 you pass the ruin of a cabin that may date to the mining era. About 700 m later, the trail narrows and soon breaks out onto the beginning of the cliffs and ledges that are emblematic of Castle Mountain. Wildflowers thrive in these openings. You switchback a few times, and cut up through a loose gully. The trail enters a stand of whitebark pines and descends slightly to the former lookout site.

Built in the early 1940s by conscientious objectors, the Castle Mountain fire lookout was one of seven in Banff National Park. In the 1970s, Parks Canada began using helicopters for smoke patrols and the lookout was abandoned. It burned in 1983 after hikers inadvertently set fire to it. Everything but the concrete footings of the main building has since been removed. Take care at the cliff edge.

Castle cliffs

Saws, Castles, and Troughs

The views from the lookout site are grand and varied, in no small part due to the tremendous variety of the structural geology included. The Simpson Pass Thrust angles across the Bow Valley just south of here, dividing the front ranges, to the south and east, from the main ranges, to the west and north. Storm Mountain (3158 m), just west of the fault, is prominent in the view southwest. You can look farther west through Vermilion Pass (1680 m) to the peaks of the Rockwall in Kootenay National Park. Looking north in the Bow Valley, the massive hulk of Mt. Temple (3544 m) dominates. But my favourite view is looking southeast into the sweeping maw of the Bow Valley (p. 61), with the Sawback Range of the front ranges on the east, and Pilot Mountain (2954 m) in the Massive Range on the skyline in the west. In the distance, you can see the Sundance Range near Banff town and, if the day is very clear, peaks of the Fairholme Range near Canmore. The forested jumble of the Hillsdale Slide covers the valley floor in the mid-distance. If you are visiting in late June or early July on a windy day, you may see clouds of yellow tree pollen near the valley bottom. It's a big view. Just think: during the peak of the Late Wisconsin Glaciation, ice filled this valley to just about the elevation where you now stand.

You can pick out two cliffs on Castle Mountain – the lower, closer one is Cathedral Formation limestone; the upper one, set farther back, is Eldon Formation limestone. Between them is a terrace of Stephen Formation shale, known as Goat Ledge. Mountain goats are less common than in the past. The only time I have seen goats here is through binoculars, from the highway. A climber's hut on the terrace serves as a base for a series of classic rock climbing routes on the upper cliff.

ON THE EDGE

Whitebark pines thrive on the cliff edge at the lookout site. Whereas the mountain pine beetle holds the collective attention of many forest watchers in the Rockies, whitebark pines are being clobbered primarily by another affliction – this one introduced from Europe. White pine blister rust (see photo, p. 99) arrived in North America on a shipment of tree seedlings in 1906. It has taken a century for the rust to wreak its havoc to the crests of mountain ridges in western North America, but the damage is now done. In the Waterton-Glacier area, one researcher claims that the whitebark pine is "functionally extinct." Almost all of the trees there are infected; many are already dead. Seedlings succumb quickly. You will see dead whitebark pines near the lookout site, killed by the rust. In some areas, Parks Canada plans to use prescribed burns to help eliminate diseased trees in the hope that healthy seedlings can regenerate. The whitebark pine is known as a "keystone" vegetation species. Among other species affected, its disappearance will have profound impacts on Clark's nutcrackers and grizzly bears, which rely on whitebark pine seeds for food.

13. The Beehives and Plain of the Six Glaciers

Lake Louise from the Big Beehive

If you have time for only one hike near Lake Louise, this should be your choice. Views from the modest summits of Little Beehive and Big Beehive reveal much of the area's spectacular scenery. The outing culminates with a point-blank view of the glacier-draped headwall beneath Mt. Victoria. However, this is not a hike for solitude. The outing incorporates two of the more popular trails in the Rockies – Lake Agnes and Plain of the Six Glaciers. The trail on the north side of Big Beehive is often snowbound into July. If you are counting on the tea houses being open, check at the Lake Louise park information centre.

Trailhead to Little Beehive

The broad Lake Agnes trail climbs steadily through subalpine forest for 1.6 km to a switchback that overlooks Lake Louise and the delta at its inlet. If the glacial melt season is on, you may see plumes of glacial sediment dispersing into the lake. The quartzite cliffs of Fairview Mountain (2744 m) rise across the lake. The trail narrows, turns sharply north and crosses a section of the wooden pipeline that provided drinking water from Lake Agnes to the Chateau during its early days. At the horse-hiker barrier, turn west (left) to reach Mirror Lake. The quartzite buttress of Big Beehive forms the backdrop for this pond, which is impounded by moraine and has no visible surface outlet. Mirror Lake and nearby Lake Agnes were referred to by the Canadian Pacific Railway as "the

TRAIL THUMBNAIL

Day-hike

Route	Elev. (m)	Dist. (km)
Parking area	1735	0
Trailhead	1732	0.6
Mirror Lake	2027	3.0
Little Beehive jct	2104	3.7
Lake Agnes connector jct	2170	4.2
Little Beehive	2253	4.8
Lake Agnes	2118	5.8
Big Beehive jct	2260	7.1
Big Beehive	2270	7.4
Highline jct	2010	8.9
Plain of the Six Glaciers jct	1950	10.7
Plain of the Six Glaciers teahouse	2135	12.1
Victoria Glacier viewpoint	2150	13.7
Parking area	1735	21.2

Trailhead

From Lake Louise Village, follow Lake Louise Drive 5.5 km to the parking areas at the lake. Paved walkways lead to the lakeshore. Walk along the lakeshore to the trail junction west of the Chateau. You want the Lake Agnes trail. It branches uphill to the north (right).

Maps

NTS: 82 N/8

Gem Trek: *Lake Louise and Yoho* or *Best of Lake Louise*

Best lighting: most features are best lit in the morning

VARIATIONS

- The many junctions make numerous variations possible. Here are two:
- Exit from the Highline junction; 12.0 km total.
- Exit from the Plain of the Six Glaciers junction; 15.0 km total.

> *For some time we sat and smoked and gazed at the gem of beauty beneath the glacier [Lake Louise]. My Stoney guide told me that higher up were two smaller lakes, one of which his people called the "goat's looking glass," [Mirror Lake] as the goats came down to it to use it as a mirror while they combed their beards.*
>
> Tom Wilson, quoted in *Trail Blazer of the Rockies*

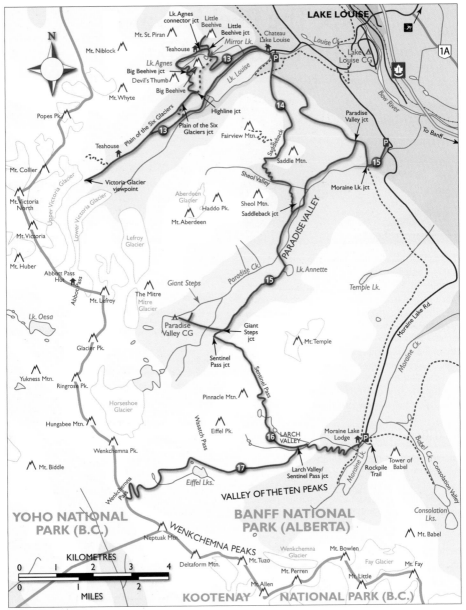

lakes in the clouds" in promotional material in the late 1800s.

The trail continues north from Mirror Lake, switchbacking through larch trees on an avalanche slope on Mt. St. Piran. The mountain commemorates the English parish that was the birthplace of Willoughby Astley, the first manager of Chalet Lake Louise. In the 1890s, Astley supervised the cutting of many trails in the area, including this one.

At the junction at km 3.1, turn sharply northeast (right) onto the Little Beehive trail. You ascend higher onto the avalanche slope, where western anemone,

Sitka valerian, arnica, common fireweed, common yarrow, white rhododendron, fleabanes, dwarf dogwood, cinquefoil, and pink mountain heather grow. There are fine views southwest to Big Beehive, Fairview Mountain, Haddo Peak (3070 m) and glacier-clad Mt. Aberdeen (3152 m). The icy summit of Mt. Temple (3544 m) rises above them all.

After 500 m you reach another junction. Turn northeast (right), and follow the trail 700 m across an avalanche slope onto the larch covered knoll of Little Beehive. You can see Lake Louise and the Chateau from the cliff edge at the far side of the avalanche

Lake Agnes

slope. Partway across, you pass a large quartzite boulder that is surrounded by red-stemmed saxifrage.

Little Beehive commands a superlative view of the Bow Valley, from Hector Lake in the north to Pilot Mountain (2954 m) in the south. The spot was an obvious choice for a fire lookout, which operated

from 1942 until 1978. Parks Canada removed the lookout building in 1985 and has since installed a display that describes the role of forest fires in this ecosystem.

Little Beehive to Lake Agnes

On your descent from Little Beehive, keep straight ahead at the first junction. As you approach the Lake Agnes teahouse, the trail passes alongside a bluff of Gog Formation siltstone. As with most rocks in the area, the bluff dips to the southwest. Within this overall plane, some layers of sediments are at widely varying angles. This is called cross-bedding. These layers record the edges of shifting deltas when the sediments were deposited in the Early Cambrian, or where streams cut through sediments after the sediments had been deposited. Beyond the bluff, the trail climbs a staircase to the teahouse on the shore of Lake Agnes.

Lake Agnes

Walter Wilcox, an early visitor to Lake Agnes, called it "a wild tarn imprisoned by cheerless cliffs." True to Wilcox's description, the lake is a glacial tarn, 20.5 m deep. The wilderness character of the lake is now lost to the throngs of visitors, but the scene is impressive nonetheless. From south to north, Big Beehive (2270 m), Devil's Thumb (2458 m), Mt. Whyte (2990 m), and Mt. Niblock (2976 m) form a tight cirque around the lake. Sir William Whyte was a vice-president of the CPR. John Niblock was a railway superintendent in the 1890s. The lake was their favourite fishing hole in the Rockies. Fishing is no longer allowed.

The Lake Agnes teahouse was one of a series constructed by the CPR to entice its hotel clients into the mountains. The first structure here was built in 1901. The present teahouse was privately reconstructed in 1981. It is open daily from mid-June to early October, serving lunch, refreshments, and baked goods. You can learn more about the history of the teahouses at an interpretive display on the south side of the lake's outlet. Look for striations – grooves etched by glacial ice – in the quartzite bedrock nearby.

The upper subalpine forest at Lake Agnes provides the seeds, berries, fungi, and insects eaten by Clark's nutcrackers, gray jays, golden-mantled ground squirrels, Columbian ground squirrels, least chipmunks, and red squirrels. Please do not feed these birds and animals. Your "kindness" may ultimately kill them. Reliant on handouts, the non-hibernating species may not cache enough food to tide them through the winter. Those that do hibernate may go to sleep with bodies run-down by junk food diets, never to reawaken.

WHO WAS AGNES?

Lake Agnes is named for Lady Susan Agnes Macdonald, wife of Prime Minister John A. Macdonald. Lady Agnes had been informed by the CPR that when she visited the lake in 1890, she would be the first woman to do so. Unfortunately, chalet manager Willoughby Astley, unaware of the arrangement, had guided another woman to the lake a few days earlier. By coincidence, the other woman's first name was Agnes. A member of the first lady's party defused the apparent consternation, pointing out that by giving the name "Agnes" to the lake, everyone would be kept happy.

Lake Agnes to Big Beehive

If the trail over Big Beehive is snowbound, cross the bridge at the lake outlet, descend a staircase and hike beneath quartzite cliffs to Mirror Lake in 400 m. Turn south (right) and take the Highline trail – with its great view of Lake Louise – 800 m to the Highline junction. Skip ahead to that point in the description. This will shorten the outing by 1.9 km.

From the teahouse, head west through boulderfields along the north shore of the lake. Hoary marmots and pikas are common here. Damp areas support dense growths of false hellebore and red-stemmed saxifrage. At the west end of the lake, the trail swings south beneath the shattered cliffs of the Devil's Thumb. Use caution if you must cross any lingering snow. The coarse sand eroded from the quartzite bedrock will scrunch under your feet.

The trail switchbacks steeply up to the saddle between Big Beehive and Devil's Thumb. Take care not to dislodge rocks onto people below. Scan the cliffs of Mt. Niblock and Mt. St. Piran (2625 m) opposite, for mountain goats. From the crest of the climb, rough paths lead northeast (left) for 300 m to a shelter on the Big Beehive. Here, you obtain a stunning overview of Lake Louise, more than 500 m below. Lake Louise is 2 km long, has an area of 85 ha, and a maximum depth of 70 m. It is the 11th largest lake in Banff National Park. The lake occupies a hanging valley, dammed by a moraine that was pushed up alongside the Bow Valley Glacier during the Late Wisconsin Glaciation.

LATERAL DAMAGE

The lateral moraine on the south side of Plain of the Six Glaciers reveals an interesting snapshot of local glacial history, involving two rock glaciers on the lower slopes of Mt. Aberdeen. Victoria Glacier overran the more easterly of these two features during the Little Ice Age advance. The lateral moraine towers over it. The westerly rock glacier was also shorn during the advance, but has since re-accumulated enough mass to spill over the lateral moraine.

Big Beehive to Plain of the Six Glaciers

Return to where the main trail cuts across Big Beehive and turn south (left). The trail switchbacks steadily down to join the highline route from Lake Agnes to the Plain of the Six Glaciers. Turn southwest (right), and follow this trail 1.8 km to the Plain of the Six Glaciers trail junction. Turn southwest (right).

The view to the south features The Mitre (2890 m), named for its resemblance to a bishop's hat. At the series of switchbacks just before the teahouse, look upslope for mountain goats. Common butterwort, one of seven species of carnivorous plants in the Rockies, grows in the seeps nearby. Golden eagles have nested nearby in recent years. Look for them overhead.

Swiss guides employed by the CPR built the Plain of the Six Glaciers teahouse in 1924. The building is just out of harm's way, beside a large avalanche path. Originally, the teahouse served as a staging area for mountaineers. Overnight accommodation is no longer offered. You can purchase lunch, refreshments and baked goods in season, which generally runs from mid-June to late September.

A MEAT-EATING VEGAN

Butterwort is a small, attractive plant with a tallish stem for its size. It sports a purple flower and a rosette of pale green, basal leaves. Nothing peculiar so far, but the common butterwort is a plant that could have come from a John Wyndham novel. Although it also practices photosynthesis, it is one of seven insectivorous plants in the Rockies. Common butterwort grows on soils that are poor in nitrogen, so it supplements its supply through carnivory. Its leaves are coated in a sticky, acidic enzyme that traps and digests insects, turning them into bug slurpee. Yum. The exoskeletons cannot be digested, and so remain as black specks on the leaves. Although the butterwort's table of insect fare necessarily includes only small insects, occasional prey may have just finished pollinating the plant's flower. How's that for gratitude?

Victoria Glacier moraines and Lake Louise

GLACIER TYPES

Glacial ice forms in areas where more snow accumulates in winter than melts in summer. The shape of a glacier depends on its location and on features of the surrounding landscape. *Icefields* form on flat areas at high elevation. *Outlet valley glaciers* flow from icefields into valleys below. *Alpine valley glaciers* occupy high mountain valleys and are not fed by icefields. *Cirque glaciers* occupy and erode bowl-shaped depressions in mountainsides. A small cirque glacier is called a *pocket glacier*. *Catchment glaciers* form at high elevations where indentations in a mountainside trap windblown snow. If the indentation is deep, the glacier may be called a *niche glacier*. Where ice tumbles from a cliff edge and coalesces on the valley floor, the resulting body of ice is called a *regenerated glacier*.

Any of these glacier types can also be called a *hanging glacier* if the ice terminates on a cliff. A *rock glacier* is a lobe-shaped accumulation of rock that insulates permanent ice within. Except for icefields and outlet valley glaciers, you can see all these glacier types from the Plain of the Six Glaciers trail.

Teahouse to Victoria Glacier Overlook

The teahouse is the ultimate destination for many hikers. But if you have the legs, consider extending this hike southwest for 1.6 km to the exposed crest of a lateral moraine that overlooks the Lower Victoria Glacier. Here, you are face to face with an ice age landscape. Massive limestone and quartzite cliffs glisten with glacial ice. Rockfalls and avalanches echo about. The moraine at trail's end is ice-cored. Use caution. Keep off the glacier.

In the view southwest, Abbot Pass (2920 m) separates Mt. Lefroy (3442 m) and Mt. Victoria (3464 m). Abbot Pass Hut, built by Swiss guides in 1921-22, sits atop the pass. Although most of this building is made from stone quarried on-site, the guides packed more than two tonnes of supplies by horse across the glacier, and then winched and carried the stuff the remaining distance to the pass. Named for Phillip Stanley Abbot, who died on Mt. Lefroy in 1896, the hut was the highest inhabitable building in Canada until the Neil Colgan Hut was constructed above Moraine Lake in 1982.

It is 7.5 km to the parking area via the Plain of the Six Glaciers trail. Keep straight ahead at all trail junctions. If the short section of trail along the edge of a bluff (equipped with a cable handrail) is not to your liking, you can bypass it on moraines to the south. If you reach the lake in early evening, you may witness the comings and goings of beavers. They often venture onto the trail to nibble the shoreline willows, oblivious to human traffic. The displays of red-stemmed saxifrage at the base of the lakeside cliffs are the best that I have seen in the Rockies.

14. Saddleback

Mt. Temple and larches

BANFF NATIONAL PARK

TRAIL THUMBNAIL

Day-hike; see map, p. 64

Route	Elev. (m)	Dist. (km)
Parking area	1735	0
Trailhead	1738	0.1
Saddleback	2330	3.8
Saddleback jct, Paradise Valley	1845	7.6
Moraine Lake trail jct	1814	10.4
Parking area	1735	14.9

Trailhead
Enquire at the Lake Louise park information centre about any restrictions on this trail. From Lake Louise Village, follow Lake Louise Drive 5.5 km to the parking areas at the lake. Paved walkways lead to the lakeshore. The Saddleback trailhead is southeast of the World Heritage Site monument, near the boathouse.

Maps
NTS: 82 N/8
Gem Trek: *Lake Louise and Yoho* or *Best of Lake Louise*

Best lighting: any time

Cleared in 1893, the trail to Saddleback was among the earlier recreational hiking trails in the Rockies. Its ascent has since served many as an introduction to the alpine wonders of the Lake Louise area, and as a test of fitness. Few trails are so intent of purpose. With an average grade of 16 percent, this trail makes a beeline for the "saddle" connecting Fairview Mountain and Saddle Mountain, leaving many hikers breathless along the way.

Lake Louise to Saddleback

The first hundred metres set the tone for this outing, as you toil upward across the shaded northeast slope of Fairview Mountain. More than 4 m of snow falls here annually. The damp, climax, subalpine forest of Engelmann spruce and subalpine fir has not burned since 1630. Feathermosses are prominent in the undergrowth.

Keep straight ahead at the Fairview Lookout and Moraine Lake trail junctions. The trail crosses a broad swath in the forest, created by avalanches from the quartzite cliffs of Fairview Mountain. From the switchback at the south edge of this avalanche path, look back for the view of Chateau Lake Louise and distant Mt. Hector (3394 m), rising above the expansive, glacially carved trough of the Bow Valley.

At about km 2, the trail forks. Both trails lead to Saddleback, converging again in 400 m. The left-hand trail is less steep and offers views across the Bow Valley to the Slate Range. You can see the slopes of Whitehorn Mountain (2621 m), criss-crossed by the ski runs of the Lake Louise ski area. After it

swings south to approach the pass, the trail crosses more avalanche terrain and switchbacks through the first stands of Lyall's larch. The winding route into the pass circumvents snow patches that linger in early summer. Please do not shortcut the switchbacks.

The icy crest of Mt. Temple (3544 m) looms majestically over a foreground of larch trees on Saddleback. The dark, rocky peak to the west of the pass is Sheol Mountain (2776 m). *Sheol* is the Hebrew abode of the dead. The mountain was named because of its gloomy appearance when viewed from the valley at its base.

The CPR built a teahouse on Saddleback in 1922. It had an unreliable water supply and operated for only one summer. You may find weathered boards in various locations on the pass – the remains of

VARIATIONS

- Hike to the pass and back; 7.6 km return.
- Cross the pass to make a loop through lower Paradise Valley; 14.9 km.
- Competent hikers can add an ascent of Fairview Mountain; 3.0 km return from the pass.

> *Lake Louise was in the door-yard, and Fairview the house-top from which we descended to seek the fields beyond the bounding sky-line.*
>
> James Monroe Thorington; *The Glittering Mountains of Canada*

the building's siding. Sections of the water line from Sheol Valley still run across the flanks of Fairview Mountain.

Fairview Mountain (2744 m)

From the cairn on the pass, a steep track leads 1.5 km northwest onto the slopes of Fairview Mountain. First climbed by surveyor J.J. McArthur in 1887, Fairview is today the most frequently ascended mountain in the Rockies. Its summit is the 2nd-highest point reached on the Classic Hikes. During good weather, when the slopes are free of snow, virtually any reasonably fit and well-prepared hiker can make the ascent. As the mountain's name implies, the summit panorama is among the finer near Lake

Louise. Be sure to descend from Fairview by retracing your route of ascent. Accidents, sometimes fatal, are common on this "easy" mountain when hikers attempt to "take a shortcut" down the northeast face to Lake Louise. Hardly a summer goes by without a call for rescue specialists to pluck off-route hikers, stranded on the cliffs. Lightning killed an experienced hiker on Fairview's summit in 2002.

Loop Hike Option

Continue southwest over Saddleback to descend the switchbacks into Sheol Valley. As you lose elevation, the relatively minor summit of Sheol Mountain gains in stature, gloomily blocking the afternoon sun. The trail crosses the creek that drains Sheol Valley. The descent continues to the Paradise Valley trail junction, 3.8 km from the pass. Turn northeast east (left) and follow this pleasant trail 3.1 km to the Moraine Lake trail junction, making two crossings of Paradise Creek. Turn northwest (left) at the junction, from where it is 4.4 km through subalpine forest to the parking area near the trailhead. See Classic Hike #15 for information on Paradise Valley.

EEEEP!

Often heard but seldom seen, the shrill "eeep" of the tiny pika (PEE-kah or PIE-kah) will tell you that this member of the rabbit family is nearby. The pika lives among the blocks and rubble of boulderfields and rockslides. With a minuscule tail, big round ears, and a gray coat, it looks like a tennis ball with ears. Its folk name is "rock rabbit."

The pika inhabits a small home range. It scurries about during daytime, gathering grasses, lichens, leaves, and wildflowers; drying them on boulders then stashing the hay within the boulderfield. The pika does not hibernate. During the winter it uses rocky corridors under the snow to reach its food caches. It also eats partially digested pellets of its own dung. Yum.

A large boulderfield may be home to a colony of pikas, who take turns acting as lookouts. The pika's call warns its fellows of approaching danger. Eagles and hawks can pick-off a pika from above. More dangerous are martens and weasels that hunt the pika through its boulder home. As the Earth's climate warms, pikas are encountering major stresses. Higher summer temperatures are cooking them in their rocky warrens; decreased winter snowpacks are causing them to freeze. As treeline shifts upwards, pikas that lived at lower elevations and in warmer sites are dying off, unable to migrate to where conditions are favourable.

FROM YALE TO PARADISE

Sheol, Fairview, Saddle, Paradise and many other names in the Lake Louise area were given by members of the Yale Lake Louise Club. These five school mates spent a blissful and somewhat perilous summer on the heights around Lake Louise in 1894. Although most of them lacked significant mountaineering experience, their adventures included the first ascents of Mt. Temple and Mt. Aberdeen, the discoveries of Paradise Valley and Moraine Lake, and the first crossings of Sentinel, Wasatch, Wenkchemna, and Mitre passes. Two members, Walter Wilcox and Samuel Allen – who had visited the Rockies together in 1893 – each published maps of the area. Wilcox (seated on the right in the photo) also authored *Camping in the Rockies* – later called *The Rockies of Canada* – a best selling book that went through numerous printings and editions, establishing him as the authority of the day on the Canadian Rockies.

15. Paradise Valley

Paradise Creek

TRAIL THUMBNAIL

Day-hike or overnight; see map, p.64

Route	Elev. (m)	Dist. (km)
Trailhead	1729	0
Moraine Lake trail jct	1799	1.1
Paradise Valley jct	1825	1.3
Saddleback jct	1845	4.2
Lake Annette	1980	5.8
Giant Steps jct	2119	8.5
Paradise Valley CG jct	2012	10.2
Paradise Valley CG	2020	+0.3
Giant Steps	2012	10.5

Special considerations

The Paradise Valley campground may be closed. The trail may be subject to a minimum group size. Enquire at the Lake Louise park information centre.

Trailhead

From Lake Louise Village, follow Lake Louise Drive 3 km to the Moraine Lake Road. Turn south (left). Follow this road 2.3 km to the Paradise Creek trailhead.

Maps

NTS: 82 N/8
Gem Trek: *Lake Louise and Yoho*

Best lighting: morning

With its alluring combination of forest, lakes, glaciers, meadows, waterfalls, and imposing mountains, Paradise Valley provides one of the more complete hiking experiences in the Canadian Rockies. From the backcountry campground at the head of the valley, you can explore the Giant Steps, Sentinel Pass, Wasatch Pass, and Horseshoe Glacier. This outing is an excellent choice for novice backpackers, and is best between mid-July and mid-September.

Trailhead to Lake Annette

The outing begins with an ascent over forested moraines. The open subalpine forest features yellow columbine, false hellebore, fleabane, arnica, and dwarf dogwood. Club mosses, spike mosses, feathermosses, grouseberry, and false azalea comprise the undergrowth.

Keep straight ahead at the bike-ski trail junction. The trail follows the crest of an ancient creek bank through a doghair pine forest to the Moraine Lake trail. Turn north (right). Follow this trail 200 m to the Paradise Valley junction, ascending a rolling sequence of ancient creek terraces. Turn west (left) at the junction. The Paradise Valley trail climbs a short distance over moraines, and then begins a gradual descent to the first crossing of Paradise Creek.

Boggy areas along the south bank of Paradise Creek feature elephant-head, cotton-grass, fleabane,

cinquefoil, and yellow paintbrush. The trail recrosses the creek to reach the Saddleback junction. Keep straight ahead. At the Lake Annette junction, 1.5 km further, turn south (left), and again cross Paradise Creek. The trail climbs moderately to the outlet of Lake Annette. White mountain heather covers the slope west of the trail. White globeflowers grow along the outlet stream. Look for dippers here.

Bordered by boulderfields, moraine and larch forest, Lake Annette sits at the base of Mt. Temple's stupendous north face. A kruppelholz forest of

VARIATIONS

- Hike to Lake Annette; 10.6 km return.
- Hike to the Giant Steps; 21.0 km return.
- Use the campground as a base to explore the upper valley.
- Add a visit to Sentinel Pass; 5.4 km return from the Giant Steps jct. See Classic Hike #16.

Lake Annette

Porcupine

subalpine fir rings the north shore. The upper part of each tree is a lifeless spike, killed by the chilling blast of avalanches from Mt. Temple. The gnarled mat of the lower trees has survived, insulated within the snowpack. Walter Wilcox named Lake Annette for a woman he presumed was the wife of Willoughby Astley, the first manager of the Chalet Lake Louise. Annette was Astley's mother.

MT. TEMPLE –
A MOUNTAIN CRUCIBLE

The north face of Mt. Temple (3544 m) dominates the view south from the first bridge over Paradise Creek. Mt. Temple is the highest peak in the Lake Louise area, 3rd-highest in Banff National Park, 6th-highest in Alberta, and 11th-highest in the Rockies. The summit rises more than 1700 vertical metres above the valley floor.

Mt. Temple has long been a testing place for mountaineers. It was first climbed in 1894 by members of the Yale Lake Louise Club, led by schoolmates Walter Wilcox and Samuel Allen. They followed a route from Sentinel Pass on the opposite side of the mountain. The imposing north flank was first climbed in 1966, and now features many challenging routes. George Dawson named the mountain in 1884 for Sir Richard Temple, patron of a British scientific expedition to the Rockies.

Lake Annette to Upper Paradise Valley

From Lake Annette the trail climbs steeply southwest onto a bench covered in rockslide debris. This is a good place to see pikas, and perhaps a wolverine. This section of trail is usually snowbound and muddy until mid-July. The apex of the trail features a grand prospect ahead to the tremendous cirque of Horseshoe Glacier and the peaks that surround the head of Paradise Valley. Highest is Hungabee Mountain (Hun-GAH-bee) (3490 m), the 16th-highest peak in the Rockies. Samuel Allen applied this Stoney name in 1894. Appropriately, it means "Chieftain." You can see the Slate Range to the northeast, and the glacier serac wall on the north face of Mt. Temple, high above to the southeast.

Near the end of the 2.7 km traverse beneath Mt. Temple, the quartzite towers that flank Pinnacle Mountain (3070 m) come into view. Highest of the pinnacles is the Grand Sentinel. At the base of Mt. Lefroy, across Paradise Valley, "Mitre Glacier" terminates in a classic moraine-dammed lake. The cliffs of Ringrose Peak (3292 m), Glacier Peak (3302 m), and Mt. Lefroy (3442 m) are alive with snow avalanches on warm afternoons. At the Giant Steps junction, turn northwest (right), and descend to a bridge over Paradise Creek. Keep straight ahead to the Paradise Valley campground junction. Turn northeast (right) for the Giant Steps, reached in 300 m.

Almost everyone who has camped in Paradise Valley has a good (bad?) porcupine story. Porcupines

> ..we saw a new group of mountains in the distance, while a most beautiful valley lay far below us. Throughout a broad expanse of meadows and open country, many streams were to be seen winding through this valley, clearly traceable to their various sources in glaciers, springs and melting snowdrifts.
>
> Walter Wilcox; *The Rockies of Canada*

eat leaves and the tender cambium layer within tree bark. They also have a taste for anything salty. Boots and pack straps are prime porcupine cuisine, especially at night. Keep your boots inside your tent and don't go barefoot.

To exit from Paradise Valley, retrace your route to the trailhead. If you want to tag Sentinel Pass, head west (right) at the Giant Steps junction for 400 m to the Sentinel Pass junction. Turn south (left) for the gritty, blocky, and sometimes snowy, 2.3 km climb to the pass. From the crest of Sentinel Pass, it is shorter (5.8 km) to head down to Moraine Lake, but you will need to have arranged transportation. See Classic Hike #16.

THE GIANT STEPS

The Giant Steps cascade over a series of gently dipping, quartzite slabs in the north fork of Paradise Creek. Scratches on the slabs are striations, caused by rocks embedded in the underside of Horseshoe Glacier when it most recently advanced across this area. Depressions in the slabs have filled with thin soils that support miniature gardens of lichens, mosses, and wildflowers. Please avoid stepping on them. The trail emerges at the uppermost cascades. To reach the lower falls, backtrack to the approach trail and follow faint paths downstream. Use caution on the slippery rock, and be watchful for ice on cold days.

16. Sentinel Pass

Sentinel Pass

TRAIL THUMBNAIL

Day-hike or overnight; see map, p. 64

Route	Elev. (m)	Dist. (km)
Trailhead	1888	0
Larch Valley-Sentinel Pass jct	2241	2.7
Sentinel Pass	2612	5.8
Sentinel Pass jct (Paradise Valley)	2119	8.1
Giant Steps jct	2120	8.5
Lake Annette	1966	11.2
Paradise Creek trailhead	1729	17.0

Trailhead
From Lake Louise Village, follow Lake Louise Drive 3 km to the Moraine Lake Road. Turn south (left). Follow this road 12 km to its end at Moraine Lake. The trailhead is on the lakeshore, south of the lodge.

Special considerations
The Paradise Valley campground may be closed. The trail may be subject to a minimum group size. Enquire at the Lake Louise park information centre. On the final approach to Sentinel Pass, and on the north side of the pass, you are exposed to avalanche and rockfall hazards. Use caution crossing snow patches.

Maps
NTS: 82 N/8
Gem Trek: *Lake Louise and Yoho*

Few destinations better exemplify the primal nature of the Rockies than the barren cleft of Sentinel Pass. Sandwiched between the shattered ramparts of Pinnacle Mountain and Mt. Temple, the pass is the 4th-highest point reached on the Classic Hikes. It offers you a toehold in the domain of mountaineers. The steep slopes on either side of the pass can be treacherous when snow covered. Most years, if you hike this trail before mid-July, you should carry an ice axe and be proficient in its use.

Trailhead to Sentinel Pass

From the trailhead kiosk in front of the lodge, follow the trail southwest for 35 m to a junction. The Sentinel Pass-Wenkchemna Pass trail branches north (right), and immediately begins its steep climb. In the next 2.5 km, the trail gains 352 m to the entrance to Larch Valley. You can see Moraine Lake through the trees. Listen for hermit thrushes, yellow-rumped warblers, and golden-crowned sparrows. The climb – which takes you to the crest of an ancient lateral moraine of the Wenkchemna Glacier – concludes with a series of ten switchbacks that lead to a trail junction and a well-placed bench. The trail to Larch Valley and Sentinel Pass branches north (right).

MR. FAY'S MOUNTAIN

By most accounts, Professor Charles Fay of Tufts University was a gentleman and an accomplished mountaineer. Founder of the Appalachian Mountain Club and the American Alpine Club, Fay made 25 visits to the Rockies between 1894 and 1930, the year of his death. However, there is one story that portrays Fay out of character. To honour Fay's contribution to the exploration of the Rockies, the Geographic Board permitted him to choose a mountain to name for himself. Fellow mountaineer, C.S. Thompson, suggested the peak above Moraine Lake that Samuel Allen had first called Heejee ("Peak One.") Fay concurred, thus supplanting Allen's name; the first of seven times that this would happen in Valley of the Ten Peaks.

On his visit in 1904, Fay intended to make the first ascent of "his mountain." Two guides, the Kaufmann brothers, based at Chalet Lake Louise, apparently conspired to rob him of this prize. While one of the guides led Fay on a poor route destined for certain failure, another led British mountaineer, Gertrude Benham, to success by a different route. Although there is no official record of what transpired, it is thought that Fay was so incensed that he promptly had the Kaufmanns fired by their employer, the Canadian Pacific Railway. Fay considered applying to have the name Mt. Fay bestowed upon another peak so that he might attempt its first ascent. This he did not do, settling instead for a consolation prize, the second ascent of Mt. Fay, two weeks after Benham's.

Larch Valley occupies a broad glacial cirque, centered on a bedrock fault south of Sentinel Pass. The trail winds its way into the lower valley and crosses a footbridge to a meadow. As early morning visitors will discover, the meadow is a frost hollow where cold air collects. Trees along the northern edge of the meadow display branches stunted by the cold. The meadow contains earth hummocks, caused by repeated freezing and thawing of the soil when it was underlaid by permafrost. To the southwest is Deltaform Mountain (3426 m), highest of the Wenkchemna Peaks, and the 14th-highest mountain in Alberta. American explorer, Walter Wilcox, named the mountain for its resemblance to delta – Δ – the fourth letter of the Greek alphabet.

The trail swings north and climbs to treeline, passing some ancient larches and glades filled with western anemone. Following several bear encounters here in the early 2000s, Parks Canada pruned the trees at trailside to improve sight lines. Samuel Allen, a companion of Walter Wilcox, named the three lakes in the tundra below Sentinel Pass, Minnestimma Lakes. *Minnestimma* is Stoney for "sleeping waters." From the outlet of the middle lake, the trail heads east and begins the stiff climb along the lower flank of Mt. Temple to the switchbacks that lead into Sentinel Pass. Use caution on the snow patches and keep your ears keen for rockfall from above.

Sentinel Pass

Sentinel Pass was first reached in 1894 by Samuel Allen, who ascended from a camp in Paradise Valley. A few days later, Allen, Wilcox, and L.F. Frissell returned to the pass and climbed Mt. Temple, the first time a mountain exceeding 3353 m (11,000 ft) had been climbed in Canada. Theirs has become "regular route" on the mountain. On a fair summer day, as many as a hundred mountaineers may make the trip to Mt. Temple's summit by this route.

The pass is a vast ruin of nature indeed. The chief agent of erosion at work here is mechanical weathering. Water expands nine percent when frozen. The repeated freezing and thawing of water forces cracks open. Eventually, boulders, cliffs, and mountainsides succumb to this incessant process. Mountains become molehills.

> *Opposite was a pinnacled mountain stained red and gray, rent into thousands of narrow gullies or beetling turrets by the wear of ages. It was a vast ruin of nature, a barren mass of tottering walls and cliffs, raising two lofty summits upwards.*
>
> Walter Wilcox; *The Rockies of Canada*

The view south from the pass features the Wenkchemna Peaks, from Mt. Fay (3234 m) in the east, to Deltaform Mountain in the west. The large pinnacle to the north of the pass is the 120 m high Grand Sentinel, a favourite objective of rock climbers.

Optional Exit: Sentinel Pass to Paradise Valley

North from the pass, the trail is poorly defined as it switchbacks steeply down through scree and boulders (and probably snow) on the west side of the valley. Take care not to dislodge rocks onto people below. After the initial descent, the trail angles across the valley floor (follow cairns) to the east side. The grade lessens and the way becomes obvious. The pinnacles on the north slope of Pinnacle Mountain may be silhouetted against the sky or looming from the mist, offering intriguing possibilities to photographers.

Paradise Valley Options

At the trail junction 2.3 km north of Sentinel Pass, turn northeast (right) for 400 m to the Giant Steps junction. If you would like to visit the Giant Steps or camp in the backcountry campground in Paradise Valley, turn north (left). Otherwise, keep straight ahead on the highline route beneath the north face of Mt. Temple to Lake Annette, and then to the Moraine Lake Road (8.2 km). (See Classic Hike #15.) You should have transportation prearranged. (Stash a bike?) The Paradise Creek parking area is 9.7 km by road from Moraine Lake, and 5.3 km from Lake Louise Village.

The Grand Sentinel

VARIATIONS

- Hike to the pass and return the same way; 11.6 km
- Cross Sentinel Pass to Paradise Valley. Exit from Paradise Valley via Lake Annette to the Moraine Lake Road; 16.4 km. See Classic Hike #15.
- Cross Sentinel Pass to Paradise Valley. Visit the Giant Steps and exit via Lake Annette to the Moraine Lake Road; 20.4 km. See Classic Hike #15.
- Same as previous, but camp at the Paradise Valley campground; 21.0 km. See Classic Hike #15.
- Strong hikers can combine this outing with Wenkchemna Pass; 26.2 km. See Classic Hike #17.
- You can begin this outing with a short sidetrip (500 m return) along the interpretive trail to the top of the Moraine Lake Rockpile. See Classic Hike #17.

LYALL'S LARCH – GOLD IN THE HILLS

Larch Valley is named for the tree, Lyall's (LIE-alls) larch – also called subalpine larch, and alpine larch. Of the three larch species in Canada, Lyall's is the least extensive in range. In the Rockies, you won't find it north of Clearwater Pass, 28 km north of Lake Louise. It grows only in the upper subalpine forest, frequently forming pure stands at treeline. The mature tree is 5-10 m tall and has a ragged top, and brown bark highlighted with reddish-purple tones. Bright green needles grow from black, knobby twigs that are covered in dark woolly down. The wood burns easily, but because the tree usually grows in rocky terrain, forest fires rarely consume larch forests. Some trees in Larch Valley may be more than 400 years old.

The Lyall's larch is a deciduous conifer – it sheds its needles in late summer. Then the tree goes dormant with the buds for next year's growth already formed. Before shedding, larch needles turn golden yellow, transforming the treeline forests of the southern Rockies into a wonderful sight. Visitors flock to Larch Valley at that time by the hundreds. Steer clear. There are other, better places to see larches, but I won't name them here, lest they also become overrun. Eugene Bourgeau catalogued the tree. Its taxonomic name, *Larix lyalli*, commemorates David Lyall, a Scottish surgeon and naturalist who explored in the Arctic, Antarctic, New Zealand, and British North America in the mid-1800s.

17. Wenkchemna Pass

Eiffel Lakes

Day-hike; see map, p. 64

Route	Elev. (m)	Dist. (km)
Trailhead	1888	0
Larch Valley-Sentinel Pass jct	2241	2.7
Eiffel Lakes	2287	6.0
Wenkchemna Pass	2604	9.7

Trailhead
From Lake Louise Village, follow Lake Louise Drive 3 km to the Moraine Lake Road. Turn south (left). Follow this road 12 km to its end at Moraine Lake. The trailhead is on the lakeshore, south of the lodge.

Special considerations
The trail may be subject to a minimum group size. Enquire at the Lake Louise park information centre. Early season hikers should be prepared for travel on snow and the risk of avalanche danger.

Maps
NTS: 82 N/8
Gem Trek: *Lake Louise and Yoho*

The Wenkchemna Pass trail travels the length of the Valley of the Ten Peaks to a barren, rocky saddle on the crest of the continental divide. The north faces of the Wenkchemna Peaks loom over this hike. But if the sun breaks through, even that imposing mountain wall brightens, becoming a backdrop for sublime scenery. Forests of Lyall's larch, intriguing geology, and human history add to the appeal of this outing. Wenkchemna Pass is the 5th-highest point reached on the Classic Hikes. In most years it is snowbound well into July.

Trailhead to the Eiffel Lakes

From the trailhead kiosk in front of the lodge, follow the trail southwest for 35 m to a junction. The Sentinel Pass-Wenkchemna Pass trail branches north (right), and immediately begins its steep climb. In the next 2.5 km, the trail gains 352 m to the entrance to Larch Valley. You can see Moraine Lake through the trees. Listen for hermit thrushes, yellow-rumped warblers, and golden-crowned sparrows. The climb – which takes you to the crest of an ancient lateral moraine of

the Wenkchemna Glacier – concludes with a series of ten switchbacks that lead to a trail junction and a well-placed bench. The trail to Larch Valley and Sentinel Pass branches north (right). Keep straight ahead (west) for Wenkchemna Pass.

For the next 2 km, the trail travels at treeline across the southern flank of Eiffel Peak (3077 m), offering

WHEN IS A MORAINE NOT A MORAINE?

You can begin this hike with a short sidetrip (500 m return) to the top of the Moraine Lake rockpile. Samuel Allen called the lake, Heejee Lake, in 1893. Walter Wilcox paid the first visit to its shores in 1899. He called it Moraine Lake because he thought that the rockpile was a glacial moraine. Geologists now generally agree that the rockpile is rockslide debris, although some think that it may have been transported on the surface of a glacier – which would make it a rockslide, a moraine, and a pile of erratics. So, maybe Wilcox was wrong and right.

Most of the boulders in the rockpile are Gog Formation quartzite and siltstone. You can see fossilized worm burrowings and an example of

ripple rock. This rock records the action of wavelets on a prehistoric shoreline, 560 million-years-ago.

views ahead to Wenkchemna Pass, and back to the western end of Moraine Lake. Parks Canada pruned trees at trailside here to improve visibility after several bear encounters in the early 2000s. In 1893, Walter Wilcox and colleague Samuel Allen were the first to see the upper part of this valley. Wilcox was so taken aback by the austere appearance of the Wenkchemna Peaks and the chaos of rubble at their bases, that he coined the name Desolation Valley.

Samuel Allen named ten of the mountains in this valley with Stoney words for the numbers, 1 to 10. *Wenkchemna* means "ten." Allen's nomenclature was arbitrary, as eighteen mountains flank the valley. Only three of the Wenkchemna Peaks still bear the original names. Tonsa or "Peak 4" (3053 m) is south across the valley from Eiffel Peak. Wenkchemna Pass is bordered by Wenkchemna Peak (3206 m) on the north, and by Neptuak Mountain, "Peak 9" (3241 m), on the southeast.

After you cross an avalanche slope, the Eiffel Lakes come into view. These lakes, fringed with larch trees, occupy depressions in rockslide debris. They were a favourite destination of Wilcox, who would pack his large format camera here late in the summer, when he thought the scenery was at its best. Wilcox called the lakes the "Wenkchemna Lakes." The name "Eiffel" refers to a tower of rock, not visible from here, on the north side of Eiffel Peak. This tower supposedly resembles the well known structure in Paris. The lakes are fish-less.

The Eiffel Lakes nestle in the debris of two massive rockslides; one from the north face of Neptuak Mountain, the other from near Wenkchemna Pass. One of the boulders has an estimated weight of more than 1000 tonnes. The total volume of the rockslides is more than 10 million cubic metres. The prominent peak to the northwest is Hungabee (hun-GAH-bee) Mountain (3490 m). *Hungabee* means "Chieftain." The mountain is the 2nd-highest in the area, after Mt. Temple, and commands the head of nearby Paradise Valley.

Eiffel Lakes to Wenkchemna Pass

West of the Eiffel Lakes, the trail is rough as it crosses boulderfields. The going becomes easier as the trail winds through an upper subalpine meadow bisected by several streams – the last water sources before the pass. From the meadows, the trail angles southwest and then switchbacks upward through more boulderfields. The quartzite boulders underfoot rest on the surface of a rock glacier – an accumulation of ice that allows the entire mass to creep slowly downhill. There are several small kettle lakes northwest of the trail. You may see white-tailed ptarmigan as you approach the pass. These ground-dwelling, grouse-like birds feature plumage that changes from white in winter, to a mottled brown, gray and black in summer. The tail is always white. On the final section of trail you toil across a scree slope before descending slightly onto Wenkchemna Pass. That's the official

A VALLEY OF ROCK AND ICE

Most of the rubble on the floor of the Valley of the Ten Peaks is surface moraine that covers the 4 km² Wenkchemna Glacier. This peculiar body of ice is sustained primarily by snow and ice avalanches from couloirs on the north faces of the Wenkchemna Peaks. The more easterly part of the glacier is now stagnant and detached from the active glacial ice. Insulated by the moraine on its surface, this huge mass of ice will slowly melt if the glacier does not advance again and reincorporate it.

The rubble-covered glacier features conical talus (TAY-luss) piles, mounds of rock created by avalanches. These piles have been carried from the base of the cliffs by the moving ice. Kettle ponds, formed by slumping and melting of ice-cored moraines, dot the glacier's surface. A sinuous terminal moraine winds along the glacier's northern margin like an ice-age dragon. Walter Wilcox was right – it is a scene of desolation, but not without beauty.

VARIATION

- Strong hikers can add a visit to Sentinel Pass; 26.2 km total. See Classic Hike #16.

The day had perhaps fifteen minutes of bright wonder and we were there for all of them. A quick glissade down the snow patch and we were back in the dismal soup. The sunlight continued to scatter itself about the day, but we had drunk our fill. Time had stopped up there, as occasionally it does in mountain places. We had transcended summer, autumn, spring and winter. Yea, it is barren, but it is so beautiful.

Jon Whyte; *Mountain Chronicles*

MEADOW CHALICE

Wenkchemna Pass

The meadows on this hike are flush with western anemone. You will have to arrive early in the hiking season to see the showy, creamy-white blooms – sometimes tinged with blue – that poke through the edges of receding snowbanks. Most hikers only ever see the seedheads that endure the remainder of the season. When covered with dew or backlit, these shaggy tops are a favourite with photographers. Anemone is derived from the Greek, *anemos*, which means "wind." "Chalice flower" is one of the folk names for this plant – a reference to the deep, cup-shaped bloom. The confines at the centre of the flower trap solar heat, evidently making the location more attractive to pollinating insects, thus helping to ensure propagation.

route, however if snow covers the area, you will probably follow whatever track has been beaten. Perhaps you will even follow the track of a wolverine, as I once did. Be careful on any snowslopes.

The trackless west slope of the pass plunges to the upper reaches of Tokumm Creek in Yoho National Park. The rock formation in the meadows there is called Eagle Eyrie. Golden eagles do frequent this area, and when seen from ground level, the rock formation resembles a bird of prey. The summit of Neptuak Mountain, southeast of the pass, is the only point in Canada where the boundaries of three national parks meet – Yoho, Banff, and Kootenay. Looking northeast, the massive bulk of Mt. Temple (3544 m) dominates all other mountains in the area.

18. Skoki

Mt. Richardson, Corrall Creek

The area known as Skoki (SKOWE-key) encompasses a series of compact, lake-dotted valleys – Ptarmigan, Baker, Skoki, and Red Deer – in the Slate Range northeast of Lake Louise. Although peopled, the Skoki area backs onto the wilderness of northeastern Banff. Grizzly bears, wolves, moose, wolverines, mule deer, elk, coyote, bighorn sheep, and mountain goats frequent these valleys. Much of the hiking is at or above treeline.

This outing describes a counter-clockwise loop hike. You can add day-hikes from the campgrounds. Mountaineers can make straightforward ascents of more than a dozen nearby summits. Completing the charm of the Skoki area is its vibrant human history. You share the entire loop with horses.

Trailhead to Boulder Pass

The Skoki trail commences with a stiff climb along the Temple access road. Don't let the road and its occasional traffic fool you; grizzly bears frequent

TRAIL THUMBNAIL

Overnight, 3-5 days

Route	Elev. (m)	Dist. (km)
Trailhead	1698	0
Temple Research Station	1990	3.7
End of gravel road	1995	3.9
Halfway Hut	2195	7.1
Hidden Lake CG jct	2195	7.2
Hidden Lake CG	2198	+0.1
Boulder Pass	2340	8.7
Deception Pass jct	2348	10.5
Baker Lake CG	2210	13.2
Baker Creek jct	1955	13.9
Baker-Red Deer Divide	2180	15.0
"Jones' Pass" jct	2160	16.7
Red Deer Lakes CG	2088	+2.3
"Jones' Pass"	2210	19.0
Skoki Valley jct	2195	19.6
Skoki Lodge	2164	20.0
Merlin Meadows CG	2119	21.2
Skoki Valley jct	2195	22.8
Deception Pass	2475	25.8
Boulder Pass	2345	28.2
Trailhead	1698	36.9

Trailhead
From the Lake Louise interchange on Highway 1, turn east onto Whitehorn Road and follow signs for the Lake Louise ski area. Turn south (right) after 2 km onto the Fish Creek road. Follow this gravel road 1 km until it becomes restricted access. Park in the parking area (right).

Special consideration
Parks Canada is considering restricting access in the Skoki area. Check at the Lake Louise park information centre.

Maps
NTS: 82 N/8, 82 N/9, 82 O/5, 82 O/12
Gem Trek: *Lake Louise and Yoho* or *Banff and Mt. Assiniboine*

Every time we go to Skoki we carry along the same old stories, but each trip to Skoki seems to provide a new story which becomes part of the accumulation. The greatest thing about stories is their lightness and portability. I've seen people with seven kilo packs, but they've packed a couple of gross [of] stories into the map flap, and the pack seems inexhaustible.

Jon Whyte; *Mountain Chronicles*

this area. Travel accordingly. Views are limited, except from the top of "Ford Hill," where you may see Mt. Victoria (3464 m) and other summits near Lake Louise to the west. Keep straight ahead at junctions until the road ends 200 m beyond the Temple Research Station at the Lake Louise ski area. Angle steeply uphill across a ski run to where the trail proper begins.

From here to near Boulder Pass, the trail follows Corral Creek through upper subalpine forest. You may see red squirrels, porcupines, gray jays, Clark's nutcrackers, American martens, and mule deer. Some work on the Skoki trail was done by Ukrainian prisoners during WWI. At km 6.8, the forest thins. Cross Corral Creek to its west bank. Use caution if the bridge is frosty. Ahead are the three highest summits of the Slate Range, from west to east – Mt. Richardson (3086 m), Pika Peak (3023 m), and Ptarmigan Peak (3059 m). James Hector named Mt. Richardson for John Richardson, surgeon and naturalist with the Franklin Arctic expeditions of 1819 and 1825. The Slate Range is reportedly home to approximately 40 mountain goats, but it recent decades their numbers have dwindled.

Halfway Hut (also called Ptarmigan Hut) is the next waypoint on the trail. The cabin was constructed in 1931 as a stopover for ski guests of Skoki Lodge, and for guides and packers making supply trips. The building is halfway between the Lake Louise railway

VARIATIONS

- Day-hike to Hidden Lake and Boulder Pass; 20.0 km return.
- Day-hike to Boulder Pass and Deception Pass; 22.0 km return.
- Hike the loop in reverse.
- Base yourself at one of the four campgrounds and visit other destinations as day-hikes.

HIDDEN LAKE, 1.3 KM

I recommend the sidetrip to Hidden Lake if you are staying at the nearby campground, or are day-hiking from the trailhead to Boulder Pass. The trail departs from the campground and follows the north fork of Corral Creek. Wildflowers fill the glades in the treeline larch forest. Rock-hop the stream just below the lake's outlet, and follow the wet track to the lakeshore.

Hidden Lake is a typical glacial tarn, 32.3 m deep. Cutthroat trout inhabit the waters. Mountain goats and bighorn sheep ramble along the cliffs north of the lake. Redoubt Mountain looms across the valley to the southeast.

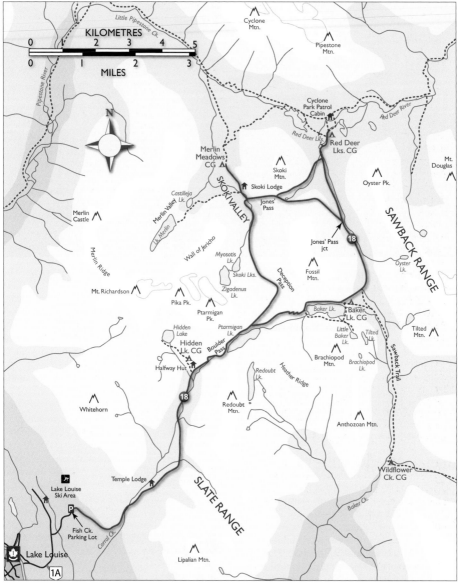

KILOMETRES

0   2   3   4   5

0   1   2   3

MILES

N

Little Pipestone Ck.

Cyclone Mtn.

Pipestone Mtn.

Red Deer River

Cyclone Park Patrol Cabin

Red Deer Lks.

Red Deer Lks. CG

Pipestone River

Merlin Meadows CG

Skoki Mtn.

Skoki Lodge

Oyster Pk.

Mt. Douglas

Castilleja Lk.

Merlin Valley

Jones' Pass

SKOKI VALLEY

SAWBACK RANGE

Merlin Castle

Lk. Merlin

Jones' Pass jct

18

Oyster Lk.

Merlin Ridge

Wall of Jericho

Myosotis Lk.

Fossil Mtn.

Deception Pass

Mt. Richardson

Skoki Lks.

Zigadenus Lk.

Pika Pk.

Ptarmigan Pk.

Baker Lk.

Baker Lk. CG

Sawback Trail

Tilted Mtn.

Hidden Lake

Ptarmigan Lk.

Little Baker Lk.

Tilted Lk.

Hidden Lk. CG

Boulder Pass

Halfway Hut

Brachiopod Mtn.

Brachiopod Lk.

Redoubt Lk.

Heather Ridge

Whitehorn

Redoubt Mtn.

18

Anthozoan Mtn.

Wildflower Ck. CG

Baker Ck.

Temple Lodge

SLATE RANGE

Lake Louise Ski Area

P

Fish Ck. Parking Lot

Corral Ck.

Lake Louise

1A

Lipalian Mtn.

station and Skoki Lodge. Many sober and reputable travellers have reported unusual sights and sounds in and near Halfway Hut. The ghosts of four skiers killed nearby in avalanches are said to haunt the building. They schuss down from Ptarmigan Peak to convene a nightly poker game in winter. Today, the hut is a day-use shelter only. It is located on the site of a prehistoric encampment. There are fine views of Mt. Temple (3544 m) and some of the Wenkchemna Peaks from the meadows nearby. Porcupines and Columbian ground squirrels frequent the area. I have seen a female wolverine with three cubs here.

The Hidden Lake junction is 100 m north of Halfway Hut. The adjacent backcountry campground

is less than four hours travel from the trailhead for most hikers, making it possible to start this hike late in the day in early summer, with the assurance of reaching a campground before dark.

The initial 500 m of trail between Halfway Hut and Boulder Pass can be muddy. Some ancient stumps at trailside may have been sources for some of the logs in the walls of Halfway Hut. The final kilometre to the pass winds through massive quartzite boulders of rockslide debris from Redoubt Mountain (2902 m). The mountain was named because of its "redoubtable," fortress-like appearance. If you look back during the climb, you may see the large boulder that mimics the shape of distant Mt. Temple. Keen

Ptarmigan Lake

observers may also pick out a dry stream course – probably an ancient drainage from Ptarmigan Lake. Some rocks at trailside contain fossilized corals.

Boulder Pass is a gateway to the front ranges of northeastern Banff. The centrepiece in the view is Ptarmigan Lake, which laps against the eastern side of the pass. On rare calm days, the lake mirrors Fossil Mountain (2946 m) and the distant summits of Mt. Douglas (3235 m) and Mt. St. Bride (3312 m), the two highest mountains in the Sawback Range. True to the name of the lake and nearby peak, you may see white-tailed ptarmigan – a ground-dwelling, alpine grouse – on the pass.

Boulder Pass to Baker Lake

The Skoki trail is rocky and wet in places as it undulates along the north shore of Ptarmigan Lake. Kruppelholz tree islands of spruce and fir dot the tundra. Cotton-grass grows along the lakeshore. You should be prepared for poor weather in this vicinity. When the clouds are down on the hills, Ptarmigan Lake ranks among the bleaker places in the Rockies. Summer snowfalls are common and winds are often strong and bitterly cold. However, on fair days, this piece of trail is upper subalpine heaven. The Deception Pass junction is 1.9 km from Boulder Pass. Keep straight ahead for Baker Lake.

The trail contours through several shale gullies southwest of Fossil Mountain, before descending through stunted subalpine forest to Baker Lake. Follow the north shore of the lake through willows to the Baker Lake campground near the outlet. The lake is popular with backcountry anglers, and with bugs. Porcupines and snowshoe hares frequent the tenting area. Look for dippers in the outlet stream.

Baker Lake to Red Deer Lakes

At the junction 50 m east of Baker Lake campground, keep northeast (left). From the junction, the trail contours through open subalpine forest dotted with larches, and then descends to the treeless tundra of the valley floor and another junction. Turn north (left). The wildflowers here are exceptional, and include elephant-head and dense clumps of vibrantly coloured paintbrush.

Cyclone Mountain (3042 m) and its eastern outlier, Pipestone Mountain (2972 m), are prominent to the north. A mountaineering party named Cyclone Mountain in 1910. A thunderstorm gathered over its summit as they were deliberating how to climb it. The sedimentary formations of Pipestone Mountain feature an anticline.

About 2 km from the campground, you cross the unremarkable height of land that separates Baker

---

LITTLE BAKER LAKE, 1.2 KM

Little Baker Lake is one of three lakes tucked under the east flank of Brachiopod Mountain. Rock-hop the outlet of Baker Lake and follow beaten paths through larch forest to the southeast. Look back at Fossil Mountain to see the incredible Z-shaped, overturned fold in the upper part of the south face.

The maze of paths here defies sensible description. Pass a small unnamed pond (not shown on the topographic map) along its east shore, and continue to Little Baker Lake. You have views to Tilted Lake en route. Brachiopod Lake is farther south. This seasonal pond usually dries up by late summer.

A TEXTBOOK LANDSCAPE

The vicinity of Ptarmigan Lake marks the transition from the eastern main ranges to the front ranges. The eastern main ranges were created 100 million-years-ago. The mountains contain resistant limestone, dolomite, and quartzite cliffs alternating with layers of recessive shale. The strata are horizontal or dip slightly to the southwest.

If you look at Ptarmigan Peak, you can see that it rests on a massive sandwich of alternating resistant and recessive sedimentary layers. This rock sandwich is the Pipestone Pass Thrust, an assemblage of rocks that slid 60 km during mountain building, upward and over younger rocks. The steep drop between Ptarmigan Lake and Baker Lake marks the leading edge of this thrust sheet.

In contrast, the younger rocks of mountains farther east were thrust skyward 80 million-years-ago as the front ranges. The sedimentary formations of front range mountains, like Fossil Mountain, dip steeply to the southwest, creating sawtooth and dip-slope mountain forms.

In few places in the Rockies is it as easy to grasp the complex concept of thrust sheets, and the differences between the eastern main ranges and front ranges, as it is by looking at the profile of Ptarmigan Peak from the shore of Ptarmigan Lake, and comparing it with mountains to the east. The names of some peaks in the Slate Range pay tribute to fossils found on their slopes: Fossil, Oyster, Brachiopod, and Anthozoan.

Creek (Bow River watershed) from the Red Deer River. Perhaps because it is almost unrecognizable as a mountain pass, this well-travelled feature is not officially named – locals call it "Cotton-grass Pass." Broad mountain passes are frequently boggy like this one. Without a steep gradient to direct the flow of streams and springs, water collects into pools and marshes. The sedges and willows that grow in these areas make them excellent habitat for moose.

At the trail junction 3.5 km from Baker Lake campground, turn west (left) if you do not want to include the Red Deer Lakes in this outing. The trail climbs over the shoulder of Fossil Mountain into "Jones' Pass."

To continue to Red Deer Lakes, keep straight ahead at this junction, and the one following. The trail enters a 250 year old spruce-fir forest where the tread soon deteriorates into horse-churned muck. You must make several awkward stream hops during the next 700 m, after which the sidetrail to Red Deer Lakes campground branches east (right).

The nearby Red Deer Lakes are popular fishing holes, and were formerly stocked to promote angling. Research has indicated that the rainbow trout, eastern brook trout, and cutthroat trout present are no longer reproducing. Mt. Hector (3394 m), the highest peak in this part of Banff National Park, and the 17th-highest in Alberta, is prominent in the view west. The Cree knew the Red Deer River as "Elk River," because of the numerous elk (wapiti) in the upper reaches of the watershed. Europeans refer to elk as "red deer," so the first explorers applied this name to the river and lakes.

KEN JONES: THE MOUNTAIN LIFE

Jon Whyte suggested the unofficial name for the pass between Skoki and Fossil mountains. In 1936, Skoki Lodge was enlarged and a new ridgepole was sought for the roof. Outfitter and woodsman, Ken Jones, scoured the Skoki area for a tree of suitable length, finding one at Douglas Lake, more than 13 km to the east. Using a horse team, it took Jones a week to skid the tree to Skoki Lodge via "Jones' Pass." Jones transformed his love for the mountains into a career, becoming the country's first Canadian-born mountain guide. He was a testimony to the youth-giving properties of a mountain life, making his last visit to Skoki Lodge in the spring on 2002, at age 89. Ken died at Nanton, Alberta, in 2004.

SKOKI LODGE

The party of J.F. Porter made the first detailed exploration of the Skoki area in 1911. Porter bestowed many names still in use today. *Skokie* is an aboriginal word that he brought from his Illinois home. It means "marsh." He gave it to the wet meadow near today's Merlin Meadows campground.

In 1930, ski enthusiasts Cliff White and Cyril Paris of Banff sought a place to build the first ski lodge in the Rockies. With its abundant snowfall and variety of skiing slopes, they chose the Skoki

Valley. Originally intended to be a ski club cabin only, the lodge opened in the winter of 1931 and soon became a commercial enterprise. It now operates seasonally in summer and winter. Tea, coffee, soup and baked goods are usually available to hikers for a fee during posted hours – usually late morning to late afternoon – just the thing to cheer up a rainy day. Call 403-522-7248 before you hit the trail if you are counting on the lodge being open.

LAKE MERLIN, 2.9 KM

In a landscape overflowing with lakes, Lake Merlin is the most scenic. The trail to the lake is an up-and-down affair, routed across boulderfields and up a steep limestone headwall. The destination more than compensates for the demands of the approach. Lawrence Grassi (see p. 207), renowned for his trail construction in the Lake O'Hara area in Yoho, worked on part of this trail.

The trailhead is at creekside, opposite the front door of Skoki Lodge. The purplish rock in the creek bed is ancient Miette Formation shale. The trail winds through pleasant upper subalpine forest for 300 m to a junction. Turn west (right). You then climb onto a sideslope of quartzite boulders that have appropriately tumbled from the Wall of Jericho. The blooms of red-stemmed saxifrage, mountain sorrel, yellow columbine, and arnica brighten the rocky slopes. Views north include Mt. Willingdon (3373 m), Cataract Peak (3333 m), Cyclone Mountain, and unnamed summits on the west side of the Drummond Icefield.

The trail crosses a low ridge west of the boulderfield. I have encountered a wolverine here. It fled off-trail into a dead end and turned to face me, snarling. I timidly backed away to let the animal escape. It was gone in a flash. Descend from the ridge on a rocky trail, following cairns where necessary. Unfortunately, a number of paths have been marked, only serving to confuse the route. During the descent, your eyes will probably be fixed on remarkably coloured Castilleja (cass-TIH-lee-ah) Lake – named for the genus of the wildflower, paintbrush.

The trail draws alongside the south shore of Castilleja Lake before commencing a steep climb south on scree slopes. At the top of this climb, follow cairns west to the Lake Merlin headwall. Ascend a scree gully through the headwall and then descend west over limestone pavement to the lakeshore. Take care not to knock rocks onto your companions while you are in the gully. With your boots, you've just traced a dominant theme of eastern

main range mountains: the alternation of resistant and recessive formations of rock. Castilleja Lake is set in blocky Gog quartzite. The gully is crumbly shale of the Mt. Whyte Formation. The solid pavement is Cathedral Formation limestone.

The glaciated north face of Mt. Richardson creates an exceptional backdrop for Lake Merlin. The lake takes its name from nearby Merlin Castle, an assembly of quartzite pinnacles that J.F. Porter likened to an Arthurian castle. Merlin was a prophet and magician of Arthurian legend. Porter may have had another intention in mind when he gave the name, for Lake Merlin demonstrates some of nature's magic. If you walk along the lake's northeast shore, you may be puzzled at the absence of an outlet stream. But you probably noticed that Castilleja Lake received an inlet stream from above. As with many lakes set in limestone in the Rockies, Lake Merlin it drains underground through the underlying Cathedral Formation.

When Porter's party visited the lake, they noticed evidence of an abandoned surface outlet, along with driftwood that marked an ancient high water level. The driftwood is still there. This indicates that Lake Merlin's subterranean outlet is, in geological terms, of recent origin. With care, you can search the upper headwall northeast of the lake for a natural "window" that allows a glimpse within the bedrock to the underground stream. It's a remarkable sight, for the stream is an underground waterfall. Merlin, indeed!

Red Deer Lakes to Merlin Meadows Campground

From Red Deer Lakes campground, backtrack south 700 m to a junction. Turn west (right), hop the creek, and follow the trail heading west into "Jones' Pass." The trail from the Baker-Red Deer Divide merges with this trail at an avalanche slope just before the crest of the pass. This area is often fragrant with the resin of trees downed in avalanches during the previous winter. Straight ahead (southwest) is the Wall of Jericho (2910 m), and Ptarmigan Peak. West from the pass, sections of trail have been gravel-capped. The trail swings northwest and descends to the Skoki Valley junction. Turn north (right). You reach Skoki Lodge in 400 m. Merlin Meadows campground is 1.2 km farther north.

Return

The homeward trail departs south from Merlin Meadows campground. Keep straight ahead at the junction 400 m south of Skoki Lodge. The trail climbs 300 m in the next 3 km, to Deception Pass. Cyril Paris named the pass for a reason that will soon be obvious: it's farther to the crest than it looks.

Deception Pass provides a tremendous panorama of the Slate Range, Ptarmigan Lake, the Bow Range near Lake Louise, and more distant points north and south. White-tailed ptarmigan are common here. Skiers in winter find ascent and descent of this pass either a peril or a pleasure, depending on their fondness for terminal velocity.

Descend south on slopes of compacted shale to the Boulder Pass trail. Turn west (right). The remainder of the trail covers familiar ground, retracing the first 10.5 km of this outing along the shore of Ptarmigan Lake and over Boulder Pass, to the Fish Creek parking area.

19. Mosquito Creek

Upper Fish Lake

With its high starting elevation, the Mosquito Creek trail grants quick access to a lofty and sublime alpine environment with many pockets to explore. I have stomped and skied along this trail perhaps twenty times and still never tire of its destinations. You share all routes with commercial horse parties, so avoid this trail during wet weather when muck and mire prevails. Grizzly bears frequent the valley, meadows, and passes. Travel accordingly.

Trailhead to Molar Pass Junction

The trail climbs steeply up the bank of Mosquito Creek – the steepest grade in the first 7 km – and then angles across the right of way cleared in the 1930s for the "Wonder Road," precursor of the Icefields Parkway. The next 1.9 km is through open coniferous forest

TRAIL THUMBNAIL

Day-hike or overnight

Route	Elev. (m)	Dist. (km)
Trailhead	1828	0
Mosquito Creek CG	1990	5.4
Molar Pass jct	2195	6.9
Molar Pass	2360	+3.4
"Mosquito Lake"	2302	8.8
Molar Meadows	2310	9.0
North Molar Pass	2590	11.5
Upper Fish Lake CG	2210	14.8

Trailhead
Mosquito Creek on the Icefields Parkway, 23.6 km north of Highway 1. The parking area is on the west side of the Parkway, south of the bridge. The trailhead is on the east side of the Parkway, north of the bridge. Use caution crossing the road.

Maps
NTS: 82 N/9
Gem Trek: *Bow Lake and Saskatchewan Crossing*

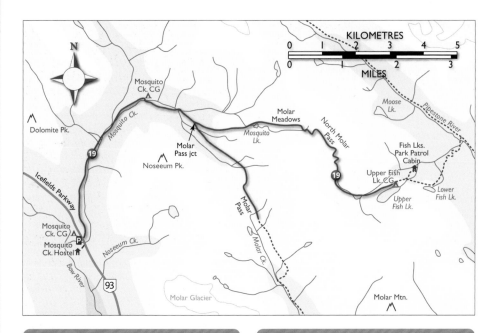

A COLD AND ROCKY HOME

At approximately km 3, the trail crosses an alluvial fan where a tributary stream enters from the north. Vegetation on this fan is scant. Not only does the rocky soil make tree growth difficult here, but the tributary stream and Mosquito Creek channel cold air into the valley bottom, shortening the growing season.

Mountain fireweed (riverbeauty), yellow mountain saxifrage (photo), red-stemmed saxifrage, yellow paintbrush, elephant-head, and common butterwort are wildflowers that thrive in this cold, damp environment. Common butterwort is one of seven insectivorous plant species in the Rockies. The pale green leaves at the base of the plant trap and digest insects.

This habitat is also good for sedges. Sedges resemble grasses, but have triangular, solid stems. One of the more common sedges in the Rockies is cotton-grass. Its brilliant white tufts contain minuscule flowers. The tufts grace the banks of subalpine streams and marshes in late July and August.

AQUATIC GARDENS

Upper subalpine areas with limestone bedrock often contain seeps – outlets for rain water and snowmelt that have drained underground. As the water percolates downwards, resistant rock layers intercept it and channel the water laterally to the surface. The bedrock underfoot on the way to Molar Pass is Gog Formation quartzite, but the culprit limestone is just uphill to the east. When the trail has been churned into quagmire by horses, no amount of drainage control and no heat spell will keep the incessant trickles from collecting on the tread. This failure of trail design brings some joy along with wet boots – tiny gardens of moisture-loving plants that thrive in and around the slop. Look for elephant-head, white globeflower, yellow paintbrush, dwarf false asphodel, red-stemmed saxifrage, yellow mountain saxifrage, cotton-grass, fringed grass-of-parnassus, and mountain marsh-marigold (photo). Step gently.

Molar Pass

with a variety of subalpine wildflowers. The forest in this valley last burned in 1830, in a large fire that also consumed much of the upper Bow Valley. The rooted and rocky trail drops to creekside and then travels across willow plain. Rock-hop as necessary.

The trail crosses the north fork of Mosquito Creek on a log bridge, and continues through forest to the Mosquito Creek campground at km 5.4. The campground is set among Eldon Formation boulders that tumbled in a rockslide. Given the horse traffic in this area, you should treat all drinking water here.

The trail beyond the campground is notorious for its muck holes and braiding, especially during early summer and after rains. The trail crosses the creek on a bridge and follows the bank for roughly 1 km. It then recrosses the creek, reaching the Molar Pass junction 500 m farther.

Molar Pass Junction to Molar Pass

For 1.5 km beyond the junction, you hike on a wet and sometimes sketchy trail through glades of open upper subalpine forest. The exceptional wildflower displays here more than compensate for the poor trail. The cliffs to the west are part of the group of summits at the head of Noseeum Creek. The northeast cliffs of the highest peak, "Noseeum Peak" (2987 m), feature a niche glacier. The craggy entrance to Molar Pass looms ahead.

The grade steepens as the trail climbs onto drier ground above the creek. Rock-hop a stream that cascades down titled slabs of quartzite bedrock. Mountain sorrel, leather-leaved saxifrage, alpine forget-me-not, and dense blooms of yellow columbine grow here. The trail switchbacks cleverly through the cliff at the northern entrance to Molar Pass. From the top of this climb you have an exceptional view north over upper Mosquito Creek, and onto the extensive, rolling alpland of Molar Meadows to the northeast.

Molar Pass is a heath and avens tundra – 2 km long – that separates the headwaters of Mosquito Creek and Molar Creek. The view south improves as you traverse the hillside on the east side of the pass. We once watched a grizzly bear here from a kilometre away. Eventually, you can see the summit of Mt. Hector (3394 m), the peaks of the Slate Range, Molar Mountain (3022 m) and its outlying tower (2901 m). James Hector named Molar Mountain in 1858 as he trooped by in the Pipestone Valley. When viewed from there and also from near Lake Louise, the mountain and its tower bear resemblance to pointed teeth.

VARIATIONS

- Day-hike to Molar Meadows; 9.0 km.
- Day-hike to Molar Pass; 10.3 km.
- Day-hike to North Molar Pass; 11.5 km.
- Camp at Mosquito Creek campground and explore both passes.
- Backpack to Fish Lakes campground; 14.8 km.

Sometimes, a north-south pass separated summer, on its sun-exposed southern approach, from winter, on its shaded north slope. Other times, a pass was a narrow, somber defile, home to only shadows and chill, a keyhole that triggered more questions than it answered, a place where to linger was to be mournful of high places. And still other times, certainly less often, the crest of a pass was an utterly tranquil, blissful, sun-drenched place, close to heaven, a bridge between earth and sky.

Graeme Pole; *Healy Park*

Most of the bedrock in Molar Pass is Cathedral Formation limestone. The axis of the pass lies along a bedrock fault. To the west, above the pass, a ledge of Stephen Formation shale is topped by massive cliffs of Eldon Formation limestone. This sequence – Cathedral-Stephen-Eldon – is the "Middle Cambrian sandwich" of sedimentary formations that builds many mountain walls in the central Rockies. The fissured limestone pavement of the pass is known as a "clint and grike" landscape. The "clints" are limestone blocks and the "grikes" are karst fissures that separate them. The words come from the dialect of Yorkshire, England, where this kind of landscape is common. True to karst fashion, the four lakelets on the benches west of the pass drain underground.

When you start to descend into the upper reaches of Molar Creek, it's time to turn around. Your ramblings in Molar Pass will add a few kilometres to the length of this hike.

Molar Pass Junction to North Molar Pass

Keep straight ahead at the junction and begin a steep climb through treeline. Above is the exquisite alpine tundra of Molar Meadows. The flower-filled meadows are a favourite haunt of grizzly bears. An unnamed quartzite spire rises to the south. The castellated towers of Dolomite Peak (2950 m) are prominent in the view west. "Mosquito Lake" (unnamed on the topographic map), its shores fringed with cottongrass, completes this idyllic scene. The lake is a great place to rest before the hard work ahead – the climb to North Molar Pass – 280 m of elevation gain in the next 2.7 km. Of course, you could simply park it here in wildflower heaven.

Rock-hop the lake's outlet and climb away from the north shore. The trail crosses a beautiful alpland, the match of any in the Rockies. On the final approach to North Molar Pass, you may be intrigued by the two rock types visible: weathered and lichen-covered blocks of Gog Formation quartzite, to the south of the trail; pink and buff coloured fragments of Cathedral Formation limestone, to the north.

The ascent culminates in a steep track, scraped out of the rubble. The narrow, barren crest of North Molar Pass (2590 m) is the 6th-highest point reached on the Classic Hikes. The pass is named for its proximity to Molar Mountain, the summit of which is framed in the view southeast, just before you cross the pass. After taking in the view, those day-hiking from the Icefields Parkway should turn back. If you are day-hiking from the Mosquito Creek campground, assess your stamina for the 373 m descent to Upper Fish Lake, which you will have to climb on your return.

North Molar Pass to Upper Fish Lake

A perennial snow and ice patch clings to the southeast side of North Molar Pass. Give this feature a wide berth by crossing high on the slope to the north, then descending to pick up the trail. After an initially abrupt drop, you cross the stream that drains the pass. The trail then begins a rambling, braided descent through sedge and heath meadows toward Upper Fish Lake. Where the trail again angles to the edge of the stream, rock-hop to the east side. A cairn sometimes marks this crossing point; otherwise, it is easy to miss. Cross the stream again in 1 km on a log bridge upstream from a small canyon cut into Cathedral Formation limestone.

From the rise just beyond this crossing, you get your first full view of Upper Fish Lake, 100 m below. Cataract Peak (3333 m) rises beyond the lake on the east side of the Pipestone Valley. Cataract is among the higher mountains in the front ranges. It is surprising that this fine peak was not climbed until 1930.

The Upper Fish Lake campground is set in a grove of spruce, fir, and larch, 100 m north of the upper lake. The larch trees here are near the northern limit for the species. Angling is no longer allowed in the lakes. A park patrol cabin is 200 m north of the lake.

If you would like to add more distance to your outing, rock-hop the outlet of Upper Fish Lake and continue to Lower Fish Lake in 1 km. The trail beyond – one of the muddier in the Rockies – descends steeply to the Pipestone Valley.

THE GHOST DEER

The **Clearwater-Siffleur** caribou herd was the most southerly in the Rockies. When the first edition of *Classic Hikes* went to press in 1994, the herd contained about two dozen animals and appeared to be expanding its range. I had seen caribou tracks in the upper valley of Mosquito Creek in 1990. Reports of sitings came from the Skoki area, near Lake Louise, and along Bath Creek. At the time, there was a legendary member of the herd – a white bull that I had seen in 1990 and in 1992. The ghostly appearance of that bull may have been an omen. The population of the herd dwindled steadily for 15 years; in some years no sitings were reported. By 2008, the herd was thought to number five, a few of which were radio-collared. In the spring of 2009, researchers discovered the remains of four caribou – including the radio-collared animals – in an avalanche deposit along Molar Creek. No caribou have been seen in Banff since. This probably marks the first extirpation of a large mammal species in a Canadian national park.

20. Dolomite Pass

Helen Creek meadows

TRAIL THUMBNAIL

Day-hike or overnight

Route	Elev. (m)	Dist. (km)
Trailhead	1944	0
Lake Helen	2363	6.0
Trail summit	2500	6.9
Lake Katherine	2370	8.1
Dolomite Pass	2395	8.9

Trailhead
East side of the Icefields Parkway, 32.5 km north of Highway 1; opposite the Crowfoot Glacier viewpoint.

Maps
NTS: 82 N/9
Gem Trek: *Bow Lake and Saskatchewan Crossing*

For more than 5 km, the Dolomite (DOE-loh-mite) Pass trail traverses an exceptional alpine environment. The wildflower displays in the meadows south of Lake Helen are superb. Dolomite Pass and the valleys it connects are travel routes and prime summer habitat for grizzly bears. Fortunate hikers may also see wolves. You share the trail commercial horse parties.

Trailhead to Lake Helen

You ascend steadily for the first 3 km as the trail contours around the south end of an outlying ridge of Cirque Peak. In 2000, Parks Canada set a prescribed burn above the trail to help regenerate whitebark pine. From treeline you have great views into the Bow Valley. Mt. Hector (3394 m) is the prominent

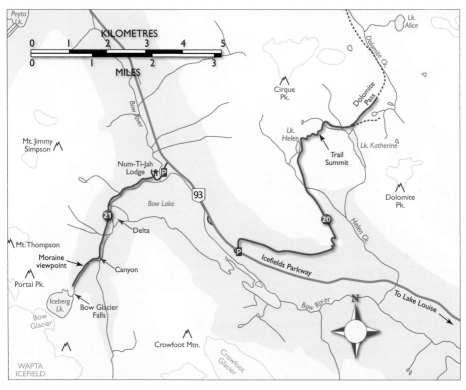

Crowfoot Glacier

glacier-clad peak, 14 km south. Crowfoot Glacier is west, above the outlet of Bow Lake. Early travellers in the Bow Valley called it "Trident Glacier" because its terminus featured three separate lobes of ice, two of which draped the headwall toward Bow Lake. The present name likens the glacier's form to the foot of the American crow, which has three splayed toes. The extent of glacial recession makes the origin of the name less obvious today, as climate warming has trimmed two of the "toes." One lobe of ice fell off in the 1920s, in an avalanche reportedly (but not likely) heard at Lake Louise.

After a series of switchbacks, you make a hairpin turn north into the valley of Helen Creek. Cirque Peak (2993 m) is straight ahead, and the castellated summits of Dolomite Peak (2950 m) tower over Helen Creek to the east. The true summit of Dolomite Peak is the fourth tower from north. It was first climbed in 1930. Some of the other towers were first ascended on days-off by workers employed in the construction of the original Icefields Parkway, between 1931 and 1939.

The meadows nearby are a sea of colour in mid- to late-July, packed with an array of upper subalpine wildflowers: western anemone, bracted lousewort,

paintbrush, fleabane, glacier lily, Sitka valerian, mountain heather, yellow columbine, and arnica. After the first frosts of August, the pungent stench of valerian fills the air – one of the harbingers of autumn in the Rockies.

The trail crosses the base of a quartzite rockslide – a good place to look for hoary marmots – and then descends into a ravine. Rock-hop the stream and continue north on a braided trail across the alpine tundra toward Lake Helen. Braids develop when hikers and horses avoid muddy sections of trail. As few as 20 pairs of feet travelling across untracked tundra may create a permanent trail. Despite trail restoration efforts, thoughtless hikers and riders continue to beat new braids into the meadows here. Please – get your boots wet and muddy – keep to the most beaten path, thereby preventing the development of additional braids, and allowing the marginal braids to recover.

For many, Lake Helen is the ultimate destination on this hike. The knoll just south of the lake provides pleasing views south to the Bow Valley. The lake-dotted alpland in the foreground is reminiscent of highland Britain. Indeed, one member of the first party to cross Dolomite Pass suggested the name "Doone" for features in this area. *Doone* is Gaelic for "down." Confusingly, "The Downs" are limestone uplands of central Britain. Golden eagles use the quartzite cliffs at the head of the valley as nesting grounds.

THE CROWFOOT DYKE

The Crowfoot Dyke is the most accessible exposure of igneous rock in the central Rockies. You can see it on the Icefields Parkway – a dull, green outcrop of diabase – 1.1 km south of the trailhead. A dyke is an intrusion of molten rock that flowed underground along cracks in existing sedimentary rock, and then consolidated. The Crowfoot Dyke formed between 570 and 730 million-years-ago. It extends 2.8 km east from the outlet of Bow Lake to the banks of Helen Creek, passing beneath the trail.

LAKE HELEN OR HELEN LAKE?

Most locals, and those who make the trail signs, refer to Lake Helen as "Helen Lake." In the case of geographical features (other than rivers and passes) that were named in English to honour people, the generic part of the name is supposed to come first, followed by the specific. So... Lake Louise, Mt. Victoria, Mt. Stephen. When the feature is not named for a person, the arrangement is supposed to be the other way around: Glacier Lake, Castle Mountain, Saskatchewan Glacier. Scan your maps and you'll find many exceptions to the rule, but Lake Helen follows it.

VARIATIONS

- Hike to Lake Helen; 12.0 km return.
- Experienced backpackers may random camp in the valley of Dolomite Creek, north of the pass.

At last one of the party put the question flatly to me: "Have you any idea where we are?" I replied: "I know perfectly well where we are; we are between the valley of the Pipestone and the Bow. What I do not know is where we are going to come out."

Ralph Edwards; *The Trail to the Charmed Land*

Dolomite Peak

Lake Helen to Dolomite Pass

The trail to Dolomite Pass continues north from Lake Helen to the base of Cirque Peak. The switchbacking climb over the mountain's south ridge is the high point on this hike. The rock underfoot is brownish limestone of the Pika Formation. Views of Dolomite Peak and the environs of Dolomite Pass are superb. On clear days, you can see Mt. Assiniboine (3616 m), 110 km to the south. Many hikers are confused as to why they must now *descend* to approach Dolomite Pass. The explanation is simple. Unlike most trails that follow streams to their sources on mountain passes, this trail traverses into Dolomite Pass

DOLOMITE PEAK

Dolomite formed when water seeped into limestone sediments before those sediments turned to rock. Calcium in the limestone was replaced with magnesium. The magnesium-enriched rock – more properly described as a mineral – is usually tougher than the original limestone, and more colourful too. Dolomite Peak does not contain massive dolomite cliffs like its namesake mountains in the Italian Alps. However, it does display an interesting sequence of sedimentary formations. From the shore of Lake Katherine to the summit of the peak, the formations are Pika Formation limestone, Arctomys Formation shale, Waterfowl Formation limestone, Sullivan Formation shale, and finally, cliffs of Lyell (lie-ELL) Formation limestone. These formations are Middle Cambrian to Late Cambrian in age. The recessive shales have been eroded into ledges; the more resistant limestones have endured as cliffs. Their alternation creates the "layer cake" or castellated form of Dolomite Peak.

from another drainage, crossing this high ridge on the way.

The steep descent east from the ridge crosses an outcrop of purple Arctomys (ARK-toe-miss) shale. In the southeast face of Cirque Peak you can see a prominent anticline, or arch-shaped fold in a layer of this formation. From the meadows at the north end of Lake Katherine, Mt. Temple (3544 m) is visible to the south, as is the glaciated horn of Mt. Daly (3148 m). You may be surprised to see hoary marmots in these open meadows, away from their customary sanctuary of boulderfields. It seems that these particular animals are content to burrow deeply into the meadows, rather than use boulders for partial cover.

Rock-hop the lake's inlet and climb the hillside to the east into Dolomite Pass. The trail becomes vague. The travelled route is on the rise north of the small lake that drains east into Dolomite Creek. Random camping is allowed east and north from this point, but is not recommended unless you pack a bear barrel to store your food in. There are no trees from which to rig a food storage system.

Dolomite Pass was first crossed in 1898 by a party from Boston's Appalachian Mountain Club. The mountaineers named a number of nearby features for family members. Alice was the wife of party leader, Reverend H.P. Nicholls. Helen and Katherine were two of his daughters. Other names were given for descriptive reasons: Observation Peak (3174 m) for the view from its summit; Cirque Peak for the cirque glacier on its north flank; and Dolomite Peak for its resemblance to The Dolomites, a group of mountains in The Alps, renowned for their sheer north facing cliffs. If you continue 1 km northeast from Dolomite Pass, you will be rewarded with views to the south of another lake and the glacier on the northeast side of Dolomite Peak.

21. Bow Glacier Falls

Bow Glacier Falls

TRAIL THUMBNAIL

Day-hike; see map, p. 87

Route	Elev. (m)	Dist. (km)
Parking area	1940	0
Trailhead	1938	0.4
Bow Lake delta	1938	2.4
Mouth of Bow Canyon	1966	3.6
Moraine viewpoint	1996	4.0
Base of Bow Falls	2103	5.0

Trailhead
West side of the Icefields Parkway, 35.1 km north of Highway 1. Follow the Num-ti-Jah Lodge access road west for 400 m to the public parking area. Walk the gravel road west toward the lake, curving northwest (right) in front of the lodge to the trailhead on the lakeshore.

Maps
NTS: 82 N/9, 82 N/10
Gem Trek: *Bow Lake and Saskatchewan Crossing*

Best lighting: before early afternoon

For more than a century, the shores of Bow Lake have been a favourite stopping place. No wonder. This relatively short hike is packed with variety – it offers a lakeshore stroll with fine views, an ascent alongside a canyon, a rough track across a moraine field, and a spray-filled vista of a thundering waterfall. Despite the attractions, on a fair morning with the lake calm, you'll be tempted to plunk down at your first view of the lakeshore and go no farther. The landscape is much less claustrophobic than at Lake Louise and Moraine Lake; the scenery on par. But the environs of Num-ti-Jah Lodge are teeming, and you will soon want to move on to escape the throngs just discharged from their buses. Don't worry; most of them are heading to the restroom and won't be joining you.

Trailhead to Moraine Viewpoint

As you walk past the lodge, you may see barn swallows overhead; they nest in the various buildings. The rocky and rooted trail follows the north shore of Bow Lake at the base of Mt. Jimmy Simpson (2966 m), crossing the runouts of avalanche slopes and rockslides. Most of the rocks are quartzite of the Gog Group of formations. Look and listen for pikas. Flag trees dot the lakeshore. Bearing branches only on their leeward sides, they "flag" the prevailing wind

JIMMY SIMPSON

Trail guide and outfitter, Jimmy Simpson, spent the winters of the early 1900s hunting and trapping in the remote country north of Bow Lake, and came to know the area better than anyone. His adventures are legendary. They include his poaching of what was then a world record bighorn ram, and Jimmy claiming that he heard heavenly music coming from the sky one winter night. Simpson said that he regularly dreamed of the locations of sheep and goats. Next day he would lead his clients there for a successful hunt. (This area was not part of Banff National Park at the time.) In 1920, Simpson began construction of a simple log cabin on the lakeshore. The rustic abode became popular with mountaineers. During construction of the Icefields Parkway in the 1930s, Simpson built the forerunner of today's Num-ti-Jah (numm-TAH-zjaah) Lodge. The lodge's name is a Stoney expression for the American marten, a member of the weasel family common in subalpine forest. The original octagonal cabin, known as "The Ram Pasture," still stands.

DELTAS

Many streams and rivers in the Rockies are glacially fed. Where the angle of a stream bed is relatively steep, the water moves cobbles and gravels. Where the angle lessens, larger particles drop out of the flow, creating a rocky, fan-shaped landform. If this landform occurs on the side of a valley, it is called an alluvial fan. If it occurs on the shore of a lake, it is known as a delta. The name comes from the resemblance of the landform to delta – Δ – the fourth letter of the Greek alphabet.

Bow Lake features two deltas. The most obvious is on the northwest shore, where meltwater from Bow Glacier enters the lake. The growth of vegetation is hindered by the constant deposition of silt and gravel, by the shifting of the meltwater streams, and by the cold air channelled along the water.

Less obvious is the delta where the lodge sits. The stream that created this delta is now but a trickle. It no longer transports glacial sediments. Vegetation has stabilized the underlying gravels. This delta was probably created thousands of years ago by a meltwater surge from a glacier near Bow Pass. The glacier has since disappeared.

LIONS AND TIGERS AND... ZEBRAS?

Lion rock

Tiger rock

Zebra rock

The Middle Cambrian formations of the central Rockies contain a colourful assortment of rocks. The moraines on this hike are one of the better places to go on safari to appreciate them. Gray Eldon Formation limestone provides the surface onto which the Mixmaster of the Bow Glacier has dumped, among others: two-tone, tan-coloured Cathedral Formation dolomite (lion rock); black Cathedral limestone striped with apricot dolomite (tiger rock); and gray Lyell (lie-ELL) Formation limestone striped with buff dolomite (zebra rock).

from the Wapta Icefield. This wind whips whitecaps on the lake in summer, and shapes frozen waves of snow, called sastrugi, in winter. Bow Lake is frozen, on average, from the first week of November until the second week of June. A superb array of wildflowers colours the trail margins. Look for the intricate blooms of shooting stars. When the lake level is high, you may get your feet wet on a few short sections.

The pyramid-form of St. Nicholas Peak (2970 m), is prominent in the view southwest across the lake. St. Nicholas was the Swiss birthplace of Peter Sarbach, the guide who led the first mountaineers onto the Wapta Icefield, in 1897. *Wapta* is Stoney for "river." Jean Habel, a German mountaineer, named the feature in 1897, but his reason for applying the generic name "river" to an icefield is not clear. Perhaps he meant "river of ice." To the southeast, glacier-clad Mt. Hector (3394 m) dominates the upper Bow Valley. J.N. Collie named this fine peak for James Hector, naturalist, geologist, and doctor of the Palliser Expedition.

You reach the delta on the west shore of the lake at km 2.4. A short section of trail here may be flooded, especially in late afternoon on a hot day. Skirt the wet area by keeping right, against the base of the cliffs. Elephant-head grows in the glacial silt at the water's edge. The trail carries on along the inlet stream. I have seen dippers and a solitary sandpiper here.

You climb over the first of three forested moraines and drop back to the floodplain. Cross a small tributary stream on a log bridge. The trail skirts the end of a second forested moraine 400 m later, by hugging the bank of the stream. If the water level is high, an alternate trail climbs over and descends the moraine. Keep to creekside for 200 m to where the trail reaches the third forested moraine. Skirt this along the creek or climb over it. Another 400 m stretch of floodplain, carpeted with mountain avens, intervenes before the trail delivers you to the mouth of Bow Canyon.

The climb alongside the canyon is withering but short. Use care if the trail is wet or snowy – especially on the way down. The canyon is about 20 m deep, and is carved into Eldon Formation limestone. Its central portion features a chockstone that spans the chasm. The trail levels near the upper end of the canyon, with a pleasing view ahead – past an ancient whitebark pine – to Bow Glacier Falls. Carry on for 50 m to the viewpoint on the crest of the Little Ice Age moraine of Bow Glacier.

Viewpoint to Bow Glacier Falls

Bow Glacier is one of four principal outlet glaciers of the 40 km² Wapta Icefield. The viewpoint marks the glacier's halting place in about 1850 – the end of the Little Ice Age. The terminal moraine of that advance is smeared against the knoll under your feet. Just over 1 km away, Bow Glacier Falls thunders down a cliff of Pika Formation limestone. If you study the cliffs

At the W. [west] end of the Upper Bow Lake a gap is torn in the mountain-wall, and through this gap the snow is pressed in a fine glacier which descends in two large ice-falls to the valley.... Crossing a low wooded spur – once the terminal moraine of the glacier – we descended into a stony valley left by the retreating ice.

Harold B. Dixon; "The Ascent of Mt. Lefroy, and Other climbs in the Rocky Mountains," *Alpine Journal 1898*

ILL WINDS

Atmospheric contaminants – including DDT, toxaphene, and PCBs – are present at low concentrations in the snow and ice of Bow Glacier. These pollutants are carried from as far away as Eurasia before condensing on the icefields of the Rockies. Deep layers of the icefields were contaminated more heavily in the mid-20th century, when these chemicals were also widely used in North America. With climate warming, some of the contaminated deeper layers are beginning to melt, releasing the pollutants into headwater streams. These streams also carry radioactive fallout from the atmospheric nuclear bomb tests of the 1950s and 1960s.

The pollutants are currently present at concentrations measured in parts per trillion – not high enough to render the water unfit to drink. But this might change as climate warming accelerates the melting of glaciers. Because of their tendency to accumulate in the fatty tissues of cold water organisms and to be biomagnified in food chains, toxaphene and other chemicals can reach fairly high concentrations in the lake trout of Bow Lake – 10-20 times higher than in nearby lakes that don't receive glacial meltwater. A similar process of atmospheric pollution and biomagnification in long food chains is taking place in the Arctic, where concentrations of pollutants can reach values high enough to be of concern to people who eat fish and marine mammals.

VANISHING ACT

Bow Glacier, 1897

Bow Glacier, 2002

The first mountaineers to travel the Wapta Icefield did so by ascending Bow Glacier in 1897. When I first learned of their route, I thought it preposterous, plagued with cliffs, steep moraines, and even steeper ice. But I wasn't thinking Little Ice Age. Those mountaineers ascended Bow Glacier just after that mini-ice age had loosened its grip and the glacier began to recede from the vicinity of today's viewpoint. They did have to deal with steep ice on the headwalls, but getting that far was a relatively easy glacier plod. As the accompanying photographs show, the change in the landscape in just over a century is astounding.

Photographs taken about 1930 show that the toe of the glacier had receded partway up the lower headwall, where the falls are today. Today, the glacier has almost receded to the top of the second headwall, and its terminus is thinning rapidly. The basin between the two headwalls contains a tarn known to locals as "Iceberg Lake."

alongside the upper cataract of the falls, you will see why the water flows where it does. Trace one of the layers in the cliff, from south to north (left to right). You will see that the layers are offset at the waterfall, indicating that the stream course has been captured by a fault in the rock. Mt. Thompson (3089 m) and its outlier, Portal Peak (2926 m), flank the falls to the north. The peak to the south of the glacier is officially unnamed. Locals know it variously as "Polaris," "The Hamburger," and "The Onion." Yellow columbine, pink wintergreen, white camas, daisy fleabane, and arrow-leaved groundsel grow at the viewpoint. Be careful not to trample them.

The viewpoint provides the postcard shot of the falls, but for the full sensory experience, you'll want to pick your way across the forefield and immerse yourself in the spray. Head north (right) from the viewpoint a short distance, then descend sharply west (left) from the moraine crest to the forefield. A promising track heads toward the falls, but where a tributary stream comes down from Mt. Thompson, piling rubble into the valley, the route becomes vague. Rock-hop and boulder-hop as required. You may get your feet wet, but the direction to your destination is obvious. Pick your way carefully to avoid trampling the moisture-loving plants that grow here.

Any of the thousands of boulders at the base of the falls can serve as your ultimate stopping place. The closer you get to the stream, the wetter you will likely be, as spray from the falls coats the area – not such a bad thing on a hot day. But if it's cold, watch for ice on the rocks. Keep off snow patches. Lesser waterfalls cascade over the colourful, banded cliffs to the north. This amphitheatre was one of the honing grounds for waterfall ice climbers in the late 1970s, during the development of that pursuit.

22. Chephren Lake – Cirque Lake

Chephren Lake

What makes a hike "classic?" Is it the trail itself – its location and route; its history? Or is it the scenery, the vegetation? Is it sharing the experience with a companion, or is it a welcome period of solitude accompanied by exertion? It can be any or all of these things, and it can be different from day to day on the same trail. What is a certainty about this excursion is that it is not the trail itself that makes this hike a classic. I won't belabour descriptions of the muck and mire that await. At best, you will have damp feet by day's end; after a rain, you will likely be soaked – as I once was – from the elbows down. But the twin destinations – two gems tucked away in their glacial pockets – are classic in every regard, and the austere mountain walls echo with the history of early pack trips along Bear Creek (the Mistaya River).

TRAIL THUMBNAIL

Day-hike

Route	Elev. (m)	Dist. (km)
Trailhead	1684	0
Mistaya River bridge	1661	0.4
Chephren-Cirque jct	1737	1.7
Chephren Lake	1720	3.9
Chephren-Cirque jct	1737	6.1
Cirque Lake	1791	9.0
Chephren-Cirque jct	1737	11.9
Mistaya River bridge	1661	13.2
Trailhead	1684	13.6

Trailhead
At Waterfowl Lake campground, on the west side of the Icefields Parkway, 56.4 km north of Highway 1. Don't go into the campground, but continue south (straight ahead) on the access road for 400 m. The trailhead is at the southwest corner of the parking area.

Maps
NTS: 82 N/15
Gem Trek: *Bow Lake and Saskatchewan Crossing*

Best lighting: morning

VARIATIONS

- Hike to Chephren Lake; 7.8 km return.
- Hike to Cirque Lake; 9.2 km return.

Trailhead to Chephren-Cirque Junction

The trail begins as a gravel path that skirts the south edge of the campground. As with most campgrounds on the Icefields Parkway, this one occupies an alluvial fan – in this case created by Noyes Creek. The bulk of this landform was deposited by a surge in glacial melt at the end of the Crowfoot Advance, 6000-7000 years ago. The fan spans most of the floor of the Mistaya Valley, impounding the waters of Upper Waterfowl Lake.

After 400 m, you reach the bridges that cross the narrows between the Waterfowl lakes. Those staying in the campground can begin the hike here. Bears frequent the campground and surrounding area. Travel accordingly.

The trail climbs south from the bridges, initially through open spruce-fir forest, with buffaloberry, dwarf dogwood, feather-mosses, and clubmosses in the understory. The forest here last burned in 1858. Listen for varied thrushes and robins. A section of pine forest follows, with an understory that features prolific blooms of Labrador tea. On my last visit, I heard a loon calling from

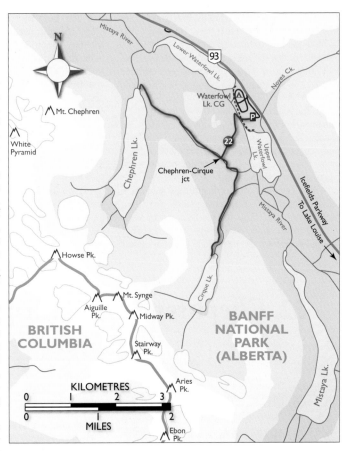

From the Bow Pass a long march brought us to our old beautiful camping-ground near Waterfowl Lake at the foot of Pyramid and Howse Peak. Those two cloud-compelling mountains were, as usual, veiled in mist when we arrived; but they were nearly clear next morning, and old Dave's wonder and delight at the grim black precipices and stately glacier-crowned peaks knew no bounds.

Hugh Stutfield and J.N. Collie; *Climbs and Exploration in the Canadian Rockies*
[Dave Tewksbury was a horse packer on Collie's 1902 expedition]

THE TRAIL NORTH

The first packtrains to travel north in the Mistaya (miss-TAY-yah) Valley did so on a difficult trail along the east side of the river. The trip from Lake Louise to Saskatchewan River Crossing required five to seven days. Upon reaching the North Saskatchewan River, travellers were obliged to make three hazardous fords – Mistaya River, Howse River, and North Saskatchewan River – in order to continue their journey north. In 1923, Jimmy Simpson cut a trail along the west bank of the Mistaya River in the lower part of the valley. Packtrains could then ford the river easily between the Waterfowl lakes, eliminating one of the trio of crossings downvalley. The first party to use the new route was that of mountaineer James Monroe Thorington, guided by Simpson, while they were on their way to the first ascents of Mt. Saskatchewan and North Twin, and ascents of Mt. Athabasca and Mt. Columbia. The Chephren Lake trail follows the 1923 route as far as the sharp turn just before the lake.

Upper Waterfowl Lake. The trail angles southwest and begins to climb and descend a series of terraces – probably the courses of ancient creeks that once drained the glaciers west of here. Fringed grass of parnassus, elephant-head, rein orchids, and hooded ladies' tresses grow in the intervening pockets of wet meadow. Finally out of earshot of the Icefields Parkway, you cross three of these meadows before reaching the Chephren-Cirque junction at km 1.7.

Junction to Chephren Lake

Turn northwest (right) for Chephren Lake. Patches of ground lichens of the *Cladonia* genus cover the forest floor, along with clubmosses. Such ground cover is atypical for this low an elevation at this latitude, and results from the glacial chill and abundant precipitation here. Much of the trail is routed alongside wet meadows. The saturated soil, the tree roots, and the lack of significant grade on the tread hinder drainage. Things soon go from wet to wetter. Persevere; it's worth it. Views of Howse Peak (3295 m) with its niche glaciers, and Mt. Chephren (3274 m), along with displays of orchids, provide distraction. Watch your step to avoid squashing the orchids. Look for the tracks of deer and moose in the mud. You might hear rockfalls from the flanks of the mountains.

About 2 km from the junction, the trail turns sharply southwest (left), and descends steeply to the logjam at the outlet of Chephren Lake. In terms of straight-line distance, you aren't far from the highway, but in just over an hour, the trail has transported you to a very lonely piece of the Mistaya Valley.

Chephren Lake is 2.6 km long and 750 m wide. Fed principally by meltwater from two glaciers nestled under Howse Peak, the lake sports the blue-green hues typical of glacial lakes. Two meltwater streams drain the glacier south of the lake, bisecting a red quartzite cliff. A prominent lateral moraine flanks the east side of the glacier. Above, Aiguille (eh-GEEL) Peak (3001 m) – *aiguille* is French for "needle"– looms over the southeast ridge of Howse Peak. Joseph Howse was a trader for the Hudson's Bay Company. He crossed Howse Pass – at the western base of the peak – in 1810. If it has snowed recently, you may be treated to avalanches from Howse Peak's northeast face. Looking west, you can see a small cirque glacier beneath Mt. Chephren, along with the horseshoe moraine it has pushed up. The view north down the outlet stream includes Mt. Murchison (3337 m) and its many outliers. To the northwest, you can see the summit of Epaulette Mountain (3094 m), named for the glacial crest on its "shoulder." Kingfishers, sandpipers, and violet-green swallows frequent the lake.

SWAMP CRITTERS

What better place than in the shadow of majestic glacier-clad mountains, to talk about herptiles, the universally overlooked creatures of the slime? Herptiles include two classes of species, both of which are cold-blooded: amphibians – which have smooth skin, soft eggs, a larval stage, and an adult stage; and reptiles – which have scaly skin, hard-shelled eggs, and only one life stage. There are four amphibian species in this part of the Rockies. You are most likely to see the boreal toad. You'll find it near water in mid- to late-spring, when it mates. The female deposits the eggs in gelatinous strings in the water. Later in the summer, you might find toads well away from water. They seem to enjoy trail edges. The Columbia spotted frog is the larger of the two frog species in this part of the Rockies. It is greenish-brown with dark spots. The wood frog is the other hopping amphibian of the central Rockies. Identify this small, brownish frog by its black mask. It has a remarkable winter survival strategy – it freezes solid. The long-toed salamander is a carnivorous, lizard-like creature about 10 cm long, with glossy dark skin, and a yellowish-green stripe down the back. Although not often seen, it is most often found in low elevation valleys. Of reptiles there is but one – the wandering garter snake. Nowhere common, it prefers montane woods. It grows to a length of 45-107 cm.

Herptiles are barometer species for the well-being of wetlands. Some herptile populations have disappeared since the global amphibian crash began in the late 1970s. Habitat loss – the draining of wetlands – has been a key factor in the decline, but climate warming, water pollution, competition with introduced species, disease, and an increase in UV radiation may also be factors. All of the herptiles mentioned here are pushing the elevational limits for their species, making them particularly vulnerable to environmental stresses. In the Rockies, comprehensive baseline data from which to plot any trend in the populations does not yet exist. But the swamp critters of Banff are being systematically studied by volunteers, who slosh through the woods from puddle to puddle, slough to slough, with, notebook, thermometer, and magnifying glass in hand.

Cirque/Chephren trail sign

Mountaineers and anglers have beaten paths along both shores, but if you found the travel this far to be exasperating, don't consider exploring them.

After you've had your fill of mountain watching and lake watching, return to the Chephren-Cirque junction. You'll be pleasantly surprised at the subtle, downhill grade. Turn northeast (left) if you've had enough; head southeast (straight ahead) to carry on to Cirque Lake.

Junction to Cirque Lake

The Cirque Lake trail, initially much drier than the route to Chephren Lake, descends through open forest. Dwarf dogwood, wild strawberry, feather-mosses, and clubmosses grow in the understory. Early season hikers will be treated to the blooms of calypso orchids. Red squirrels are numerous. At the bases of many conifers you will see piles of scales shucked from cones by the squirrels as they harvest the seeds. Rock-hop the outlet of the wet meadow that extends toward Chephren Lake. A little farther on you walk on a creekbank between two streams. Rock-hop the second stream and continue southeast a short distance to where the trail swings southwest (right), about 1.1 km from the junction. Wild rose and pink wintergreen grow nearby.

The climb begins and soon delivers you to a small pond, impounded by grasses and sedges. Moose frequent this area. Views northwest include White Pyramid (3219 m). Just beyond, the trail cuts through an ancient stand of Engelmann spruce, with arnica and horsetails beneath. You climb steeply up a forested moraine along the outlet stream from Cirque Lake. The cool of the creekbank is wonderful on a hot day. The trail makes a short switchback away from the creek. At the top, keep straight ahead and sidehill just above the water. I have seen spruce grouse here.

This is a trail where the view of your final destination is delivered in increments. At first you see the headwall at the southeast end of Cirque Lake, but it takes some time to reach the lakeshore. Look back for views of Mt. Noyes (3085 m) and the unnamed towers above Noyes Creek. There are pleasing trailside

groupings of yellow columbine and hybrid yellow-western columbine, along with twinflower, false hellebore, and orchids. Near the outlet of the lake, you cross the base of an avalanche slope. Beside the trail, the water flows through an extensive meadow of sedges before the creek proper begins. Trail's end is a quartzite boulderfield on the northwest shore of the lake. The slope above is excellent bear habitat.

Cirque Lake is scarcely a third the size of its northern neighbour but shares a similar setting. Your eye will be drawn to the hanging niche glacier between Aries Peak (3012 m) and Stairway Peak (3000 m), and to the valley glacier at the far end of the lake. *Aries* is Latin for "ram," in this case, referring to bighorn sheep. The name was given to balance features to the south named *Capricorn*, Latin for "goat." Midway Peak (2923 m) is so named because it lies about halfway between Stairway Peak and Mt. Synge (2957 m). This latter mountain commemorates an Irish engineer who, in 1852, drew a map showing a railway route across Canada. He was ridiculed at the time – principally because he never travelled west of Ottawa. Thirty years later, after the expenditure of many millions of dollars in surveying and the loss of at least 38 surveyors, Synge's route was essentially adopted.

Take care on the steep sections during your return. They can be slick when wet.

THE MATTERHORN OF THE MISTAYA

Mt. Chephren (KEFF-ren) is a prominent landmark in the Mistaya Valley and the upper North Saskatchewan Valley, visible from Bow Pass to Parker Ridge. It is a classic horn mountain, its crest whittled from horizontal layers of limestone and quartzite by the action of glaciers on two of its three flanks. J.N. Collie named it Black Pyramid in 1898, to contrast it with glacier-capped White Pyramid to the southwest. The name was changed in 1918, to prevent confusion with its neighbour and with Pyramid Mountain in Jasper. Chephren was the son of Cheops, builder of the Great Pyramid. He reigned in the 26th century BC, and was apparently immortalized in the face of the Sphinx. The first ascent of Mt. Chephren was made in 1913.

23. Sarbach Lookout

Mt. Murchison

Banff's fire lookout system, completed between 1941 and 1950, contained seven lookouts. Connected to warden stations in the valleys below by telephone, the keepers who staffed the lookouts were often able to provide early warning of forest fires. Aerial smoke patrols during times of high fire hazard rendered the lookouts obsolete in the 1980s. Although the lookout towers in Banff were all abandoned by 1978 and removed by 1985, the trails to most lookout sites are still maintained. They provide easy access to lofty viewpoints. The Sarbach (SAR-back) Lookout site is unique in that it grants an overview of three of Banff's larger valleys.

Trailhead to Mistaya River

The initial 450 m of trail is road width as it descends to Mistaya Canyon. Across the bridge, turn north (right) in 15 m. The trail ascends a bank of glacial till. Till overlies the bedrock here to a depth of more than 30 m. Because most till in the Rockies came from limestone bedrock, it contains a high percentage of calcium carbonate (lime). Water percolating through the till creates a natural cement that binds the rock

> *Bear Creek [Mistaya River] safely crossed, we pushed on up the main valley of the Saskatchewan to the westward. On the 25th we climbed a peak 10,700 feet high, which was named after our guide, Sarbach. The first thousand feet was through primeval forest; then up a steep gully in a limestone escarpment, and over steep screes to the foot of the final peak.*
>
> Hugh Stutfield and J.N. Collie; *Climbs and Exploration in the Canadian Rockies*

particles together. In places along the Mistaya River, rainwater and snowmelt have eroded hoodoos into the till banks.

At the junction in 200 m, turn southwest (left) onto the Sarbach Lookout trail. The forest on this river terrace is an ancient one of Engelmann spruce and lodgepole pine that last burned in 1640. The lodgepole pines here are as old and as tall as you will see anywhere in the Rockies. One spruce at trailside shows charred heartwood exposed by a lightning strike. At first glance, the tree appears dead. However, a few upper branches are still growing. In the absence of recent fire, new habitat in this forest is created by blowdowns that remove weakened trees. The downed trees are piled like jackstraws. They provide abundant fuel for the inevitable day when the forest will burn.

At km 1.7, the trail regains the bank of the Mistaya River, from where you have a fine view south to the tremendous mountain wall along the west side of the Mistaya Valley. The glacier-draped cliffs of White Pyramid (3219 m), Epaulette Mountain (3094 m), the Kaufmann Peaks (3110 m and 3094 m), and Mt. Sarbach (3155 m) create an archetypal Rockies image. If you were to keep going straight ahead here, you wouldn't get far – trust me – but you would be following the original trail on this side of the valley, cut in 1923. It hasn't been cleared since the Icefields Parkway opened.

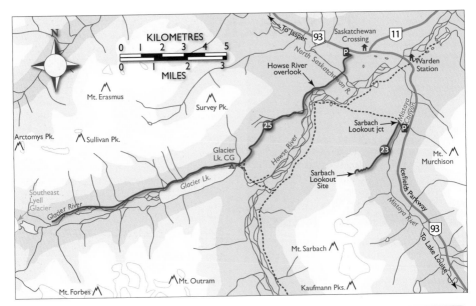

Mistaya River to Sarbach Lookout

The trail veers southwest (right) from the river. For the next km you cross boggy terrain toward the north ridge of Mt. Sarbach. You may see moose here. The "snow course markers" on trees indicate locations where the Water Survey of Canada collected snow core samples. By melting the snow, its water equivalent was determined. Data obtained from snow at these sites was combined with other data from the Rockies, allowing a prediction of the annual run-off to be calculated. The project was abandoned in the early 1980s.

To this point, the trail from the Mistaya River has climbed gradually. Now the hard work begins, 370 m of gain spread over 2.5 km. There are limited views before the lookout site. However, the blooms of arnica, few-flowered anemone, and calypso orchids brighten the trailside. The relentless climb nears its end where the trail swings onto the north end of the ridge, and whitebark pine becomes the most common tree in the surrounding forest.

The last 200 m of trail is bordered with rocks – the handiwork of a lookout keeper. Snow patches linger until early July. Remarkably, there is a record of mountain caribou tracks here. A Sacramento rain gauge, tree stumps, and the cabin foundation are now all that remain of the fire lookout, which was built in 1943, and saw use until 1971. Even without the advantage of a tower, the site commands a grand perspective of the three valleys that merge below – the Mistaya to the south, the Howse to the west, and the North Saskatchewan to the north and east.

The mountains of the Amery Group are to the north. Mt. Wilson (3260 m) looms to the northeast,

MISTAYA CANYON

Mistaya (miss-TAY-yah) Canyon is cut into Cambrian aged Eldon Formation limestone. The canyon features a natural arch and potholes eroded by rocks trapped in depressions. The river has exploited the weakness presented by a joint set – an arrangement of parallel cracks in the bedrock. This creates the dogleg course of the canyon, visible north of the bridge. In places, the canyon is scarcely 2 m wide. Rather than attempting to cross the Mistaya River in places where it was wider, Stoney First Peoples would cross here on fallen trees during their hunting trips into the mountains. *Mistaya* is a Stoney word for "grizzly bear."

above the right-angle bend in the North Saskatchewan River. The mountain commemorates Tom Wilson – trail guide, outfitter, and the first white visitor to the shores of Lake Louise.

Mt. Murchison

The stupendous form of Mt. Murchison (3337 m) fills the view across the Mistaya Valley. Mt. Murchison is a *massif*, a miniature mountain range that contains ten summits. James Hector reported that First Peoples considered Mt. Murchison to be the highest mountain in the Rockies. The impression is understandable although far from true – Mt. Murchison does not even rank among the 50 highest summits. However, the summit towers 1924 m above the North Saskatchewan River – one of the greater valley-bottom-to-peak differences in the Rockies. Although the first ascent of Mt. Murchison was claimed in 1902 during an ascent of the north summit, the slightly higher south summit was probably not climbed until 1985.

Mt. Murchison is a wonderful example of a castellated mountain. Resistant limestone and dolomite cliffs alternate with recessive ledges of shale. If you trace the sedimentary formations on the lowest tier of cliffs, you will see where they become fractured vertically, and offset in a normal fault. The formations on one side of the fault have moved downward relative to the other.

Glaciers have eroded cirque basins into Mt. Murchison's flanks. Waterfalls cascade from them. The largest is "Murchison Falls" – a winter playground for ice climbers. The mountain's many summits are glacially sculpted horns. Farther south in the Mistaya Valley, Mt. Chephren (KEFF-ren) (3274 m) and the White Pyramid also exhibit horn mountain shapes.

The summit of Mt. Sarbach is hidden from view, 5 km south of the lookout site. The mountain was first climbed in 1897 by J.N. Collie, George Baker, and Peter Sarbach, the first Swiss Guide to work in Canada. He spent only one summer in the Rockies, during which he led a number of other important first ascents, including Mt. Lefroy and Mt. Victoria at Lake Louise, and Mt. Gordon on the Wapta Icefield. You may be fortunate to see mountain goats on the slopes above the lookout site. On one visit, as I gazed across the valley at Mt. Murchison, my eye caught movement downslope, where a large grizzly bear was feeding on buffaloberries.

WHITEBARK PINE

Whitebark pine is an indicator tree of the upper subalpine life zone. The tree bark is silver and smooth on young trees, gray and scaly on older trees. Needles are in bunches of five. The tree is extremely slow growing and may not produce cones until it is 80 years old. The whitebark pine helps to stabilize steep slopes, moderate the rate of snow melt, and provide food, cover and shelter for many species of wildlife. Botanists call it a keystone species, vital to the ecosystem. Found throughout mountainous western North America, whitebark pine is declining over much of its range; threatened by blister rust (see. p. 62), fire suppression, and mountain pine beetles.

The cones of the whitebark pine do not open on their own to disperse seeds. Enter the Clark's nutcracker. The bird relies on the tree to provide its food – pine nuts – and the tree relies on the pointy-beaked bird to crack the seeds from their casings and disperse them. A Clark's nutcracker can hold up to 100 seeds in a pouch under its tongue. It caches the seeds – 22,000 to 33,000 per summer (yes, someone has counted them) – in various places to tide it through the winter. Usually, the bird chooses sun-exposed sites that are likely to be snow-free. These are just the locations that the tree prefers, so when the nutcracker forgets to come back to a particular site, some of the seeds – which it has buried at the perfect depth for germination – begin to grow into trees. Grizzly bears raid the seed caches in quest of the protein-rich pine nuts.

The stand of whitebark pine on Mt. Sarbach exhibits the diverse forms possible for this species. The tree is a gnarled and twisted kruppelholz where fully exposed to the elements. Where protected in the forest it has a robust form, attaining heights of 10-12 m. "Spike tops" indicate where the crowns of trees have suffered die-off from the chill of winter winds. The whitebark pine is one of the longer-lived tree species in the Rockies. Ages in excess of 1000 years have been recorded.

A GEO-POLITICAL RIFT

James Hector named Mount Murchison for Roderick Murchison, President of the Royal Geographical Society in 1856, and the man who had recommended Hector to the Palliser Expedition. Murchison was no piker when it came to geology, having authored and co-authored the original geological theories of, respectively, the Devonian and the Silurian periods. Hector was a keen observer of geology and landforms – he later went on to head the Geological Survey of New Zealand. Palliser described him as "the most accurate mapper of the original country I have ever seen." Everywhere in his travels in the Rockies, Hector made journal entries that described the effects of glaciation, against whose evidence he bumped his moccasins day after day. Of glacial markers in the landscape near the Waterfowl Lakes, he wrote: "... all point to a time when the glaciers which now only occupy the higher valleys were more extended."

This makes the naming of Mt. Murchison ironic. Because back across the pond, Murchison was staunchly resisting the theories of Swiss-born naturalist, Louis Aggasiz (ah-GASS-ee), who in 1837 had proposed that much of the landscape of Europe looked the way it did because of ice-age glaciations. Aggasiz, like Hector, had rock-solid evidence: striations – grooves in bedrock, scratched by rocks embedded in moving ice, far distant from any then-current glaciers; glacial erratics – oddball rocks dropped far from their places of origin; and moraines that were far removed from any then contemporary glaciers. Of course, it all seems so obvious today. But Murchison's intolerance caused heated disputes among European geologists, and contributed to a scientific rift on the Continent that still has not healed.

Murchison never saw "his" mountain. If he had, he might have hopped off his high horse in a moment, for Mt. Murchison is as ice-embattled, cirque-pocked, and crest-whittled a mountain as any – a billboard for ice-age glaciations.

24. Glacier Lake

Glacier Lake

TRAIL THUMBNAIL

Day-hike or overnight; see map, p. 98

Route	Elev. (m)	Dist. (km)
Trailhead	1443	0
North Saskatchewan River bridge	1418	1.1
Howse River overlook	1433	2.3
Glacier Lake CG	1457	9.1
Head of Glacier River valley	1493	18.6

Trailhead
West side of the Icefields Parkway, 1.2 km north of the junction with Highway 11, 76.4 km north of Highway 1, 148.8 km south of Highway 16.

Maps
NTS: 82N/15, 82 N/14
Gem Trek: *Bow Lake and Saskatchewan Crossing*

Best lighting: morning at Glacier Lake

When fur trader and map maker David Thompson visited Glacier Lake in 1807, he wrote: "all the Mountains in sight from the end of the Lake are seemingly of Ice." Thompson saw the Little Ice Age maximum of the glaciers, but even after two centuries of glacial recession, the colossal icefall of the Southeast Lyell (lie-ELL) Glacier – which tumbles from Division Mountain west of the lake – remains an archetypal Rockies sight.

Howse Valley

The Glacier Lake trail is often snow-free early in the hiking season. Although the trailhead and destination are at nearly equal elevations, there is enough up and down to make the outing an ideal early season "shake down" trip. You may random camp in the valley west of the lake. Bears frequent the area.

Trailhead to Glacier Lake

The trailhead is in a dense lodgepole pine forest, the product of a July 1940 forest fire – the Survey Peak Burn. It consumed 40 km^2, and forced closure of the Icefields Parkway. Buffaloberry and bearberry, whose fruits are favourite foods of bears, are common in the undergrowth near the trailhead. I have often seen ruffed grouse along the first kilometre of trail.

The trail descends a series of ancient river terraces to an I-beam bridge over the North Saskatchewan River at km 1.1. Here, the river's course has been captured by a bedrock fault, creating a small canyon. The North Saskatchewan River is 1216 km long. More than 80 percent of the water it carries to Hudson Bay (via Lake Winnipeg and the Nelson River), originates in glaciers. The 49 km section within Banff National Park was proclaimed a Canadian Heritage River in 1989. Canadian Heritage Rivers are those that have played an important role in the human and natural history of Canada. The trail climbs away from the river and continues through burned forest to the edge of a terrace above the Howse River at km 2.3.

This terrace "feels" different than most at similar locations in the Rockies. Usually what's immediately underfoot on the bank of a glacial river is the rubble of moraine. Not here. This riverbank, and those across the valley, are silty. The silt is called loess (LURSS). Scoured over millennia from the valley floor by the prevailing southwest wind, it is piled here into dune-like mounds where the river turns east. These loess

THE HOWSE VALLEY: A ONCE AND FUTURE HIGHWAY?

As its heavily braided appearance suggests, most of the flow of the Howse River comes from glaciers. Meltwater from three icefields, that cover more than 100 km^2 – Freshfield, Mons, and Lyell – combine to form the river. As it is one of the lower passes in the Rockies, Howse Pass (1530 m), 16 km south, was part of the first fur trade route across the Rockies. It saw use from 1800 until 1810, when the Piikani First Peoples blocked it. The Howse Valley is a haven for many large mammals: elk, mule deer, moose, black bears, grizzly bears, wolves, mountain goats, and coyotes. Joseph Howse was a fur trader who crossed the pass in 1810.

Although the Banff National Park Management Plan precludes the construction of new roads, two communities east of the Rockies – Red Deer and Rocky Mountain House – continually advocate extending Highway 11 across Howse Pass. (It doesn't help that Parks Canada itself promoted the idea in 1971.) Such a highway would decrease transportation times and costs between some places in Alberta and BC, but would destroy one of the last wilderness enclaves in the Rockies while diverting only eight percent of the traffic from Highway 1. An economic analysis of the proposed highway's effects has also shown a net economic loss for communities in central Alberta, because the road would divert traffic from the Highway 2 corridor. The idea of constructing a road over Howse Pass has very little support in BC.

deposits are the most extensive in Banff. The lower Howse Valley is also noted for its kettle lakes. Seven appear on the topographic map.

To the southwest, Mt. Outram (OOT-rum) (3245 m) commemorates reverend and mountaineer James Outram, who made first ascents of many high peaks in the Rockies in 1901 and 1902. Tucked in behind Mt. Outram is Mt. Forbes (3617 m), the 7th-highest mountain in the Rockies, the 4th-highest in Alberta, and the highest mountain entirely within Banff National Park. James Outram teamed up with the party of mountaineer J.N. Collie, to make the first ascent. James Hector of the Palliser Expedition named the mountain – not for the eminent geologist of his day – but for Edward Forbes, Hector's professor of natural history at the University of Edinburgh.

The trail swings west from the viewpoint and descends to riverside. Look back to the many-summitted massif of Mt. Murchison (3337 m), which towers above the mouth of the Mistaya Valley. The trail veers away from the river. You spend the next 5 km climbing and descending a forested spur of Survey Peak to reach the shore of Glacier Lake and the campground near its outlet.

Glacier Lake is 3.75 km long, 750 m wide, and with an area of 263 ha, is the 4th-largest lake in Banff National Park. A glacial moraine dams its waters. James Hector named Glacier Lake in 1858. Hector also named a mountain north of the lake for John Sullivan, mathematician and secretary to the Palliser Expedition. Hector and a companion climbed the peak, wearing only moccasins on their feet, so it is not likely that the challenging mountain that we call Sullivan Peak (3022 m) today was their objective. You may see osprey circling over the lake, in quest of lake trout, rocky mountain whitefish, and bull trout.

The Glacier River Valley

The rough trail along the north shore of Glacier Lake originated in the early 20th century as a mountaineering approach to Mt. Forbes and the Lyell Icefield. Although the trail is infrequently cleared and is sketchy in places, the route is obvious. Beyond the inlet, the trail works across alluvial flats, following the north bank of the Glacier River and passing the site of the 1940 Alpine Club of Canada Camp. At about the 9.5 km mark, look for a faint track that climbs steeply northwest (right) onto a series of knife-edged, lateral moraines. From this hard-won vantage you have astounding views of the icefall of the Southeast Lyell Glacier and its marginal lake, along with the tremendous glaciated fang of Mt. Forbes.

GLACIERS: THE BEGINNING AND END OF LAKES

If you look at the topographic map, you will see that Glacier Lake occupies the eastern end of a 13 km long plain. At the conclusion of the Late Wisconsin Glaciation, the lake may have filled the entire valley. Over time, rubble and sediment carried by the Glacier River have filled much of the lake. As with most glacially formed and fed lakes in the Rockies, if glacial recession continues, the day will come when the filling will be complete or the glaciers will vanish. Either way, Glacier Lake will cease to exist.

THE SOUTHEAST LYELL ICEFALL: A CASCADING RIVER OF ICE

Just over a century ago, the head of the Glacier River Valley was buried in glacial ice. Mountaineers J.N. Collie and Hugh Stutfield described the icefall in 1902: "Incomparably the finest we have seen in the Rockies, it is a larger scale than anything of the kind in Switzerland. It is of immense width, with a band of cliffs, surmounted at their northern end by blue ice-pinnacles, dividing the upper from the lower glacier for the greater part of the distance. The meltings of the higher snows fall over these cliffs in a series of waterfalls, and the roar of the ice avalanches was constant and deafening."

We fished, and set lines in the lake, but without success. It appears to be very deep, and the south shore is almost precipitous. In the afternoon violent gusts of wind occasionally blew down the valley raising the water into large waves; but the evening was calm, and the reflection of the opposite mountains was wonderfully clear.

James Hector; September 11, 1858,
Papers Relative to the Exploration of British North America

25. Sunset Pass – Sunset Lookout

Sunset Lookout

TRAIL THUMBNAIL		
Day-hike or overnight		

Day-hike or overnight

Route	Elev.	Dist.
	(m)	(km)
Trailhead	1438	0
Sunset Lookout jct	1860	2.9
Sunset Lookout site	2043	+1.6
Norman Lake CG	1973	3.6
Sunset Pass	2060	7.6
Pinto Lake viewpoint	2035	8.2

Trailhead
East side of the Icefields Parkway, 91.6 km north of Highway 1; 16.4 km north of the junction with Highway 11; 32.9 km south of the Icefield Centre; 133.6 km south of Highway 16.

Maps
NTS: 83 C/2
Gem Trek: *Bow Lake and Saskatchewan Crossing*

The Sunset Pass trail is a backcountry artery into the remote northeast corner of Banff National Park, used principally by backpackers and horse parties bound for Pinto Lake in the adjacent White Goat Wilderness Area. But the two destinations within Banff make fine outings. The sidetrail to Sunset Lookout offers a breathtaking prospect over the North Saskatchewan Valley. The willow meadows of Sunset Pass typify the upper subalpine life zone. Strong hikers can visit both destinations in a long day.

Trailhead to Sunset Lookout Junction

With no preamble, the trail climbs steeply away from the parking area. The climb abates where the trails cuts through an old stream course, but then resumes

VARIATIONS

- Hike to the lookout site; 9.0 km return.
- Hike to the pass; 15.2 km return.
- Visit both destinations; 18.6 km return.
- Camp at Norman Lake and explore.

Not far from its head Cataract River forks, one branch coming from a splendid valley to the south, where it begins in an exquisite lake about a mile long and broad, fed by an enormous spring forty feet wide. Pinto Lake, as we named it, is 5,850 feet above the sea, and on three sides of it mountain walls rise to seven or eight thousand feet, making a wonderful amphitheatre....

A.P. Coleman; *The Canadian Rockies, New and Old Trails*

with purpose. The surrounding forest is an open one, dominated by lodgepole pine. Buffaloberry, dwarf dogwood, wild strawberry, and birch-leaved spirea are common in the undergrowth. The glossy leaves of buffaloberry are pale and fuzzy on the underside, with rust-coloured spots. By late July, the yellow flowers yield red and amber berries – a staple food of bears. If the berry crop is on, you should make lots of noise and look for recent bear sign. I have surprised a grizzly bear here. The bear made a no-contact charge, passing within two metres. There are many rub-trees and scratch-trees alongside the trail. Some clearly show the claw marks of bears.

As you ascend this slope, you'll notice that the ridges of limestone bedrock, crossed by the trail, are upturned to the southwest. This is not common in the main ranges, where the strata usually lie in horizontal layers or dip slightly to the southwest. These rocks are in the western arm of the Mt. Wilson Syncline, a U-shaped fold whose axis runs through the meadows just this side of Sunset Pass. When you reach the meadows near Norman Lake, you'll be able to see the syncline in the slopes of Mt. Coleman, to the north.

The steep slope on which you have been travelling is a product of glacial overdeepening of the North Saskatchewan Valley. Tributary valleys, such as Norman Creek, were not as deeply eroded by glacial ice during the Late Wisconsin Glaciation, and were left hanging above the main valley floor. With the energy created by its steep gradient, Norman Creek has carved an impressive canyon, with a series of waterfalls. Just after km 1.0, three sidetrails lead south from the corners of switchbacks to the edge of the canyon. The second sidetrail has the best view. Use caution; the area is unfenced. The creek may have been named for John Norman Collie, one of the leading alpinists of his day. Collie climbed extensively in the European Alps, in Norway, on Nanga Parbat in the Himalaya, and made six mountaineering trips to the Rockies between 1897 and 1910.

From the canyon, the trail works its way north before switchbacking upward to the Sunset Lookout junction. A few stately Douglas-fir trees grow among the pines on this slope. This may be the northern limit for the Douglas-fir in Banff National Park. Wildflowers here include fine displays of arnica and glacier lilies. The forest becomes more enclosed and the grade moderates just before the Sunset Lookout junction. Turn north (left) for the lookout.

Sunset Lookout

The sidetrail to Sunset Lookout makes a rambling ascent through old subalpine forest. Squirrel middens, valerian, fleabanes, arnica, bracted lousewort, grouseberry, and patches of glacier lilies dot the forest floor. I've heard blackpoll warblers here. You'll know that you are just about at the lookout site when you see stumps at trailside. The trail angles west to the cliff edge and descends steeply for 60 m to the lookout site, with its staggering view of the North Saskatchewan Valley, more than 500 m below. This is no place for acrophobics; it is more suited to mountain goats, which are often seen nearby. The foundations and lightning conductor cables of the lookout pose a genuine tripping hazard. Be careful.

On my last visit, I spooked a golden eagle during my descent to the lookout site. The raptor took off, banking away to the south. As I marvelled at its flight, the bird was joined by a lesser shape – a rough-legged hawk. For the next five minutes, I was witness to their territorial duel as they scrapped – talon, beak, and feather – over the void.

Sunset Lookout was built in 1943. It operated until 1978, when smoke patrols by helicopter rendered it and the other towers in the fire lookout system obsolete. The site was well chosen. Mt. Saskatchewan (3342 m), guardian of the southeastern edge of the Columbia Icefield, dominates the view west, where the upper reaches of the Alexandra River are visible. The valleys of the North Saskatchewan, Mistaya, and Bow align to the south, allowing an unrestricted view to Bow Peak, 60 km distant. Some glaciologists speculate that before mountain building, the North Saskatchewan River flowed south along this alignment, rather than beginning its exit from the mountains at Saskatchewan River Crossing. The northern vista includes Hilda Peak, Nigel Pass, and the environs of the Columbia Icefield. Few other places in

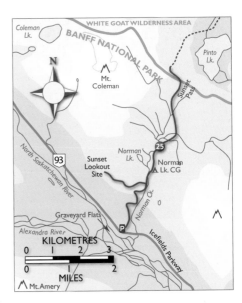

THE GRAVEYARD

From Sunset Lookout you can compare the North Saskatchewan River and the Alexandra River, which merge below on the Graveyard Flats. The North Saskatchewan is a glacially charged stream, with multiple braids and extensive gravel flats. Although it too has glacial origins, the Alexandra River shows a more meandering course, with abandoned channels, ox-bow lakes, and sloughs. Pick a channel on the Alexandra and follow it. See if it rejoins the main river or dead-ends in a pocket of moose habitat.

The gravels of the Graveyard Flats offered the best camping place in the upper North Saskatchewan valley. First Peoples dressed the kills of their hunts there. Explorer Mary Schäffer named the flats after she found animal skeletons in 1907. *Saskatchewan* is Cree for "swift current." The North Saskatchewan River is 1216 km long. The portion within Banff National Park was designated a Canadian Heritage River in 1989. Princess Alexandra was the wife of King Edward VII.

Bearberry

the Rockies reveal the trough-like, glacially-scoured form of the major valleys so clearly.

The limestone of the lookout site is a miniature rock garden. Look for these wildflowers: stonecrop, harebell, yarrow, paintbrush, dwarf raspberry, yellow-flowered false dandelion, Mackenzie's hedysarum, four-parted gentian, wild strawberry, bearberry, daisy fleabane, red-stemmed saxifrage, cinquefoil, and woolly pussytoes. The orange-coloured lichen, *Xanthoria elegans*, grows on the rock. On the trail nearby, you'll brush your pack against whitebark pines. Note the needles in bunches of five. Clark's

MR. AMERY'S MOUNTAIN

The prominent mountain to the southwest of Sunset Lookout – its flanks riddled with glacial cirques – is Mt. Amery (AY-muh-ree) (3329 m). The mountain was named in 1927 for L.S. Amery, a British statesman, publisher, and mountaineer. Two years later, Amery came to Canada with the express purpose of making the first ascent of "his" mountain. In wretched weather, guide Ernest Feuz (FOITS) Jr. led Amery and a partner by a difficult route to the summit – or so they thought. A 1985 ascent found no evidence of the cairn they claimed to have built, and no suitable rocks with which to build one. Ditto for a fair weather ascent in 1994. In the poor visibility of his ascent, it is possible that Mr. Amery did not quite reach the true summit.

nutcrackers frequent the area, gleaning the seeds from the cones of this tree. (See pages 62 and 99.)

Sunset Lookout Junction to Sunset Pass

Keep straight ahead at the lookout junction. (If you are returning from the lookout, turn northeast, or left.) The trail undulates through flower-filled glades to the edge of a large subalpine willow meadow, and an unsigned junction. Keep right and descend to a bridge over Norman Creek. The campground is in the stand of trees just beyond.

Mt. Coleman (3135 m) dominates the north side of the valley. A.P. Coleman was a geology professor from the University of Toronto. He made seven journeys into the hinterland of the Rockies between 1884 and 1908, naming many features and contributing greatly to the growing knowledge of the landscape. His book of 1911, *The Canadian Rockies, New and Old Trails*, is a landmark of Rockies' history. The north side of the mountain features a spectacular glacier and two large lakes that drain underground.

The trail to Sunset Pass follows the southeast side of wet meadows and willow plain for several kilometres, before angling northeast into forest. You might get your feet wet here and there, as you hop channels in the wet meadows. The trail reaches the height of land and the national park boundary to the north of Sunset Pass proper. It then descends slightly onto a limestone bench above the headwaters of the Cline River. Michael Cline was a fur trader in the Rockies in the early 1800s, when he made annual trading trips through the front ranges from Jasper House to the Kootenay Plains.

Pinto Lake Viewpoint

After you travel 600 m along the bench northeast of Sunset Pass, walk east from the trail to the edge the cliff. This provides a wonderful prospect over Pinto Lake and the Cline River valley. The lake commemorates one of A.P. Coleman's most troublesome packhorses on the 1893 expedition. Pinto went missing on the journey home. None was sad to see him go. Still, to quote Coleman: "... we immortalized him by giving his name to an exquisite lake near the head of Cataract River." If you are day-hiking, do not descend to Pinto Lake. It's much farther than it looks (5 km), and – if you have also been to the lookout site – will result in a 34 km outing by the time you return to the Icefields Parkway, possibly today, probably tomorrow.

26. Saskatchewan Glacier

Saskatchewan Glacier

Few people travelling the Icefields Parkway at "The Big Bend" realize that they are within 7 km of Saskatchewan Glacier, one of the larger glaciers in the Rockies. This trail grants access to the forefield of the glacier, where you can explore the rough terrain of a recently glaciated landscape. This is an unmaintained route. Originally bulldozed as a jeep road in 1941, the North Saskatchewan River and the surrounding forest are reclaiming the tread. Although most of the route is easy to follow, there are specific hazards on this hike, beginning with the walk along the Icefields Parkway. Along the way you will find an unfenced canyon, unsigned junctions, an overgrown section, an avalanche slope, high water levels, and washouts. For these reasons, this hike is recommended to experienced hikers only.

Trailhead to Saskatchewan Glacier Forefield

Cross the old bridge over the North Saskatchewan River. The bridge was completed in 1938 during construction of the "Wonder Road," the precursor to the Icefields Parkway. Fifteen metres south of the bridge, look for a faint trail that climbs the slope and then angles upstream above the west bank of the river. Don't use the lower trails as they take you close to the brink of the canyon, and because farther west they may be flooded by the river. The silver spar trees of the surrounding forest resulted from a 1905 forest

---

Through the trees we caught glimpses of magnificent scenery: the uniting streams in the canyon bottom, the mountain sides heavily timbered or rising into snow summits, and to the west an immense glacier, which was the source of the largest stream.

Walter Wilcox; *The Rockies of Canada*

TRAIL THUMBNAIL

Day-hike

Route	Elev. (m)	Dist. (km)
Trailhead	1599	0
Crest of knoll	1765	1.9
Valley floor	1737	2.5
End of defined trail	1768	5.6

Trailhead
You have two parking choices on the Icefields Parkway. Add either of these distances to the length of the hike. Please use care when walking along the roadside.

1. In the Cirrus Mountain viewpoint 600 m east of the trailhead; 107.6 km north of Highway 1, 16.9 km south of the Icefield Centre, 117.6 km south of Highway 16.
2. At the "Big Bend" parking area, 750 m west of the trailhead; 108.9 km north of Highway 1, 15.6 km south of the Icefield Centre, 116.2 km south of Highway 16.

From either parking area, walk on the gravel highway shoulder, facing traffic, to the sideroad that descends south to an old bridge. Use caution when crossing the highway. Do not attempt to park at the bridge. There is insufficient room for vehicles, the grade is steep, and access to and from the modern road is hazardous.

Maps
NTS: 83 C/3
Gem Trek: *Columbia Icefield*

Best lighting: morning and early afternoon

---

fire. The understory features bearberry, the leaves of which turn bright red in late summer.

After 400 m, keep right where the jeep track comes in from the south. Follow the riverbank, and descend northwest (right) onto the river flats 300 m later. Follow cairns across the flats for 400 m to the edge of the forest. If you look back to your left, you can see "Sideways Falls" at the lip of the valley north of Mt. Saskatchewan. The track makes a sharp turn southeast (left) into the forest and begins its winding ascent over the knoll that conceals Saskatchewan Glacier. Before you duck into the trees, look back for a fine view of the twin summits of Cirrus Mountain (3270 m), with the Mt. Wilson Syncline evident in its slopes.

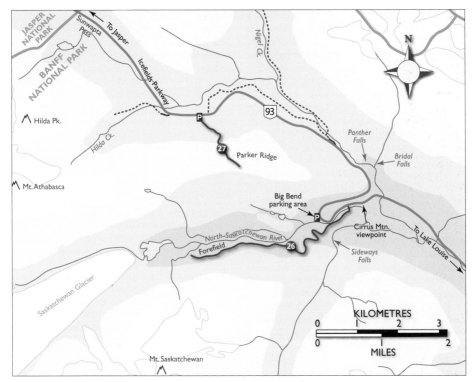

After a climb of about 1 km, the trail descends the west side of the knoll onto an avalanche slope that may be covered with snow or debris. There are fine views ahead to a cascading glacier on the southeast slopes of Mt. Andromeda (3450 m). Look and listen for the Clark's nutcrackers that frequent the whitebark pines nearby. This place, with its double-whammy of avalanches and catabatic winds, is a tough place to be a tree. One massive whitebark pine stands miraculously as a survivor in the middle of the avalanche path.

The descent concludes at the former site of the Saskatchewan Glacier Hut. You can make a detour north on a beaten path for 150 m to river's edge for a fine view upvalley. Back on the main trail you head west but the promise of easy travel is short-lived. The track is washed away 300 m beyond. There is a maze of trails here, covering about 600 m through the shin-tangle of willows and pines on the riverbank. The best way to negotiate the first part of this mess is to skirt it by heading south for 30 m to the edge of a rockslide. Head west along the rockslide until it ends and then make your way back toward the riverbank. Eventually, the willows thin and you walk through open pine and spruce forest. About 1.5 km from the hut site, a prominent cairn marks the descent from the riverbank to the forefield. Here, unless the ice recedes another 500 m before this book goes to print, you may obtain your first view of Saskatchewan Glacier.

NORTH SASKATCHEWAN RIVER CANYON

The canyon at the trailhead is a masterpiece of natural sculpture, eroded into fossil-rich dolomite of the Flume Formation. In depth and beauty, it is as impressive as many of the better known chasms in the Rockies. At its narrowest, the canyon is less than half a metre wide. (Don't think of it!) The silt-laden waters of the North Saskatchewan River have eroded many potholes and fanciful shapes into the resistant rock. If the day is typical, glacier-driven, catabatic winds will fling the spray skyward, creating rainbows that dance in the air. Please use caution here – the canyon is unfenced.

Saskatchewan Glacier Forefield

Low mounds of rubble and the odd cairn define the track across the forefield. After about a kilometre of bouldery travel, the track passes through an area of recessional moraines that date to the 1920s. I have seen a mountain goat here on the valley floor. There are several drumlins to the north – piles of teardrop-shaped glacial debris. The blunt end of each drumlin faced into the flow of ice; the tapered end faced away. Glaciologists cannot agree as to how drumlins formed, but it may be that they were created from deposits made by subglacial streams.

The point where the bulldozer track reverts to a footpath marks the location of the glacier terminus in the early 1940s. Follow cairns west from here, keeping to the south edge of the forefield. Snowmelt from the cirques above streaks the dark cliffs with waterfalls. Rock-hop the tributary streams as required. Many of the larger boulders in the forefield show striations – scratches and grooves caused by rocks embedded in the underside of the moving ice. Mountain fireweed and yellow mountain saxifrage decorate the gravels. On my last visit, I watched an American pipit here, hanging like a kite on the glacial wind. This is also good habitat for horned larks.

The more you walk toward the glacier, the farther away it seems to get. Blame it on glacial recession. Some hikers are content not to travel all the way to the marginal lake near the glacier toe. About 5.4 km from the trailhead, a faint path veers north, descending at first, and then climbing onto a knoll of debris near the centre of the valley. The cairn here offers a fine viewpoint. The strip of lengthwise rubble visible on the northern edge of Saskatchewan Glacier is a medial moraine, created where two tributary glaciers merge. If you look back at Parker Ridge on the north side of the valley, you can count six sedimentary formations from valley bottom to ridgecrest – most dating to the Late Devonian.

It is 1.7 km from the knoll to the shore of the marginal lake. If you choose to carry on and are confronted with a river crossing, don't force the issue. Glacial rivers are difficult and dangerous to ford. The lake fills a depression in the bedrock. Marginal lakes are common in the Rockies – Athabasca, Bow, Robson, and Cavell glaciers also feature them. Since the bed of this lake was uncovered in the 1960s, the glacier has receded almost 3 km. Islands in the lake are the crests of submerged recessional moraines. On

my most recent visit, I marvelled at the presence of a nesting pair of spotted sandpipers. Hummocks and hollows near the lake are miniature kames – conical shapes of moraine – and kettles – depressions where detached ice blocks melted during glacial retreat.

If you are thinking about a glacial stroll, don't; access to the glacier has become difficult and dangerous in recent years, and is not possible from the south side of the river. To complete your appreciation of Saskatchewan Glacier, I recommend a visit to Parker Ridge, Classic Hike #27.

THE SASKATCHEWAN GLACIER HUT

In 1942 the U.S. Army constructed buildings near Saskatchewan Glacier to serve as a base for testing oversnow vehicles called "Weasels." Snow flattened the base the following winter. The remains were salvaged by the Canadian Army, which built a hut for mountain warfare training in 1943. This building was leased by the Alpine Club of Canada the following year, and became known as the Saskatchewan Glacier Hut. By the 1960s, the building was in disrepair, and the river began to undermine its foundation. Parks Canada did not renew the lease in 1972. The hut was demolished and the access road was closed to vehicles. A clean-up in 1994 removed almost all traces. The small log frame structure that remains predates the hut. Analysis of the logs in this building (see the "Tree-time-knowledge" sidebar) indicates that it was probably built in 1926. It may have housed camping supplies for outfitters using the Glacier Trail. If you poke around, you might find other, more recent relics, including the leaf springs of a truck.

A MIGHTY RIVER OF ICE

Saskatchewan Glacier is one of eight outlet valley glaciers of the Columbia Icefield. The glacier extends almost 7 km from the icefield rim, making it the longest glacier in the Rockies. Its meltwaters create the first reach of the North Saskatchewan River, and eventually flow to Hudson Bay.

The most recent significant advance of glaciers in the Rockies was during the Little Ice Age, which began at approximately 1050 AD, and ended in the mid-1800s. Saskatchewan Glacier reached its maximum later than most other glaciers. In 1854, the toe extended to where the track descends from the knoll to the forefield.

A glaciated valley often preserves evidence of the former size of a glacier. A terminal moraine marks the greatest advance of the glacier, and recessional moraines mark positions of halt during its retreat. The maximum thickness of the ice is revealed by a feature called trimline. The obvious

trimline on north side of this valley is more than 100 m above the valley floor, giving an approximate indication of the thickness of Saskatchewan Glacier in the mid-1800s. The moving ice obliterated forest within the trimline. In this peri-glacial climate and on poor soils, the forest has not had time to become re-established.

Today, in the lower reaches of the valley, the Saskatchewan Glacier forefield lacks prominent terminal and lateral moraines, such as those that flank Athabasca Glacier. Lateral moraines are created when the ice fills a valley from side to side. Here, the lateral moraines were undercut when the ice retreated. They collapsed onto the glacier's surface and became part of the ground moraine – the chaos of rubble on the valley floor. Closer to the glacier you can see the lateral moraine on the north side of the valley. If you detect a glistening in its slope, you're right – it's ice-cored.

TREE-TIME-KNOWLEDGE

Most coniferous trees in the Rockies are long-lived. Those that grow near glaciers help to reveal much about the climate and glacial events of the recent past. Glaciologists look for ice-contact trees – those killed or scarred by ice during glacial advances. By coring the trees and count-

ing the tree rings, and by comparing the findings to master keys derived from other sites in the Rockies, they can assign probable dates to former positions of the ice. The process is called dendrochronology, a name derived from three Greek words – *dendros* for "tree," *chronos* for "time," and *logos* for "knowledge" – tree-time-knowledge.

The current spate of glacial retreat in the Rockies offers glaciologists an exceptional window into the past. If you hike to the marginal lake you may see driftwood piled into the bays along its eastern edge. Upvalley, there is no forest, so

trees could not have been avalanched into the lake. How did the wood get here? This is glacier-released wood, freed from Saskatchewan Glacier as the ice receded. Glaciologists have studied this wood, dating the oldest fragment to 3180 years BP – indicating that the trees, from forests that once grew upvalley, were overrun during what is known as the "Peyto Advance." In 1999, a meltwater shaft in the terminus of the glacier revealed the fossilized stumps of a forest shorn by the ice. Subalpine fir was the dominant species. Downvalley, ice-contact trees on the glacier's lateral moraine indicate three glacial advances during the Little Ice Age. Saskatchewan Glacier reached its maximum size roughly a century after the other major outlet valley glaciers of the Columbia Icefield.

WITNESS

Saskatchewan Glacier, 1924

Saskatchewan Glacier, 2010

Twenty-seven years of acquaintance with a glacier is not much of an interval, geologically speaking, on which to base a description of significant change. My first visit to this valley was in May 1984, during a ski mountaineering trip to Castleguard Mountain. I hiked to the toe of the glacier, put on my skis, and ascended the ice without difficulty. On repeat visits, including two more ski mountaineering trips in successive years, I noted degrees of glacial recession, and how access to the ice was becoming more difficult. Nothing prepared me for the jolt when I visited this valley in July 2002, after an absence of nine years. The toe of the glacier, which in 1984 was in contact with the marginal lake, had receded fully 1 km. (It has since receded

more than another kilometre.) Mountaineering access to the ice now appears impossible on the south, and is hazardous on the north. The lake is much smaller. The river, on a hot day at the end of a month-long heat wave, was much lower than I had expected. At a braided section in the forefield, I was able to ford it at two in the afternoon – something that should be unthinkable. I wish that this was merely a point of interest only to mountaineers, glaciologists, and curious guidebook authors, but Saskatchewan Glacier testifies to monumental effects of climate change. The core glacier system of the Canadian Rockies, the source of three of the continent's great rivers, is rapidly dwindling.

27. Parker Ridge

Saskatchewan Glacier from Parker Ridge

TRAIL THUMBNAIL

Day-hike; see map, p. 107

Route	Elev.	Dist.
	(m)	(km)
Trailhead	1997	0
Ridgecrest	2285	1.9
Saskatchewan Glacier viewpoint	2270	2.4

Trailhead
South side of Icefields Parkway, 115.5 km north of Highway 1; 9 km south of the Icefield Centre; 109.6 km south of Highway 16.

Special consideration
The trail may be closed until most of the winter snowpack is melted – early July in most years.

Maps
NTS: 82 C/3
Gem Trek: *Columbia Icefield*

Best lighting: morning

My visit to Parker Ridge during fieldwork for the second edition of this book was an afterthought. I had been to the ridgecrest perhaps a dozen times before; why go again? But as I drove by on a fair day, I couldn't resist. I thought that I would nip up and down in an hour and a half. I spent four. The day was jewel-bright, cut from perfection. The meld of mountain, meadow, and ice in view was quintessential Rockies. And miracle of all, there was no wind. I have been up the ridge four times since. I never tire of this outing.

> *The prospect was astounding. Ice, ice, ice, as far as the eye could reach. Great peaks rose all about us, seamed with glaciers, crowned with eternal snows. And at the glacier's head a vast ice cap covering the landscape to the southwest, reaching away into the unseen distance, the Columbia Ice Field. It is at times such as this that one realizes to the full the privilege of living.*
>
> B.W. Mitchell; *Trail Life in the Canadian Rockies*

Trailhead to the Ridgecrest

The trailhead is located in a treeline forest where vegetation growth is hindered by high elevation, cold glacial air, near constant winds, poor soils, avalanches, and a northeast aspect. From the parking area, the trail crosses a subalpine meadow – a frost hollow, typical of areas adjacent to glaciers. Cold air from Hilda Glacier collects here, creating a local growing season so short, that mature trees cannot develop.

The horn mountain shapes of Mt. Athabasca (3442 m) and its outlier, Hilda Peak (3058 m), are prominent to the west. The summits of these mountains protruded above the kilometre thick ice sheets of the Late Wisconsin Glaciation. Since the retreat of the ice sheets, alpine glaciation has continued to whittle away at the upper mountainsides, creating the horns.

The climb begins across the meadow. The trail enters ancient forest. At one point you squeeze between two massive Engelmann spruce trees that are probably at least 400 years old. However, most of the vegetation here is in stunted, kruppelholz form. (*Kruppelholz* is a German term that means "crippled wood.") The gnarled, dense, evergreen mats with silvery bark are subalpine fir trees. Taller, Engelmann spruce grow from within the mats. Although they appear to be shrubs, these are mature trees, possibly hundreds of years old.

Fossil coral

The treeless areas on the northeast slope of Parker Ridge are either avalanche swept rock, or tundra comprised of sedges, white mountain-avens, mountain heather, snow willow, arctic willow, moss campion, woolly everlasting, and purple saxifrage. Vegetation here is low in stature to reduce wind exposure, and to enable the plants to absorb heat from the dark soils. Thick, waxy leaves help retain moisture. Fuzzy stems are natural insulation.

More than 6 m of snow falls annually at Parker Ridge. Because of the shaded, northeast aspect – and

ROCK LICHENS: OLD TIMERS

In some areas, the thin soils of Parker Ridge support little but rock lichen colonies. A rock lichen is a symbiotic relationship that contains fungus and algae. The fungus houses the algae, and the algae produces food for both. One byproduct of this relationship is humic acid, which accelerates the chemical breakdown of rock and the creation of soil. Rock lichens grow outward at an incredibly slow, consistent rate, so the diameter of a lichen patch can be used to estimate its age and the dates of recent glacial retreats. It is thought some rock lichen colonies in the Rockies may have begun life at the end of the Late Wisconsin Glaciation, 11,000 years ago. Two of the more common rock lichens are the brilliant orange *Xanthoria elegans*, found on a variety of rock types; and the green and black map lichen (*Rhizocarpon geographicum*), found principally on quartzite boulders.

cold temperatures resulting from the elevation and the proximity to Columbia Icefield – this snow takes a long time to melt. A few of the drifts at trailside are perennial features. Needless to say, the slopes of Parker Ridge are popular with skiers in winter and spring. If you look north you may be able to pick out the summit of Mt. Alberta (3619 m), the 6th-highest peak in the Rockies; and the 3rd-highest peak in Alberta.

The Ridgecrest

A blast of icy wind may greet you where the trail gains the open ridgecrest. Follow the beaten path southeast (left) for 500 m for a full view of Saskatchewan Glacier. With a length of almost 7 km, this outlet valley glacier of the 230 km² Columbia Icefield is the longest in the Rockies. It descends 750 m in elevation from the icefield rim to terminate in a marginal lake, the principal headwaters of the North Saskatchewan River. The braided river courses through the rubble of the valley below, an area occupied by the glacier less than a century ago.

Compared to Athabasca Glacier, the surface of Saskatchewan Glacier is relatively unspectacular. It has no icefalls and few large crevasses. Of interest is a medial moraine, a strip of lengthwise rubble on the glacier's surface. This type of moraine forms where two tributary glaciers merge. *Saskatchewan* is a Cree word that means "swift current." Mt. Saskatchewan (3342 m) is the high peak protruding above rounded summits, 8 km south of Parker Ridge.

Immediately south (left) of the head of the Saskatchewan Glacier is Castleguard Mountain (3083 m). South of this mountain is the entrance to Castleguard Cave, one of the larger cave systems in Canada, and the 3rd-deepest in Canada and the U.S.. More than 18 km of passages have been explored.

KEEPING ON TRACK

The Parker Ridge trail was built in the 1960s with ease of access in mind. Gentle switchbacks carved the slope. Unfortunately, those impatient with the trail have shortcut the switchbacks, creating trenches that channel runoff. On your way to the ridgetop you will see dozens of signs that block the shortcut trails, encouraging you to keep on track. The signs were installed when the trail was rehabilitated in a costly project in the 1980s. Seeds from plants on Parker Ridge were grown in greenhouses, and the resulting seedlings were transplanted back to the ridge to revegetate redundant trails. Three decades later, the trail requires another overhaul. Many of the trail posts now lean downhill – evidence of soil creep. Please help to protect this fragile landscape by keeping to the gravelled path.

Some of these follow ancient drainages beneath Columbia Icefield to terminate in dead-ends that are choked with glacial ice. If the day is clear, the view beyond Castleguard Mountain will include the lofty summit of Mt. Bryce (3507 m), the 13th-highest peak in the Rockies, and the 14th-highest peak in BC; 19 km distant.

If you look uphill (west) along the crest of Parker Ridge, you will notice how the outlying ridge is rounded in appearance, becoming much more rugged toward Mt. Athabasca. The rounded parts of the ridge were completely covered by moving ice during the Late Wisconsin Glaciation, while the jagged areas were probably not. If you choose to explore along the ridge to the cairn at the high point (2255 m), please stay on the beaten path. The ridgecrest features kruppelholz forms of whitebark pine, a common tree in windy locations. The limestone bedrock of the Southesk Formation contains coral-like fossils called *Syringopora*. Please do not remove the fossils.

Mountain goats, white-tailed ptarmigan, gray jays, Clark's nutcrackers, pikas, and ravens are among the frequently observed wildlife on Parker Ridge. If you are fortunate, a grizzly bear or wolverine may lumber over the crest, or a golden eagle may wheel overhead. I have seen a harrier skim by. The ridge was probably named for Herschel Parker, an American mountaineer who made several first ascents of mountains near Lake Louise at the turn of the century.

THE GLACIER TRAIL

Mountaineering parties in the early 1900s, intent on ascending peaks at the southern edge of the Columbia Icefield, followed the Alexandra River southwest to a base camp in Castleguard Meadows. If they wanted to continue farther north, they were obliged to return along the Alexandra River to the North Saskatchewan River, before crossing Sunwapta Pass – a journey of approximately three days. This backtracking frustrated outfitter Jimmy Simpson and his clients, who felt that the supplies used descending the Alexandra could be better used exploring new ground. On the 1923 expedition of mountaineer James Monroe Thorington, Simpson took a one-day shortcut from Castleguard Meadows to Sunwapta Pass – he led the packtrain down the Saskatchewan Glacier and over Parker Ridge.

It was a day-long effort. The horses fussed, but less than expected. Simpson repeated the ploy on the Smithsonian Institution, Columbia Icefield expedition of 1924. For two decades thereafter, the crossing of Saskatchewan Glacier with horses became standard fare. In the late 1920s, outfitter Jack Brewster incorporated a visit to Castleguard Meadows via Saskatchewan Glacier into his pack trips from Jasper to Lake Louise – an outing known appropriately as "The Glacier Trail."

Wilcox Pass

Jasper National Park

Established in 1907 as Canada's sixth national park, Jasper is the largest of the mountain national parks. It includes 10,878 km² of the front ranges and eastern main ranges and has almost 1000 km of maintained trails. The Classic Hikes in Jasper are a mix of long backcountry outings and day-hikes to spectacular alpine landscapes.

Jasper town provides a full range of supplies, accommodation, and services, 362 km west of Edmonton on Highway 16; and 237 km north of Lake Louise via the Icefields Parkway. Access is by car, passenger bus or train. The park information centres are in Jasper town and at Columbia Icefield, 102 km south of Jasper; 126.5 km north of Lake Louise.

BC established Mt. Robson Provincial Park in 1913 as its second provincial park. The park includes 2172 km² at the headwaters of the Fraser River. The two frontcountry campgrounds at Robson Junction, 84 km west of Jasper, are the usual assembly places for those hiking the Berg Lake trail. The park information centre is nearby. Robson Junction is a Greyhound bus flag-stop. The park is in the Pacific time zone, one hour behind Jasper and Banff.

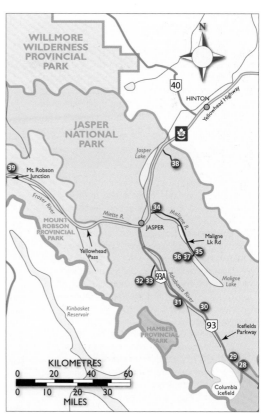

28. Brazeau

Upper Brazeau River

TRAIL THUMBNAIL

Overnight, 5-7 days

Route	Elev. (m)	Dist. (km)
Trailhead	1864	0
"Camp Parker"	1910	2.1
Nigel Pass	2195	7.2
Boulder Creek CG	2030	10.7
Four Point CG	1910	13.9
Jonas Pass jct	1910	14.0
Jonas Pass	2301	23.8
Jonas Shoulder	2490	29.6
Jonas Cutoff CG	2140	32.8
Poboktan Creek jct	2115	33.0
Poboktan Pass	2454	36.0
John John CG	2020	40.3
John John Creek bridge	1830	44.5
Brazeau Lake outlet bridge	1805	48.3
Brazeau Lake CG	1805	+0.4
Brazeau Valley jct and bridge	1720	51.2
Brazeau River CG	1720	51.3
Brazeau River east bank	1790	54.5
Wolverine South CG	1860	59.8
Brazeau River west bank	1875	62.1
Four Point CG	1910	66.2
Boulder Creek CG	2030	69.3
Nigel Pass	2195	72.8
Trailhead	1864	80.0

Trailhead
East side of the Icefields Parkway at Nigel Creek, 111.8 km north of Highway 1; 113.4 km south of Highway 16; 12.7 km south of the Icefield Centre. If you are southbound, use caution making the awkward turn into the parking area.

Maps
NTS: 83 C/3, 83 C/6, and 83 C/7

The Brazeau (brah-ZOE) Loop traverses three upper subalpine passes, the shattered crest of a mountain ridge, and the delightful, broad Brazeau Valley – with a stop a one of the larger backcountry lakes in the Rockies. The area is home to grizzly bears, elk, moose, wolf, coyotes, wolverines, cougars, deer, and mountain caribou. This is a great hike for birding. Take your time and enjoy this exquisite landscape. Backpacking in the Rockies does not get any better.

Trailhead to Nigel Pass

Fifty metres north of the parking area, the trail crosses to the east bank of Nigel Creek. For the next 7.1 km you follow the creek to its sources in the northeastern corner of Banff National Park. In the early going, the trail alternates between ancient upper subalpine forest and avalanche slopes, with exceptional wildflower displays. At km 2.1 the trail climbs onto the

VARIATIONS

Locals are split on which direction to hike this loop. If the forecast is for a few days of fair weather, hike it in the direction described so as to have good weather (albeit heavier packs) on the passes. If the forecast is not so good, hike it in the opposite direction and hope for improvement.

- Day-hike to Nigel Pass; 14.4 km return.
- For a fine three-day trip, camp at Boulder Creek (10.7 km) and spend a day exploring near Nigel Pass.
- For a superb three-day trip – perhaps the best in the Rockies – camp at Four Point (13.9 km) and day-hike to Jonas Pass (9.9 km) and Jonas Shoulder (15.7 km).
- Exit from Jonas Cutoff campground along Poboktan Creek to the Icefields Parkway; 54.1 km.

Crossing the barren pass next morning, we followed a creek flowing north-west toward a wide river valley which we had looked at longingly from a mountain-top some days before. We named the pass and creek Poboktan, from the big owls that blinked at us from the spruce trees...

A.P. Coleman; *The Canadian Rockies, New and Old Trails*

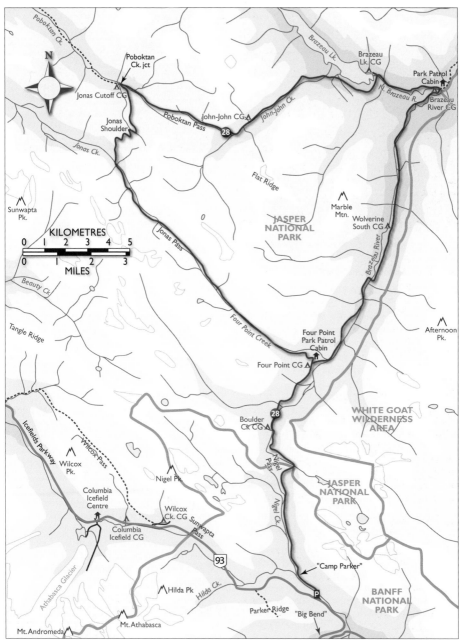

bank above the confluence of Hilda Creek and Nigel Creek. This is "Camp Parker." Many trees nearby feature carvings – the handiwork of travellers along the Icefields Parkway in the 1940s. In the days before the road was paved, the 237 km journey from Lake Louise to Jasper was at least a two-day adventure. This grove of trees was near the halfway point, and was a popular camping place. Please don't add graffiti – many of the older carvings have been disfigured in recent years.

The horn shapes of Mt. Athabasca (3442 m) and its outlier, Hilda Peak (3058 m), form the backdrop to the west. To the northwest, the southern summit of Nigel Peak displays the U-shaped fold of the Mt. Wilson Syncline.

The trail swings north into the upper valley of Nigel Creek. Although close to the Icefields Parkway, this area is frequented by grizzly bears – I have hiked here perhaps a dozen times and have had three bear experiences. Make lots of noise while you cross the

Tree carving at "Camp Parker"

Grizzly bear along Nigel Creek

avalanche slopes. The last kilometre of the climb is on a steep, eroded trail that leads to a craggy limestone bluff that overlooks the Brazeau River. This point is 1 km to the east of, and slightly higher than Nigel Pass proper. Here, you are astride the boundary between Banff and Jasper, and between two geological provinces – the eastern main ranges to the west, and the front ranges to the east.

Parker Ridge, Mt. Saskatchewan (3342 m) and the rounded peaks adjacent to Saskatchewan Glacier are prominent in the view south. To the southeast, you can see Cataract Pass (2500 m) and the southerly source of the Brazeau River. The glaciated summit of Nigel Peak (3211 m) rises above massive limestone cliffs in the view west.

BACKCOUNTRY CONSTRUCTION, AU NATUREL

The use of natural materials for bridges prevails in Jasper's backcountry. In other parks, pressure-treated wood structures – designed to the specifications of lawyers – have become the norm. By the time pressure-treated wood is purchased and flown to the work site (along with the trail crew), these structures involve a tremendous expense. Although supposedly "maintenance free" for 30-50 years, pressure-treated wood structures succumb to the vagaries of flash-floods and undercut stream banks, and to heavy snow loads, just as readily as bridges built from materials found on-site. The chemical compound typically used in the wood – copper-chromate-arsenic – is a lethal poison. All good reasons to go primitive and use natural and "found" materials for trail structures in the backcountry.

Nigel Pass to Four Point Campground

Drop to the Brazeau River and rock-hop or make a straightforward ford. We were once entertained here as a ptarmigan hen, fleeing our presence, coerced her chicks into crossing the river. Ptarmigan are ground-dwelling birds. However, as this hen and her brood demonstrated, they are capable of short bursts of flight when threatened.

The trail climbs away from the river and for the next kilometre winds through rockslide debris dotted with hardy alpine flowers – moss campion, saw-wort, cinquefoil, white mountain-avens, and yellow hedysarum. Just before it commences a steep descent, the trail crests a small bluff that offers a panorama of the upper Brazeau Valley. This is a graphic dip-slope landscape – the steeply tilted southwest facing slopes of the front range peaks terminate on northeast facing cliffs. The colourful quartzite ridge to the north divides the drainages of Boulder Creek and Four Point Creek. Particularly pleasing are the meanders, verdant wet meadows, and waterfalls along the Brazeau River. The meadows are lush with the showy white tufts of cotton-grass in late summer.

The trail descends to those meadows and delivers you to a bridge across the Brazeau River. Boulder Creek campground is on the far bank. Beyond the campground, the trail undulates in forest alongside a canyon, with many rocks and roots underfoot. Buffaloberry bushes line the trail. You cross Boulder Creek in 600 m, on a log bridge.

Most hikers travel as far as Four Point campground on the first day. Although it is a pleasant place, nestled in pine forest near the river, the campground shows the wear and tear of heavy use. Please do your part to minimize impacts at the campgrounds on this loop.

Four Point Campground to Jonas Cutoff Campground

As camping is not allowed in Jonas Pass, you must complete the 18.9 km to Jonas Cutoff campground on the second day. All but the concluding 3.2 km are uphill. Start early to allow plenty of time to enjoy the alpine glory of Jonas Pass.

Nigel Pass

MOUNTAIN CARIBOU

The caribou is a deer family member that has a brown coat with lighter patches on the neck, rump, belly, and lower legs. The neck is fringed on its underside. The word "caribou" is probably derived from the Micmac name for this animal, *Xalibu*, which means "the one who paws."

Male and female caribou each grow antlers that feature a forward-reaching "shovel." In summer, it is usually the females that carry antlers. Their "rack" is smaller than that of mature males. When they run, caribou carry their heads high and tilted back, and lift their legs in a distinctive prance. If you are close enough you will hear the clacking made by tendons in the animal's legs. The caribou's large hooves help to support it in deep snow, and leave a track that is more rounded than that of other deer family members. The wolf is its principal predator.

Some caribou migrate between high alpine meadows in summer and low elevation forests in winter. Others range high up. Caribou paw through the snow to obtain ground lichens in winter, and depend on deep winter snow to give them a step up to snag tree lichens. In the northern part of Jasper, the caribou migration takes the animals out of the park onto provincial lands where they are not protected. One of Jasper's herds – the one you may see on the Brazeau loop – does not migrate out of the park, making its 100 animals the only fully protected mountain caribou in Canada. Nonetheless, the population of this herd declined 50 percent between 1988 and 2004. Alberta's caribou population has decreased from more than 9000 animals to less than 1000 animals since 1960. Population estimates for the herds in Jasper suggest 200 to 350 animals.

Canada's southern mountain caribou are listed as "threatened" populations. Clear-cut logging on provincial lands has fragmented caribou

habitat and has destroyed much of the old-growth forest that provides winter range. Logging roads have also opened habitat to hunting and to poaching. Helicopter-accessed recreation takes people quickly into remote caribou habitat. Climate change is reducing the summer snow cover that caribou require to help regulate their body temperature. When a constellation of stresses such as this aligns, it may trigger an "extinction vortex" – a situation in which a species' natural breeding rate cannot keep pace with deaths resulting from natural and unnatural causes. Thirty of Canada's 57 mountain caribou sub-populations have already crossed that threshold.

Some wildlife biologists predict that the southern Jasper herd will be extirpated by 2045. The crisis that caribou face in the Rockies is dire, but so far Parks Canada and Alberta provincial agencies have responded with only token actions and recommendations. (BC is doing better, with a formal recovery plan for the species in place since 2007.) In 2009, the Clearwater-Siffleur caribou herd of Banff became the first sub-population of a large mammal species to be extirpated from a Canadian national park. A single avalanche wiped out the herd. (See p. 86.)

The Jonas Pass junction is 100 m northeast of Four Point campground. Turn northwest (left). The trail climbs into the hanging valley of Four Point Creek over a series of recessional moraines. Each marks a position of temporary halt during the northward retreat of the glacier that once filled the valley. In the forest and on the river flats nearby, you might spot several tree-covered drumlins – teardrop shaped mounds of glacial debris.

After a steady climb of 4 km, the trail levels in open forest. The valley bottom east of the trail is a frost hollow, devoid of trees, but bedecked with wildflowers. The shrub thickets and tundra here are important habitats for mountain caribou. On our first visit to Jonas Pass, we watched in amazement as a lone caribou descended the slopes east of the pass. From behind a boulder we observed the animal at close range for 15 minutes.

As it approaches Jonas Pass, the trail is routed between Four Point Creek and a rocky bench. Glacial cirques riddle the cliffs on the west side of the valley. Meltwater from these glaciers is the source of the five silty, tributary streams that you must rock-hop. The third stream is among my favourites in the Rockies. It cascades over the quartzite bedrock, its banks coloured by dense blooms of mountain fireweed, paintbrush, and groundsel. Look for the mauve blooms of alpine harebells on drier slopes nearby.

The crest of Jonas Pass typifies upper subalpine passes in the Rockies. Four lakelets and numerous seasonal ponds mark the imprecise height of land. Trees cannot grow in the pass itself because the soil is frozen for much of the year, preventing the supply of water required for tree growth. However, just upslope on either side of the pass, a few islands of kruppelholz mark the uppermost limit of the forest. Alpine gentians grow in profusion among the boulders in the pass. I have seen horned larks and a pair of green-winged teals. In 1992, a group of hikers watched spellbound as a cougar stalked a caribou herd nearby.

From Jonas Pass, the trail angles away from the upper reaches of Jonas Creek toward Jonas Shoulder. Several small tributary streams filter from the base of rockslides and cross the trail. These are the last water sources for 5 km.

A.P. COLEMAN, A PROFESSOR OF MOUNTAINEERING

A.P. Coleman led the first party of white people to cross Jonas Pass, in 1893. Coleman was a geology professor at the University of Toronto. He made seven trips into the uncharted wilds of the Rockies between 1884 and 1907. Initially, his quest was to find Mt. Hooker and Mt. Brown, the fabled guardians of Athabasca Pass, and reputed to be the highest mountains in the Rockies. In his last expedition, he made an attempt on Mt. Robson.

During his journey of 1893, Coleman received advice on the route from a Stoney elder, Chief Jonas. Coleman honoured his benefactor by naming a few features for him. Coleman named many other features using Stoney, Cree, and Iroquois words. His book of 1911, *The Canadian Rockies, New and Old Trails*, is one of the classics of Rockies history.

BEAUTY, EH?

The pinkish-purple bloom of mountain fireweed is often the only splash of colour on the gravels of glacial streams. About one-tenth as tall as common fireweed, its blooms endure the summer. This plant has other common names – alpine fireweed, broad-leaved willowherb, and the one that best describes it – riverbeauty. No matter whether you view dense blooms covering river gravels or the flowers of an individual plant, you'll agree.

Poboktan Pass

After an initially steep climb, the trail toward Jonas Shoulder moderates as the trail contours north. You can see three rock glaciers across the valley, extending onto the meadows near Jonas Creek. A rock glacier is an assemblage of rockslide debris that contains just enough ice to allow the entire mass to creep downhill. One study found 119 rock glaciers in Jasper National Park, but there are probably more than that. Many are stagnant or in decline, but these rock glaciers may be advancing.

During this climb, you enjoy a wonderful prospect south to Jonas Pass. The ridge east of the pass culminates nearby in a striking quartzite tower. Sunwapta Peak (3315 m), its north face cloaked in glacial ice, looms to the west. Jimmy Simpson made the first ascent of the mountain in 1906. An unwilling mountaineer but a legendary guide and hunter, Simpson was probably lured summitward while in pursuit of mountain goats or bighorn sheep. Use binoculars to look for caribou in the upper reaches of Jonas Creek.

The climb ends even more steeply than it began, on the crest of Jonas Shoulder – the ridge that separates the Jonas and Poboktan (poh-BOCK-tan) valleys. This is the 13th-highest point reached on the

Classic Hikes. *Poboktan* is Stoney for "owl." A.P. Coleman gave the name in 1892, when his party saw owls in the valley below.

The trail on the Poboktan side of Jonas Shoulder will be snow-covered in early summer. Descend with care. The trail angles sharply south (right), then switchbacks steeply down on scree. After crossing an intervening ridge, the trail rambles over boggy meadowland, paralleling the stream and descending rapidly north toward Poboktan Creek. Please keep to the beaten path to avoid creating braids in the trail. You will get your boots wet here. Shortly after you enter forest, look for a signed trail that branches west (left) to Jonas Cutoff campground, 200 m before the Poboktan Creek bridge and trail junction. It's not often that a campground, set in the ravine of a creek, is a pleasant place, but this one certainly is. Miette Formation shales colour the creek bed.

Jonas Cutoff Campground to Brazeau Lake

The splendours of this loop hike continue into the third day. At the Poboktan Creek junction, turn southeast (right), to commence the climb to

THE BRAZEAU LAKE SLIDE: THE WALLS CAME TUMBLING DOWN

When park warden Charlie Matheson rode down John-John Creek on a routine patrol in July 1933, he was the first person to see the aftermath of the tremendous Brazeau Lake Slide. He found the trail obliterated by a morass of mud and rocks. The debris was "still quivering." The backcountry telephone line was destroyed. Matheson reported that the water of Brazeau Lake had an odd taste for about a month, probably due to sediments from the slide.

The Brazeau Lake Slide is the largest landslide in the Rockies that was known to have occurred

in the 20th century. Because the dead trees in the slide debris lie parallel to the direction of flow, the slide was probably not an instantaneous catastrophe, such as the Frank Slide. (The wind blast from an instantaneous slide flattens trees at right angles to the flow.) The conical mounds in the runout of the slide are *mollards*. Vibration of the ground during the slide caused sifting and sorting of rock and sediments, building the mollards. As unlikely as it seems, the effect has been duplicated in laboratory experiments.

Brazeau Lake

Brazeau Valley

Poboktan Pass. The trail crosses and recrosses the creek on bridges, and then angles steeply away from the east bank to climb through treeline. We have had a head-on encounter here with a grizzly bear. (See, *Bears, Bears, Everywhere*, p. 276.) During the ascent you will see weathered posts, 5 m long, lying near the trail. These were formerly part of a backcountry telephone system, erected by park wardens in the 1920s. Park staff in the backcountry now pack satellite phones.

Poboktan Pass is the third upper subalpine setting on this hike; a heath and avens tundra, dotted with kruppelholz, carpeted with wildflowers and frequented by caribou and grizzly bears. The pass divides waters that flow north to the Arctic Ocean via the Athabasca, Slave, and Mackenzie rivers, from waters that flow east to Hudson Bay via the Brazeau, Saskatchewan, and Nelson rivers. Duncan McGillivray, a fur trader with the North West Company, was probably the first white man to reach Poboktan Pass, in 1800. Flat Ridge (2820 m), southeast of the pass, features several rock glaciers on its north slopes.

The trail from Poboktan Pass descends at first gradually, then abruptly into the forest along John-John Creek. John-John Harrington was father of Mona Matheson, Jasper's first female trail guide. She married Charlie Matheson, a park warden who was stationed in the Brazeau District during the 1930s. For those who have wiled away the hours on Poboktan Pass, or who would otherwise like a short day on the trail, John-John campground makes a pleasant, creek-side stopping place.

From the campground, the trail follows the north bank of John-John Creek toward Brazeau Lake. Look for golden eagle nests in the cliffs on the north side of the valley. As the John John valley opens into the valley of Brazeau Lake, the trail descends steeply through a forest of spruce and lodgepole pine. You cross John-John Creek and enter the debris of the Brazeau Lake Slide.

From the slide, look across Brazeau Lake for "the mark of Zorro" – a z-shaped, reddish-coloured fold in an unnamed peak. The trail continues southeast, climbing into lodgepole pine forest that offers only partial views of nearby Brazeau Lake. A steep descent

east through spruce-fir forest leads to the lake's outlet – the beginnings of the Northwest Brazeau River – and a bridge that provides easy passage over the torrent. Look for harlequin ducks in the fast-flowing water, and bald eagles in the nearby trees. Across the river, turn northwest (left) to reach Brazeau Lake campground (400 m) and the trail to the lakeshore. Turn southeast (right) to continue the loop.

From the campground, a rough track leads along the northeast shore of Brazeau Lake. With a length of 5 km, a maximum width of 900 m, and an area of 360 ha, the lake is one of the larger ones in the backcountry of the Rockies. It is fed by meltwater from the 25 km^2 Brazeau Icefield, to the north. In that direction you can see Mt. Henry McLeod (3315 m) – named for a railway surveyor who was the first white man known to have seen Maligne Lake. Look for moose in the bay across the lake. This is a fine campground in a wonderful setting. If you wanted to build a "day off" into this outing, this would be the place to take it.

JOSEPH BRAZEAU

The features bearing the name "Brazeau" commemorate Joseph Brazeau, a trader, clerk, and postmaster with the Hudson's Bay Company. Brazeau worked at fur trade outposts along the eastern edge of the Rockies from 1852 to 1864. With his knowledge of native languages, Brazeau was a great help to the Palliser Expedition. James Hector named the river for him in 1860. The lake and mountain were named by A.P. Coleman in 1892 and 1902, respectively. The mountain had appeared on earlier maps as "Mt. McGillivray," commemorating fur trader, Duncan McGillivray.

Brazeau Lake to Four Point Campground

From the outlet of Brazeau Lake, follow the river southeast for 2.9 km to a junction. Turn south (right), and cross the river on a high bridge to the Brazeau River campground. The following 3.2 km of trail undulates over ancient rockslides forested with lodgepole pine.

After traversing high above the cleft of a canyon, the trail descends to the main branch of the Brazeau River and crosses to its east bank. The hiking immediately improves, with expansive vistas of the broad Brazeau Valley and surrounding peaks. Marble Mountain (2962 m) is to the north. By technical definition, "marble" is limestone or dolomite that has been recrystalized through heat or pressure. True marble is rare in the Rockies. However, marble can also refer to any carbonate sedimentary rock that can be polished. Glacial polishing has created an abundance of this kind of "marble" in the Rockies.

The Brazeau River cuts across the northwest-southeast grain, or strike of the Rockies. The Bow, Athabasca, North Saskatchewan, Red Deer, and Clearwater rivers also do this. These rivers are older than the mountains. Their downward erosion kept pace with uplift during mountain building, allowing the rivers to maintain their unlikely courses.

Wolverine South campground is a wonderful stopping place for those who would like to extend their time in the Brazeau Valley. Views to the southwest include Mt. Athabasca (3442 m) on the fringe of the Columbia Icefield, 20 km distant. We have seen a golden eagle and a Swainson's hawk here. Wolf tracks often decorate the mud. Look for harlequin ducks. The trail recrosses the Brazeau River on a bridge, and alternating between shrub meadows and pine forest, completes the loop back to Four Point campground. From here, it's a day's hike over familiar ground to the Icefields Parkway via Nigel Pass.

29. Wilcox Pass

Wilcox Pass

When Walter Wilcox travelled north from Lake Louise in 1896, his party hit a roadblock in the upper Sunwapta Valley. The terrific jumble of the Mt. Kitchener Slide, and the resulting gorge on the Sunwapta River, made direct travel from Sunwapta Pass into the Sunwapta Valley impossible for horses. Wilcox's guide, Fred Stephens, detoured by climbing over a pass to the northeast, to regain the Sunwapta Valley farther north. The Wilcox Pass-Tangle Creek trail retraces this historic route, offering panoramic views of the peaks and glaciers near the Columbia Icefield. If you plan to descend into Tangle Creek, pre-arrange transportation for the end of the hike. Those who don't mind a stiff hill climb (followed by a bigger downhill!) after a good hike, might consider stashing a bike.

TRAIL THUMBNAIL

Day-hike

Route	Elev. (m)	Dist. (km)
Trailhead	2040	0
Wilcox Pass	2375	4.5
North end of pass	2320	7.4
Tangle Falls	1830	12.0

Trailhead
At Wilcox Creek campground, on the east side of the Icefields Parkway; 121.5 km north of Highway 1; 103.7 km south of Highway 16; 3.0 km south of the Icefield Centre. The trailhead is on the north side of the campground access road.

Maps
NTS: 83 C/3, 83 C/6
Gem Trek: *Columbia Icefield*

Best lighting: any time

VARIATIONS

- Hike to the pass; 9.0 km return.
- Hike to the north end of the pass; 14.8 km return.
- Traverse the pass to Tangle Falls; 12.0 km.

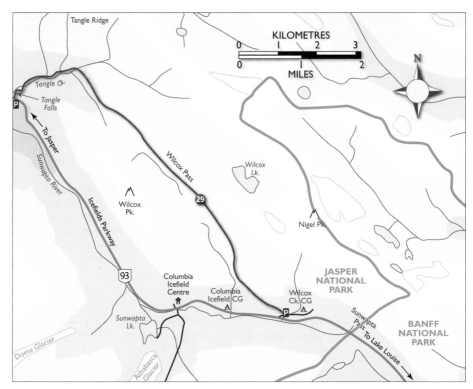

Trailhead to Wilcox Pass

From the trailhead at the entrance to Wilcox Creek campground, the trail climbs steeply into an ancient forest of Engelmann spruce. They aren't giants, but many of these trees – stunted by the glacial chill – are 300 years to 350 years old. The oldest known Engelmann spruce in Jasper National Park – approximately 700 years – grows 3 km west of here. The high stumps you see are from trees cut for bridge timbers during construction of the original Icefields Parkway in the late 1930s.

You reach treeline in just 1 km, on a cliff edge that overlooks the Icefields Parkway. In the view south, from left to right, the features are Mt. Athabasca

(3442 m), Mt. Andromeda (3450 m), Athabasca Glacier, Snow Dome (3451 m), Dome Glacier, and Mt. Kitchener (3480 m). J.N. Collie and Hermann Woolley made the first ascent of Mt. Athabasca in 1898. From its summit, they claimed the "discovery" of the Columbia Icefield. Today, Mt. Athabasca is probably the most frequently ascended alpine peak in the Rockies. Look for climbers on the icy faces of this mountain, and on Mt. Andromeda.

GOOD STEW, NIGEL!

Nigel Vavasour was the cook on the 1898 expedition that made the first ascent of Mt. Athabasca and claimed "discovery" of the Columbia Icefield. The expedition included mountaineers John Norman Collie, Herman Woolley, and Hugh Stutfield, with guide Bill Peyto (PEE-toe). On the way north from Lake Louise, the party lost many supplies when testy pack horses plunged into the North Saskatchewan River. The larder was almost empty before serious climbing could begin. While Collie and Woolley claimed glory on the heights of Mt. Athabasca, Stutfield and Peyto bagged bighorn sheep near Nigel Pass, in an area that they called the "Wild Sheep Hills." The sheep stew that became the party's staple for the next two weeks must have been a success, for Collie applied the cook's name to several features nearby.

There remained a high grassy pass to the right, and here after reaching an elevation of 8000 feet, we were encouraged by seeing a long valley running north-west, which we knew must be some part of the Athabasca River. Thus the most critical part of our expedition, the discovery of a pass between the Saskatchewan and Athabasca, was safely accomplished.

Walter Wilcox; *Camping in the Rockies*

Bighorn ram

pass include mountain goat, grizzly bear, moose, wolverine, and golden eagle. I have seen falcons, killdeer, and green-winged teals. In early August, the showy, white tufts of the sedge, cotton-grass, decorate many of the ponds in the height of the pass. If you do not wish to carry on to Tangle Creek, retrace your route to the trailhead.

Wilcox Pass to Tangle Falls

The trail becomes indistinct as you head northwest across the pass. Work your way upslope toward Wilcox Peak – following occasional cairns – to gain the rocky bench about 20 m above the level of the pass. Please walk side by side and spread out to avoid repetitive trampling of vegetation. Continue north on this bench, usually without benefit of defined trail. The blooms of sawwort, dwarf columbine, stonecrop, and alpine hawksbeard colour the screes.

At the north end of the bench, look for a faint track that descends northeast to upper Tangle Creek. This track soon becomes a well-beaten trail. The glaciated summits of Mt. Woolley (3405 m), Diadem Peak (3371 m) and Mushroom Peak (3210 m) are grouped together in the northwest. *Diadem* is Latin for "crown," and refers to the snowy crest of the mountain. Mountaineer, N.E. Odell named Mushroom Peak for another snow feature – a cornice that he noticed when he made the first ascent, solo, in 1947.

The trail veers north from the edge of the cliff and begins a rambling ascent through stands of ragged kruppelholz, along the principal stream that drains Wilcox Pass. Nigel Peak (3211 m) rises to the east.

Wilcox Pass is alpine tundra at its best – a broad, U-shaped valley, 3 km in length. The large cairn that marks the height of land is the ultimate destination for most hikers, but the slopes either side of the pass beckon. You might consider following a faint trail that curves around the end of the northwest ridge of Nigel Peak to Wilcox Lake. Wildflowers and wildlife abound. Flocks of bighorn sheep – often exclusively composed of rams – congregate on lingering snow patches, seeking escape from heat and bugs. I have only taken the safety off a bear spray a few times in the backcountry. Once was here, when a bighorn ram approached head down, with menace in his eye. I finally scared him off by calling him things that I won't repeat. Other wildlife species that frequent the

DISAPPEARING ICE AND DISAPPEARING WATER

Ice abounds in the view south and west from the approach to Wilcox Pass; some of the glaciers are officially named, some have nicknames. Boundary and "Little A" glaciers cloak Mt. Athabasca. The "A-A glacier" lies between Mt. Athabasca and Mt. Andromeda, which sports two unnamed glaciers. Athabasca Glacier is the principal glacier in view. "Little Dome" and Dome glaciers cascade from Snow Dome. Athabasca Glacier receded 1.6 km, and decreased 57 percent in area, and 32 percent in volume between 1870 and 1971. Glaciologists estimate that in the summer of 1998, the glacier lost 5 percent of its mass.

All of these glaciers are directly or loosely connected with the Columbia Icefield – the largest icefield in the Rockies. Meltwater from this 230 km2 body of ice feeds three of the continent's great river systems: the Columbia, the Saskatchewan, and the Athabasca/Mackenzie; and thus three oceans: the Pacific, the Atlantic, and the Arctic.

The glacially streamlined form of Wilcox Peak (2884 m) borders the west side of Wilcox Pass. Walter Wilcox and his companion, R.L. Barrett, made the first ascent in 1896. Wilcox Lake is concealed from view on the east side of the pass, at

the foot of Nigel Peak. The lake has no surface outlet, indicating underground drainage in the limestone bedrock. A large spring along Nigel Creek, 5 km south, is thought to be the emergence of the underground stream.

Tangle Falls

The domed summit of Tangle Ridge (3000 m) is due north. Later in the descent, you obtain a view of Mt. Alberta (3619 m), tucked in behind Mt. Woolley. Mt. Alberta is the 6th-highest mountain in the Canadian Rockies and is one of the more difficult to climb. This, and Parker Ridge, are the only maintained hiking trails from which you can see it.

You reach the sources of Tangle Creek in a large willow meadow. After entering the forest and crossing the creek to its south bank, the trail comes to an opening on a rise. In the view west beyond the icebound summits of Stutfield Peak (3450 m), you might pick out the shoulder of North Twin (3731 m), the 3rd-highest mountain in the Rockies, and the 2nd-highest in Alberta. There is an old campsite in the clearing below this rise, with tepee poles still stacked against the trees. The following clearing contains the ruins of a cabin. Jimmy Simpson or Bill Peyto may have built it in the early 1900s, to serve them on their winter trap lines.

The trail soon emerges from forest at the top of a grassy slope, 120 m above the Icefields Parkway. Bighorn sheep frequent this area. Descend south to the grade of the "Wonder Road," forerunner of the Icefields Parkway. Follow this track north (right) to Tangle Falls and trail's end. The bedrock of the falls is Cambrian-aged, Mistaya Formation limestone. Outfitters call untracked bush "shin tangle." Mary Schäffer named Tangle Creek and falls in 1907 after a trying descent from Wilcox Pass. From Tangle Falls it is 9.8 km south along the Icefields Parkway to the trailhead.

30. Maligne Pass

Maligne Pass

On a fair day, Maligne (mah-LEEN) Pass is a glory – the match of any alpine environment in the Rockies. Although only a single ridge separates you from the Icefields Parkway, the pass is a remote place, the wilderness haunt of grizzly bears and caribou. You share the trail with horses.

TRAIL THUMBNAIL

Day-hike or overnight

Route	Elev. (m)	Dist. (km)
Trailhead	1540	0
Maligne Pass jct	1710	6.1
Poboktan Creek CG	1765	+1.3
Avalanche CG	2040	11.2
Maligne Pass	2220	15.2

Trailhead
South side of Poboktan Creek on the east side of the Icefields Parkway; 69.9 km south of Highway 16; 30.8 km north of the Icefield Centre; 155.3 km north of Highway 1.

Maps
NTS: 83 C/6, 83 C/11, and 83 C/12

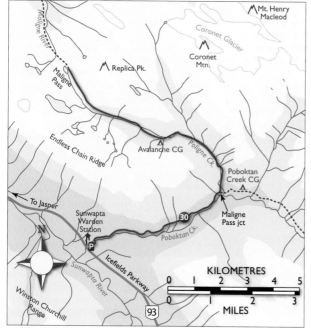

KILOMETRES

0 1 2 3 4 5

0 1 2 3

MILES

Trailhead to Maligne Pass Junction

In 2010, the bridge across Poboktan (po-BOCK-tan) Creek, adjacent to the trailhead, was decommissioned. If the bridge has not been replaced, use the highway bridge to cross the creek. Hike between the warden station and the creek to meet the trail proper in about 125 m. If the hiker bridge has been rebuilt,

VARIATIONS

- Day-hike the pass; 30.4 km return.
- Camp at Avalanche CG and explore the pass over the next day or two.
- If you are getting a late start, you can go as far as Poboktan Creek campground on the first day. This will add 2.6 km to the outing.

The new pass was a duplication of all other passes, soft and spongy; our aneroid showed the altitude as 7200 feet. Long patches of snow made the travelling very heavy, but the pass was a short one, and, with the saddle-horses ahead breaking the way, we were not long in getting over.

Mary Schäffer; *Old Indian Trails of the Canadian Rockies*

use it to cross the creek, then turn east (right).

For decades, the Poboktan Creek trail has been an artery into the Brazeau backcountry. In places, the wide trail isn't pretty – it's chewed by horse traffic – but the vegetation at trailside provides distraction. You begin in a forest dominated by Engelmann spruce. Twinflower, northern gentian, dwarf dogwood, yellow columbine, and fireweed grow in the understory. After about 700 m, the trail draws alongside the rambunctious creek. If the water is up you may hear boulders rolling down the creekbed. For once, the native name for this creek does not mean "turbulent water." *Poboktan* is a Stoney word for "owl." Mountaineer, A.P. Coleman, gave the name to the creek, and to the pass at its head, in 1892.

The first 2 km of trail reveals a subtle aspect of the geological blueprint of the Rockies. You are hiking beside Poboktan Creek, so you might expect that you are ascending the Poboktan Valley. But take a look at the topographic map. You are still in the Sunwapta Valley. The ice-age glacier that most recently carved this valley was much larger than the glacier that carved the Poboktan Valley. At the end of the Late Wisconsin Glaciation, Poboktan Creek probably emptied from its valley in a waterfall. Subsequent downward erosion of the creek has blurred that abrupt transition. Between the trailhead and the mouth of the Poboktan Valley, you climb over a series of low rises. These could be old river terraces of the Sunwapta River. (Yes, *Sunwapta* is Stoney for "turbulent water.")

If you look south through the trees, you may catch glimpses of the rim of the Columbia Icefield on Mount Kitchener (3480 m). The trail contours around the edge of a quartzite boulderslide on the southeast end of Endless Chain Ridge and enters an open forest of mature lodgepole pines. You will see small pines growing in the understory. When a forest survives long enough for trees of the same species to propagate, it is said to be a climax forest. The lodgepole pine is a fire-dependent species and is relatively short-lived in the Rockies – 75-200 years. It is not often that lodgepoles form a climax forest. However, lodgepoles have an affinity for quartzite bedrock, so this type of forest is more common in the front ranges of Jasper than elsewhere in the Rockies. Bracted lousewort, Labrador tea, fleabanes, white camas, paintbrush, dwarf blueberry, wild strawberry, and crowberry grow beneath the trees. I have seen a

Maligne Pass

pair of ravens here, gleaning tiny, red grouseberries from trailside.

About 5 km from the trailhead, you have views southeast through the trees to Poboktan Mountain (3323 m), the highest peak in the valley. The trail draws alongside the creek again at a small beach – a pleasant place to take a break. Looking down the creek, you can see the northerly peaks of the Winston Churchill Range on the west side of the Sunwapta Valley. The British statesman did not climb in those mountains, but he did climb the Matterhorn when a young lad. In a wet spot just beyond the beach, I saw the tracks and leavings of a large wolf and a smaller one, and a moose. You climb away from the creek again – travelling a section of trail that has been ditched and mounded to improve drainage – to where Poligne Creek comes

STRAIGHT UP AND NARROW

Lodgepole pine forests cloak the major valley bottoms of the montane life zone in the Rockies. Such forests often indicate where large forest fires occurred in the recent past. Lodgepole cones require temperatures above 45°C to release their seeds; hence the tree's reliance on forest fires for propa-

gation. The resulting doghair forests of tightly-spaced saplings crowd out other tree species. The long needles of the lodgepole pine are in pairs. In late June, lodgepoles release their pollen in thick clouds. That's the yellow scum you see on lakes and puddles. This tree is not the same as jack pine, which grows east of the Rockies.

Lodgepoles are susceptible to infestation by mountain pine beetles, which have affected more than half of the trees in some valleys. The beetles engrave tunnels beneath the cambium layer of the tree, in the sapwood that sustains new growth. The tunnels cut off the sap flow, killing the tree. The foliage will be reddish-brown in the summer after the attack; changing to gray the following summer.

Parasitic, pine dwarf mistletoe also afflicts lodgepole pines, sometimes causing a tree's branches to grow in dense clumps called brooms.

For First Peoples who travelled in the mountains, lodgepole pines offered poles for making travois and tepees. A mature tree, unless it is slow-growing, is free of branches on the lower two-thirds of its trunk. European explorers copied the practice of tent-making with this tree. I have seen stacks of ancient poles in many places along trails in the Rockies. You may be puzzled by the contradiction inherent in the typically arrow-straight trunks of this tree species, and its Latin species name, *contorta*. The tree was first catalogued in coastal California, where it is typically twisted in form. The coastal variety is now known as shore pine.

The oldest recorded lodgepole, a tree in Yoho's McArthur Creek valley, was 454 years when cored in the late 1980s. The tallest lodgepole known is 46.34 m, in BC's Manning Provincial Park. The lodgepole pine is the provincial tree of Alberta.

rushing down from the north. Turn north (left) at the junction just before the creek. If you would like to camp nearby, you can use Poboktan Creek campground, 1.3 km to the south (right).

Maligne Pass Junction to Avalanche Campground

Poligne (derived from POboktan and MaLIGNE) is a better handle than "Maboktan" would have been, but it seems a shame that more imagination did not go into naming the creek. By the time you reach the pass, you will be well acquainted with this watercourse – having crossed it and its tributary eight times on bridges. The first of these is just 200 m north of the junction, where the creek emerges from a slabby canyon. Grind away up the east bank on the steepest grade of the hike.

CARTS BEFORE HORSES

If you have been to Maligne Lake, you may have wondered at the skookum bridge over its outlet. It looks out of place. It is. In 1971, Parks Canada unveiled its Provisional Master Plans for the four mountain parks. Conceived by bureaucrats without any involvement of the public, the plans called for the upgrading of existing fireroads and the construction of new roads. Lots of them: Howse Pass, Cascade Valley, Red Deer-Pipestone, Fortress Lake, Redearth Creek, Wapta Falls, Ottertail, Amiskwi, Otterhead, Kicking Horse, Beaverfoot, Yoho Valley, and Maligne Pass-Poboktan Creek. Some of the road alignments were partially cut – the first km of the Wapta Falls trail in Yoho is an example. The public responded with outrage and the feds dropped the plans. Those who love wild places owe a great deal to the fledgling environmentalists who spoke out against those proposals more than four decades ago. The public consultation process we have today, although not ideal, is a legacy of the debacle of 1971. That and a bridge built for a road that – thanks to subsequent legislation – should never again be entertained.

At the top of this climb, the trail swings north (left) and descends slightly. Note the transition in the forest that took place on the climb, from lower subalpine to upper subalpine. You soon cross to the west side of the creek to bypass a section where avalanche slopes run right to the valley floor. The trail is rough here and wet. Judging from the tracks I saw, caribou are frequent visitors. Perhaps they enjoy munching on the sedges. The third crossing of Poligne Creek delivers you onto the shingle flat of a tributary that emerges from a rock glacier. There are boulders of Gog conglomerate here – 600-million-year-old concrete made from pebbles cemented together with quartz. The fourth creek crossing spans the mouth of the north fork of Poligne Creek, a tributary that has a reputation as a bridge basher. When I last hiked it, the trail had been re-routed north to bypass a spot where the old bridge was washed out and partially buried. Note how most backcountry bridges in Jasper are built from trees felled on-site. The locations of usable trees often dictate the placement of the resulting bridge.

You now have creeks on either side of you for a short distance, as the trail swings northwest. Cross Poligne Creek again to its west bank. The forest thins as you traverse a sideslope, with the boulder gardens and the cascades of the creek below. The bedrock here is Gog Formation siltstone and conglomerate. Look and listen for dippers. Coronet Mountain (3152 m) is to the east. American alpinist, Howard Palmer, named it for the shape of a snow formation high on the peak. Another footbridge takes you over to the east bank, with a view upvalley and across valley to the "back side" of Endless Chain Ridge. But what will likely catch your eye is underfoot – a bank of rusty, quartzite sand, eroded from the Gog bedrock. I saw stonecrop growing here, its yellow bloom flaming against the reddish-brown sand. The trail becomes something akin to muskeg just before it crosses Poligne Creek above a small canyon. Avalanche Campground is 40 m downstream on the west bank, set in a small clearing.

Avalanche Campground to Maligne Pass

The trail beyond the campground is an immediate disappointment and may try your patience. Sketchy, vague, spongy, mucky – it's all these things. But when there is this much moisture in the subalpine life zone there is usually a great display of wildflowers, and in this regard you won't be disappointed. Frosted paintbrush, valerian, elephant-head, arnica, fleabane, bluebottle gentian, groundsel, alpine speedwell, and bracted lousewort cover the tread. Watch where you step.

If you have hiked Jonas Pass from south to north, you may get a sense of the familiar as you approach Maligne Pass. The aspect is similar, as is the elevation, and the fact that both passes are sandwiched between quartzite mountains. Another similarity – caribou and grizzly bears frequent both passes.

About 1 km beyond the campground, you make the last bridged creek crossing of the ascent. The trail is very poor just beyond but then improves as it climbs away from the valley bottom – something it probably should have done a kilometre back. Lakes on the west side of the valley drain into Poligne Creek in a series of waterfalls. Pause during the climb to look downvalley for the great view toward Poboktan Pass. At the conclusion of the climb, you leave the last of the trees behind and begin a sidehill traverse into the pass. On my second visit I got hung up in traffic here. A large porcupine set off – as porcupines often do when fleeing – directly along the trail. I was finally obliged to say, "Excuse me," as I stepped around it in order to carry on.

Maligne Pass

Like a blue gem dropped into a setting of green, an unnamed lake, about 350 m long and ringed by rock on two shores, nestles in Maligne Pass. When you first see the lake, you also get your first view north to the glaciated summit of Mt. Unwin (3268 m). Sid Unwin was guide to Mary Schäffer in 1908, in her quest for Maligne Lake. After weeks on the trail with no sight of the fabled lake, Unwin set off alone one afternoon to ascend the eastern side of the upper Maligne River valley, hoping for an instructive view. In this he was successful. Schäffer named the peak for him, and Unwin has been credited with the first ascent, although it is more likely that he reached the lesser, subsidiary summit to the west. As was the case with so many of his contemporaries, Unwin fell in combat in WWI.

The trail skirts above the lake's east shore to the crest of the pass, which is marked with an artful cairn. Views ahead now include the series of peaks that flank the east side of the upper Maligne River. Closest is the massive humpback form of Mt. Mary Vaux (3201 m), named by Schäffer for her companion on the expeditions of 1907 and 1908. A member of a Philadelphia family famous for its interest in glaciers of the Rockies and Selkirks, Mary Vaux also had a keen interest in botany. She was the first woman to climb a mountain over 10,000 feet in Canada (Mt. Stephen). She later married Charles Walcott, director of the Smithsonian Institution. Vaux named Llysyfran Peak (3141 m), also in view, for a Welsh relative. Mt. Charlton (3217 m) is partially visible, to the east of Mt. Unwin. Henry Charlton was the advertising agent for the Grant Trunk Pacific Railway. Mary Schäffer named the peak for him in 1911, when the GTPR subsidized her second trip to Maligne Lake. On the west side of the pass, the Endless Chain Ridge carries on with no end in sight. Schäffer named the

ridge in 1907. She watched it parade by for the better part of a week as she rode the trail in the Sunwapta Valley.

The lake on the pass drains south into Poligne Creek. The tiny creek that crosses the trail just north of the cairn, drains north – the first gatherings of the Maligne River. *Maligne* is one of the older place-names in the Rockies. It's French for "wicked." The name was already in use when Father Pierre-Jean De Smet travelled the Athabasca Valley in 1846. Wicked is hardly a sentiment for the environs of the pass; "maligne" refers to the difficult ford of the river's mouth.

I have seen horned larks and American pipits in the meadows near the lake, and a mother blue-winged teal with a brood of six ducklings on the water. Other birds I have heard near the pass are white-crowned sparrows, boreal chickadees, and mountain chickadees. Judging from my informal census, the benches west of the pass may be the hoary marmot capital of the Rockies. Scan the wet meadows north of the pass carefully – this is great habitat for caribou.

The steep screes of Replica Peak (2794 m) rise east of Maligne Pass. Mountaineer Howard Palmer applied the name in 1923 to a presently unnamed mountain to the northeast, which he thought to be a replica of Coronet Mountain. As is often the case, a cartographer put the name in the wrong place and there it stuck. A trek to the summit of Replica Peak – best accomplished from a departure point downvalley to the south – will probably be on the minds of mountaineers. For those more content to ramble the meadowlands and benches, I'll let Maligne Pass divulge its many secret places to you.

ALPINE SPEEDWELL

Many flowering plants of the alpine life zone have blue or purple flowers, which helps them to withstand intense solar radiation. You'll have to take off our sunglasses to spot the tiny blooms of alpine speedwell. The common name of this plant recalls its use as a folk medicine cure. Tinctures and powders were prescribed for everything from blood disorders to kidney stones.

31. Fryatt Valley

Fryatt Valley

After a long approach during which the scenic interest builds gradually, the Fryatt Valley hike culminates in a wonderland of lakelets, pools, meadows, glaciers, disappearing rivers, and savage peaks – all that is classic about the Canadian Rockies. Black bears and grizzly bears frequent the approach trail. You share the trail with mountain bikers as far as the first campground.

Trailhead to Lower Fryatt Campground

The outing begins with an easy fireroad walk along the west bank of the Athabasca River through a fire succession forest of lodgepole pine. The resin-sealed cones of the lodgepole generally require the heat of a forest fire to open, resulting in a mass seeding that produces even-aged stands of trees. The fire that helped create most of these trees took place in 1889, when much of the Athabasca Valley in what is now Jasper National Park burned.

Wetlands flank the trail. These sloughs were formerly kettle lakes, created by melting blocks of ice at the end of the Late Wisconsin Glaciation. The lakes have filled with sediments that now support aquatic vegetation – creating good habitat for moose. At km 2.0 the trail crosses the braided outlet stream from the Geraldine Lakes. Over millennia, the stream has built an alluvial fan from the shales it has carried down the mountainside. It sometimes knocks out the trail bridges and turns the tread into a watercourse.

> On the Athabasca side, glaciers occupy the heads of the gorges... With the many lakes it is an attractive corner of the range and in future should become a worth-while objective for mountain travelers.
>
> Howard Palmer; *Appalachia 1926*

TRAIL THUMBNAIL

Overnight, 3-4 days

Route	Elev. (m)	Dist. (km)
Trailhead	1215	0
Athabasca River	1210	7.2
Athabasca Valley viewpoint	1240	8.6
Lower Fryatt CG	1280	11.6
Fryatt Creek bridge	1605	15.9
Brussels CG	1660	17.2
Fryatt Lake	1715	18.7
Headwall CG	1780	21.1
Sydney Vallance Hut	2000	22.0
Upper Fryatt Valley	2035	23.2

Trailhead
Follow the Icefields Parkway to the junction with Highway 93A at Athabasca Falls, 29.8 km south of Highway 16, 70.9 km north of the Icefield Centre. Turn west and follow Highway 93A, 1.1 km to the Fryatt Valley-Geraldine Lakes road. This gravel road may be gated, however the gate should not be locked unless the area is closed. Follow this road 2.1 km south to the signed trailhead for Fryatt Valley.

Maps
NTS: 83 C/12, 83 C/5

You may have to rock-hop the stream and pick your way for a short distance. Trembling aspen and cottonwood poplar trees grow here.

The pleasant stroll through the forest continues. At km 7.2, the trail draws alongside the Athabasca River, with the Icefields Parkway just 150 m away on the opposite bank. The sediment-choked waters are a formidable barrier to travel. In the 1800s, the voyageurs of the fur trade called their route across Athabasca Pass, *la grande traverse* – "the great crossing" – in reference to the difficult ford of this river. From the riverbank, you can imagine the harrowing prospect of having to cross this torrent on foot, on horseback, or in a makeshift raft.

At km 8.0 the trail veers away from the river and climbs over a knoll covered in a doghair forest of lodgepole pine. The trail emerges from the forest above the confluence of Lick Creek and the Athabasca River, atop a bank of glacial till. Till is a thick blanket of sediment and rubble left behind by glaciers and, here, it is rich in sulphur-bearing minerals. Deer, elk, and mountain goats congregate here to lick at the sediments, thereby obtaining a natural dietary supplement. The minerals are especially important to mountain goats during late spring, when they shed their winter coats. You may see goat wool on the shrubs and tree bark, and goat tracks and their pellet-like droppings on the trail nearby.

The tremendous breadth of the Athabasca Valley fills the view south. It is hard to imagine that this valley was filled with glacial ice a kilometre thick during the Late Wisconsin Glaciation. You reach Lower Fryatt campground at km 11.6. This stopping place is on an alluvial fan beside the considerable torrent of Fryatt Creek. It is likely to be chilly here at night, as cold air will drain along Fryatt Creek. This is the end of the mountain bike trail.

Lower Fryatt Campground to Upper Fryatt Valley

Cross the creek on a good bridge. The forest becomes subalpine in character as you ascend the shaded slope toward the mouth of the Fryatt Valley. A quartzite spire to the north stands guard over the entrance to the valley. The layers of rock on this outlying peak of Mt. Fryatt dip steeply to the southwest, indicating that they are part of the western arm of an anticline. The Athabasca Valley has been eroded downward through this massive, arch-shaped fold. There are many streams to hop at the valley mouth. Two of these are silty. They drain a glacially fed lake on the north slope of Mt. Christie.

The grade eases, and the trail soon crosses to the northwest bank of Fryatt Creek. From here you obtain your first, tantalizing views of the upper Fryatt Valley. Although the surrounding mountainsides rise steeply, the valley floor here feels open after travel through the confined forest below. The trail is rocky and vague in places. Rock-hop and follow cairns. I recommend Brussels campground if you want to day-hike to the upper Fryatt Valley. Although Headwall campground is closer to the main attractions, it is a poor camping place, best avoided.

The alluvial fan beyond Brussels campground is a product of debris flows and meltwater surges from the tributary valley to the north. The fan almost completely fills the valley floor, forcing Fryatt Creek

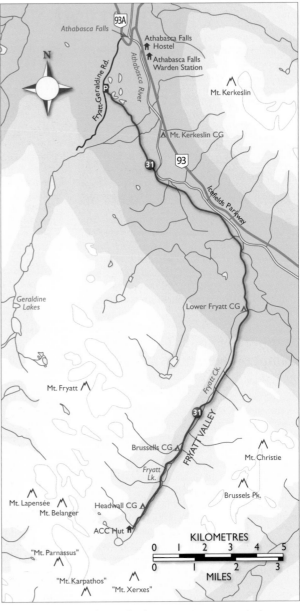

to the south. The constriction impounds the waters of Fryatt Lake. You obtain your first view of this beautiful body of water as the trail climbs over the fan. The waterfall that drains the upper valley graces the headwall beyond. The glaciated summits are the "Three Blind Mice" (2720 m) to the south (left), and "Mt. Xerxes" (ZURK-seas) (2970 m). Brussels Peak appears formidable viewed from here. At the base of its southwest ridge you can see a series of pinnacles that resembles a miniature Stonehenge.

Rock-hop streams on the alluvial fan, and descend to Fryatt Lake. Follow a rough track along the northwest shore to Headwall campground. Headwall is a graphic example of where *not* to place a campground. It is among cow parsnip at the base of a large avalanche slope, a possible haven for grizzly bears. Tent sites are close to the trail. The campground is shaded in the evening and in the early morning. Brrrr!

Beyond the campground, you climb steeply to the base of the 200 m high headwall that separates the upper and lower valleys. This headwall is one of the more unpleasant sections of "trail" in the Rockies. Outrageously steep and poorly defined in places, the ascent is more a scramble than a hike. But the grunt is over in less than a kilometre. From the top of the climb, you are rewarded with magnificent views northeast over Fryatt Valley. But you will soon want to turn your back on them. The views are even better to the southwest.

Upper Fryatt Valley

From the top of the headwall, the raw beauty of the Rockies unfurls with splendour and grace in the upper Fryatt Valley. Fryatt Creek collects in a small pool known as "The Roman Bath." Fringed with meadow and subalpine forest, this pool creates an idyllic foreground for the exquisite arrangement of glaciated mountains beyond. Switching themes from Roman to Persian to Greek to voyageur, the mountains are, from south to north: "Mt. Xerxes" (ZURK-seas) (2970 m), named for the ruthless Persian king of 486-465, BC; "Mt. Karpathos" (2987 m), named for a Greek island; "Mt. Parnassus" (2905 m), named for a Greek mountain of the same name; and Mt. Belanger (bell-ON-zjay) (3120 m), named for André Belanger, a fur trader who crossed Athabasca Pass in 1814, and

BEAR ALLEY

Buffaloberry is a common shrub in the pine forests that cloak the Athabasca Valley, and is a principal reason why bears frequent the Fryatt Valley trail. The shrub's glossy, dark green leaves are pale and fuzzy underneath, with rust coloured dots. The red and amber berries, which ripen in late July and early August, are a summer staple of bears. At that time, they may comprise up to 95 percent of a black bear's diet. An adult grizzly bear may eat 200,000 of these berries a day – a fact that will leave you asking two questions. How does a bear eat something as small as a buffaloberry? Not one at a time. It threshes the branches of the shrub through its jaws, getting a mouth full of berries and leaves. How do we know that a bear eats that many berries? Some dedicated researcher followed a bear around, picked through its scats, and, using some unknown formula, rendered the estimate. To us, the buffaloberry is sweet, but has a repulsive aftertaste.

If the berry crop is on, you should make lots of noise while hiking this trail. Bears will often be preoccupied with feeding, and may not hear you approach. If a bear perceives you as a threat to its food source, it might become aggressive. Scats containing red berries, tracks in muddy areas, and damage to the shrubs will warn you that a bear is nearby.

FROM ICEFIELD TO OCEAN

From its sources on the northern edge of the Columbia Icefield, the Athabasca River flows 1230 km to Lake Athabasca in northeastern Alberta. Its waters eventually reach the Arctic Ocean via the Mackenzie river system. *Athabasca* is Cree for "place where there are reeds," referring to the delta at the river's mouth. (Unfortunately, the namesake plants are sedges, not reeds.) The name was one of the earlier to be used by Europeans in the Rockies, possibly in 1790. The 168 km section of the Athabasca River within Jasper National Park was designated a Canadian Heritage River in 1989.

who subsequently drowned in the Athabasca River just east of the Rockies.

The Alpine Club of Canada's Sydney Vallance Hut, built in 1970, is located nearby. To carry on, follow the trail southwest from the hut to the first tributary stream. Keep straight ahead, hop the stream and cross a wet meadow to cliffs where cairns define the route.

The limestone bedrock of the upper valley exhibits remarkable karst features. The first example was the pool above the headwall. It drains underground into the waterfall. Now you will see where Fryatt Creek disappears into, and emerges from, various underground channels. The final act in the scenic drama of the Fryatt Valley is revealed when the trail winds through a boulder garden, and descends to the shore of an unnamed lake at the foot of extensive moraines below "Mt. Karpathos." This is the arrangement of cliff, tarn, meadow, and glacier that, for so many hikers, epitomizes the Canadian Rockies.

The upper Fryatt Valley offers tremendous opportunities for wandering and exploration. If you choose to travel off-trail, please spread out to avoid repetitive trampling of the fragile upper subalpine vegetation. Do not venture onto glacial ice unless you are experienced and properly equipped for glacier travel.

LEFT HANGING

Fryatt Valley is a textbook example of a hanging valley. During the Late Wisconsin Glaciation, glaciers in tributary valleys did not erode as deeply as did the ancestral Athabasca Valley glacier. As a result, when the glacial ice receded, the tributary valleys were left hanging above the floor of the Athabasca Valley. Have a look at the topographic map. The contour lines on the southwestern slope of the Athabasca Valley – either side of Fryatt Creek – describe a uniform cliff, more than 15 km in length. Through this cliff, Fryatt Creek and the streams that drain other valleys to the north and south, plunge toward the Athabasca Valley.

32. Tonquin Valley

The Ramparts from Surprise Point

The lofty, unbroken precipice of The Ramparts, towering over the Amethyst Lakes, is the prize vista of the Tonquin Valley. It's a postcard view, known around the world. If you can time your visit to the lakes to coincide with fair weather, you will grab the prize and rave about the place. If you show up during a wet spell, you may find that the crowds, the muck, and the mosquitoes take the shine off things. The Tonquin Valley receives twice as much precipitation as Jasper town. There is no question that solitude is hard to find, except perhaps late in the season. Keep alert. Bear warnings are often posted

for the Astoria, Portal, and Eremite valleys. Jasper's only known instance of a human death caused by a grizzly bear took place on this loop.

Trailhead to Surprise Point Junction

The road-width trail descends to the outlet of Cavell Lake. From the bridge, you have an inspiring view south to Mt. Edith Cavell (3363 m), the highest mountain in this area, and the 19th-highest in Alberta. Surveyor A.O. Wheeler named the mountain for an English nurse, Edith Cavell. Remaining

One realizes instinctively in the valley of the Tonquin that the carving of its great rock spires is still in the formative stage. The work is still going on; the mountains are but roughly hewn out, with an impressionistic technique as fantastic as it is fanciful.

James Monroe Thorington; *The Glittering Mountains of Canada*

TRAIL THUMBNAIL

Overnight, 3-5 days

Route	Elev. (m)	Dist. (km)
Astoria trailhead	1738	0
Astoria CG	1692	6.8
Chrome Lake jct	1695	8.2
Switchback CG jct	2100	13.8
Switchback CG	2100	+0.2
Surprise Point jct	1979	16.8
Clitheroe CG	1980	+0.1
Surprise Point CG	1900	+2.2
Amethyst Lakes CG	1982	20.2
Moat Lake jct	1985	22.7
Maccarib CG	1997	23.6
Maccarib Pass	2210	31.1
Portal Creek CG	1980	33.5
Portal trailhead	1480	43.7

Trailhead

Follow the Icefields Parkway 6.7 km south from Jasper to Highway 93A. Turn right and follow Highway 93A south for 5.2 km. Turn right onto the Mt. Edith Cavell Road, and follow this 12 km to the Tonquin Valley trailhead parking area, opposite the youth hostel. Large recreational vehicles and trailers are not allowed on the Mt. Edith Cavell Road. Use the trailer drop-off. A shuttle service is available from Jasper (fee charged).

Maps

NTS: 83 D/9 and 83 D/16
Gem Trek: *Jasper and Maligne Lake*

in Brussels after it fell in WWI, she was executed in 1915 for allegedly assisting the escape of prisoners of war. Cavell is properly pronounced with an emphasis to rhyme with "gravel."

Keep right at the junction across the bridge. The next 4.7 km are a novelty for the beginning of a hike. The trail descends gradually over this distance, crossing Verdant Creek on the way. The mature forest at trailside consists of Engelmann spruce and whitebark pine, with an understory dominated by

VARIATIONS

- Hike the route in reverse.
- Approach Surprise Point by way of Chrome Lake, adding 2.3 km to the total outing.
- Camp at Clitheroe (16.9 km) or Surprise Point (19.0 km), and explore.
- Day-hike from Portal trailhead to Maccarib Pass; 25.2 km return.
- Backpack to Portal Creek campground and day-hike to Maccarib Pass.

buffaloberry. This shrub's red and amber berries are a favourite food of black bears and grizzly bears. You may see bear scats and tracks along the trail. Throne Mountain (3120 m) is the prominent peak to the west. A deep glacial cirque between the two northeast-trending ridges creates the mountain's "arm rests" and "seat".

Cross the Astoria River on a bridge and follow the north bank 1.8 km to Astoria campground. The fruits of crowberry, grouseberry, bearberry, and bunchberry (dwarf dogwood) colour the undergrowth nearby in late summer. Because horses frequent the Tonquin loop, you should treat water from all sources before consumption. Be sure to take your water upstream from the trail at this campground, to minimize the chance of contamination by horse dung and urine.

The trail is poor and wet beneath the quartzite rockslide on Oldhorn Mountain (2990 m). A new slide covered the trail here in 2010. On the west side of this slide, the trail switchbacks to gain entry to the Tonquin Valley. By the early 1980s, the trail here was so ruined by horse use that extensive rehabilitation was necessary. Parks Canada flew in heavy machinery, and sections of trail were crowned and ditched to improve drainage. Crews installed soil blanket beneath the tread to prevent deep mud holes from re-developing. Much of the tread surface is gravel, transported here by helicopter. Although the expensive finished product looks out of place in the subalpine meadows, it has – although it's hard to believe it on some days – significantly reduced the muck and mire underfoot.

The trail levels near the Switchback campground junction, from where you obtain your first, tantalizing view of The Ramparts and Amethyst Lakes. Continuing northwest, the trail makes a treeline traverse through delightful meadowland on the slopes beneath Oldhorn Mountain. The views continue to improve, and now include Chrome Lake to the south, and Moat Lake to the northwest. After a short

OCEAN-GOING, INLAND

In an attempt to compete with the Hudson's Bay Company and North West Company, American fur trade entrepreneur, John Jacob Astor, established Fort Astoria in 1811 near the mouth of the Columbia River. *The Tonquin* was one of Astor's sea vessels. How did the names, Tonquin and Astoria, navigate upstream to the Rockies? The Athabasca Pass fur trade route crossed the Rockies 30 km south of the Tonquin Valley. Some of Astor's employees crossed that pass in 1813. If those connections seem tenuous, consider this: Tonquin Creek does not flow in the Tonquin Valley, nor into any river in Jasper. The creek is across the continental divide, in BC.

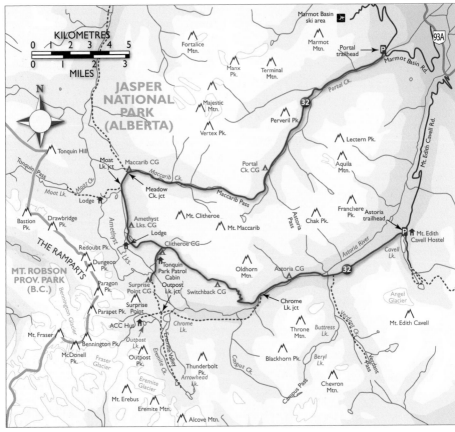

descent, the trail reaches the Surprise Point junction. You have three options for camping nearby. The Amethyst Lake campground is 3.4 km north (right); Surprise Point campground is 2.2 km southwest (left); and Clitheroe campground is 100 m west (left). *Clitheroe* is an Old English name, with Germanic origins and various translations – "hill by the water," "song thrush hill," and "hill of loose stones." All of them fit.

Surprise Point Junction to Surprise Point

The trail to Surprise Point campground passes through Clitheroe campground and soon deteriorates into a horse-churned quagmire. The character of the trail improves slightly as it angles south into a large meadow that contains the Tonquin park patrol cabin. In front of the cabin, turn west (right) into forest, and follow signs for Surprise Point.

CHROME LAKE APPROACH

Unless you plan to go no farther than Surprise Point campground, keep straight ahead at the Chrome Lake junction. The approach to Chrome Lake from this junction is on a poor trail, but it will save you 2.1 km and some climbing if you use it to reach Surprise Point campground. Chrome Lake is 6.5 km along the trail. The Eremite Valley junction is 300 m farther. Turn north (right) to climb to Surprise Point campground in 1.9 km. If you use this option and continue with the remainder of the Tonquin loop, you increase the total distance to 46.0 km.

A MOUNTAIN FORTRESS

The Ramparts are a precipice of Gog Formation quartzite – 900 m high in places – that extends in an arc for 14 km along the continental divide. Seven of the named summits exceed 3050 m. The surveyors of the Interprovincial Boundary Survey were inspired by the fortress-like appearance of the mountain wall, and so coined the names: Parapet, Dungeon, Redoubt, Drawbridge, Bastion, Turret, and Barbican. Moat Lake, at the foot of the northern Ramparts, completes the motif.

CHROME LAKE-OUTPOST LAKE-EREMITE VALLEY, 20.8 KM RETURN FROM SURPRISE POINT CAMPGROUND

If you don't mind rough trails and are competent at fording glacial streams, you can combine these three destinations into an energetic and rewarding day-hike from either Surprise Point or Clitheroe campgrounds.

Upper Eremite Valley

Chrome Lake

Head south on a rooted, rocky and muddy trail, that descends 2.1 km to a junction northwest of Chrome Lake. A 200 m sidetrip to the east (left) takes you to the swampy lakeshore. Look for bog orchids and spotted frogs. The upper Eremite Valley, your ultimate destination on this day-hike, is to the south. Backtrack to the junction, and head west on the Outpost Lake trail for 400 m to another junction.

Outpost Lake

Turn west (right) if you would like to make the 2.4 km return sidetrip to Outpost Lake. The trail crosses Penstock Creek and climbs steeply onto a knoll of rockslide debris and the forested lakeshore. The Alpine Club of Canada's, Wates-Gibson hut is nearby. The building is named for Cyril Wates and Rex Gibson, two mountaineers who were active in this area from the 1920s to the 1940s. The present hut is the third structure in this vicinity; it dates to 1967. You'll find the foundation and chimney of its predecessor, constructed in 1947, along the east shore of the lake.

Outpost Lake contains the only non-silty water on this hike. There are many mountaineer's paths in this area. One leads to a sedge meadow south of Surprise Point. I have seen northern bog lemmings here. This rodent prefers damp habitats in the upper subalpine life zone. Backtrack to the Outpost Lake junction. Turn south (right) for the Eremite Valley.

Eremite Valley

As you follow Penstock Creek south, look west to see Bennington Peak (3260 m), named for Bennington, Vermont, the birthplace of fur trader and explorer, Simon Fraser. Meltwater from glaciers on the north side of the peak is a principal source of the 1280 km long Fraser River.

The origin of Penstock Creek's unusual name is soon revealed. Just north of its confluence with Eremite Creek, Penstock Creek flows underground through a cave – a natural penstock. Cross the creek easily on the natural bridge that results. You must then cross Eremite Creek – usually a challenging ford – possibly a show-stopper. After crossing, do not follow the well-beaten trail east toward Chrome Lake. Pick up a faint trail heading south. It is on the west side of the bedrock ridge that separates Eremite Creek from Chrome Lake.

After a kilometre of hiking through willows, the trail ascends slightly into a flower-filled glade, before descending again to the creek. This area has been the site of five Alpine Club of Canada mountaineering camps since 1941. Camping and fires are no longer allowed here, nor anywhere else in the Eremite Valley. Beyond, the trail climbs steeply into upper subalpine forest. Eremite Glacier occupies a deep cirque to the west. Fine waterfalls cascade over the ice-worn cliffs beneath it. Where the trail drops into a small draw, take the east (left) branch, and resume the climb over rockslide debris and through a shintangle of kruppelholz fir.

Upper Eremite Valley

Spectacular scenery packs the upper valley. A chaos of moraines marks the maximum advance of various glaciers during the Little Ice Age. Arrowhead Lake is dammed by the curving east lateral moraine of Eremite Glacier. The lake is not a typical glacial tarn, but a murky, shallow flat where sediment-choked meltwater collects.

About 4.5 km south of the Outpost Lake junction, the Eremite trail disappears in a meadow bisected by meltwater streams. Boulder-hop the streams, and scramble onto the moraines to the south for a marvelous view of the peaks, glaciers, and tarns at the head of the valley. An *eremite* is a religious recluse, or hermit. Surveyor M.P. Bridgland applied the name in 1916 to the 2910 m mountain west of the valley. Bridgland considered the mountain to be "a solitary peak."

The trail emerges from the forest into an extensive wet meadow on the east shore of Lower Amethyst Lake. Look for fish and waterfowl in the larger stream channels. Follow metal markers across a cotton-grass bog to the bridged outlet of the lower lake. I once saw a solitary mountain caribou here. This vantage offers one of the finer prospects of The Ramparts. Surprise Point campground is 400 m beyond, set on a rocky knoll, surrounded by wetland.

The campground provides a panoramic view of the Tonquin Valley and the upper Astoria Valley. From here, Mt. Edith Cavell is almost unrecognizable – a rocky chisel scraping the sky. Unfortunately, the campground is often teeming with bugs. The only appealing water source is Lower Amethyst Lake, more than 200 m distant. (Bring a water billy.) Surprise Point (2400 m), southwest of the campground, was named because a party from the Interprovincial Boundary Survey was surprised at how long it took them to reach its lowly summit.

Surprise Point Junction to Maccarib Creek Campground

The Tonquin loop continues north from the Surprise Point junction on a rocky trail that descends toward the peninsula that separates the two Amethyst Lakes. The buildings in view are part of a horse outfitter's lodge. After it gains the east shore of Upper Amethyst Lake, the trail swings north alongside a marsh to the Amethyst Lake campground. Across the lake, you can see six glaciers on The Ramparts. Four of these glaciers created horseshoe-shaped terminal moraines during the Little Ice Age.

If you choose to camp here, be aware that outfitters graze their horses nightly along the east and north shores of Upper Amethyst Lake. In a national park, the horses – an introduced species – compete for scant food with mountain caribou – a species at risk. The jingle-jangle of horse bells will likely put a hole in your planned solid night's sleep.

A braided trail leads north from the campground. A.Y. Jackson captured the view of the northwestern arc of The Ramparts from here, in his 1924 painting, "The Ramparts." Jackson was a member of The Group of Seven – artists who specialized in Canadian landscapes. The highest peak of The Ramparts, Mt. Geikie (GEEK-ee) (3270 m), is entirely in BC. It commemorates Scottish geologist, Sir Archibald Geikie.

You'd never guess it, but on this section of trail, you cross a watershed divide. The Amethyst Lakes drain southwest into the Astoria River. To the north, waters flow into Meadow Creek. That's right; the Amethyst Lakes occupy a mountain pass.

The Tonquin loop climbs away from the northeast shore of Upper Amethyst Lake through open spruce forest, and then descends to Maccarib (mah-KAH-rib) Creek. Cross the bridge and turn east (right) at the Meadow Creek junction. The sidetrail to Maccarib Creek campground is 50 m farther. Hikers and non-commercial horse parties share the campground. Situated on a bench above the north bank of Maccarib Creek, it offers exceptional views west to The Ramparts, and east to Maccarib Pass. *Maccarib* is Quinnipiac for "caribou."

Maccarib Campground to Portal Trailhead

The trail to Maccarib Pass ascends gradually through upper subalpine wet meadows, crossing Maccarib Creek and its tributaries numerous times on bridges. Most of the trail has been rehabilitated. Gravel cap has been laid over soil blanket, and the edges have been reinforced with timber, creating a finished product called "turnpiking." Mt. Clitheroe (2749 m) forms the southern slope of the valley. It features a sizeable rock glacier, comprised of quartzite boulders.

Groundsel and fireweed grow at trailside on the final climb to Maccarib Pass. The tundra of the pass stretches almost 2 km over the divide between Maccarib Creek and Portal Creek. Low-lying areas feature earth hummocks, created by repeated freezing and thawing of the soil when permafrost underlaid the area. The hummocks are vegetated with western anemone, woolly everlasting, and mountain heather. Snow willow, arctic willow, white mountain-avens, and moss campion grow in the hollows between them. White-tailed ptarmigan, Columbian ground squirrels, and mountain caribou are three of the creatures you may see on the pass. You can see Mt. Edith Cavell again to the southwest, over Astoria Pass.

From Maccarib Pass, the trail switchbacks down to Portal Creek through rolling subalpine meadows. You reach the Portal Creek campground in 2.4 km. Most of the surrounding mountains are composed of reddish, Gog Formation quartzite. In 1916, surveyor M.P. Bridgland named two mountains along the creek for golden eagles he saw in the vicinity – Chak

---

MOAT LAKE, 3.5 KM

The Moat Lake junction is 2.5 km north of Amethyst Lake campground. Although the sidetrip to the lake is worthwhile, horses have wrecked the trail. The final 1.5 km involves a poorly defined track across a boulder meadow covered in willows. However, the rewards are a close-up view of the northern Ramparts, and a pleasing prospect of Mt. Clitheroe and Majestic Hill if you return in the light of late afternoon.

Maccarib Pass

GOODAIR'S FINAL RESTING PLACE

The grave of park warden, Percy Goodair, is just north of Maccarib campground. Goodair was district warden in the Tonquin Valley in the 1920s, and worked from a cabin located here. On September 12, 1929, Goodair died just outside the cabin door. Although the cause of death was never determined, his body had been mauled and scavenged by a grizzly bear.

Mountaineer, James Monroe Thorington, characterized Goodair in 1925. "A quiet, pleasant man, he had had the usual interesting career of those whom one runs across in the far places. Studying medicine in London, he enlisted and went to Africa during the Boer War, remaining afterward in the South African diamond fields, wandering as a prospector to strange corners of the earth, and at last finding a life in the Canadian wilderness that pleased and held him. We could quite understand it, and not without a touch of envy."

Peak (2775 m) and Aquila Mountain (2840 m). *Chak* is Stoney for eagle, and *Aquila* is Latin. The slopes of Chak Peak contain a large rock glacier. Farther down the valley you might pick out Lectern Peak (2780 m), named for the rostrum of rock at its summit. On the horizon, far to the northeast, you can see the gray limestone peaks of the Colin Range, beyond Jasper.

Just over halfway down the valley, the trail ascends onto a rocky sideslope and contours across the flank of Peveril Peak, before descending steeply through lodgepole pine forest to cross the westerly tributary of Portal Creek. The remaining 3.7 km continues the steady descent, passing beside two outcrops of glacial till. Numerous animal trails and tracks indicate that goats and deer use these outcrops as mineral licks. From the second outcrop, you have a fine view west along Portal Creek to Peveril Peak (2660 m). This mountain's unusual name was in the title of a novel written by Sir Walter Scott. The last interesting feature on the Tonquin loop is a mass of downed trees to the south of the trail. The weathered trees appear to be ancient avalanche debris from the opposite side of the valley. This slope has since revegetated with mature forest, indicating that the avalanche probably took place at least 200 years ago.

Cross the bridge to the south bank of Portal Creek. The Tonquin loop ends a few hundred metres later at a parking area on the Marmot Basin Road. Turn east (right) to descend this road, 6.5 km to its junction with Highway 93A. At this junction, turn north (left) for Jasper, or south (right) for the Mt. Edith Cavell Road junction. You should prearrange transportation for the conclusion of this hike. Otherwise, avoid arriving at the Marmot Basin road late in the day.

33. Cavell Meadows

Cavell Meadows

Day-hike

Route	Elev. (m)	Dist. (km)
Trailhead	1762	0
Cavell Meadows/ Path of the Glacier jct	1795	0.5
1st loop jct	2006	2.0
Angel Glacier (#1) viewpoint	2029	2.4
Cavell Meadows (#2) viewpoint	2119	2.8
2nd loop jct	2126	3.1
3rd loop jct	2181	3.5
End-of-trail (#3) viewpoint	2228	3.9
4th loop jct	2118	4.6
1st loop jct	2006	5.1
Path of the Glacier jct	1795	6.6
Cavell Pond	1808	6.9
Trailhead	1762	7.7

Trailhead

Follow the Icefields Parkway, 6.7 km south from Jasper to Highway 93A. Turn right and follow Highway 93A south for 5.2 km. Turn right onto the Mt. Edith Cavell Road, and follow this 14 km to the Mt. Edith Cavell parking area. The Path of the Glacier-Cavell Meadows trailhead is at the southeast corner of the parking area. Large recreational vehicles and trailers are not allowed on the Mt. Edith Cavell Road. Use the trailer drop-off opposite the beginning of the road. A shuttle service is available from Jasper (fee charged).

Special considerations

Check at the park information centre regarding trail closures. You may be exposed to the threat of ice avalanches on the Path of the Glacier trail. Don't walk around the west shore of Cavell Pond or ascend the moraines beneath Angel Glacier.

Maps

NTS: 83 D/9
Gem Trek: *Jasper and Maligne Lake*

Best lighting: morning

On the rolling alpland of Cavell Meadows, Angel Glacier and the precipitous north face of Mt. Edith Cavell (3363 m) provide the backdrop for a stunning mid-summer display of wildflowers. This loop outing begins on the Cavell Meadows trail and returns via the Path of the Glacier. The Friends of Jasper National Park and Parks Canada completed an extensive restoration of the Cavell Meadows trail in 2004. To spare the meadows and to honour the work, please keep to the maintained trail.

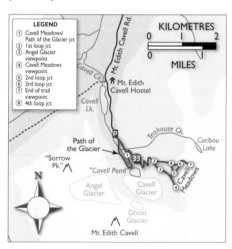

LEGEND
① Cavell Meadows/ Path of the Glacier jct
② 1st loop jct
③ Angel Glacier viewpoint
④ Cavell Meadows viewpoint
⑤ 2nd loop jct
⑥ 3rd loop jct
⑦ End of trail viewpoint
⑧ 4th loop jct

KILOMETRES
MILES

Mt. Edith Cavell Rd.

Cavell Ck.

Mt. Edith Cavell Hostel

Cavell Lk.

Path of the Glacier

Teahouse Ck.

Caribou Lake

"Sorrow Pk."

"Cavell Pond"

Angel Glacier

Cavell Glacier

Cavell Meadows

Ghost Glacier

Mt. Edith Cavell

N

Trailhead to Cavell Meadows

From the parking area, the trail climbs over a terminal moraine and works its way south through the quartzite rubble of the glacier forefield. Life is slowly taking hold. A cottonwood poplar grows from the rocks, right on the trail. At the junction in 600 m, turn east (left). The Cavell Meadows trail climbs steeply over a lateral moraine. Cavell Glacier created this landform, and the terminal moraine you crossed earlier, during the Little Ice Age. The coarse, quartz sand underfoot has been eroded from the quartzite boulders. Least chipmunks, golden mantled ground squirrels, and pikas live in the nooks and crannies of this moraine. Please don't feed them.

The top of the moraine marks an abrupt transition to subalpine forest. This is the trimline of Cavell Glacier. A century and a half ago, the ice of the glacier was thick enough to reach this far up the side of the valley, obliterating mature forest. Some trees near

Pink mountain heather

Moss campion

trimline show evidence of roots and trunks damaged by the moving glacial ice. You can see where two, lesser moraines nest within the outer moraine. Together, they record three glacial advances of nearly equal magnitude. There once were two terminal moraines near the trailhead, nested one inside the other, but the older, outer moraine – which dated to 1705 – was destroyed when the parking area was built in the 1970s.

Dwarf false asphodel, cotton-grass, and red-stemmed saxifrage grow in wet areas, competing for you attention with the views of Angel Glacier. After paralleling the moraine crest for a few hundred metres, the trail switchbacks east (left) into the trees. The forest here is an ancient one, dominated by Engelmann spruce and subalpine fir. One fir is half a metre thick at its base. In the winter of 1990-91, a snow avalanche from the north face of Mt. Edith Cavell created a windblast strong enough to topple some of these trees. One tree cut from the debris by chainsaw showed 232 concentric rings, each recording a year's growth. Arnica and valerian comprise most of the ground cover. Red-breasted nuthatches and Clark's nutcrackers are common, along with red squirrels.

Keep right at the first loop junction. At km 2.4, you reach the first of the new viewpoints, which provides an excellent view of Angel Glacier. The ice cliffs are 40 m thick. Angel Glacier formerly merged with Cavell Glacier; however, glacial recession caused it to break contact in the 1940s. After a few decades when the Angel hovered in equilibrium, it began winging up the cliff. As with many glaciers in the Rockies, it is disappearing. You can see the lichen trimline of Angel Glacier clearly to the north of the hanging body of ice. The Cavell (Little Ice Age) Advance scoured the lichens from the rock, which now lies bare as the ice has receded.

The forest soon becomes a patchwork of tree islands separated by glades of subalpine meadow. Although the elevation here (2060 m) is low for treeline, the chilling effects of glacial ice, the north-facing slope, and the winter-long shade of Mt. Edith Cavell, combine to inhibit the growth of forest. Soon the trail emerges from the trees. Fleabane, paintbrush, Sitka valerian, western anemone, arnica, alpine veronica, bracted lousewort, groundsel, everlasting, and white mountain-avens are just a few of the many wildflowers that grow here. Amateur botanists are particularly fond of these meadows for their displays of mountain heather – pink, yellow, and white. In most years, the blooms peak in late July.

At km 2.8, you reach the Cavell Meadows viewpoint. If you are tired, turn back here and retrace your steps to the trailhead. For those wanting to go higher,

THE ANGEL OF MERCY

Today, "Angel" seems a most appropriate name for the wing-shaped glacier. However, the glacier's appearance did not prompt the name. Mt. Edith Cavell commemorates an English nurse who worked behind the lines with the Belgian Red Cross in WWI. She tended to the injured of both sides, but was executed for allegedly assisting the escape of captive troops. It was popular to refer to nurse Cavell as "the angel of mercy," and this is how the name first became associated with the glacier. According to Edith's brother, their family name is properly pronounced and emphasized to rhyme with "gravel."

From the foot of the glacier to the top of the peak there is not a single speck of vegetation, not a blade of living green; but almost at one's feet, within a space formed by the glacier's escaping streams, lies a tiny emerald island, a veritable little oasis, like a patch of lawn left in the ruins of a battlefield.... this little meadow is a perfect garden of wild flowers.

Mabel Williams; *Jasper National Park*

139

please refer to the map. Keep right at junctions after you leave the second viewpoint, to reach the end-of-trail viewpoint in 1.1 km. As you ascend the quartzite screes of the ridge, you may have the pleasure of placing your feet in the "Sasquatch tracks" – footprints made by the many thousands of hikers who have preceded you.

The upper meadows are part of the alpine life zone, and are occasionally visited by mountain caribou and grizzly bears. Some hollows here may hold snow until mid-August. The trickle of snowmelt on warm days provides water for moisture loving plants such as leather-leaved saxifrage, white globeflower, and red-stemmed saxifrage. The reddish tinge in snowbanks is watermelon snow, caused by algae with a red pigment. Some of the steep slopes above the meadows contain rock glaciers – accumulations of rock that contain just enough ice to allow the whole mass to creep downhill.

Cavell Meadows to The Path of the Glacier

Descending from the end-of-trail viewpoint, keep straight ahead (west) at the next three junctions to reach the Path of the Glacier junction in 2.7 km. Turn south (left). The trail descends to "Cavell Pond" in the cirque at the base of Mt. Edith Cavell. Retreating ice uncovered the hollow that contains this lake in 1963. Icebergs or "growlers" calve from the toes of the Angel and Cavell glaciers, and are often afloat in the water. The surface of Cavell Glacier contains several talus (TAY-luss) cones, piles of rocky avalanche debris, transported from the base of Mt. Edith Cavell's north face by the moving ice.

The trail returns to the parking area along the outlet from the pond. The rocky soils and cold

Angel Glacier

environment make it difficult for vegetation to become established here. The rambunctious creek plays havoc with the trail. Willows, sedges, mountain fireweed, and a few stunted spruce trees are all that have taken hold. Barring another glacial advance, it will be centuries before this forefield supports mature subalpine forest again.

THE LITTLE ICE AGE: COOL DETECTIVE WORK

The most recent advance of Cavell Glacier took place during what is often called the Little Ice Age, which lasted from 1050 AD to the mid 1840s. Glaciologists have gained much of their understanding of that recent glaciation in the Rockies from studies carried out here, so they often refer to the Little Ice Age as the "Cavell Advance."

Glaciologists use vegetation near glaciers to help them assign dates to glacial events. They take core samples from mature trees near trimline. By counting the tree rings in the core, and cross-referencing to a master key for the area, they can determine the approximate ages of the trees. If a tree is 300 years old, glacial ice has not covered its location for at least 300 years. This process is called dendrochronology. (See p. 109). By sampling many trees close to a glacier, the date and extent of the most recent glacial advance can be plotted. Trees that grow on moraines formed during the Cavell Advance, or those obviously damaged by glacial ice, are particularly useful in this process.

Rock lichens also provide an accurate means for dating glacial events. The rock lichen known as map lichen (*Rhizocarpon geographicum*, see p. 111), grows at a known rate. These lichens have been growing on boulders in the forefield since the ice withdrew. By measuring the diameter of the lichens, glaciologists can determine how long it has been since the adjacent area was covered by ice.

What have glaciologists learned about Cavell Glacier? Between 1888 and 1975, the glacier receded 988 m. The maximum of the Cavell Advance here took place in 1705. This was the greatest advance of Cavell Glacier during the previous 2600 years.

34. Maligne Canyon

Maligne River

TRAIL THUMBNAIL

Day-hike

Route	Elev. (m)	Dist. (km)
Sixth Bridge trailhead	1015	0
Fifth Bridge	1030	1.6
Fourth Bridge	1055	2.9
First Bridge	1140	3.5
Upper trailhead	1145	3.7

Trailhead
Follow Highway 16, 3.7 km east of Jasper to the Maligne Lake Road. Turn east, cross the Athabasca River, and follow the road 2.3 km to the turnoff for Sixth Bridge. Follow this sideroad 1.2 km to the Sixth Bridge picnic area.

Maps
NTS: 83 D/9 and 83 C/13
Gem Trek: *Best of Jasper*

Best lighting: Cloudy days provide the best detail in the canyon.

Whether you are a seasoned backpacker or a novice hiker, Maligne (mah-LEEN) Canyon is one of Jasper's "must see" places. The canyon's popularity is justly deserved. If you hike the full length, it rates as a stellar natural history walk. When you are storm-bound in Jasper, this is a great outing to make while you wait for the weather to clear in the high country. You share the first 1.3 km with bikers; the first 1.6 km with horses. If you take young children on this hike, hold their hands. Although the trail is fenced in many places, the route is often alongside the swift-flowing river or along the maw of the canyon – places not without hazard.

[We felt] compelling admiration for its gloomy splendour, its ebony walls so close together in spots that one could almost jump across, not merely perpendicular but sometimes overhanging, so that creeping to the edge and leaning over one looked down to the centre of the stream roaring a hundred feet or more below.

Lawrence J. Burpee; *Among the Canadian Alps*

Trailhead to Fourth Bridge

From the parking area, cross the bridge to the northeast bank of the Maligne River. Turn southeast (right). Jesuit missionary, Pierre-Jean De Smet, referred to the river in 1846, using the French word "maligne," which means "wicked." Imagine the bridge removed; contemplate the crossing, and you can appreciate the sentiment. The first 800 m along the riverbank is on a wide, flat, trail through a montane forest of white spruce, lodgepole pine, trembling aspen, and a few Douglas-firs. The fire-scarred trunks of the Douglas-firs testify to their ability to withstand moderate ground fires. I have met a black bear here. (Of course, I had left the bear spray in the truck.) Prickly juniper, buffaloberry, wild onion, bearberry, and very tall, Scouler's willow make up most of the sparse ground cover. Red squirrels chatter from the trees. Short spur trails lead to pleasing views of the river. Look for dippers. The building on the opposite bank of the river was formerly the warden office and, before that, the park fish hatchery. In the early 1930s, fish fry raised in this building were introduced into the fish-less rivers of the Maligne Valley. Sigh.

The pleasant preamble done with, you soon reach the mouth of the canyon. Note the change in the character of the forest. Dampness and chill prevail; Engelmann spruce, subalpine fir, and lodgepole

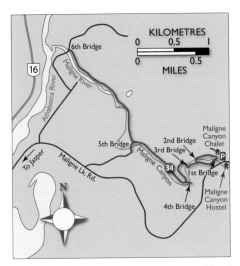

Maligne Canyon

pine dominate. The trail climbs over a jumble of limestone boulders, from which issues a bit of the mystery and magic of the Maligne Valley. Yes, it's a spring, but it also has been proven to be an outlet for the underground drainage of Medicine Lake, 17 km southeast. This outlet, called an emergence, is one of more than twenty between here and Fourth Bridge. They gush when Medicine Lake is full; they trickle as the lake level drops.

Horsetails – a favourite springtime food of bears – grow alongside the first emergence. I have seen bear scats and tracks in the sand nearby. White birch also grows here. Please don't peel the bark. At km 1.3 the bike trail veers left. Keep straight ahead. At km 1.6, the trail from Fifth Bridge comes in from the west (right). Angle left, upstream, and turn right at the horse-hiker separation in 50 m.

The trail traverses an exposed till bank that is being colonized by trembling aspen, juniper, and wild rose. Across the river, you can see the sedimentary layers of the bedrock. They dip slightly to the north, but what is more important to the creation of the canyon is that the bedrock on the west side of the river is higher than that on the east side – by about 3 m. This offset is a normal fault – a fracture in the bedrock that occurred after mountain building. The rocks east of the fault dropped relative to those on the west. A lateral moraine deposited by the ancestral Maligne Glacier diverted the Maligne river onto the fault, where the flowing water readily exploited the weakness. In no time, geologically speaking – less than 10,000 years – Maligne Canyon came into being.

That's one canyon-creation theory. Another proposes that Maligne Canyon is itself the course of an ancient underground stream, exposed to daylight by glacial erosion during the Late Wisconsin Glaciation.

The trail descends into the damp forest at riverside. This is my favourite part of the canyon. Two of the larger emergences from the Maligne karst system enter beneath an overhang on the opposite bank. Beaten paths lead to the riverbank in places, but the wet, silt-covered rock is certain death if you misplace a step. The canyon winds; the trail makes brief climbs and descents, passing from open slope to confined chasm – a patchwork of micro-habitats. On the opposite bank, a waterfall cascades from the ancestral lateral moraine on the canyon rim, scouring away the soils to reveal a complete exposure of the bedrock. Fourth Bridge takes you across the canyon but the trail does not continue on that bank.

Above Fourth Bridge

The bedrock geology changes above the Fourth Bridge. The canyon narrows dramatically as a result. Downstream, the river is eroding the relatively weak shales of the Banff Formation. Upstream, the river has a tougher time with the more resistant limestone of the Palliser Formation. This limestone is fossil-rich, containing snail-like gastropods, clam-like brachiopods, squid-like cephalopods, crinoids (related to sea-stars), and corals.

The Maligne River takes a mighty drop beneath Third Bridge, where the canyon's depth is 10 m and you cross to the opposite bank. Here, the air also changes. Below the bridge, it's cool and damp where you've been hiking within the canyon. From here on, you climb along the canyon rim, where the air is noticeably warmer. If you've had any solitude on the trail to this point, you probably won't now, as many people hike here from the upper parking area. Note

Whitewater!

"Rawk!" (Common raven)

THE INVISIBLE RIVER

Two rivers flow through Maligne Canyon. If you were to compare the volume of flow at Sixth Bridge with the volume at First Bridge in mid-summer, you would see that the lower canyon contains eight times as much water as the upper canyon. The emergences of the Maligne karst system pump 24,000 litres per second into the canyon. This underground river may be the largest in the world. The entrances to the karst system – called sinks – are upvalley on the floor of Medicine Lake. It takes 70 hours for the water to travel from there to Maligne Canyon. Other emergences of the underground river feed some of the lakes near Jasper town.

how the bedrock has been polished smooth in places by the shuffling of millions of feet, some, amazingly, clad in high heels. The large boulders at trailside are glacial erratics, dropped here when the Maligne Valley glacier last receded, some 12,000 years ago.

Nooks and crannies on the opposite wall of the canyon are nesting places for ravens. Maligne Canyon is also one of three known nesting places in Alberta for black swifts. Look for them on the wing in the evening. They are easy to recognize in flight, having been described as "cigars with wings." The canyon is deepest – 55 m – at Second Bridge. It's so deep, it's hard to grasp the scale. Locals know the pocket of ice on the wall below as "The Icebox." (If you are wondering, yes, people venture onto the canyon floor on guided walks in the winter.) A damp, canyon forest of spruce and subalpine fir grows on the shaded, south side of the river, whereas a drier forest of lodgepole pine and Douglas-fir grows on the sunny, north side of the river.

Don't cross Second Bridge but carry on to First Bridge, where the canyon is 38 m deep and the entire river is forced through a 1 m slot. A chockstone spans the canyon just downstream; you get to cross on a bridge. Although the canyon is shallow from here on, it features wonderful potholes – circular depressions drilled into the limestone by boulders caught in eddies – a process that requires thousands of years. Some of the potholes now lie in abandoned channels. The depressions are gradually filling with soils to become miniature gardens. Alas, the upper canyon is showing the abuses of heavy visitation. Graffiti has appeared on rocks in the river bed, and a fenced area that displays fossils has been walked on so much, the outlines of the fossils have been obliterated.

Return

I recommend that you walk back down the canyon, as you are certain to see things that you missed on the way up. Loop around the parking area to recross the canyon at Second Bridge. If nothing else, you get to spend more time in the company of the lower Maligne River, a ribbon of blue-green beauty.

35. Opal Hills

Opal Hills

The Opal Hills are a delightful island of green set amidst the gray limestone mountains that flank the east side of the Maligne (mah-LEEN) Valley. This steep loop hike features interesting geology and, with a little extra effort, an exceptional view of Maligne Lake.

Trailhead to Opal Meadows

From the trailhead, descend through lodgepole pine forest into a clearing known as the "hummock and hollow meadow." Keep left at the junction 200 m from the parking area. You can see the Opal Hills through the treetops, but you'll soon have your head down as you begin a steep climb on a poorly conceived and heavily eroded trail. Persevere; the views ahead are worth the effort.

A MADE-OVER MOUNTAIN

Where are those drab gray limestones, so typical of the Queen Elizabeth Ranges on the east side of the Maligne Valley? Has Opal Peak had a facelift? No, it was more like a face-drop. The Palliser and Rundle formation limestones, along with the Gog Formation quartzite that was beneath them, now rest on the floor of the Maligne Valley. All that rock went there in one or more colossal landslides, sometime after the Late Wisconsin Glaciation, following the retreat of the ancestral Maligne Valley glacier, some 10,000 years ago. The volume of the landslides is estimated at 498 million cubic metres, making it the second largest landslide complex yet identified in the Rockies. Although it isn't a gardener's first choice, the Sulphur Mountain Formation siltstone exposed by the landslide offers – after the weathering of millennia – much better soil than the limestones. Thus, the green meadows that contrast beautifully with the reddish-brown siltstone. Add the white snowbanks in the gullies, and you can see why Mary Schäffer coined the name, Opal Hills.

TRAIL THUMBNAIL

Day-hike

Route	Elev. (m)	Dist. (km)
Trailhead	1700	0
Schäffer Viewpoint jct	1695	0.2
Loop trail jct	1900	1.6
Maligne Lake viewpoint	2150	2.6
Summit of meadows	2160	3.2
Loop trail jct	1900	6.6
Trailhead	1700	8.2

Trailhead
Follow Highway 16, 3.7 km east from Jasper to the Maligne Lake Road. Turn east (right). Follow the Maligne Lake Road 44 km to parking areas on the east side of the lake. The trailhead is at the northeast corner of the uppermost parking area.

Maps
NTS: 83 C/12 , 83 C/13
Gem Trek: *Jasper and Maligne Lake*

Best lighting: afternoon

ALPINE LOUSEWORT

The Opal Hills feature an inordinate number of blooms of alpine lousewort. You have to get nose to meadow to appreciate these tiny (5-15 cm tall), pinkish-purple beauties. The leaves are fern-like and, together with the stem, are covered in tiny filaments that help insulate the plant from the wind. There are nine lousewort species in the Canadian Rockies, including two that are more familiar – bracted lousewort and elephant-head. The name, "lousewort," comes from a falsely-held belief that domestic animals that ate the plants of this genus would become infested with lice. Anything that eats large quantities of these plants is, however, likely to become very sick. They are poisonous.

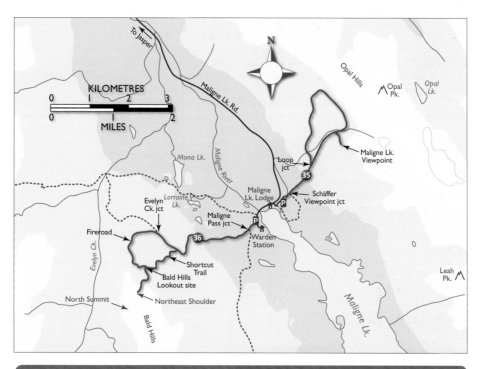

MOUNTAIN WOMAN

Mary Schäffer was a Quaker from Philadelphia who made her first visit to the Rockies in 1889. After a few summers of adjustment, she took to the backwoods life with passion and ease, and endeared herself to Stoney First Peoples, who called her *Yahe-Weha* – "mountain woman."

Following her husband's death in 1903, Schäffer made annual pilgrimages to the Rockies. Her initial focus was to collect botanical samples for a wildflower guide, which she was to illustrate. With the necessary collecting completed in 1905, adventure became the motivation. She journeyed to Wilcox Pass in 1906, and in 1907 made the first attempt to find a large lake known to the Stoneys as *Chaba Imne*, which means, "Beaver Lake." Using a crude map drawn by Stoney chieftain Sampson Beaver, Schäffer reached the lake from the south on her second attempt, in 1908. Her party built a raft and spent three days mapping and exploring the lake, and naming many features. She returned in 1911, this time approaching from the recently completed Grand Trunk Pacific Railway, at Jasper. The accounts of her journeys, published in magazines and journals, made her a celebrity. Her book of 1911, *Old Indian Trails of the Canadian Rockies*, vividly conjures trail life in the early days.

145

You reach the loop junction at km 1.6. The route described here takes the right-hand branch. The remainder of the climb is at times withering – a 25 degree grade in places – but you hike downhill later on a trail less steep, which is consequently safer and easier on your knees.

Beyond the junction, the lodgepole pines give way to a mature forest of Engelmann spruce and subalpine fir. The trail parallels a shale ravine during the final climb to the meadows that surround the Opal Hills. Looking west from the meadows, you have a fine view of the Maligne Valley. The Opal Hills are hummocks of landslide material from Opal Peak (2789 m). You won't find opals. Mary Schäffer named the hills for their colours – reddish rock and green tundra, striped with snow. But you will find gems of a different sort in the meadows – exquisite wildflower displays.

From the first junction in the meadows, a faint track climbs south onto a knoll. By contouring farther south, you are rewarded with a panoramic view of Maligne Lake, more than 400 m below. Maligne Lake is by far the largest of Jasper's 778 mapped lakes and ponds, and is the largest natural lake in the Rockies – 22 km long and 96 m deep, with an area of 2066 ha. It is fed by meltwaters from the 25 km^2 Brazeau (brah-ZOE) Icefield, and by many other glaciers. *Maligne* is French for "wicked" – a reference to the difficult ford at the mouth of the Maligne River, 40 km north of here.

The loop trail keeps left at the viewpoint junction, crosses the shale ravine, and soon branches north into the meadows. With its abundance of upper subalpine and alpine wildflowers, and krummholz tree islands, the shallow, meadowed vale between the Opal Hills and Opal Peak is a delight. Bears like it, too. Keep alert.

Return

At the north end of the meadow, the trail curves west and then south, re-entering the forest to commence the sideslope descent to the loop junction. Use caution on the steep grade to the parking area, especially if the trail is wet.

> *In the spring of 1908 a small party of six... unnoticed by a solitary soul, slipped quietly away from civilisation and were lost, so far as the world was concerned, in a sea of mountains to the north. Our quest was a mythical lake spoken of by the Stoney Indians....*
>
> Mary Schäffer; *The 1911 Expedition to Maligne Lake*

HUMMOCKS, HOLLOWS, ROCKSLIDES, AND MOOSE

In the Rockies, "hummock and hollow" landscapes – such as the meadow near the trailhead – usually resulted from the melting of detached blocks of rubble-covered glacial ice at the end of the Late Wisconsin Glaciation. However, the mounds in this meadow are the remains of frost-shattered boulders of landslide debris. The hollows are probably bedrock karst features called dolines (DOLE-eens). The Maligne Valley contains the second largest measured landslide in the Rockies. Depressions in the debris have filled with water, creating many lakes and ponds. The wet shrub thickets that develop nearby are excellent moose habitat. The Maligne Valley supports one of the few remaining concentrations of moose in the Rockies.

MOUNTAIN HEATHER

Plants of the heath family are emblematic, evergreen shrubs of the alpine life zone, that create extensive mats above treeline. Botanists often call such an area a heath tundra. There are four species of heather in the Rockies; two white, one yellow, and one pink. All have nodding, urn-like flowers, but none bear fruit. If you see small berries on a heath-like plant, you are looking at either crowberry or grouseberry, other common plants on the heath tundra.

36. Bald Hills

Maligne Lake from Bald Hills

TRAIL THUMBNAIL

Day-hike; see map, p. 145

Route	Elev. (m)	Dist. (km)
Trailhead	1697	0
Maligne Pass jct	1710	0.3
Shortcut trail jct	1940	2.5
Evelyn Creek jct	1960	3.2
Lookout site	2170	5.2
End of fireroad	2180	5.7
Northeast shoulder	2280	6.2
North summit	2320	7.1

Trailhead

Follow Highway 16, 3.7 km east from Jasper to the Maligne Lake Road. Turn east (right). Follow the Maligne Lake Road 44 km to the bridge over the lake's outlet. Cross the bridge and follow the road 250 m to the parking area on the west shore of the lake. There are two trailheads west of the parking area. The one for Bald Hills is to the south (left).

Maps

NTS: 83 C/12

Gem Trek: *Jasper and Maligne Lake*

On a fair day, it would be difficult to pick a finer destination than the Bald Hills. Few viewpoints in the Rockies, reached in such a short distance, offer such a great panorama. Adding to the attractions are interesting geology and tremendous wildflower displays. You share the fireroad with horses.

Trailhead to Lookout Site

Although all are unanimous in extolling the destination, I have heard some describe the hike to the Bald Hills as a boring fireroad plod. The tread is hard and you may have to dodge commercial horse parties, but if you look around, you will see much of interest during the ascent.

The forest is a near-homogenous stand of lodgepole pine, which indicates a large forest fire in the not-too-distant past. You can see charred logs and stumps. Golden-crowned kinglets and black-capped chickadees buzz through the trees. Two plants prevalent in pine forests are everywhere in the understory – twinflower and Labrador tea. Arnica, fleabane, buffaloberry, dwarf dogwood, northern sweetvetch, and various willows are also common, along with invasive plants borne in the feed and dung of horses – dandelion, buttercup, and clover. Ruffed grouse and spruce grouse make occasional trailside appearances. Fritillary butterflies – smallish, with orange wings dotted with black – seem partial to this fireroad; perhaps attracted by various goodies in the horse dung.

VARIATIONS

- You can make a loop to and from the lookout site by ascending the fireroad and descending the shortcut trail, or vice versa. The loop will be 1.3 km shorter than the out-and-back distance along the fireroad. If you use the shortcut trail up and down, your outing will be 2.6 km shorter.
- Ascend the north summit, 1.8 km return from the lookout site.

You reach the Maligne Pass junction in 300 m. Keep straight ahead. A series of outbuildings – a horse staging area, a helipad, and a pumphouse – borders the right-hand side of the fireroad over the next 400 m. Ahead, you have a glimpse of the ultimate destination. Looking back, you can see the mountain known as the "Sinking Ship," on the east side of Maligne Lake.

The fireroad veers north and winds through an area of rocky hummocks. These hummocks are landslide debris known as mollards. (See p. 119). The debris came from the vicinity of the Opal Hills on the east side of the valley, in a series of monumental rockslides that followed the retreat of the main valley glacier after the Late Wisconsin Glaciation. Some of the debris dammed the outlet of Maligne Lake.

The fireroad levels just before the shortcut trail junction at km 2.5. The shortcut trail is steeper than the fireroad, and is rockier and rooted. It is a toe-jammer and knee-cruncher on the way down, but if you use it on the ascent, it cuts the remaining distance to the lookout site from 2.7 km to 1.4 km.

Beyond the shortcut junction, the fireroad undulates for 700 m to the Evelyn Creek junction. Keep left for the Bald Hills. I have seen the tracks of moose and deer here. The steepest section of fireroad follows, yielding a fine view back to the Opal Hills. Note the

Northeast summit

transition in the understory; pink mountain heather and yellow mountain heather are now common, marking the lower subalpine life zone. Views to the north begin to open, with the Queen Elizabeth Range visible across the Maligne Valley, and Little Shovel Pass in the Maligne Range visible to the north. This snippet of view encapsulates the two great themes of the local geology – younger, gray, front range limestone to the east; older, colourful, main range quartzite underfoot. Mona Lake, named for Mona Harrigan, Jasper's first female trail guide, is revealed as a blue gem in the green mantle of the valley floor.

The grade moderates as the fireroad curves southwest to enter treeline glades. You pass a small pond. White mountain avens and white mountain heather are common. In this transitional forest, I heard a surprising chorus of birdlife: juncos, hermit thrushes, a golden-crowned sparrow, ruby-crowned kinglets, and a Cooper's hawk.

A hitching rail marks the lookout site. Prompted by extensive forest fires in 1936, Parks Canada constructed a fire lookout system in the national parks in the late 1930s and early 1940s. With only a few exceptions, the structures – which saw use until the 1970s – have been removed. But without exception, all were well sited, as this view attests. To the southeast, you see most of the length of Maligne Lake. From north to south, the peaks in view on the east side of the lake are: Opal Hills, "Sinking Ship," Leah Peak (2801 m), Samson Peak (3801 m), Maligne Mountain (with glacier, 3200 m), Mt. Paul (2850 m), Monkhead Mountain (3219 m), and Mt. Warren (3362 m). Mt. Charlton (3217 m) and Mt. Unwin (3268 m), on the near shore, complete the visible lakeside peaks.

Lookout Site to North Summit

To carry on, take the left-hand of the two tracks that branch from the hitching rail. This track is the proper continuation of the fireroad. It initially heads south, passing the junction with the shortcut trail in 75 m (marked only by a cairn), before looping west to end at the base of the north summit. (If you come up the

shortcut trail, turn south onto the fireroad if you want to go to the summit; otherwise turn north to descend the fireroad.) The meadows here are flush with the best displays of white mountain heather and blue-bottle gentian I have seen in the Rockies.

If you are hiking early in the season, the slopes above may be entirely snow covered. Otherwise, a beaten track ascends steeply south on the screes, turning west at its steepest point to gain the shoulder of this modest summit. From there, the grade relents as you walk onto the domed high point, with its panoramic views.

The rounded shapes of the Bald Hills indicate that they were completely covered by glacial ice during the Late Wisconsin Glaciation. With their harsh edges removed, the connecting ridges to the middle and south summits beckon to competent ramblers. I have fond memories of our eldest daughter, then just five, tagging these peaks during a 17 km day (photo, above.). I couldn't keep up. To reach the middle summit, make a slight descent west to gain the well-beaten path on its north ridge. Views southwest from the middle summit include the head of Evelyn Creek, with a prominent rock glacier above its southerly fork. To the south, keen eyes will discern Mt. Columbia (3741 m), North Twin (3731 m), and Mt. Alberta (3619 m), respectively, 2nd-, 3rd-, and 6th-highest peaks in the Rockies; and 1-2-3 in Alberta.

We had read Mrs. Schäffer's enthusiastic description of the lake, but were hardly prepared for the perfectly glorious sight that lay before us: a lake of the most exquisite blue, mirroring on one side a high ridge clothed to the water's edge in dark green timber, and on the other a noble range of mountains climbing up and up in graceful towers and pinnacles sharply outlined against a cloudless sky.

Lawrence J. Burpee; *Among the Canadian Alps*

37. Skyline

Apex of the Skyline trail

For almost two-thirds of its length, the Skyline travels at or above treeline. Rambling through expansive meadows, crossing high passes, and traversing ridgecrests of the Maligne (mah-LEEN) Range, it provides panoramic views of the Athabasca and Maligne valleys, and the surrounding mountain ranges. It's no wonder that the Skyline is the most heavily travelled backcountry trail in Jasper.

Given its high elevation, in most years you should not hike the Skyline until after mid-July, when most of the snow will have melted. Avoid this outing during poor weather. If it's stormy in Jasper, it will be miserable on the exposed ridges of the Maligne Range. Although you can complete the trail in two days, I recommend spending more time. The summits of the Maligne Range offer many possibilities for ridge walking and straightforward mountaineering.

Trailhead to Little Shovel Pass

From the trailhead, a broad path climbs through an open coniferous forest dominated by lodgepole pine. The undergrowth features buffaloberry, feathermosses, twinflower, common fireweed, rocky mountain goldenrod, and grouseberry. The sweet, red fruit of this heath family member is a favourite food of ruffed grouse. You may see these birds here.

The trail winds through hummocky terrain, debris from the Maligne Lake landslides. At km 2.2 and km 2.4, short sidetrails branch, respectively, southwest (left) to Lorraine Lake, and north (right) to Mona Lake. These lakes occupy hollows in the debris of the rockslide Mona Harrigan Matheson was Jasper's first licensed female trail guide. Lorraine Magstad's parents worked at the Maligne Lake chalet in the late 1920s.

At km 4.8 the trail crosses Evelyn Creek to the first campground. "Evelyn" was one of two persons – the wife of the first resident Superintendent of Jasper National Park in 1913; or the Duchess of Devonshire, who visited Jasper in 1920.

The trail climbs steeply away from the campground. Although the elevation here is subalpine,

lodgepole pine is still the dominant tree. Engelmann spruce and subalpine fir are typically more common in the subalpine, however the combination of quartzite soils and southerly exposure here create a perfect niche for lodgepole pines. Many of the pines are twisted and stunted, products of the colder climate

TRAIL THUMBNAIL

Overnight, 2-4 days

Route	Elev. (m)	Dist. (km)
Maligne Lake trailhead	1690	0
Lorraine Lake jct	1755	2.2
Mona Lake jct	1755	2.4
Evelyn Creek CG	1810	4.8
Little Shovel CG	2155	8.3
Little Shovel Pass	2220	10.3
Snowbowl CG	2080	12.2
Big Shovel Pass	2300	17.5
Watchtower jct	2280	17.9
Wabasso jct	2240	19.5
Curator CG	2120	+0.8
The Notch	2510	22.1
Trail summit	2530	24.2
Tekarra CG	2060	30.9
Signal CG jct	2020	35.7
Signal CG	2015	+0.1
Signal Mountain trailhead	1160	44.1

Trailhead

To take advantage of the higher starting elevation, most people hike the Skyline from south to north. Follow Highway 16, 3.7 km east from Jasper to the Maligne Lake Road. Turn east (right). Follow the Maligne Lake Road 44.3 km to the parking area on the west side of the lake. The Skyline trailhead is the most northerly of the two trailheads on the west side of the parking area. A shuttle service is available from Jasper (fee charged).

Maps

NTS: 83 C/12, 83 C/13, 83 D/16
Gem trek: *Jasper and Maligne Lake*

VARIATIONS

- Hike the trail in reverse.
- Day-hike to Little Shovel Pass; 20.6 km return.
- Camp at Snowbowl campground (12.2 km) and explore.
- Hike in from the north, camp at Tekarra campground (13.2 km) and explore.

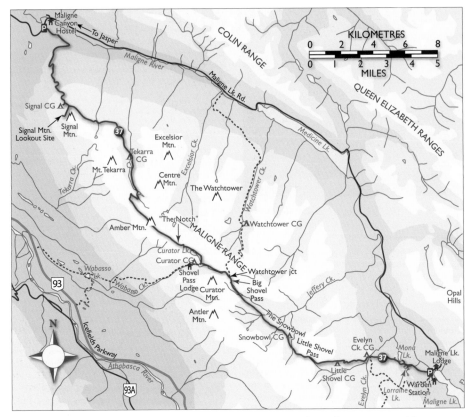

at this higher elevation. Two more members of the heath family are now common in the undergrowth – crowberry and blueberry.

Beyond Little Shovel campground, the trail swings north onto the alpine tundra that leads to Little Shovel Pass. The blooms of ragwort, yellow paintbrush, and mountain fireweed colour the banks of the stream that drains the pass.

Looking southeast from the crest of Little Shovel Pass, the ragged limestone summits of the Queen Elizabeth Range rise above Maligne Lake. Most prominent is Mt. Brazeau (brah-ZOE) (3470 m), highest mountain in the front ranges, 10th-highest in Alberta, and 20-th highest in the Rockies. The pass

THE MAKING OF THE SKYLINE

The section of the Skyline south of Big Shovel Pass was first travelled by Mary Schäffer's expedition to Maligne Lake in 1911. Outfitter Fred Brewster developed the northern part of the trail in 1937. Brewster's patrons journeyed by road from Jasper to Medicine Lake. From there, they were ferried across the lake. They then boarded horse-drawn carts to lodging at Maligne Lake. Return was on horseback along the Skyline to Jasper.

is home to a colony of hoary marmots. Marmots usually prefer the protection of boulderfields. Here, in the absence of protective rocks, they excavate deep burrows on open ground, to remain out of the grasp of grizzly bears, their principal predator.

Little Shovel Pass to Curator Campground

The steady descent north from Little Shovel Pass leads to an extensive upper subalpine basin known as The Snowbowl. Sedges and willows here are important summer foods for mountain caribou. Snowbowl campground makes a good base for day-hiking toward Antler Mountain (2557 m) at the head of the valley. Beyond the grove of trees that harbours the campground, the trail descends north into meadows, and begins its rambling and often muddy ascent toward Big Shovel Pass. Moisture-loving wildflowers and sedges thrive here – fleabane, Sitka valerian, western anemone, ragwort, shooting star, white globeflower, mountain marsh marigold, cotton-grass, and elephant-head. The pink petals of elephant-head have three lobes, which create the ears, trunk, and mouth of the "elephant." Several dozen miniature "elephant-heads" are arranged atop each spike of this showy wildflower. The Latin species name,

MALIGNE LAKE, THE HARD WAY

In 1908, outfitter Billy Warren led a party organized by Mary Schäffer to Maligne Lake. They reached the lake from the south, constructed a raft, explored the waters and named many surrounding features. Schäffer's account of the journey was widely circulated and well received, and brought an unwanted celebrity status.

With the completion of the Grand Trunk Pacific Railway as far as Jasper in 1911, the Canadian government sought to publicize the newly created Jasper Forest Park. Mary Schäffer was invited to return to the lake, to make an accurate map of it. Schäffer, who lamented the coming of the railway and the changes it would bring to the mountains she dearly loved, reluctantly agreed.

Instead of building another raft on the shores of the lake, it was decided that materials for a boat would be packed on horseback from Jasper. Rather than tackle the trackless wilds of the Maligne Valley with such a load, outfitter Jack Otto chose to cross the crest of the Maligne Range. After ascending Wabasso Creek, Otto led the party along the southern part of today's Skyline to the north shore of Maligne Lake.

This unlikely journey was undertaken at an even more unlikely time of year, mid-June, when snows were still deep in the high country. Otto sent an advance party to pack a trail over the high passes. Finding the snow more than they could handle, his men fashioned two impromptu shovels from spruce trees, and used them to scoop out a trail across the passes. The shovels, which Schäffer at first mistook for distant sheep, were left on the high point to greet the following party.

Surveyor A.O. Wheeler subsequently proposed the name "Bighorn Pass" for Big Shovel Pass, because sheep abound in the area. However, Schäffer's place name has endured. The original shovels are now in the collection of the Jasper-Yellowhead Historical Society.

groenlandica, means "Greenland." That's where the species was first catalogued.

Curator Mountain (2624 m), west of Big Shovel Pass, was named for its position as custodian of the pass. An ice apron clings to its eastern slope; its cornice bears the unmistakable brilliant blue of perennial snow.

On the north side of Big Shovel Pass, the trail is a faint path beaten into the screes – easily lost when snow covered. The trail forks. Keep right. Although the rocky slopes appear barren, closer inspection will reveal the blooms of moss campion, alpine harebell, Lyall's goldenweed, golden fleabane, and alpine hawksbeard.

About 400 m north of Big Shovel Pass, the trail from the Watchtower Basin descends the ridge from the east. Scamper up to the ridgecrest for the view over the hanging valley of Watchtower Creek. The striking summit of The Watchtower (2791 m) was first climbed in 1951. Watchtower Basin offers an escape route from the Skyline. It might get you out of the weather quickly, but the route, at least in the early going, is not easy. The initial descent is north. Then the trail switchbacks tightly to the south to contour around the swampy basin at the head of the valley. It is 13.2 km to the Maligne Lake Road.

The Skyline descends to the Wabasso junction. Turn south (left) to camp at Curator campground. This badly eroded sidetrail loses 120 m of elevation in just 800 m. The pleasant campground is set in a grove of trees beneath a waterfall. Shovel Pass Lodge is in the meadow below the campground. Parks Canada claims that the drinking water at this campground is safe, which is surprising, as horses from the lodge

VENERABLE MOUNTAINS

The Maligne Range is part of the eastern main ranges. Elsewhere in the Rockies, these ranges are usually high and rugged. The modest elevations and rounded summits of mountains along the Skyline indicate that they were completely covered by glacial ice during the Late Wisconsin Glaciation – when valley glaciers were a kilometre thick.

Most surface rocks in the Maligne Range are early-Cambrian, Gog Formation quartzite. Map lichen (see p. 119) grows profusely on this rock, making it appear dark from a distance. However, quartzite can be colourful when viewed close-up – buff, pink, purple, and white. Fresh exposures often feature reddish-orange stains caused by iron oxide. The Maligne Range mountains are in marked contrast to the higher, sawtooth and dip-slope mountains of the younger front ranges to the east, which are composed principally of drab, gray limestones.

Curator Lake

The next 5 km are the apex of the Skyline, as it follows the backbone of the Maligne Range across the summit ridge of Amber Mountain at 2530 m – the 10th-highest point reached on the Classic Hikes. Do not attempt this section of trail during electrical storms. Even non-mountaineers will be tempted to walk (no trail) the few hundred metres to Amber Mountain's highest, most northerly point (2565 m). To the east, four parallel ranges of sawtooth mountains rake the sky like rocky waves. You can see Jasper town to the north. Amber Mountain was named because of the colour of its weathered screes. If you study these screes carefully you will see a geologic feature called patterned ground. The soil here is permafrost, although the surface screes thaw for part of the summer. These freeze and thaw cycles churn the top layer of the screes, separating larger particles from smaller ones. On flat terrain this creates shapes called polygons; on slopes it creates stone stripes. This is a place where a single bootprint can literally destroy a century's worth of a miraculous natural process.

From the ridge north of Amber Mountain, the trail leaves the "skyline" and switchbacks down

wander through it. Unless you want to go thirsty, you'll be obliged to sample the cocktail. Boil it first. This is the headwaters of Wabasso Creek, which Mary Schäffer followed to the Skyline in 1911. *Wabasso* is Cree for "rabbit." The Wabasso trail offers a 13.8 km exit from the Skyline to the Icefields Parkway.

Curator Campground to Tekarra Campground

From the Curator campground junction, the Skyline winds north through boulderfields beside Curator Lake, and then climbs steadily to The Notch (2510 m). This pass often sports a cornice of snow on its east side. Give it a wide berth.

The scree summits that flank this lofty pass are walk-ups that offer superb views of the Athabasca Valley. Mt. Edith Cavell (3363 m) is the prominent peak to the southwest. The Ramparts of the Tonquin Valley are beyond. Views south include Mt. Christie (3103 m) and Mt. Fryatt (3361 m), Brussels Peak (3161 m), and the northern fringe of the Columbia Icefield. Directly below, Curator Lake sparkles like a blue gem in a setting of barren stone. On clear days, Mt. Robson (3959 m) towers above the horizon, some 90 km to the northwest.

> *A mile from the summit... Jack rather excitedly called our attention to two tiny specks on the skyline and, though he remained sweetly non-committal and suggested they might be a horse or two men, we knew he meant "sheep," and sheep they promptly became.... Then we came close enough to analyze our two immovable sheep – only to find them a pair of abandoned shovels which had been hewn from a tree and, in case we needed the same, left standing conspicuously in the snow.*
>
> Mary Schäffer; *The 1911 Expedition to Maligne Lake*

PART ROCK, PART ICE

The valleys east of Amber Mountain contain a number of tarns whose blue-green waters indicate glacial sources. However, you won't see any obvious glacial ice. The meltwater comes from rock glaciers, piles of rockslide debris that insulate ice within. There are 119 catalogued rock glaciers in Jasper National Park. The photograph shows one on Centre Mountain.

Tekarra Meadows

toward Centre Lake. On the west slope of Centre Mountain (2700 m), you can see the rock glacier that feeds this lake. Bighorn sheep, mountain caribou, white-tailed ptarmigan, and hoary marmots frequent this area. Mount Tekarra (teh-CAR-rah) (2694 m), with its massive east facing cliffs of Gog Formation quartzite, dominates the view north. *Tekarra* was James Hector's Iroquois guide when the Palliser Expedition travelled to Athabasca Pass in 1859. During your descent to Centre Lake, you pass a gigantic limestone boulder – a glacial erratic. It's a good place to find shade on a hot day, or to take shelter from the wind.

The remaining 2 km to Tekarra campground involve delightful upper subalpine hiking. Mountain fireweed and cotton-grass bloom in the adjacent stream course. The campground is located at the creek crossing, 500 m below the outlet of Tekarra Lake. From this convenient base, mountaineers may make ascents of Mount Tekarra, Centre Mountain, and Excelsior Mountain.

Tekarra Campground to Signal Mountain Trailhead

From Tekarra campground, the trail ascends to treeline and contours around the north flank of Mount Tekarra. The sawtooth limestone slabs of the Colin Range are prominent across the Maligne Valley. Between 1835 and 1849, Colin Fraser was in charge of Jasper House, a Hudson's Bay Company outpost in the Athabasca Valley. James Hector named a mountain for him in 1859.

Signal Mountain – formerly the site of a fire lookout – is the northern outlier of Mt. Tekarra. Its slopes command remarkable views north along a 30 km length of the Athabasca Valley, and west beyond Jasper into the Miette Valley. The mountains northwest of Jasper are the Victoria Cross Range. Five summits in this range were named for Canadian soldiers who were WWI recipients of the Victoria Cross, Britain's highest award for military valor.

Turn north (right) where the trail joins the Signal Mountain fireroad. The Signal campground junction is in 50 m. The Skyline concludes with an 8.4 km fireroad walk, that descends steadily to the Maligne Lake Road. On the way you have views of Roche Bonhomme (ROSH-bun-OMM) in the Colin Range. The mountain's French name means "good fellow rock," and was probably given by the voyageurs of the fur trade in the early 1800s. The strata near the summit bear a striking resemblance to the face of a man, looking skyward. After you spot this old man, you will see many others in Jasper's front ranges. The patch of dead trees below the summit is the remains of a 1985 forest fire.

SIGNAL MOUNTAIN LOOKOUT, 0.9 KM

If you want to top off the Skyline with one last great view, turn southwest (left) at the junction with the Signal Mountain fireroad. Follow the culmination of the fireroad as it climbs the last 100 m to the lookout site, with its grand prospect of the Athabasca and Miette valleys. Built in 1941, Signal Mountain Lookout was the first operational lookout in the national parks. This sidetrip is a particularly good option if you camp at Signal campground. You could nip up to the lookout site for sunset or sunrise, or both.

38. Sulphur Skyline

Sulphur Skyline

TRAIL THUMBNAIL

Day-hike

Route	Elev. (m)	Dist. (km)
Trailhead	1372	0
Sulphur Skyline jct	1508	2.6
Sulphur Ridge summit	2060	4.6

Trailhead
Follow Highway 16 east from Jasper, 42.9 km to the Miette (mee-YETT) Hot Springs Road. Turn south (right) and follow this road 19 km to its end at the Miette Hot Springs parking area. Two trails depart. You want the trailhead that is south (right) of the hot springs pool entrance. Some of the park trail signs refer to this outing as "Sulphur Ridge."

Maps
NTS: 83 F/4
Gem Trek: *Jasper and Maligne Lake*

Best lighting: afternoon

A handful of trails in the front ranges of Jasper and Banff climb from valley bottoms in the montane life zone to alpine ridges or summits. None does so as quickly as the Sulphur Skyline trail. The stiff ascent rewards you with a panoramic view of the wildly contorted peaks in northeastern Jasper. The ridgecrest is usually windy. Carry warm clothing and drinking water.

Trailhead to Sulphur Skyline

Make an end-run around the sheep in the parking area to reach the trailhead. The trail begins as a broad, paved lane, leading southeast from the hot pool building. The mixed forest contains tree species of the montane and lower subalpine life zones, but with an overall ambience that is more damp that usual for the front ranges – Douglas-fir, cottonwood poplar, trembling aspen, lodgepole pine, and white spruce. Scouler's willow – a tall shrub – is abundant, as is common juniper. Wildflowers include northern bedstraw, camas, arnica, yarrow, and harebells. Keep straight ahead where the paved surface ends at the water supply for the hot springs. The trail narrows. Keep left at the subsequent, unsigned junction. From open slopes you can look south to a shallow cirque. The dome to the east (left) of the cirque is your destination.

The trail contours into the pass that separates Sulphur Ridge from the unnamed peak to the north. At the fork junction in the pass, keep south (right) and commence a steep climb. If you have your head down on this section you will miss the rapid transition from lower subalpine to upper subalpine forest. Kruppelholz spruce and fir trees testify to the windiness of this location. A band of bighorn sheep frequents these slopes. This trail was rebuilt in the 1990s; log benches block the old switchbacks. White rhododendron grows here, along with a rarity on the Classic Hikes – the nodding, purple bloom of monkshood. You may also see a beautiful hybrid form of columbine that has a yellow flower head and mauve sepals. I have not seen this elsewhere.

The trail curves south as it gains treeline on the east shoulder of Sulphur Ridge, revealing a spectacular view southeast over the Fiddle River valley and the Nikanassin Range. The Nikanassin and the adjoining Miette Range to the north are oriented along the strike of the Rockies, northwest-southeast. The mountains consist of resistant rocks in the upturned edge of a thrust sheet. The valleys on either side have been eroded into the weak shales along the thrust faults, and are known as strike valleys. Looking north, you can see how Fiddle River valley aligns with the Moosehorn valley, northwest

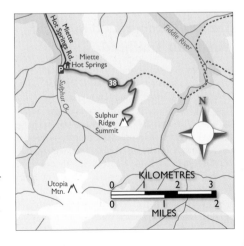

Hybrid columbine

of the Athabasca River. The Athabasca is an antecedent stream. It cut through the strike alignment as the mountains were being created, making two sidevalleys out of what would have been one valley, and bisecting the parallel ranges of mountains.

The trail levels briefly at treeline in a meadow with a white quartzite boulder at trailside, and quartzite rubble underfoot. If you think that the boulder looks out of place among the surrounding siltstone – you're right. The boulder is a glacial erratic, transported by glacial ice some 30 km from the main ranges to the west, and deposited here when the ice receded. Erratics provide glaciologists with clues as to the ice age origins of ice age glaciers. On one visit, a mule deer was hanging around here, obviously accustomed to hand-outs. On another visit, 32 bighorn sheep crowded this meadow and the slopes nearby.

The trail leaves the windblasted kruppelholz to traverse west beneath the summit dome of Sulphur Ridge, which sits atop the crest of an anticline. It then switchbacks tightly upslope to the summit – a tough climb on a rough track. To the east, foothills and prairie stretch to the horizon. A sea of rugged front limestone peaks floods the view in all other directions. Ashlar Ridge (1700 m) will catch your eye to the north. "Ashlar" is a form of masonry – thin

THE MIETTE REEF: LEGACY OF ANCIENT OCEAN

The mountains near Miette Hot Springs contain a remarkable formation called the Miette Reef. This reef was built by encrusting colonies of sponges – called stromatoporoids (strome-at-oh-PORE-oids) – that lived in warm, shallow seas during the Late Devonian. The Miette Reef amassed to a thickness of 200 m before being entombed in sediments that killed the stromatoporoids and the other reef-building lifeforms. The reef was once again brought to the earth's surface during mountain building; this time, high and dry. The principal rocks are the gray and black dolomite of the Cairn Formation and the pale limestone and dolomite of the overlying Southesk Formation. The Miette is but one reef in a larger system called the Fairholme Reef Complex, into which most of southern Alberta's oil and gas wells have been drilled. Less than 10 km east of Sulphur Ridge – outside Jasper National Park – drilling crews are active, tapping petroleum resources in the foothills. You can see the seismic lines – narrow strips in the forest cut during petroleum exploration. You can't drill for oil or gas in the park, but if you tried, you'd go bust. The oil has long since drained from the Miette Reef.

Bighorn sheep on Sulphur Ridge

FIRST RANGE AND FIRST FIDDLE

Nikanassin is Cree for "first range." It is the first row of the Rockies in this area when viewed from the east. In 1846, Pierre-Jean De Smet, a Jesuit missionary, called the Fiddle River, *La Rivière au Violon* (Violin River). Various origins of the river's name are given. The most far-fetched claims that the wind makes the sound of a violin when it strikes the ridge of the nearby Fiddle Range. It is more likely that De Smet – who travelled with a fur trade brigade – was entertained at camp by a fiddle-playing voyageur. De Smet's "violin" was soon corrupted to "fiddle."

Mountain meadow cinquefoil

The stiff beds of limestone, quartzite and slate of the Athabasca Mountains [front ranges] must have been buried under a far thicker load of overlying rock than was the case farther south-east to make them so much more plastic, and one must imagine them to have been thousands of feet below the original surface when they were crumpled and contorted into their present daring forms.

A.P. Coleman; *The Canadian Rockies, New and Old Trails*

dressed stones used to cover brick or rubble. The remarkable 300 m high cliff of the upper mountain is resistant Palliser Formation limestone. Utopia Mountain (2563 m) is 3 km to the southwest of Sulphur Ridge. A survey crew named the mountain because its summit provided them with refuge from the flies in the valley bottom.

Sulphur Ridge is an unofficial name for this minor summit, given in recognition of the pungent smell of Miette Hot Springs. The springs are the hottest (53.9 °C) and most aromatic in the Rockies. You won't catch a whiff of sulphur on the summit. However, on your return to the parking area, you can follow the boardwalk south past the old hot springs building. Here, at the spring outlets, the sulphur aroma is prominent, as is the yellow colour of elemental sulphur, produced as the hydrogen sulphide reacts with oxygen. Speaking of hot springs, why not grab your swim gear (you packed it, right?) and go for a dip.

Mt. Robson Provincial Park

39. Berg Lake

Mt. Robson

MOUNT ROBSON PROVINCIAL PARK

TRAIL THUMBNAIL

Overnight, 2-6 days

Route	Elev. (m)	Dist. (km)
Trailhead	862	0
Kinney Lake	985	4.2
Kinney Lake viewpoint	1006	5.2
Kinney Lake CG	990	6.8
Whitehorn CG	1138	10.9
Emperor Falls viewpoint	1493	14.7
Emperor Falls CG	1642	15.4
Marmot CG	1660	18.1
Hargreaves Glacier jct	1663	18.5
Berg Lake CG	1660	20.2
Toboggan Creek jct	1655	20.3
Rearguard CG	1659	21.3
Snowbird Pass jct	1659	21.7
Robson Pass CG jct	1655	22.2
Robson Pass CG	1655	+0.1
Robson Pass	1652	22.6

Trailhead
Follow Highway 16, 84 km west from Jasper; 18 km east from Tete Jaune Cache, BC; to the park information centre at Robson Junction. Obtain your permit here. Turn north and follow the paved sideroad 2 km to its end at the Berg Lake trailhead parking area.

Maps
NTS: 83 E/3

Towering majestically above Berg Lake, the two-kilometre-high north flank of Mt. Robson epitomizes the Canadian Rockies. Clad with a magnificent array of glaciers, this monolith of rock, snow, and ice is without equal in a range of mountains celebrated for its scenery.

The Berg Lake trail, which brings you to the foot of Mt. Robson's awesome northern rampart, is by far the most heavily travelled backpacking route in the Canadian Rockies. Four thousand people register each summer for overnight trips – they stay an average of 2.7 days each. Another 50,000 make day-hikes. Strong backpackers can reach Berg Lake in a day, but campgrounds along the way allow you to break the approach conveniently into two days.

Obtain your permit at the park information centre on Highway 16. There are 98 tent sites on the trail, 18 of which can be reserved in advance for any given day. Phone 800-689-9025. The trail is open to mountain bikes as far as Kinney Lake campground. Horse packers occasionally use the trail. Helicopters land at Robson Pass two days a week. Flightseeing traffic is common overhead.

Trailhead to Kinney Lake

The broad trail to Kinney Lake is always within sound of the Robson River. Look for harlequin ducks and dippers in the fast-flowing water. The forest features species that typify BC's Western Interior Hemlock Forest zone – western redcedar (BC's provincial tree), western hemlock, western white pine, thimbleberry, and devil's club. The trail passes through an old-growth stand of western redcedars about 2 km from the trailhead. Scan the forest for BC's provincial bird – the hooded, blue and black, Steller's jay. At km 3 the trail bisects a mineral lick used by elk, deer, moose, and mountain goats. Look for their tracks. We have seen a moose in the Robson River, just beyond this point.

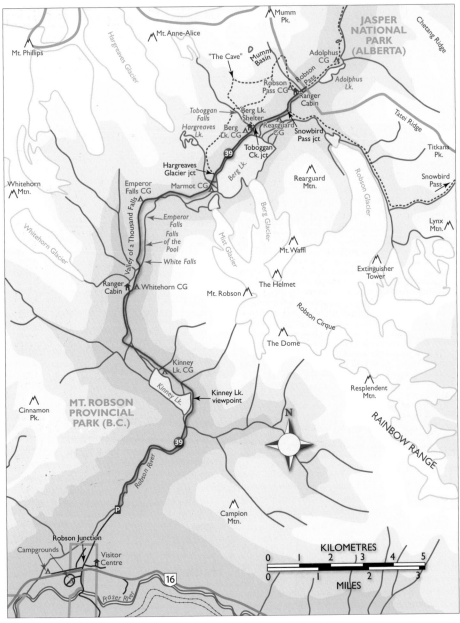

About an hour from the trailhead, you reach the outlet of Kinney Lake – sometimes referred to as "the mirror of the mount. " Just downstream from the outlet, a creek that drains the basin between Mt. Robson and Mt. Resplendent has created an alluvial fan in the Robson River. This fan holds back some of the river's energy, helping to create Kinney Lake. In recent years, the shoreline and trail near the lake have often been flooded. One of the better views of the lake is from the viewpoint on its southeast shore, 1 km beyond the outlet bridge. Avalanche slopes on Cinnamon Peak extend to waterline on the opposite shore.

Leaving the Kinney Lake viewpoint, the trail climbs over a rise and descends to the lakeshore. The remaining distance to Kinney Lake campground is across an alluvial fan that contains material eroded from the southwest face of Mt. Robson. Beyond the campground you climb through forest and then descend to cross the delta at the inlet to the lake.

THE REVEREND MOUNTAINEER

Kinney Lake commemorates Reverend George Kinney, who was in the first mountaineering party to attempt Mt. Robson. In 1907, Kinney and A.P. Coleman approached the mountain on horseback from Lake Louise – a journey that took six weeks. Poor weather and a shortage of food put end to the exploration before they could set foot on the mountain. Kinney returned in 1908 and again in 1909 when, with outfitter Curly Phillips, he nearly reached the summit by a difficult route on the west face. Given their scant equipment and Phillips' lack of mountaineering experience, it was a bold and remarkable achievement, tainted later by the fact that Kinney claimed to have reached the summit, while Phillips admitted his doubt in the matter.

THE MOUNTAIN OF THE SPIRAL ROAD

Mt. Robson (3957 m) towers 3095 m above the trailhead, yet the summit is only 8 km away. This staggering vertical relief is hard to grasp. By way of comparison, Mt. Temple rises slightly more than 2000 m from the floor of the Bow Valley near Lake Louise, and Mt. Stephen rises 1900 m above the Kicking Horse Valley at Field.

Mt. Robson is 216 m higher than Mt. Columbia, the 2nd-highest mountain in the Rockies, and 549 m higher than Resplendent Mountain (3408 m), the next highest peak nearby. Why is Mt. Robson so high? Its rock is not particularly tough. The secret is that the layers are flat-lying through the centre of the peak. Flat-lying layers are more difficult for glaciers to erode than tilted layers. This rock sandwich – almost 4 km thick – is one of the more complete, unbroken assemblages of Cambrian rock exposed anywhere on earth.

The strata bend slightly upward from the centre of the mountain toward the east and west, revealing a broad syncline. This creates the illusion of spiral ramps. Secwempc (Shuswap) First Peoples from the interior of BC knew Mt. Robson as *Yuh-hai-has-kun* – "mountain of the spiral road." As impressive as it is, Mt. Robson is not the highest mountain in British Columbia, nor is Mt. Waddington (4019 m), the other popular guess. The honour belongs to Mt. Fairweather (4671 m), on the boundary with Alaska.

The quest to find the definitive origin of Mt. Robson's name has been a bane for scholars of Rockies' history. You might think that the monarch mountain of the range was named to honour a politician, official or dignitary. Elsewhere in BC, the name "Robson" appears frequently, commemorating John Robson, provincial premier from 1889-92. However, there is no connection here.

The name "Mt. Robinson" may have been in use for the mountain as early as 1827. Scholars agree that the strongest candidate to lay claim to the name is Colin Robertson, an officer with the North West and Hudson's Bay companies. In 1820, Robertson dispatched a group of Iroquois fur traders to the area immediately west of Mt. Robson. They may have applied the name, which was subsequently corrupted – twice – through use.

Kinney Lake to Emperor Falls

From the north end of the delta, the trail climbs steeply above the west bank of the Robson River into the Valley of a Thousand Falls. As mountaineer J.M. Thorington observed in 1925: "If not quite a thousand falls come streaming down from the cliffs on either side, the number is at all events most satisfactory and surpassed only by the beauty of their height." Along the trail, you will also see three waterfalls on the Robson River – White Falls, Falls of the Pool, and Emperor Falls.

The trail descends to a suspension bridge crossing of the Robson River. It is safest to cross the bridge one at a time. Whitehorn campground is on the east bank. Emergency assistance may be available at the Whitehorn ranger cabin, on the west bank of the river, just north of the bridge. The trail recrosses the Robson River on another bridge 800 m north of the campground. Yellow lady's slipper orchids bloom on the gravels nearby in early July.

To this point the elevation changes have been gentle. In the next 4.5 km, the trail climbs 503 m. For the 1913 Alpine Club of Canada camp in Robson Pass, outfitter Curly Phillips constructed "The Flying Trestle Bridge" – a decked, log structure that made it possible for pack horses to ascend the first cliff. Viewpoints for the three waterfalls on the Robson River provide scenic distraction from the hard work. Use caution near the cliff edges.

As you approach Emperor Falls, note the abandoned river gorge east of the trail. This is a beheaded stream. The Robson River formerly flowed here but the water subsequently eroded a new channel farther east. In places, the new course of the river is above the present level of the trail. At high water, a trickle of the Robson River spills into the abandoned gorge. Emperor Falls viewpoint is 150 m east on a sidetrail.

Snowbird Pass trail

CLOUD CAP MOUNTAIN

From Emperor Falls campground, you can often see how Mt. Robson creates its own weather. Prevailing winds are from the southwest. When the west side of the mountain is clear, the north and east sides may display a banner cloud. Pluming from the summit, this cloud is created when damp air is forced to rise in order to clear the crest. It does not necessarily presage rain or snow. However, if clouds begin to mass at mid-height on the western side of the mountain, the weather is likely to deteriorate. Climbers and hikers on the east and north sides may not see this sure sign of an approaching storm, and are frequently caught in the foul weather that results.

The tendency for weather to change rapidly on Mt. Robson is one of the principal reasons why it is so difficult to climb. Most of the climbing routes require 3-5 days for a round trip from the highway. In some years, when poor climbing conditions and foul weather persist, Mt. Robson may go unclimbed despite dozens of attempts. Between 1939 and 1953, not a single mountaineering party was known to have reached the summit. When The Overlanders passed Mt. Robson in 1862, bound for the Cariboo goldfields, their native guide informed them that he had seen the summit only once in his first 29 visits. Not surprisingly, they called it "Cloud Cap Mountain."

Immediately behind us, a giant among giants, and immeasurably supreme, rose Robson's Peak. This magnificent mountain is of conical form, glacier clothed and rugged. When we first caught sight of it, a shroud of mist partially enveloped the summit, but this presently rolled away, and we saw its upper portion dimmed by a necklace of light, feathery clouds, beyond which its pointed apex of ice, glittering in the morning sun, shot up far into the blue heaven above...

Milton and Cheadle; *The Northwest Passage by Land*

The glaciers you see at Berg Lake only hint at the vast domain of glacial ice concealed on the east slopes of Mt. Robson. You get the full view from the trail to Snowbird Pass, a strenuous outing with views rarely matched in the Rockies.

Head northeast from Berg Lake campground, past the cotton-grass ponds on the Toboggan Creek alluvial fan. Continue through Rearguard campground and onto the glacial flats near Robson Pass. The Snowbird Pass trail branches southeast (right) at km 1.1, and strikes off through the forefield of Robson Glacier. The showy, twisted seedheads of white mountain-avens cover the gravels in July and August. Mountain fireweed grows along the stream courses. Lynx Mountain (3175 m) is directly ahead, between the slopes of Tatei (tat-EH-ee) Ridge (2781 m) on the east (left), and Rearguard Mountain (2744 m) on the west (right). *Tatei* is Stoney for "wind."

The most recent advance of Robson Glacier reached its maximum in 1782. Tree-ring evidence (see p. 109) from this area indicates that the glacier began advancing into living forest in 1142. In 1911, A.O. Wheeler marked two large rocks in the forefield, recording the distance from each rock to the toe of Robson Glacier. In 1911, the toe of the glacier was 53 m distant from the western rock. When last measured in 1989, the ice had receded 1249 m. In the early 1990s, farther upvalley in an area just melted out from the ice, glaciologists discovered the stumps of trees that had been overrun by the glacier more than 3700 years ago.

The rocky knoll east of the trail is a nunatak. Robson Glacier splayed around the nunatak early in the 20th century, sending meltwater streams northeast to Adolphus Lake (Arctic Ocean watershed), and southwest to Berg Lake (Pacific Ocean watershed). This was one of a few instances in the world where a single alpine valley glacier (as opposed to an icefield) fed two oceans. Why could this be significant? Well, for one thing, if it were still the case that Robson Glacier fed two oceans, the BC-Alberta boundary would run along the centreline of Robson Glacier, and the provinces would share the summit of Mt. Robson. But more importantly, the dwindling of Robson Glacier demonstrates how source water for a major river system can be shut off by a changing climate. From a precipitation point of view, it is already "dry" east and northeast of the Rockies. Take the melt of hundreds of glaciers out of the water cycle, and trouble looms.

If you explore off-trail here, you can trace the ancient meltwater courses, and you will see striations – bedrock scratches caused by stone fragments embedded in the underside of Robson Glacier. The concrete cairns in the vicinity mark the Alberta-BC boundary.

Meltwater from the terminus of Robson Glacier collects in a marginal lake. The western lobe of the glacier toe exhibits massive horizontal crevasses. As the glacier retreats, huge chunks of ice separate along these fissures, to avalanche into the lake. The dark, lengthwise strips of rubble on the glacier's surface are medial moraines, formed by the merging of tributary glaciers "upstream." On the lower mountainsides either side of the terminus, you can see the trimlines of the Little Ice Age advances. There are two trimlines here, indicating advances of different extent. The advancing ice scoured the vegetation below the trimlines. The lower icefalls on Robson Glacier feature a myriad of free-standing pinnacles of ice. These seracs (sair-RACKS) form where crevassed glacial ice plunges over irregularities in the bedrock.

The trail angles uphill through moraines east of the marginal lake. Follow cairns where necessary. The graceful horn of Resplendent Mountain (3408 m) rises from the head of Robson Glacier. Immediately east of it is Extinguisher Tower (2433 m), a minor summit named for its resemblance to a candle snuffer. Looking back, the summits north of Berg Lake rise in parallel, dip-slope ramps. The glaciated peak farthest west is Mt. Phillips (3246 m), named for outfitter Curly Phillips. Farthest east is Mumm Peak (2964 m), named for English mountaineer Arnold Mumm, who was in the party that made its first ascent in 1910, after a failed attempt on Mt. Robson.

The track climbs steeply through ice-cored moraines. Sections of the route occasionally slump where the ice melts out. The exposed ice appears black. Keep off it. A steep switchback leads through a cliff to the creek that drains Snowbird Meadows. But – as wonderful as the meadows are – you will probably be looking over your shoulder to where a chaos of cascading ice fills the view. The icefall at the head of Robson Glacier leads to the rounded summit of The Dome (3090 m). The snow and ice face above is the Kain Face, named for Conrad Kain, who guided the first ascent of Mt. Robson via this route in 1913. At the time, it was the most difficult mountaineering route in North America. Without benefit of the tools and equipment enjoyed by modern mountaineers, Kain chopped more than 600 steps in this icy slope during the ascent. His rope mates, A.H. MacCarthy and W.F. Foster, praised Kain's ability and courage. When he reached the summit, Kain stepped aside and, with customary modesty, announced: "Gentlemen, that's as far as I can take you." The Kain Face is one of two "regular routes" on Mt. Robson today.

The trail climbs east through rolling upper subalpine meadows on the north side of the creek toward Snowbird Pass. These meadows are one of two places that could lay claim to being the hoary marmot capital of the Rockies. The other is Maligne Pass. Mountain fireweed and yellow mountain saxifrage grow on the gravels in the creek. Follow cairns through the final slopes of scree and boulders.

Snowbird Pass is located on the continental divide and on the boundary between Mt. Robson Provincial Park and Jasper National Park. It commands a lofty view across the 25 km2 Reef Icefield and the head of Coleman Glacier to the east. Titkana Peak (2827 m) rises north of Snowbird Pass. *Titkana* is Iroquois for "ptarmigan."

The drenching spray is a welcome relief on a hot day, but can make the viewpoint a soggy location for photographing the falls. The driest vantages for photography are on the main trail.

The trail levels and draws alongside the Robson River at Emperor Falls campground. The Emperor Ridge of Mt. Robson rises across the river. The mountaineering route of Kinney and Phillips lay slightly south of this ridge. Today, the Emperor Ridge is considered one of the harder routes on Mt. Robson, and in the Rockies. "Emperor" refers to the fact that Mt. Robson is "monarch of the Rockies."

Emperor Falls to Berg Lake

From Emperor Falls campground, the trail curves east into the upper valley of the Robson River, revealing partial views of Mist Glacier and Berg Glacier on the north side of Mt. Robson. After contouring above the river on a boulderslope – look and listen for pikas – the trail descends to the river flats. Rock-hop as necessary. In the view west, Whitehorn Mountain (3399 m) rises majestically above the Valley of a Thousand Falls. As its name suggests, the mountain is a classic, glacially carved horn.

The final kilometre to Berg Lake is routed across a large alluvial fan, created by the creek that drains Hargreaves Glacier to the north. From the crest of the fan, Berg Lake comes into view. The trail descends to the northwest shore of the lake at Marmot campground. If you stay here you will escape the crowds at campgrounds farther along the trail. However, the exposed gravels of the Hargreaves fan can be bleak during poor weather.

Berg Lake

The trail continues along the northwest shore of Berg Lake, passing the Hargreaves Glacier junction. You can now see the entire north flank of Mt. Robson. Berg Lake is the largest lake in the Rockies into which a glacier flows directly. Although Berg Glacier still reaches the lake, is considerably smaller than when

first photographed in 1908. Two lateral moraines flank the terminus and extend into the lake, giving an indication of the glacier's size during the Little Ice Age.

Tent sites at Berg Lake campground are on both sides of Toboggan Creek. The Hargreaves shelter is a day-use facility only. The building was constructed as a guest chalet by the Hargreaves family, one-time owners of Mt. Robson Ranch. It was later donated to BC Parks. The shelter is frequently overrun. Rodents pilfer the food lockers.

If the crowded environs of Berg Lake campground are not to your liking, continue to Rearguard campground or Robson Pass campground. If you really want to get away from the crowds, Adolphus campground beckons, 4.6 km northeast from Berg Lake in Jasper National Park. You'll need to book the campsite and purchase a wilderness pass at the Jasper park information centre.

HOARY MARMOTS: INDOLENT RODENTS

The hoary marmot is a large rodent that resembles the woodchuck, to which it is related. Its preferred habitat is upper subalpine boulderfields and meadows. The marmot eats grasses, leaves, flowers, and berries, never straying too far from its den. Grizzly bears, lynx, hawks, and eagles are its principal predators. The shrill whistle of the marmot warns its fellows that a threat is near, and gives rise to its folk name, "whistle-pig." "Hoary" refers to its grayish-tipped coat. The marmot disdains the hardships of winter, autumn, and spring; it hibernates nine months of the year. The Snowbird marmots have little fear of hikers, and a fondness for exploring packs, boots, and lunches without invitation. Please do not feed them.

BERG LAKE

Plan on the 2.1 km hike along the shore of Berg Lake taking longer than expected. The incredible north face of Mt. Robson will have you rubbernecking frequently. A.P. Coleman named Berg Lake in 1908, in reference to the ice bergs or "growlers" that calve from the glacier. These ice avalanches provide terrific entertainment for campers. A few hours after an avalanche, the prevailing wind usually will have carried the bergs to the lakeshore near Berg Lake campground. You bring the Scotch, the glacier provides "the rocks."

HARGREAVES GLACIER-MUMM BASIN, (2103 M) 14.5 KM LOOP

This outing undulates over diverse terrain on the slopes north of Berg Lake, providing incomparable views of Mt. Robson. From Berg Lake campground, follow the Berg Lake trail southwest for 1.7 km to the Hargreaves Glacier junction. Turn north (right). Ascend a steep track along a dry stream bed, and follow cairns to the east lateral moraine of Hargreaves Glacier. Continue to a signed, 300 m sidetrail that takes you to the crest of the moraine, from where the view opens northwest over the rocky basin that contains Hargreaves Glacier and its marginal lake.

Hargreaves Glacier 1992

Hargreaves Glacier 2010

As recently as 200 years ago, Hargreaves Glacier filled the basin to the height of this moraine. The glacier is south-facing – not a good thing for ice as the climate warms. The rapid retreat of the glacier has uncovered a fantastically smooth slab of apricot and gray limestone and dolomite of the Eldon and Pika formations. An upturned lip of this rock dams the lake. The photos, taken in 1992 and 2010, record a stunning degree of change. Note the decrease in the size and thickness of the glacier, and the appearance of small trees.

The view south from the moraine provides new detail of Mt. Robson. Mist Glacier terminates in a marginal lake, separated from Berg Lake by a horseshoe-shaped terminal moraine. The cliffs between upper Mist Glacier and the Emperor Ridge are known as the Emperor Face. This face was first climbed in 1978 and has not often been repeated. The ice sheet to the left is the true "north face" of the mountain, first climbed in 1963. A long sought after prize for extreme skiers, the face was first skied in 1995. The two glaciated peaks northeast of Mt. Robson are The Helmet (3418 m), and Mt. Waffl (2913 m); the latter named for Newman Waffl, who died in a 1930 solo attempt on Mt. Robson.

From the Hargreaves moraine, follow the cairned trail northeast to treeline. Views ahead include Adolphus Lake in Jasper National Park. The lake commemorates Adolphus Moberly, a Métis settler of the Athabasca Valley who guided A.P. Coleman to Mt. Robson in 1908. The lake's dark blue colour indicates that its water is non-glacial.

A steep descent through delightful upper subalpine meadows brings you to a crossing of Toboggan Creek, and a trail junction 150 m beyond. You can exit this hike to Berg Lake campground by following the track 1.2 km downstream (right), past Toboggan Falls – a slab waterfall that resembles a waterslide. Turn northwest (left) at this junction to continue to Mumm Basin, stopping at "the Cave." The track climbs steeply through burned forest for approximately 1.5 km to the cave entrance – a horizontal slot in the Eldon Formation limestone.

Bring a headlamp if you'd like to explore, but beware of ice on the floor. The Cave itself won't be to everyone's liking, however the panorama of Berg Lake and Mt. Robson from nearby is the climax of this outing. Group of Seven artist, Lawren Harris, depicted this scene in a work titled "Tumbling Glacier." Looking south, Resplendent Mountain fills the notch between Mt. Waffl and Rearguard Mountain. If you study the upper valley of Toboggan Creek carefully, you will see where the creek emerges from underground.

If you want to exit at this point, descend straight down Toboggan Creek to Berg Lake campground. To carry on, you can follow cairns from the Cave to contour east onto a high trail, crossing boulders, screes, and meadows toward Mumm Basin. The rocks here are all Middle Cambrian – limestones of the Chetang and Pika formations, and Arctomys (ARK-toe-miss) Formation shale. If you time it right, the wildflower displays will be superb, including clumps of fringed grass-of-parnassus, and the showy seedheads of western anemone.

Mumm Basin

The trail crosses briefly into Alberta, before commencing a steep descent to Robson Pass. After re-entering BC at boundary cairn "4U," the steep descent continues on a well-beaten trail to Robson Pass campground. Turn southwest (right) at the junction just beyond to return to Berg Lake.

Takkakaw Falls

Yoho National Park

Founded in 1886 as Canada's second national park, Yoho includes 1313 km² on the western slopes of the Rockies in BC. "Yoho" is a Cree expression of awe and wonder – sentiments affirmed by many hikers who cherish the park's 350 km of trails. The Classic Hikes in Yoho provide high-level views of the park's lake-dotted, glaciated landscape.

The village of Field is in the centre of the park; 85 km west of Banff; 26 km west of Lake Louise; and 57 km east of Golden on Highway 1. Access is by car or by passenger bus. Accommodation and basic supplies are available. The park information centre is on Highway 1 at the Field junction. Yoho is in the Mountain time zone – the same as Banff and Jasper national parks.

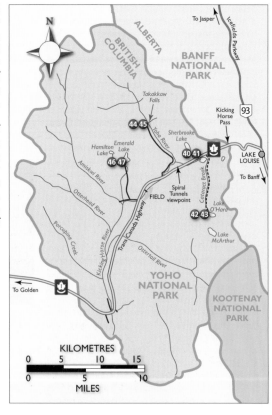

40. Paget Lookout

Paget Lookout

TRAIL THUMBNAIL

Day-hike

Route	Elev.	Dist.
	(m)	(km)
Trailhead	1616	0
Paget Lookout jct	1783	1.4
Paget Lookout	2134	3.5

Trailhead
Wapta Lake picnic area on the north side of Highway 1, 11 km east of Field; 15 km west of Lake Louise. For safety, eastbound travellers should make a U-turn at West Louise Lodge, 500 m east of the trailhead, and approach westbound. The trailhead is adjacent to the picnic shelter.

Maps
NTS: 82 N/8
Gem Trek: *Lake Louise and Yoho*

Best lighting: any time

In the aftermath of large forest fires in 1936 and 1940, the Dominion Parks Branch surveyed the mountain national parks to determine suitable sites for fire lookouts. The sites chosen each possessed unrestricted views of major valleys and were in line of sight with adjacent lookouts in the system. Connected by telephone to warden stations in the valleys below, lookout staff would phone in reports of smokes and fires. The upper slope of Paget (PADGE-ett) Peak was one of three sites chosen in Yoho National Park. Paget Lookout saw use until the late 1970s. The access trail is still maintained and the lookout building is open as a day-use shelter. From the lookout, you are rewarded with a grand overview of much of eastern Yoho National Park.

Trailhead to Paget Lookout

Hike northeast from the picnic area for 80 m to a junction. Make a sharp turn west (left). The next 1.3 km of trail ascends through subalpine forest, notable for its inclusion of cottonwood poplars and Douglas-firs; both species are near their altitudinal limits. In early summer, you may spot the blooms of evergreen violets and calypso orchids. Some trees still sport insulators from the days when the lookout was connected to the Wapta Lake warden station by telephone. You'll also see old stumps – evidence of logging during railway construction in the 1880s.

Turn northeast (right) at the junction at km 1.4. The trail crosses and recrosses an avalanche slope

> *We made the ascent of the mountain to the north across Wapta Lake... The view from this mountain presents 5 small lakes, one of which at the time of our exploration was still covered with ice.*
>
> J.J. McArthur; *Report of Department of the Interior 1887*

beneath Paget Peak. I've seen spruce grouse here. The cliffs to the north contain a sequence of Cambrian rocks – five formations in all – that dip toward the southwest.

Where the trail begins its switchback ascent through the cliffs of Paget Peak, whitebark pine trees become common. The whitebark pine grows in the upper subalpine life zone and prefers windswept locations. On younger trees the bark is smooth and silvery-gray; on older trees, it is gray and scaly. The needles are in bunches of five.

The switchbacks provide glimpses of Mt. Niles (2967 m) and Sherbrooke Lake – the third largest lake in Yoho. Mt. Ogden (2703 m) rises from the western shore of the lake. The mountain commemorates Isaac Ogden, a vice-president of the Canadian Pacific Railway. The Lower Spiral Tunnel is in the opposite flank of the mountain. I've often seen boreal toads on these switchbacks, hike-hopping along. At the top of the switchbacks the grade eases, and the trail heads northeast to the lookout. Early season hikers will be treated to displays of glacier lilies.

VARIATION

- Combine this outing with a visit to Sherbrooke Lake, 10.2 km total; or to Sherbrooke Lake and Niles Meadows, 23.8 km total. See Classic Hike #41.

Mountain goats

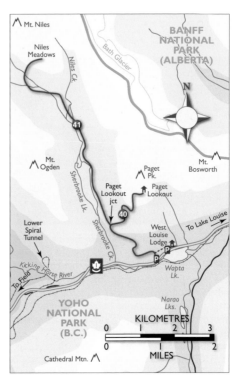

Paget Lookout commands a 180° panorama, from Mt. Richardson, the Slate Range, and the Bow Valley in the northeast; to the lofty peaks that surround Lake Louise and Lake O'Hara in the south; and to the Van Horne Range and the middle reach of the Kicking Horse Valley in the southwest. Narao Peak (nah-RAY-owe) (2973 m) peak is across the valley to the southeast. The mountain's name is Stoney for "hit in the stomach," probably a reference to when James Hector of the Palliser Expedition was kicked by his horse, near Wapta Falls in 1858. The forested slopes of Narao Peak show different shades of green, indicating tree stands dominated by different species. Most of the upper Kicking Horse Valley burned in 1889 in fires caused by railway operations. The lighter green canopy indicates stands of lodgepole pine. The darker, taller canopy indicates more ancient stands of Engelmann spruce and subalpine fir.

In the view from the lookout, you can see how the gradient of the Kicking Horse River, which flows west from the continental divide, is much steeper than that of the Bow River, which flows east. Rivers on the west slope of the Rockies flow only about 525 km straight line distance to the Pacific Ocean. East

WATERBARS: GOING WITH THE FLOW

Hiking trails disturb natural drainage patterns. The ideal slope for a hiking trail is 12°. On trails that are less steep, water may water collect in low spots. Trails that are steeper often become stream courses. Waterbars are one of several devices that trail crews use to prevent water from collecting underfoot. A waterbar is an angled log or a row of rocks embedded in the trail to divert water from the tread to an area off-trail where drainage is better. Waterbars are often installed on steep sections of trail that ascend upslope, or across a sideslope, like those on the upper part of the Paget Lookout trail. Without waterbars, these sections of trail would erode into channels. Waterbars are ideally located where there is a natural dip on the downhill edge of the trail. In the absence of such a dip, trail crews may bevel the trail where they install the waterbar, to increase its effectiveness. Waterbars are often slippery and pose a genuine tripping hazard. Step over them, not on them.

BEAUTY CONCEALED

Calypso is Greek for "concealment." You'll find the exquisite calypso orchid tucked away in damp, shaded woods, such as those along the trail as far as Paget Lookout junction. The calypso blooms soon after winter's snow melts.

KETTLES AND SINKS

Many of the major east-west passes in the Rockies (Kicking Horse, Vermilion, Yellowhead, and Crowsnest) have lakes near their summits. The massive ice sheets of the early Pleistocene glaciations scoured these passes, 1.9 million-years-ago. At the end of the most recent glaciation, the Late Wisconsin, huge blocks of rubble-covered ice came to rest atop the passes. As the ice blocks melted, the rubble slumped, creating hollows. The resulting lakes are known as kettles. Wapta Lake is a kettle, as are Summit Lake and Sink Lake farther east in Kicking Horse Pass. Sink Lake has no visible surface outlet, and may drain underground into Wapta Lake. When Highway 1 was constructed through Yoho in 1956, crews excavating a road cut near Wapta Lake found permafrost – evidence of the remnant glacial ice. *Wapta* is a Stoney word for "river." It was the original name of the Kicking Horse River.

slope rivers flow about 1500 km to Hudson Bay or 2200 km to the Arctic Ocean. A steep gradient gives a river much more energy, and enables it to erode a deeper valley. The town of Field is 16.3 km west of Kicking Horse Pass as the water flows, at an elevation of 1242 m. At an equal distance east of Kicking Horse Pass on the Bow River, the valley floor elevation is 1533 m.

You may see some of Yoho's estimated population of 400 mountain goats nearby. For decades, big-horn sheep were thought to be absent from the park. However, since the early 1990s sheep have made regular appearances at a mineral lick on the lower slopes of Paget Peak, adjacent to Highway 1. I have seen spruce grouse at the lookout.

Paget Peak (2580 m) was named for Reverend Dean Paget of Calgary, a founding member of the Alpine Club of Canada, who climbed the peak in 1904. Surveyor J.J. McArthur made the first ascent in 1886.

JAMES HECTOR

"He was admired and talked about by every man that travelled with him and his fame as a traveller was a wonder and a byword among many a teepee that never saw the man." So wrote Peter Erasmus, James Hector's assistant on the Palliser Expedition of 1857-60. Hector was but 22 when, in 1856, he was recommended to the expedition as its doctor and geologist. He had received his medical degree earlier that year – which says something of the training of the day – but his real purpose in becoming an M.D. had been to study the subjects that only enrollment in the medical college at the University of Edinburgh made available – botany, geology, and chemistry. During the expedition's travels, Hector brought his remarkable powers of observation to the unknown lands of western Canada. His journals and official reports are a mother-lode of information and detail that paint a lucid picture of the Canadian Rockies just over a decade before the railway surveyors arrived.

In addition to his scholarly work, Hector pounded along his share of tracks and trails – 900 km in one 57-day stint in 1858 alone – and made the first recorded crossings by a European of four passes – Vermilion, Kicking Horse, Pipestone, and Howse. But for all his travels, Hector is best known for a mishap that took place on August 29,

1858, when he was kicked in the chest by his horse and rendered unconscious. Two days later, his men were calling the river along which they travelled, the "Kicking Horse." Two days after that, they crossed Kicking Horse Pass. Given his injury and that his party was perpetually short of food, it is not surprising that Hector considered the pass a poor choice for a transportation route. The railway builders and politicians of the 1880s should have listened to him.

After surveying Vancouver Island and California at the conclusion of the Palliser Expedition, Hector returned to England to write his contribution to its report. He was off the following year to survey Otago Province in New Zealand, becoming director of that country's Geological Survey in 1865. He was awarded the Lyell Medal in 1875 and was knighted by Queen Victoria in 1886. Hector returned to Canada in 1903 with his son, hoping to revisit the site of his mishap near Wapta Falls and Kicking Horse Pass, where a monument to him had been installed. He was at Glacier House, near Roger's Pass, when his son took ill. Dr. Hector, then 69, did not act soon enough. His son died of appendicitis. Grief-stricken, Hector soon departed for New Zealand, never to return. He died in 1907

41. Sherbrooke Valley

Sherbrooke Lake

TRAIL THUMBNAIL

Day-hike; see map, p. 166

Route	Elev. (m)	Dist. (km)
Trailhead	1616	0
Paget Lookout jct	1783	1.4
Sherbrooke Lake	1814	3.0
Niles Meadows	2317	9.8

Trailhead
Wapta Lake picnic area on the north side of
Highway 1, 11 km east of Field, 15 km west of
Lake Louise. For safety, eastbound travellers
should make a U-turn at West Louise Lodge,
500 m east of the trailhead, and approach
westbound. The trailhead is adjacent to the
picnic shelter.

Maps
NTS: 82 N/8, 82 N/9
Gem Trek: *Lake Louise and Yoho*

Although Lake O'Hara and the Yoho Valley attract most of Yoho's hikers, the Sherbrooke Valley has a wilderness quality missing from those other areas. This outing features one of Yoho's larger backcountry lakes, excellent wildlife viewing opportunities, and classic upper subalpine meadows. It's a great pocket of bear habitat. Travel accordingly.

Trailhead to Sherbrooke Lake

Hike northeast from the picnic area for 80 m to a junction. Make a sharp turn west (left). The next 1.3 km of trail ascends through subalpine forest, notable for its inclusion of cottonwood poplars and Douglas-firs; both species are near their altitudinal limits. In early summer, you may spot the blooms of evergreen violets and calypso orchids. Some trees still sport insulators from the days when the lookout was connected to the Wapta Lake warden station by telephone. You'll also see old stumps – evidence of logging during railway construction in the 1880s. Keep straight ahead at the junction at km 1.4. The right-hand trail leads to Paget Lookout.

Between the Paget Lookout junction and Sherbrooke Lake, sections of trail have been gravel-capped. Pressure-treated wood decking has been installed to bridge boggy areas. Look for the blooms of orchids here in early summer, including tall white rein-orchid and hooded ladies'-tresses. You can see Mt. Stephen (3199 m) and Cathedral Crags (3073 m) through the trees to the southwest.

Sixty metres beyond the first blowdown, a short sidetrail leads west (left) to the shore of Sherbrooke Lake. Early morning visitors often find the lake a tranquil mirror, reflecting the colourful slabs of Mt. Ogden (2703 m) opposite, and the thumb-like form of Mt. Niles (2967 m) at the north end of the valley. The upthrust sedimentary formations in Mt. Ogden's ridge date to the Cambrian. In the sequence of five formations, the rocks become progressively younger toward the north end of the mountain.

With an area of 35 ha, Sherbrooke is the third largest lake in Yoho. It is 12 m deep, and is usually frozen until late June. Glacially formed and fed, its

VARIATION

- Combine this outing with a visit to Paget Lookout; 23.8 km total. See Classic Hike #40.

At noon we came upon a fine lake something over a mile in length, whose pale blue waters settled once for all the question as to whether our valley led directly to the glacier.

Charles Fay; *Appalachia 1898*

Niles Meadows

waters change colour from clear, to blue-green, to silty gray as the glacial melt season progresses. Lake trout and rainbow trout inhabit the waters. Surveyor J.J. McArthur named the lake in 1887 after the town of Sherbrooke, near his home in the province of Quebec.

The trail follows the east shore. You may see mountain goats high on the cliffs of Paget Peak. Extensive avalanche slopes reach down to west shore. These slopes – with their abundant browse – are good places to look for moose, deer, and elk. The avalanche slopes are also frequented by grizzly bears. At the north end of the lake, the trail passes through another blowdown. There are many dead trees in the lake, with root plates still attached. While the downed trees on shore blew over in a windstorm, those in the lake did not. They were probably uprooted by avalanches from the slope to the west. Deposited on the frozen lake surface, the trees came to rest in this shallow part of the lake when that winter's ice melted.

Sherbrooke Lake to Niles Meadows

Beyond the lake's inlet, the trail ascends beside a small canyon that contains a waterfall, and then emerges into an extensive subalpine wet meadow, dotted with massive boulders. Here Niles Creek, draining the valley to the northeast, converges with upper Sherbrooke Creek.

The trail crosses the two channels of Niles Creek and then makes several sharp turns as it works its way through willows to the north edge of the meadow. This section is difficult to describe – look for the beaten path and perhaps the odd bit of flagging tape. After a gentle switchback ascent into an ancient spruce-fir forest – tree ages of 300 years have been recorded here – the grade steepens to crest a rock step alongside a waterfall. Three hundred metres farther, cross the creek to its west bank.

The upper reach of Sherbrooke Creek is both avalanche slope and creek bed. Snow avalanches have severed many tree tops at trailside. Cross to the east side of the creek. The mountains along the west side of the valley feature wildly folded and steeply dipping rock formations. Two waterfalls cascade over the cliff to the north. The trail angles sharply to the southeast (right) and climbs an open slope, where clumps of false hellebore grow. A hundred metres after cresting this slope, the trail emerges from the trees and swings north into the meadows beneath Mt. Niles. Take note of where the trail leaves the trees. It is easy to miss on your return.

A rockslide on the west side of the meadow makes a good lunch place. Mt. Niles is the centrepiece in the view north. Its strata show the unmistakable U-shaped fold of a syncline. The mountain was named for William Niles, president of the Appalachian Mountain Club in 1898. For the adventurous, animal trails and mountaineers' paths lead above treeline onto the surrounding benches, where you can enjoy a superb view of Sherbrooke Lake and the mountains between Lake Louise and Field.

IN THE FOOTSTEPS OF PIONEERS

Surveyors of the Dominion Topographic Survey topped peaks and ridges in this valley in 1886. The next recorded travellers were mountaineers Charles Fay and party, who, without benefit of a trail, used this approach to attempt Mt. Balfour on the Waputik (WAH-poo-tick) Icefield in 1898. Although unsuccessful on Mt. Balfour, Fay's party made the first ascents of Mt. Niles and the unnamed peak immediately south of Mt. Daly. The trail we now hike originated in 1911, to provide access to the 6th annual Alpine Club of Canada mountaineering camp, which convened at the north edge of the Niles Creek meadow. Here and there you will see rotting corduroy bridges that date to the original trail construction.

BLOWDOWN

Just before Sherbrooke Lake, the trail passes through the first of the valley's blowdown areas. Many of these Engelmann spruce and subalpine fir trees were uprooted during a thunderstorm in August 1984. I was working at the Chateau Lake Louise at the time. The storm blew out windows on the ground floor, and flooded the basement. You may still be able to count the rings on some of the trees cleared from the trail here. A few of the spruces were roughly 300 years old.

Although it looks like a scene of destruction, this blowdown is one of nature's methods for revitalizing areas of old forest. In the absence of fire, blowdowns create openings in the forest canopy, allowing sunlight to reach the ground. This promotes new growth of shrubs and wildflowers that provide food for deer, elk, moose, and bears. The fallen trees eventually decompose into soil.

42. Lake O'Hara Alpine Circuit

Opabin Plateau

Lake O'Hara is the most developed and popular hiking destination in the Rockies. Within a 5 km radius of the lake, 80 km of hiking trails explore every nook and cranny of an exceptional high country landscape. The Lake O'Hara Alpine Circuit connects sections of seven trails into a rewarding loop, with views of more than a dozen lakes and ponds, and the rugged peaks along the continental divide.

Trailhead to Wiwaxy Gap

From the interpretive display, follow the lakeshore trail north (left) for 60 m to the outlet bridge. Cross the bridge, turn east (right) and follow the north shore trail 200 m to the Wiwaxy Gap junction. The "north bay" of Lake O'Hara, adjacent to this section of trail, is closed to angling to protect trout spawning and nursery habitat.

Looking west across the lake, Odaray Mountain (3159 m) may be reflected if the water is calm. Surveyor J.J. McArthur made the first ascent of the southern summit of the mountain (Little Odaray, 2962 m) in 1887. McArthur later described the area to Robert O'Hara, a retired British army colonel. O'Hara made at least two visits to the lake in the 1880s and 1890s. It became known as "O'Hara's Lake."

SPECIAL CONSIDERATIONS

Portions of this hike traverse exposed ledges. About a third of the distance is on rough trails through boulderfields and across scree slopes. In these places, you must pay careful attention to route markers. Avoid this hike during early season, poor weather, electrical storms, and after snowfalls – although for day visitors, the timing of your outing will likely be dictated by your bus reservation, not by the weather. Opabin Plateau is usually closed until the winter snowpack has melted – well into July in most years.

TRAIL THUMBNAIL

Day-hike

Route	Elev. (m)	Dist. (km)
Trailhead	2022	0
Wiwaxy Gap jct	2025	0.3
Wiwaxy Gap	2530	2.2
Lake Oesa jct	2260	4.2
East Opabin jct	2287	6.6
Opabin Lake	2285	7.1
Opabin Prospect jct	2220	8.7
All Soul's jct	2210	8.8
All Soul's Prospect	2435	9.8
Schäffer Lake	2180	11.0
Trailhead	2022	12.4

Trailhead

Parks Canada controls the number of visitors in the Lake O'Hara area through a complicated quota system. You can hike the unmaintained Cataract Brook trail (12.8 km) to Lake O'Hara campground, or walk the fireroad (10.4 km). Most folks fork over the cash and take the bus, which makes four round-trips each day. You don't need a reservation if you are hiking in and out from the parking area on the same day, but you do need to reserve if you plan on taking the bus or on camping. Reservations are accepted (and usually fill) three months in advance. A few seats on the bus and a few tent sites are available each day on a first come, first served basis – for use on the *following* day. As a last gasp, you can show up to meet the bus and hope that someone else is running late. Call 250-343-6433 well in advance for details.

To reach the staging area, follow Highway 1 to the junction with Highway 1A, 12.6 km west of Lake Louise, 13.4 km east of Field. Turn onto Highway 1A, cross the railway tracks and turn west (right) to the Lake O'Hara parking area. Meet the park attendant at the bus shelter just inside the fireroad gate, or lace up your boots to walk the road or the Cataract Brook trail. And no, you can't bike the road. The Alpine Circuit trailhead is adjacent to the park patrol cabin, 600 m south of the campground.

Maps
NTS: 82 N/8
Gem Trek: *Lake Louise and Yoho*
The Adventure Map: Lake O'Hara

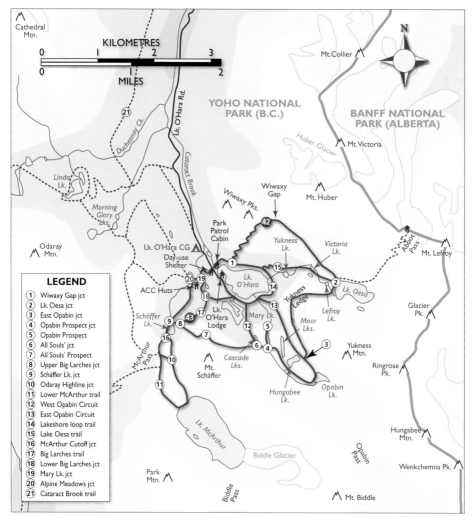

LEGEND

1. Wiwaxy Gap jct
2. Lk. Oesa jct
3. East Opabin jct
4. Opabin Prospect jct
5. Opabin Prospect
6. All Souls' jct
7. All Souls' Prospect
8. Upper Big Larches jct
9. Schäffer Lk. jct
10. Odaray Highline jct
11. Lower McArthur trail
12. West Opabin Circuit
13. East Opabin Circuit
14. Lakeshore loop trail
15. Lake Oesa trail
16. McArthur Cutoff jct
17. Big Larches trail
18. Lower Big Larches jct
19. Mary Lk. jct
20. Alpine Meadows jct
21. Cataract Brook trail

The climb from the lakeshore to Wiwaxy Gap is one of the steeper on any of the Classic Hikes – a huffing-puffing 503 m in just 1.9 km. The first leg switchbacks tightly in a gully that was swept by a debris flow in the summer of 1985. At the top of the gully, you traverse east beneath a 20 m quartzite cliff, and then ascend the cliff on ledges. The steep grade resumes. A remarkable Engelmann spruce tree towers over

the trail. Two of its roots have grown laterally out of the steep slope, and then upward to become separate trunks. The diameter of the main trunk is 1.4 m at the base. Whitebark pines also grow here.

Your rapid ascent soon provides an aerial view of Lake O'Hara. The lake has an area of 34.4 ha and a maximum depth of 38.1 m. As its vivid colour suggests, glacial meltwater collects in the lake. If you look southeast into the valley that contains Lake Oesa, you can see that Lake O'Hara is the lowest in a series of five lakes and ponds. Glaciologists call such an arrangement *paternoster lakes*, or a glacial cirque staircase. During the Late Wisconsin Glaciation, glacial ice flowed west and hollowed the basin for each lake at a progressively lower elevation. A cascading stream now connects them. As with most lakes created this way, the deepest part of Lake O'Hara is just beneath the headwall, where the glacier plunged into the valley. Across Lake O'Hara to the southeast,

VARIATIONS

- Shorten the outing by exiting from Lake Oesa (7.5 km total), East Opabin (9.7 km total) or West Opabin (10.8 km total).
- Add a visit to Opabin Prospect; 0.8 km return.
- Extend the outing by adding Lake McArthur to the end of the circuit; 15.6 km total. See Classic Hike #43.

Lake Oesa

Yukness Mountain (2851 m) scrapes the sky. The glacially sculpted horn of Mt. Biddle (3320 m) looms above Opabin Pass to the south. McArthur Pass frames the north glacier of Mt. Owen (3083 m) to the southwest.

The trail traverses across more gullies and continues its steep, sidehill ascent. Wherever the trail becomes faint or takes to ledges, look for cairns and painted markers – two vertical yellow stripes on a rectangular blue background. Although you may occasionally have to put your hands on the rock for balance, in no place does the route involve technical climbing. If you come face to face with an unscalable cliff, backtrack and look for the route markers.

Above treeline, the trail angles steeply to Wiwaxy Gap, the low point on the ridge that connects the Wiwaxy Peaks (2706 m) to the west, with Mt. Huber (3348 m) to the east. This is the 9th-highest point reached on the Classic Hikes. Daisy fleabane, golden fleabane, Drummond's anemone, spotted saxifrage, alpine arnica, moss campion, and white mountain-avens are scattered across the screes. Look for the tracks and pellets of mountain goats.

For those unaccustomed to high places, Wiwaxy Gap may seem more like a mountain summit than a pass. The view north over Cataract Brook includes Cathedral Mountain (3187 m), and the peaks on the Wapta and Waputik icefields in the northern part of Yoho National Park. Melt from Huber Glacier feeds two waterfalls on the cliff to the northeast. Above the waterfalls, the keen eye can pick out the rocky summit of Mt. Victoria (3464 m). Its western aspect

LAKE O'HARA LEXICON

Some of the unusual names in the Lake O'Hara area come from the Stoney dialect, and were given by American explorer, Samuel Allen, who visited the Rockies four times in the early 1890s. He learned the names from William Twin, a Stoney who often guided explorers.

- *Hungabee* (hun-GAH-bee): "chieftain." With an elevation of 3490 m, it is the highest mountain in the area.
- *Oesa* (owe-EE-sah): "ice" (Allen spelled it Oeesa.) The lake is usually frozen into July.
- *Opabin* (owe-PAY-bin): "rocky." This name appears often throughout the mountains of western North America.
- *Wiwaxy* (wih-WAX-ee): "windy." Allen called the valley to the north the "gorge of the winds."
- *Yukness* (YUCK-ness): "sharpened, as with a knife." The mountain owes its horn shape to glacial sharpening.
- Uncertainty surrounds the meaning of *Odaray* (OWE-dah-ray), which was named by surveyor J.J. McArthur. Four meanings have been proposed: "many waterfalls," "very brushy," "windfall" or "cone." As McArthur originally referred to it as "Cone Mountain," the latter was probably the intended meaning.

Picture the colours of morning darting from pyramid to pyramid, then slowly creeping down into the valleys, as sunlight puts a crown upon the summits, while still wrapt in the purple gloom sleep the circling glaciers, the winding stream, and the emerald water of Lake Oeesa.

Samuel Allen; *Alpine Journal 1896*

is entirely unlike the familiar view from Lake Louise. True to its name, Wiwaxy Gap is a windy place, and with the sweat you've worked up during the climb, you are not likely to linger.

Wiwaxy Gap to Lake Oesa

Head southeast from Wiwaxy Gap on the trail that aims straight for Lake Oesa. Ignore the paths that lead uphill and downhill, left and right respectively. You can see the trail ahead, scratched across the cliff edge. If this does not look to your liking or if snow lingers, turn back here. Also, beware of snow avalanche danger on this next section if you are hiking before mid-July or after a snowfall. The 2.2 km to Lake Oesa involves a descending traverse, with fine views to the chain of paternoster lakes. On a calm day, you can hear the cascading water in the cataracts that link the lakes. Across the chasm, Yukness Mountain broods in morning shadow.

The massive mountain wall that backs Lake Oesa is part of the continental divide. It extends from Mt. Lefroy (3442 m) on the north, through Glacier Peak (3302 m), to Ringrose Peak (3292 m) on the south. A small drift glacier occupies Lake Oesa's northeast shore, and a moraine-dammed lake sits above

ALPINE IMAGERY

The Lake O'Hara area has attracted and inspired many artists, among them, J.S. Sargent, W.J. Phillips, Peter and Catherine Whyte, and members of the Group of Seven, including J.E.H. MacDonald. Macdonald in particular was enchanted with Lake O'Hara. He made the first of seven visits in 1924. Several of his works include views of Mt. Biddle, Mt. Owen, and Cathedral Mountain from the trail between Wiwaxy Gap and Lake Oesa, from Opabin Plateau, and from along Yukness Ledge.

the southeast shore. A glacier-worn rock slab dams Lake Oesa.

At the first trail junction, turn southwest, downhill to the right. In 150 m you reach the Lake Oesa junction. You want the trail indicated as "Opabin Plateau via Yukness Ledge Alpine Route," which angles southeast from the junction. The trail crosses the rock slabs west of the lake and descends toward the outlet. Follow the large cairns and use caution if the rock is wet or icy. At the third cairn, the trail angles off to the south (right) across a small meadow, and then descends a short cliff to the outlet stream. Rock-hop the stream and follow the cairned route west, climbing across slabs and through boulderfields. Beware of rockfall danger here.

The trail descends a natural staircase with some awkward steps, and then switchbacks on the north end of the terrace that overlooks Lake O'Hara. Pay careful attention to the route markers here. At the next junction, turn sharply south (left). If the weather has become foul you can exit by going straight ahead at this junction. This will bring you to the Lake Oesa trail at Victoria Lake, where you turn west (left) to descend to Lake O'Hara.

For the next kilometre, the trail traverses Yukness Ledge, offering breathtaking views over Lake O'Hara. Move slowly and carefully near the cliff edge, especially if the rock is wet. You may see a sediment plume issuing from "East Opabin Creek" into Lake O'Hara, where the glacial sediment transported by the creek disperses into the lake. The finest particles, called rock flour, are suspended in the lake water. They reflect the blue and green wavelengths of the spectrum, giving the lake its remarkable colour.

Opabin Glacier comes into view straight ahead, tucked beneath the sheer flank of Mt. Biddle. Samuel Allen named the mountain for A.J. Biddle, a Philadelphia author and publisher. Opabin Plateau is west of the trail, covered with stands of larch and dotted with the Opabin Moor Lakes. When you have travelled slightly more than one half of the length above Opabin Plateau, the trail begins a winding and sometimes steep descent through rockslide debris to its junction with the East Opabin Trail. Hungabee Lake is adjacent to the junction.

Turn southeast (left), cross a rock bridge, and ascend the rise to Opabin Lake. Notice the boulders that were inlaid in the walking surface during trail rehabilitation in 1988 and 1989. The thin, clay soils here saturate with water quickly, creating a slippery, poorly drained tread. Undisciplined hikers walk off the trail, damaging the surrounding vegetation. The boulders serve as stepping stones, keeping feet dry and preserving the adjacent upper subalpine meadows.

Hungabee Mountain (3490 m), first climbed in 1903, towers to the southeast of Opabin Lake. The broad, northwest face forms part of the regular

173

mountaineering route from Opabin Pass. Although many mountaineers have this summit on their "wish list," the poor rock on the upper mountain and the frequent presence of snow and ice often thwart attempts to climb it.

The mass of rubble on the south shore of Opabin Lake is a terminal moraine, created during the Little Ice Age advance of Opabin Glacier. The moraine has partly filled the lake. Study of lake bottom sediments at Opabin Lake and Lake O'Hara indicates that the Little Ice Age was the most significant glacial advance here in the last 8500 years. Between 8500 and 3000 years ago, glaciers were absent in this area above the elevation of Opabin Lake. The upper Opabin Valley, now a chaos of moraine and ice, supported subalpine forest.

Turn sharply northwest (right) at the junction at Opabin Lake, to follow the West Opabin Circuit. The upper subalpine meadows here are flush with mountain heather, and are frequented by white-tailed ptarmigan. The occasional wolverine makes tracks through here, bound from Tokumm Creek to the McArthur Valley. The trail descends rock benches, paralleling West Opabin Creek. You can see where the silty water of Opabin Lake drains beneath a complex of moraines. The moraines record two distinct glacial advances. Rock lichens cover the lower, larger, and more darkly coloured moraine. Atop this sits the more colourful rock of the Little Ice Age moraine, created in the mid-1800s, and thus relatively lichen-free.

There are fine views ahead of Cathedral Mountain, the Wiwaxy Peaks, and the serried flanks of Mt. Huber (3348 m), reflected here and there in the numerous lakes and ponds on Opabin Plateau. Emil Huber was a Swiss alpinist who, in 1890, made the first ascent of Mt. Sir Donald, near Rogers Pass. At all trail junctions, keep to the West Opabin Circuit, which is always either left or straight ahead. After 1.6 km of delightful hiking, you reach the Opabin Prospect junction. Detour north (right) if you want to make the 0.8 km return trip to this viewpoint. The main trail begins a steep descent with views of Mary Lake and Cathedral Mountain ahead. The All Souls' Prospect junction is 80 m farther. You may exit the Alpine Circuit at this point by keeping straight. Otherwise, turn west (left), and ascend a rock staircase onto the benches beneath Mt. Schäffer (2691 m) – named for Mary Schäffer, best known for her exploration of Maligne Lake in 1908. Hoary marmots frequent these benches, and you may see mountain goats on the cliffs above.

You climb steeply to the west on scree and then traverse northwest at a more reasonable grade. Beware of rockfall danger here. The ascent brings you to All Souls' Prospect. The peculiar name of this viewpoint was given by Dr. George Link, who cleared many trails in the Lake O'Hara area. All Souls' Day is November 2 – a day of prayer for the souls of the faithful departed.

From All Souls' Prospect, you will enjoy a tremendous and lofty panorama on a clear day. The Cataract Brook Valley is to the north, leading your eye to Mt. Bosworth (2769 m) above Kicking Horse

THE GOG FORMATIONS: TOUGH STUFF

The Lake O'Hara Alpine Circuit is the only Classic Hike that features a single rock formation underfoot for its entire distance. Between lake level and approximately 2750 m, the bedrock is Gog Formation quartzite and siltstone.

Gog quartzite is a very hard, quartz-rich sandstone; the hardest rock in the central Rockies. It is composed of pebble-size, sand-size, and silt-size quartz particles eroded from the Canadian Shield, transported to the southwest by rivers, and deposited in ancient seas during the Early Cambrian, between 525 and 545 million-years-ago. The small spaces between the individual quartz grains are filled with tiny intergrown crystals of quartz that bind the sandstone together very tightly.

Green and black map lichens (*Rhizocarpon geographicum*, see p. 111) cover some exposures of Gog quartzite. Where protected from weathering, Gog quartzite is often white, pinkish or purplish; where exposed it can become stained brown and red with iron oxide. Fossil trilobites occur here and there in Gog rocks, but the fossilized burrowings of worms (*Planolites*) and of trilobites (*Rusphycos*) are much more common, as is iron pyrite ("fool's

gold") – another source of colour. Some quartzite boulders contain a conglomerate of fist-sized pebbles and rocks, bound together with quartz. At the Lake Oesa junction, trail builders have incorporated colourful ripple rock slabs of Gog siltstone into the walking surface.

Lake O'Hara from Yukness Ledge

Pass. You can see all of the principal peaks of the continental divide in this area, and to the west and southwest respectively, you have point-blank views of Odaray Mountain and Mt. Owen. Looking southeast, you can see Neptuak Mountain (3241 m) framed through Opabin Pass. From here, Opabin Plateau appears a desolate place; its meadowlands and larch forest dwarfed to insignificance by moraines and rockslides, and by the precipices that ring the valley.

Descend north from All Souls' Prospect on a rough path beaten into the screes and boulderfields. This is a bone-jarring descent, with one 2 m step that requires downclimbing. The proliferation of trails in the Lake O'Hara area has resulted in many redundant and parallel paths. If you look down to the meadows near Schäffer Lake, you can see recently gravelled trails, and older trails that have been closed and left to revegetate.

CAIRN BUILDING

The rock piles that mark the route and crown the highpoints of this hike are cairns. *Carn* is Gaelic for "pile of rocks." Cairns assist hikers and mountaineers when the way is vague or during poor weather when visibility is limited. The cairns in the Lake O'Hara area have evolved over decades. Many are "overkill" for their intended purpose, cluttering the margin of well-defined routes. Some are no more than landscape graffiti – unnecessary and inappropriate. Please do not add to existing cairns or build new ones. When you move rocks in the alpine life zone you alter drainage patterns, overturn lichens, and disrupt the formation of soils. On the small scale, you may be setting back the growth of vegetation by centuries.

The trail winds through treeline forest and passes the Big Larches junction. Keep straight ahead to the Schäffer Lake junction in 100 m. The lake is a kettle pond fringed with willows. Unless you want to add Lake McArthur to this outing, turn northeast (right) at this junction. As the trail begins its descent to Lake O'Hara, note the gradual transition from larch forest to one dominated by Engelmann spruce and subalpine fir.

The descent brings you to the "Alpine Meadow" and the Alpine Club of Canada's Elizabeth Parker Hut. The buildings date to 1926, and have been operated by the ACC since 1930. Nine other cabins formerly on this site were moved to the lakeshore and are now the outlying cabins of Lake O'Hara Lodge. Keep straight ahead at the junction adjacent to the hut.

The ACC held the first of six mountaineering camps at Lake O'Hara on this meadow in 1909. Between then and 1974, when random camping and group camping were abolished, the meadows suffered impacts from overuse. East of the hut you can see a fenced plot on a closed trail. Look at the subtle difference that four decades of natural regeneration has produced in the vegetation – a vivid indication of the harshness of the local climate.

Turn north (left) at the junction 200 m east of the hut. The trail climbs out of the creekbed, swings east, and descends to Le Relais (the day-use shelter), opposite the park patrol cabin on the fireroad. Outbound buses stop here. If you're staying at the campground, turn north (left) and walk 600 m along the road.

43. Lake McArthur

Lake McArthur

TRAIL THUMBNAIL

Day-hike

Route	Elev. (m)	Dist. (km)
Trailhead	2022	0
Mary Lake jct	2030	0.3
Big Larches jct	2050	0.6
Schäffer Lake	2180	1.7
McArthur Cutoff jct	2180	1.8
Odaray Highline jct	2325	2.3
High point of trail	2375	2.6
Lake McArthur	2260	3.3
McArthur Cutoff jct	2180	4.8
Schäffer Lake	2180	4.9
Alpine Meadows jct	2030	5.8
Mary Lake jct	2030	6.0
Trailhead	2015	6.3

Trailhead
For details on access to the Lake O'Hara area, see p. 170. The Lake McArthur trailhead is opposite the park patrol cabin, 600 m south of the Lake O'Hara campground.

Maps
NTS: 82 N/8
Gem Trek: *Lake Louise and Yoho*
The Adventure Map: Lake O'Hara

Best lighting: afternoon

Many hikers consider this short, steep trail a stairway to alpine heaven. Alpine lakes in the Rockies often "get the blues," but none in such an ethereal way as does Lake McArthur. The lake may be ice-covered until mid-July.

Trailhead to Lake McArthur

Begin opposite the park patrol cabin on the north side of Le Relais, the day-use shelter. Head west through ancient forest for 200 m. The trail turns south along the edge of the "Alpine Meadow" to reach the Mary Lake junction in another 100 m. Keep straight ahead to the Big Larches junction in 300 m. Turn southwest (right), to begin the ascent to Schäffer Lake.

The aptly-named Big Larches trail climbs around the north end of Mt. Schäffer (2691 m), through the jumbled quartzite blocks of a rockslide known as the "Devil's Rock Pile." Mt. Schäffer commemorates Mary Schäffer, the explorer known best for her trips to Maligne Lake in 1908 and 1911. It's a stiff climb, but the larch forest and the wildflowers offer many incentives to pause. The displays of western anemone are particularly fine. I have seen Columbian ground squirrels here pretending to be porcupines – climbing into the larches to eat the needles. If you don't see these wanna-be porkies, you may see the real thing.

You pass the junction with the Alpine Circuit just before the trail levels at Schäffer Lake. Walk around the north and west shores of the lake to the McArthur Cutoff junction. Take the left-hand fork, and begin climbing again. The trail crosses a geologic transition during this climb. Most of the bedrock in the Lake O'Hara basin is quartzite, sandstone, and siltstone of the Gog Group of formations. On these slopes you pass through a thin outcrop of Mt. Whyte Formation shale, with the remainder of the ascent being on Cathedral Formation limestone. The rock formations – all of them date to the Cambrian – get younger as you go uphill. Lawrence Grassi, park warden during the 1950s and early 1960s, worked on sections of this trail. The late Jon Whyte wrote of his craft: "The Rockies shall not easily wear away what he built. Centuries from now the pilgrims shall make

VARIATIONS

- Hike the loop in reverse.
- Add a visit to Lake McArthur to the conclusion of the Lake O'Hara Alpine Circuit; 15.6 km total. See Classic Hike #42.

their way to Lake McArthur along his path, and they shall wonder that one among us had so much art and skill. His name by then may be forgotten, but his art shall not." (For more on Grassi, see p. 207.)

Keep straight ahead at the Odaray Highline junction. A short distance later, the trail begins to descend and swings southeast through alpine meadows to the crags above the north shore of Lake McArthur. I can tell you that the colour of the lake is a marvel, but you really do have to see it to believe how much so. A warm summer afternoon here is backcountry heaven.

Lake McArthur

With an area of 77 hectares, Lake McArthur is Yoho's second largest lake and, for its altitude, may be the largest backcountry lake in the Rockies. Nestled between two northwest-trending ridges of Mt.

Biddle, the lake is a textbook example of a tarn – a lake that occupies a glacially-sculpted basin within a glacial cirque. The maximum depth is 84 m. The lake's size results from two features of the Cathedral Formation limestone bedrock. The rock at the northwest shore dips at an angle of about 24°, effectively damming the water. With its path blocked, the lake water has sought an underground outlet – as water often does in limestone – eroding one or more sinks in the lake bottom. Sinks usually do not drain a lake as fast as an above-ground outlet would, so the water pools before draining. This pooling probably affects the sediment load of the lake, helping to create its spectacular colour. The emergence of the underground outlet has not been determined, but it may be in upper McArthur Creek.

Mt. Biddle (3320 m) dominates the head of the cirque. If you think that its dark crest appears formidable, you're right. The upper part of the mountain is

CANADA'S FIRST ALPINIST

James Joseph McArthur was a Dominion Land Surveyor who worked in the Rockies from 1887 to 1893. His task was to survey the "Railway Belt" – the lands bordering, and given to, the recently constructed Canadian Pacific Railway. McArthur literally went above the call of duty, occupying scores of summits as survey stations. Because the peaks were often unnamed at the time, some of these ascents were not credited when the first mountaineering guidebook to the Rockies was written. Alexander Mackenzie, David Douglas, David Thompson, James Hector, and A.P. Coleman had each made sporadic ascents in the Rockies before 1887. But J.J. McArthur can lay claim to being Canada's first practiced alpinist.

McArthur's work was extremely difficult, accomplished without trails and often without the use of horses to pack gear. His journal entries sum up days of hardship in single sentences, matter-of-factly recording prodigious feats of travel at a time when summers were much more harsh than those of today. Sometimes alone, sometimes with an assistant, he would carry heavy photographic equipment to the summits, some of which were walk-ups, but a few of which – such as Mt. Stephen near Field – were not. His ascent of Mt. Stephen – with his assistant, Tom Riley – on September 9, 1887, was the first of any mountain over 10,000 feet in Canada. Clouds and firesmoke marred the view, so the duo went back in 1892. This time, they carried a tree trunk to the summit, to leave behind as a sighting pole. I have not met too many contemporary mountaineers who, with benefit of guidebooks and an approach trail, have cared to climb Mt. Stephen twice, let alone to pack a chunk of tree the second time.

McArthur's photography was used to create extremely beautiful and accurate maps. Many of the elevations we assign to features today have not been changed since those first surveys. McArthur went on to lead the Canadian contingent that surveyed the Alaska-BC boundary, and later was Canadian representative on the International Boundary Commission. His name adorns four features in Yoho – a pass, a creek, a lake, and a mountain.

Leaving our alpensticks behind, we stepped across and with face to the wall moved along the ledge to a slanting rift, up which we clambered, our entire weight sometimes dependent on the first joints of our fingers.

From J.J. McArthur's description of the first ascent of Mt. Stephen

Eldon Formation limestone, a cliff-builder just about everywhere in the Rockies, but hereabouts, loose and crumbly. The horseshoe traverse of Mt. Biddle and Park Mountain (2951 m) is a mountaineering test piece, not often accomplished. Explorer, Samuel Allen, named Mt. Biddle in 1894, for his Philadelphia friend, Anthony Biddle. "Park" refers to the park-like vegetation at Park Mountain's base.

Accounts from 1904 and photographs taken in 1909 indicate that, in those years, Biddle Glacier extended into the lake. Photographs taken in 1933 show that the ice had receded about 300 m from the lakeshore. Today, it is more than a kilometre from the ice to the water.

From one station, I counted sixteen alpine lakes, one of which is more strikingly beautiful than any other I have seen. It is about 1/2 mile in length, and lies between two high spurs to the E. of the pass [McArthur Pass], at an altitude of about 8000 ft. A steep glacier comes in at the E. end, and the water, undermining the ice, cause bodies to fall off, leaving a clear blue face, and the surface of the lake is, in consequence of the falling ice, dotted with miniature icebergs.

J.J. McArthur; *Report of the Department of the Interior 1892*

Return

In deference to the bears that frequent McArthur Pass, avoid using the Lower McArthur trail when you leave the lake. Retrace your steps to Schäffer Lake, from where you have two options: descend the Big Larches trail, or keep straight ahead at the junction on the north side of the lake, to descend to the Alpine Meadow. Keep straight ahead at the junction at the Elizabeth Parker hut, cross the meadow, turn north (left) at the Mary Lake junction, and walk out to the trailhead.

FACE TO FACIES

Biddle Pass (2613 m) is the saddle on the ridge that connects Mt. Biddle and Park Mountain. It has never seen much use as a travel route, but it is a great landmark for spotting the division between the eastern main ranges and the western main ranges. The rock of eastern main range mountains was created from sediments deposited close to shore in relatively shallow seas. Lime-producing cyanobacteria (blue-green algae) lived in those waters. Therefore limestone predominates, along with sandstone and siltstone. Farther offshore, muds sank deep into the relatively lifeless abyss, where they compacted to create shale – the primary rock, or facies, of the western main ranges. You can see the line where the facies change on Biddle Pass – dark shales to the west, lighter-coloured limestones and quartzite to the east.

44. Iceline

Iceline moraine

It was 85 years before Edward Whymper's suggestion (see p. 181) concerning a high-level hiking route in the Yoho Valley became a reality. Constructed in 1987, the Iceline quickly became perhaps the premier day-hike in the Rockies. Scratched from glacial rubble, the trail follows a sensational line, contouring the edge of Emerald Glacier for 5 km. Spectacular, close-up views of glaciers, and panoramic vistas of the Yoho Valley are your rewards for venturing into this harsh domain. Snow often clogs the trail until early July.

Trailhead to the Iceline

The trail ascends the avalanche slope above the hostel and works its way south. Look back to obtain fine views of Takakkaw (TAH-kuh-kah) Falls – 254 m high – and Mt. Balfour (3284 m). At the edge of the avalanche slope, the trail enters old-growth forest, replete with white rhododendron and devil's club. Despite the nearby peril of avalanching snow and the wind blasts it generates, some of the Engelmann spruce trees have attained diameters of 1.2 m at the

TRAIL THUMBNAIL

Day-hike or overnight

Route	Elev. (m)	Dist. (km)
Takakkaw Falls parking area	1510	0
Iceline-Yoho Pass trailhead	1520	0.6
Hidden Lakes jct	1638	1.8
Yoho Lake-Iceline lower jct	1646	2.0
Yoho Lake-Iceline upper jct	1860	3.2
Celeste Lake upper jct	2195	6.4
Trail summit	2230	7.1
Kiwetinok Pass jct	2073	10.9
Iceline north jct	2070	11.2
Little Yoho CG	2056	+0.3
Celeste Lake lower jct	1768	14.1
Whaleback jct	1768	14.2
Marpole Lake-Twin Falls jct	1814	14.8
Little Yoho jct	1608	16.4
Laughing Falls CG	1608	16.5
Takakkaw Falls parking area	1509	21.1

Trailhead

Follow Highway 1 to the Yoho Valley Road, 3.7 km east of Field, 22.3 km west of Lake Louise. Turn north and follow this road 13 km to the Takakkaw Falls parking area. Walk south; keep straight ahead at the junction that leads to the falls. Cross the Yoho Valley Road to the Iceline-Yoho Pass trailhead, just north of Whiskey Jack Hostel. Those travelling without a vehicle can use the hostel or nearby Takakkaw Falls walk-in campground as a base.

Maps

NTS: 82 N/7, 82 N/8, 82 N/10
Gem Trek: *Lake Louise and Yoho*

base. With ages of 300-400 years, these are among the older trees in Yoho National Park. I have seen moose, elk, and ruffed grouse here. The trail in this area is one of the slickest in the Rockies, especially on the way down. Step carefully.

The west slope of the Yoho Valley is terraced, with bedrock strata that dip toward the Yoho River. Just before the trail reaches the first terrace, the 300 m sidetrail to Hidden Lakes branches south. Beyond this junction, the main trail returns to the avalanche slope and ascends steeply along its southern edge. You reach the Yoho Pass-Iceline lower junction in 200 m. Yoho Lake is straight ahead. For the Iceline, turn north (right).

For the next 1.2 km, the trail climbs across a second terrace to the Yoho Pass-Iceline upper junction. You will see bedrock in the trail as you gain elevation – limestone of the Eldon Formation. At the junction, turn north (right). Here, you are slightly higher than the brink of Takakkaw Falls across the

Ascending a moraine

valley. You can see the waterfall's source in Daly Glacier. *Takakkaw* is Cree for "It is magnificent!"

The Iceline

To this point, you've been hiking sections of trail that existed before 1987. Just beyond the junction, angle northwest (left) onto the newer trail. The character of the Iceline is soon evident, as the trail ascends a rock staircase. Construction of the Iceline required imaginative trail building techniques. Crews used boulders and rock slabs to create bridges, steps, retaining walls, and drainage culverts. Where the trail crosses bedrock slabs, rows of rubble define its margin. These rocks, and many artful cairns help guide the way across the forefield of Emerald Glacier. Please refrain from building new cairns.

VARIATIONS

- Hike to the trail summit; 14.2 km return.
- Exit from the Celeste Lake upper jct via Celeste Lake to the Little Yoho trail, and on to Takakkaw Falls; 17.7 km total.
- Add a visit to Marpole Lake and Twin Falls; 25.5 km total. If you camp at Little Yoho and at Twin Falls, you can spend two nights out.
- Approach from Emerald Lake via Yoho Pass to the Yoho Lake-Iceline upper junction in 10.7 km, making the total for the outing 28.8 km. If you camp at Yoho Lake and at Little Yoho, you can spend two nights out. See Classic Hikes #45 and #46 for more options.

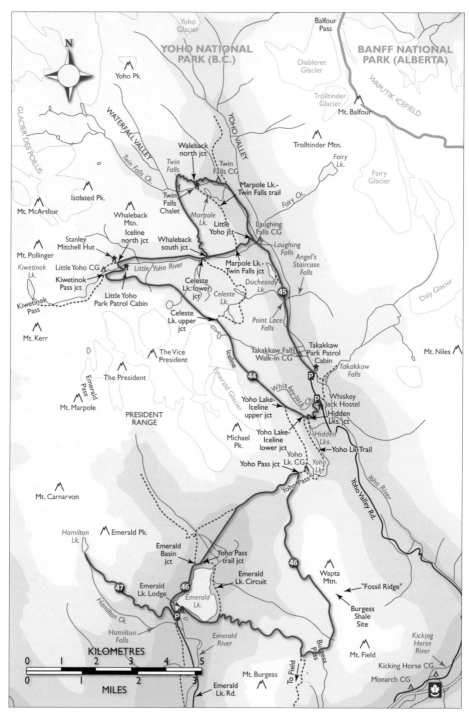

The Iceline roughly parallels Edward Whymper's route of exploration in 1901, when his party followed the edge of Emerald Glacier from Yoho Pass to the Little Yoho Valley. Whymper, famous for his first ascent of the Matterhorn in 1865, was accompanied by trail guide Bill Peyto, mountaineer James Outram, and four European mountaineering guides. During the trip, party members made first ascents of nine mountains in the Little Yoho, crossed several passes, and named many features.

Emerald Glacier

Emerald Glacier consists of several cirque glaciers tucked under the east flank of The Vice President. During their most recent significant advance – the Little Ice Age – these lobes of ice covered the area now traversed by the trail. Working its way north, the trail climbs and descends a series of lateral moraines. Between the moraines, you cross areas of recently exposed bedrock, bisected by meltwater streams. Rock-hop the streams, as necessary. The bedrock displays striations – scratches and grooves etched by stones embedded in the underside of the moving ice.

The vistas from the Iceline improve with each moraine crossed. Just before the Celeste Lake upper junction, the trail draws alongside a marginal lake – the greater "Lake in the Sky." (See the back cover photo.) The low ridge of debris north of this lake is a push moraine, created by a minor advance of the closest lobe of ice in the 1970s. To the north, across the Little Yoho Valley, you can see Mt. McArthur

(3021 m) and the rocky prow of Isolated Peak (2823 m). Surveyor W.S. Drewry made the first ascent of Mt. McArthur in 1891. He named the peak for his colleague, J.J. McArthur (see p. 177).

There is little shelter from poor weather or intense heat on the Iceline. If you are weary, you may choose to exit at the Celeste Lake upper junction. It is 11.3 km to the Takakkaw Falls parking area via Celeste Lake and Laughing Falls. Continuing on the Iceline, you begin to contour west into the Little Yoho Valley, passing the lesser "Lake in the Sky", to reach the apex of the trail on the crest of another moraine. Ahead are the northern aspects of The Vice President (3077 m) and The President (3123 m). These mountains were originally named for two officials of the CPR – President, Thomas Shaughnessy, and Vice-President, David McNicoll. It was later discovered that the men's personal names had been previously given to two mountains in Glacier National Park, BC. Thus, their titles were applied to these mountains.

SLIP SLIDING AWAY

Whiskey Jack hostel originated in 1922 as a CPR bungalow camp called Yoho Valley Lodge. Oblivious to the avalanche hazard, the builders chose the slope because it was close to a stream and offered a view of Takakkaw Falls. (You can see a section of the old water pipeline in the trail.) An avalanche damaged the lodge in the winter of 1937-38. The surviving buildings were relocated to the south, but not far enough to be out of harm's way. In 1967 another avalanche destroyed the vacant main lodge building. The surviving outbuildings became a hostel in 1969. "Whiskey jack" is a folk name for the gray jay, a crow family member that is common in the surrounding subalpine forest.

An entirely new trail was made this year... along the upper slopes of... the Yoho Valley. I suggest that this... should be completed by connecting the Upper Yoho Valley [Little Yoho] with the... trail which goes along the bottom of the valley. If this is done, tourists will be able to make a grand trip, ... and will obtain a greater diversity of views than they can by following a single route.

Letter from mountaineer Edward Whymper to Sir Thomas Shaughnessy, President of the CPR; January 3, 1902

181

Iceline trail summit

Another lobe of Emerald Glacier nestles on the north flank of The Vice President. Its meltwaters feed a lake that is backed by a lofty, 600 m long lateral moraine. The meltwater stream is building a delta into the lake. Another, smaller moraine-dammed lake lies to the north. As you descend toward treeline, Yoho Glacier, Mt. Gordon (3161 m), and Mt. Balfour are to the northeast. The north ridge of The Vice President is unofficially called "Barometer Peak." It features wildly overturned folds. Purple Arctomys (ARK-toe-miss) shale is common at trailside.

Little Yoho Valley to Takakkaw Falls

The Iceline swings behind the prominent moraine and, 500 m later, begins a steady descent through meadow and subalpine forest to the Little Yoho River and the Kiwetinok Pass junction. Turn east (right) and follow the river 300 m to a bridge. Cross it to the Iceline north junction. The Little Yoho campground is 300 m west (left). This junction is at just over the half-way point on the hike. The remainder of the distance is on good trails and can be completed fairly quickly, if desired. Head east (right) from the junction on the Little Yoho trail for 3.8 km to the Marpole Lake-Twin Falls junction. Turn south (right) and descend to the Little Yoho junction (Laughing Falls) in 1.6 km. Turn south (right) and follow the Yoho Valley trail 4.7 km to the Takakkaw Falls parking area.

If you feel like having a marathon the day, you can add visits to Marpole Lake and Twin Falls – although the falls will be shaded in the afternoon. Keep north (straight ahead) at the Marpole Lake-Twin Falls junction. It's 1.8 km to Marpole Lake, 0.7 km to Twin Falls and the Whaleback north junction. Turn east (right), passing the Yoho Glacier jct in 1.5 km, to reach the Little Yoho junction (Laughing Falls) on the Yoho Valley trail, in a further 2.0 km. (See Classic Hike #45 for more details.)

SOME ASSEMBLY REQUIRED

If you wanted to build a mountain like those that surround the Yoho Valley, your raw materials would all be at trailside on the Iceline. Because of extensive glaciation, rubble from every rock formation in the area has been hived-off and deposited here in the moraines. Limestones of every shade of gray and white, dolomites of peach and apricot, and red and amber shales – the colours and textures are marvelous. They are so great, I would recommend hiking the first 5 km of the Iceline on even a lousy weather day just to appreciate them. Most of the rocks date to the Middle- and Late Cambrian periods.

45. Yoho – Little Yoho

Takakkaw Falls

TRAIL THUMBNAIL

Overnight, 3-5 days; see map, p. 180

Route	Elev. (m)	Dist. (km)
Takakkaw Falls parking area	1509	0
Takakkaw Falls walk-in CG	1517	0.2
Yoho Valley trailhead	1520	0.4
Angel's Staircase Falls, Point Lace Falls jct	1540	2.3
Duchesnay Lake jct	1590	3.7
Laughing Falls and CG	1608	4.6
Little Yoho jct	1608	4.7
Twin Falls Creek bridge	1610	4.9
Yoho Glacier jct	1616	6.8
Twin Falls CG	1616	7.0
Whaleback north jct	1905	8.5
Twin Falls bridge or ford	1980	11.2
Whaleback trail summit	2210	12.8
Whaleback south jct	1768	15.1
Celeste Lake lower jct	1768	15.2
Iceline north jct	2070	17.8
Little Yoho CG	2073	+0.3
Kiwetinok Pass jct	2073	18.1
Iceline trail summit	2230	21.9
Celeste Lake upper jct	2195	22.6
Yoho Lake-Iceline upper jct	1860	25.8
Yoho Lake-Iceline lower jct	1646	27.0
Iceline -Yoho Pass trailhead	1501	28.4
Takakkaw Falls parking area	1509	29.0

Trailhead

Follow Highway 1 to the Yoho Valley Road, 3.7 km east of Field, 22.3 km west of Lake Louise. Turn north and follow this road 13 km to the Takakkaw Falls parking area. The trailhead is at the north end of the first parking area. Those travelling without a vehicle can use Takakkaw Falls walk-in campground or nearby Whiskey Jack hostel as a base.

Maps

NTS: 82 N/7, 82 N/8, 82 N/9, 82 N/10
Gem Trek: *Lake Louise and Yoho*

Yoho National Park takes its name from a Cree expression of awe and wonder. The Yoho Valley and Little Yoho Valley contain many of the park's wonders – waterfalls, turbulent rivers, glacier-clad peaks, and pockets of alpine meadow. You won't find solitude – except perhaps late in the hiking season – but you'll probably fall in love with the place anyway. The close spacing of campgrounds, the well-developed trails, and the convenient access to treeline and glacial environments make the area ideal for novice backpackers.

Takakkaw Falls to Twin Falls Campground

The outing begins along a gravel road to the Takakkaw Falls walk-in campground. The Yoho Valley trail departs north and heads across alluvial flats into forest. This trail originated after the expansion of the Mt. Stephen Reserve – the forerunner of Yoho National Park – as a corduroy carriage road, constructed between 1903 and 1909. In this case, the corduroy was built by laying sections of whole trees across the tread, and covering the bumpy surface with dirt. You can still see sections of old corduroy at trailside.

The Yoho Valley exemplifies the park's interpretive theme of "rockwalls and waterfalls" better than any other place. Glaciers carved the massive U-shaped valley. Tributary valleys also filled with ice, but were not as deeply eroded. When the ancestral Yoho Glacier receded, the tributary valleys were left hanging above the main valley floor.

VARIATIONS

- Camp at Laughing Falls (4.6 km), an excellent novice backpack.
- Camp at Twin Falls (7.0 km) and day-hike to Yoho Glacier and the Whaleback.
- Camp at Little Yoho (10.2 km) and explore.

It required no discussion to select a name for this wonderfully beautiful cascade. It named itself; Twin Falls it was called there and then, and so it appears on Habel's map...

Ralph Edwards; *The Trail to the Charmed Land*

Their streams now plunge toward the Yoho River as waterfalls. Takakkaw Falls (TAH-kuh-kah) cascades 254 m. The name is a Cree expression that means "It is magnificent!" You may have heard that Takakkaw Falls is the highest waterfall in Canada. It isn't; that honour clearly goes to Della Falls on Vancouver Island. Helmet Falls, in Kootenay; Hunlen Falls, in Tweedsmuir; and Takakkaw are all in the running as the next highest – depending on whether you measure all the cascades, or just the single highest drop in each waterfall. The frozen falls were one of the first "extreme" waterfall ice climbs during the development of that pursuit in the 1970s.

At km 2.3, short sidetrails branch east to the bank of the Yoho River and a view of Angel's Staircase Falls, and southwest to Point Lace Falls. The Yoho Valley trail continues north and climbs Hollingsworth Hill, named for a district warden who used dynamite to widen the right of way. The Duchesnay Lake junction is at km 3.7. The sidetrip is less than half the 400 m indicated on the park sign. In most years, the lake is dry by late summer. Moose frequent this area. Back on the main trail, you draw alongside the Yoho River at a small canyon. The tilted, potholed, rock exposed in the riverbed is Sullivan Formation limestone.

Laughing Falls campground is situated just beyond, on an alluvial fan at the confluence of Twin Falls Creek, the Little Yoho River, and the Yoho River. For the best views of nearby Laughing Falls, follow beaten paths along the north bank of the Little Yoho River.

Continue north (straight ahead) at the Little Yoho junction just beyond Laughing Falls campground. The trail crosses to the east bank of Twin Falls Creek and follows cobbled flats alongside the Yoho River. I once encountered a herd of 23 elk here. The trail turns sharply south to re-enter the valley of Twin Falls Creek, from where you have tantalizing views west through the trees to Twin Falls. At the Yoho Glacier junction, the trail to the glacier branches north (right). Turn south (left) to reach Twin Falls campground in 150 m.

Twin Falls Campground to The Whaleback

Beyond Twin Falls campground, the trail bypasses a small canyon in the creek, and climbs toward the Whaleback junction. Look for a slab of "ripple rock" in the trail. The rock's undulating surface records the action of wavelets on a prehistoric shoreline. The roar of Twin Falls increases as you approach the Whaleback north junction. Here, several of the Engelmann spruce trees are more than 1 m in diameter and 45 m tall.

Twin Falls Chalet is 80 m south of the Whaleback north junction. The Chalet originated in 1908 as a shelter built by the CPR for its mountaineering guides and clients. It was expanded in 1923. It is now a Federal Heritage Building, owned by Yoho National Park and privately operated under lease. Out the front door, Twin Falls cascades over a 180 m cliff of Cathedral Formation limestone at the mouth of a hanging valley. Paths along Twin Falls Creek provide uninhibited views of the thundering cascades, which are sunlit until mid-morning.

Head north (right) at the Whaleback north junction. The trail climbs steadily for the next 2.7 km

QUEST FOR HIDDEN MOUNTAIN

Laughing Falls brightened up the otherwise glum surroundings during the rain-plagued, first exploration of the Yoho Valley in 1897. The expedition was organized by Jean Habel (AHH-bull), a German mathematics professor and mountaineer. Habel was intent on ascending a mountain he had seen from the railway the previous year – a peak that he had called Hidden Mountain, now named Mont des Poilus.

Habel's party journeyed from Field to Emerald Lake, then over Yoho Pass to the floor of the Yoho Valley at Takakkaw Falls. This 25 km excursion, delayed by the professor's many ramblings, required eight days. Continuing north in the valley, the party was the first to see Laughing Falls and Twin Falls, and the first to set foot on Yoho Glacier. The expedition ran out of supplies before any serious attempt could be made on Hidden Mountain. However, Habel's report, published the following year in the journal *Appalachia*, created great interest in the Yoho Valley, and was instrumental in the area being added to the national park reserve in 1901.

Yoho Glacier

YOHO GLACIER, 2.3 KM

If you arrive early at Twin Falls campground, you may want to hike to Yoho Glacier after setting up camp. Backtrack to the Yoho Glacier junction and head north on a rough trail that rises and falls through an ancient forest of Engelmann spruce and subalpine fir. The trail makes a short switchback descent 2.2 km from the junction, and emerges abruptly from the forest onto a barren slope that overlooks the forefield of Yoho Glacier. The sudden transition marks the trimline of the glacier. In 1844, the ice stopped here. All forest to the north was obliterated. In this harsh climate and on these poor soils, it will take many centuries for a forest to become re-established.

Looking north, you can see Yoho Glacier notched between the cliffs of Mt. Gordon (3161 m) to the east, and the slopes and moraines of Yoho Peak (2773 m) to the west. The glacier has receded almost 3 km. Yoho Glacier is one of eight outlet valley glaciers of the 40 km² Wapta Icefield. Early in the 20th century, the glacier was the subject of intense scientific study and annual measurement. When glacial retreat made access to the ice difficult for the horses that packed the heavy survey gear, the studies were abandoned.

If you follow a rough track north from the end of the maintained trail, you can explore the colourful, ice-sculpted and water-worn slabs in the forefield of Yoho Glacier. The rock formations date to the Middle Cambrian. Mountaineers can also follow cairns to the west lateral moraine of Yoho Glacier. This knife-edge ridge of rubble provides a breathtaking panorama of the glacier, the Wapta Icefield, and the Yoho Valley.

LEAVING WELL ENOUGH ALONE

When viewed in context of the relentless force of flowing water and the shattering effects of frost, the limestone column that divides Twin Falls is a temporary feature. Even more so when you consider that unnatural forces have also been at work. In 1924, trail workers used dynamite in an attempt to equalize the volume of the two falls. Debris from the blast blocked the southerly channel and had exactly the opposite effect intended. One can well imagine the panic of the workers as they toiled in that perilous place, in their ultimately successful attempt to set matters right. In recent years, one of the falls often dwindles by August.

to the mouth of the Waterfall Valley. You have fine views east to Mt. Balfour (3284 m) – the highest peak in the area – and to the peculiar, castellated summit of Trolltinder Mountain (2912 m). The name means "Gnome's Peak." It reminded Jean Habel of a peak with the same name in Norway. Glaciers that adorn these mountains are part of the 32 km² Waputik Icefield. *Waputik* (WAH-poo-tick) is a Stoney word that means "white goat."

The trail follows the edge of the cliff south to former site of Whaleback campground. Camping is no longer allowed. Use caution if you approach the cliff edge. People have died here, from falls into the creek and over the cliff. One hiker fell into the whirlpool at the brink of the falls and survived the chill and the inevitable pull of the current for 45 minutes before being rescued. The mountain goats here are downright aggressive. A goat approached me once, with its head down, when my back was to the cliff. Mind if I butt out?

The Whaleback

In summer, a decked I-beam bridge spans Twin Falls Creek above the falls. Avalanches from Whaleback Mountain (2617 m) sweep this area. Crews install and dismantle the bridge annually to prevent its destruction. If you are hiking when the bridge is out, expect a moderate to difficult ford of Twin Falls Creek, best accomplished about 50 m above the bridge site. The water is silty and extremely cold. Mountaineer, Edward Whymper, named Whaleback Mountain. When viewed from the south, the shales of its upper slopes suggest a massive whale breaching the ocean's surface. The turreted peak at the northwest end of Whaleback Mountain is Isolated Peak (2823 m). It was first climbed in 1901 by a party that included Whymper and James Outram.

The next 1.6 km is the scenic highlight of the Yoho Valley. The trail makes a steady ascent south from the creek and winds through treeline into delightful upper subalpine meadows. Prominent in the view north from the apex is the pyramidical form of Mont des Poilus (3166 m) – Jean Habel's "Hidden Mountain." The mountain's present name commemorates French foot soldiers of WWI. Group of Seven artist, Lawren Harris, depicted this scene in a work entitled "Isolation Peak."

Meltwaters from the glacier in the foreground feed Twin Falls. Mt. Collie (3143 m) and Yoho Peak are to the northeast, separated from Mt. Habel, Mt. Rhondda, and Mt. Gordon by Yoho Glacier. To the east is Mt. Balfour. To its south are Mt. Daly (3148 m), and Mt. Niles (2967 m) at the head of Daly Glacier. Farther south the view includes Mt. Stephen, Cathedral Mountain, Odaray Mountain, Mt. Victoria, Mt. Huber, and Hungabee Mountain.

Isolated Meadows

A short distance before you reach the south end of Whaleback Mountain, the trail angles sharply right (west). However, continue straight ahead for 80 m to a viewpoint that overlooks the Little Yoho Valley. The glaciated mountains across the valley are The Vice President (3077 m) and The President (3123 m), named for executives of the Canadian Pacific Railway. The rocky bench beneath The Vice President is the route of the Iceline trail. A cairn on the viewpoint commemorates a skier, killed nearby in a snow avalanche in 1962. Whitebark pine grows in this windswept location.

The trail switchbacks steeply down an avalanche gully to reach the Little Yoho Valley in 2.1 km. Turn west (right) onto the Little Yoho trail, and keep straight ahead to the Celeste Lake lower junction just beyond. The trail climbs gradually through subalpine forest for 3.0 km to the Iceline north junction. The Little Yoho campground is 300 m west (straight ahead) of the junction. It makes an excellent base for exploration of the upper valley. Although the only "official" sidetrail is to Kiwetinok Pass, experienced mountaineers may make straightforward ascents of many of the surrounding peaks. Look for dippers and sandpipers along the Little Yoho River.

NEXT STOP, LITTLE YOHO

If the weather shuts down or if you don't want to hump a backpack over the Whaleback trail, turn south (left) at the Whaleback north junction, to take the Marpole Connector trail, 2.5 km to the Little Yoho trail. You pass Marpole Lake on the way. Richard Marpole was a CPR superintendent of operations in the early 1900s. He gave out free passes to mountaineers, got some free publicity for the railway in return, and got a lake and a mountain named for himself when the mountaineers expressed their gratitude. Turn west (right) at the junction on the Little Yoho trail, and follow it 3.9 km to Little Yoho campground. An easy day, as they go.

Kiwetinok Pass

Loop Hike Options

I recommend that you exit from the Little Yoho Valley by following the Iceline. This 11.2 km route offers spectacular, close-up views of the ice and moraines of Emerald Glacier, and high level views of Takakkaw Falls and the Yoho Valley. (See Classic Hike #44.) Much of the Iceline is on rubble and rock; if you have knee, ankle or back complaints you may find it rough going with a heavy pack. Alternate exits are: follow the Little Yoho Valley trail east to Laughing Falls, and

then to Takakkaw Falls (9.9 km); follow the Iceline to the Celeste Lake upper junction, take the connector to the Little Yoho trail, then to Laughing Falls and Takakkaw Falls (16.1 km). Those who want to add another night to this outing can follow the Iceline to the Yoho Pass-Iceline upper junction (7.9 km), and take the high trail (straight ahead) for 2 km to Yoho Lake campground. From Yoho Lake it is 4.5 km to the Takakkaw Falls parking area via the Yoho Pass trail; or 8.0 km to Emerald Lake.

KIWETINOK PASS (2469 M), 3.4 KM

From the Little Yoho campground, head east to the Iceline north junction. Cross the Little Yoho River and head west for 300 m to the Kiwetinok Pass junction. Keep straight ahead. After climbing beside a small canyon, the trail drops into the forefield of President Glacier. Rock-hop or ford (straightforward) the meltwater stream and follow cairns west across the rubble. Rock-hop or ford (moderate) the Little Yoho River 500 m later to its north bank. A steep climb on a rough track ensues, leading to the rocky basin that contains Kiwetinok Lake.

Kiwetinok is a Stoney word that means "on the north side." At 2454 m, Kiwetinok has been referred to as the highest lake in Canada. It may well be the highest *named* lake, but there is at least one unnamed lake in Banff National Park, approximately 50 m higher.

Kiwetinok Lake is often frozen until early August. The lake is partially fed by meltwater from a small glacier on Kiwetinok Peak (2909 m), hence the remarkable colour of the water. You may see white-tailed ptarmigan nearby. Because summer

is so brief here, these particular birds never fully develop summer plumage. Feathers on their bellies and legs are white year-round. Looking east down the Little Yoho Valley, you can see a tremendous overturned fold in "Barometer Peak," the ridge that extends north from The Vice President. (The peak serves as a barometer of sorts for climbers; if you can see it from the ACC hut, the day is fair enough for climbing.) Beyond is Mt. Daly and Daly Glacier.

From Kiwetinok Lake, you can scramble west over boulders to Kiwetinok Pass. Beyond is the valley of the Amiskwi River, the largest tributary valley of the Kicking Horse River. (*Amiskwi* means "beaver." The river was formerly called Beavertail.) The mountaineering party of Edward Whymper made the first crossing of Kiwetinok Pass, in 1901. They had a miserable time bushwhacking their way back to Field, as has just about everyone else who has followed since. Whymper named the mountain south of the pass for Robert Kerr of the CPR, the man who had given Whymper free train passage. Whymper named the mountain north of Kiwetinok Lake for Joseph Pollinger, one of his guides.

46. Wapta Highline

Emerald Lake

Trailhead

Follow Highway 1 to the Emerald lake Road, 2.6 km west of Field. Turn north and follow the road 8 km to its end at the Emerald Lake parking area. The paved trailhead is at the north end of the parking area, next to the bridge.

Maps

NTS: 82 N/7, 82 N/8
Gem Trek: *Lake Louise and Yoho*

The Wapta Highline completes an energetic, high-level circuit of Emerald Lake, Yoho's largest and best known body of water. If you day-hike the loop, you'll have a solid workout. As well as top-notch scenery, the hike features interesting geology and human history, and uncommon vegetation. This hike is sometimes called Burgess Highline, Wapta Triangle, or Burgess Triangle.

Trailhead to Yoho Pass

The first 1.5 km follows the Emerald Lake nature trail. The lush vegetation includes trees that are uncommon in this part of the Rockies – western redcedar, western hemlock, and western yew. At km 1.1, the trail turns east (right) onto one of the larger alluvial fans in the Rockies. Most alluvial fans were established between 6000 and 7000 years ago by meltwater surges as the Earth's climate warmed rapidly after the Late Wisconsin Glaciation. The Emerald Fan is slowly filling Emerald Lake. Aerial views indicate that 50 percent of the lake's former area is now rubble.

At the next trail junction in 200 m, branch northeast (left) onto the Yoho Pass trail. For 2 km, the trail continues across the alluvial fan, offering views north to the impressive peaks that ring Emerald Basin. The centrepiece is a hanging glacier on The President (3123 m). The original road from Field to Emerald Lake was a log corduroy affair known as the "Tally-Ho Road." You can see sections beside the trail.

From the east edge of the fan, the trail begins a steady ascent to Yoho Pass. The cliffs of The Vice President dominate the view north, exhibiting a common cliff-building sequence: Cathedral Formation limestone, Stephen Formation shale, and Eldon Formation limestone. All date to the Cambrian. The mountain commemorates David McNicoll, a vice-president of the Canadian Pacific Railway. The creek at trailside drains a glacial cirque high above. The Van Horne Range to the southwest, and Mt. Vaux (VOX) (3310 m) to the south, ring the horizon. On calm days, you will see these mountains reflected in the lake, even from this distance. Group of Seven artist, Lawren Harris, painted this scene in 1924, in a work tilted "Emerald Lake." From 1954 to 1971, the Canadian ten-dollar bill featured this view.

VARIATIONS

- If you camp at Yoho Lake, you can turn this into a two-day trip, 21.3 km. You can make a three-day trip by adding a day-hike from Yoho Lake campground to the Iceline trail summit, 11.8 km return. See Classic Hike #44.

> *After about two hours travel we arrived at a point where the ground seemed to slope downward gently on either side... About half a mile from this point we emerged from the timber on the shore of a marvelously beautiful little lake, not much larger than a little pond, but of an exquisite ultramarine colour.*
>
> Ralph Edwards; *The Trail to the Charmed Land*

Devil's club

Yoho Pass to Burgess Pass

From the junction at Yoho Pass, the Wapta Highline turns sharply south (right). After about 500 m, the trail emerges from the forest beneath the gray limestone cliffs of Wapta Mountain. This is spectacular piece of trail, with a feeling of exposure. In places, the cliff overhangs the path. You can see the Van Horne Range again to the west. To the north, "Michael Falls" drops from the cirque on The Vice President in two lofty cascades. You can see the highest mountain in the area, Mt. Balfour (3284 m), to the northeast, across Yoho Pass. Pikas live in the rocky debris downslope from the trail.

On August 25, 1988, a tremendous rainstorm struck the vicinity of Field. The west-facing slopes of Wapta Mountain caught the full brunt. The sloping bedrock funnelled the runoff into gullies. Surges of water and debris swept the mountainside below, cutting three swaths through the trail, each 4 m deep. You contour in and out of these flash-flood courses. The view west again includes Emerald Lake – largest of Yoho's 61 mapped lakes and ponds – now almost 900 m below.

The trail continues south to the avalanche gully beneath Mt. Field (2635 m). Please keep to the trail if snow patches linger. Look for mountain goats on the slopes above. Across the gully, the trail turns west into Burgess Pass. As you traverse an exposed shale slope on the south side of the pass, you have fine views of Mt. Stephen (3199 m) across the Kicking Horse Valley, Mt. Vaux (VOX) in the distant southwest, and the town of Field.

The grade eases as the trail traverses an avalanche slope, and then steepens again where it re-enters the forest. The creek here begins as an underground outlet from Yoho Lake. Yellow columbine and false hellebore are common at trailside. A horse-hiker barrier marks the entrance to Yoho Pass and a trail junction. The dense, ancient forest on the pass does not allow any distant views, but if you want to visit Yoho Lake or camp at its campground (1.4 km return), or hike the Iceline, continue straight ahead (east).

The party of Jean Habel (see sidebar on p. 184) made the first crossing of Yoho Pass, in 1897. Ralph Edwards, guide on the trip, called Yoho Lake, "Marina Lake." In 1906, it was known as "Summit Lake" when the inaugural Alpine Club of Canada camp convened on its shores. The tranquil lake is spring fed and contains eastern brook trout. The cliffs of Wapta Mountain (2782 m) loom to the south. The glacial horn of Michael Peak (2701 m), a minor eminence on The Vice President, rises to the northwest.

THE EMERALD FAN: A TOUGH PLACE TO CALL HOME

Because of poor soil, glacial winds, and a fluctuating water table, the Emerald Fan is a harsh home for vegetation. Hardy plants such as common juniper, yellow mountain-avens, white camas, and paintbrush are scattered across the gravels. The evergreen leaves of mountain-avens are lightly coloured on the underside to reflect the intense heat that can radiate from the rocks. Yellow lady's slipper blooms here from mid-June to mid-July. A few lodgepole pines, gnarled white spruce, and white birch comprise the sparse tree cover. Some of the pines have branches on their northeast sides only – they "flag" the prevailing southwest winds. Although the trees look insubstantial, some of the pines are 150 years old.

You will see various generations of bridges as you cross the Emerald Fan. Glacial melt streams fluctuate daily and seasonally, and are prone to flash-floods. The I-beam bridges were installed at great expense over streams that promptly changed their courses, leaving the structures high and dry. The "boardwalk bridges" were designed to be portable, allowing trail crews to reposition the bridges as required – a daily ritual during peak runoff in August. In practice, these heavy bridges are not portable. They frequently become buried in the debris of flash-floods. The forces at work here illustrate that nature prevails despite human efforts to forge a path. You may get your feet wet.

Western redcedar forest

Burgess Pass to Emerald Lake

The trail to Emerald Lake plunges north from the junction in Burgess Pass. The initial slopes may be snow-covered until mid-July. Most of the descent is in dense forest. The imposing north face of Mt. Burgess (2588 m) towers in profile through a break in the trees. The mountain and pass were named for Alexander Burgess, Canada's Deputy Minister of the Interior in 1886. The last 2 km of this winding and relentless descent passes through the most extensive western redcedar forest in Yoho. The western redcedar is BC's provincial tree.

Follow the Emerald Lake trail west (left) from the lakeshore junction. Keep right at subsequent junctions. Watch for moose here late in the day. The trail climbs onto the glacial moraine, or rockslide – depending which theory you believe – that dams Emerald Lake, and enters the grounds of Emerald Lake Lodge. Parks Canada thinned the forest around the lodge in 2008 to reduce the fire risk, hence the clearcut. Look for devil's club. Originally constructed by the Canadian Pacific Railway in 1902, the lodge was redeveloped in 1986. The main lodge building contains timbers used in the original structure. Complete the loop by following the gravel road through the lodge grounds to the parking area.

THE BURGESS SHALE

The ridge connecting Wapta Mountain and Mt. Field is popularly known as Fossil Ridge. Charles Walcott, of the Smithsonian Institution, discovered soft-bodied fossils on the slopes above the trail in 1909. During five subsequent summers of collecting, Walcott gathered 65,000 fossil specimens that are now housed at the Smithsonian in Washington DC. Walcott described the specimens with the knowledge of the day, assigning them to categories known from fossil finds elsewhere in the world. It was 60 years before renewed interpretation of the fossils took place, and the significance of this treasure trove of ancient species was realized.

The Burgess Shale contains wonderfully preserved remains of marine animals that lived along the edge of the continental shelf during the Middle Cambrian, approximately 505 million-years-ago. A submarine cliff, now called the Cathedral Escarpment, marked the edge of the shelf. Periodic mud flows over the cliff would bury animals living on the sea floor. As the deaths of the animals were sudden and the remains were entombed,

scavenging and decay did not take place. As a result, the fossils are preserved in exquisite detail as flattened imprints in the shale.

The Burgess Shale fossils preserve some 140 species. Paleontologists have painstakingly reconstructed the animals' appearances into three-dimensional figures. Some of the fossils represent the earliest known members of many lifeform groups (phyla) that exist today. Others are unique in the world and represent species that cannot be classified among contemporary phyla. This suggests that the variety of life at "body-plan" level was greater 505 million-years-ago than it is today. Standard evolutionary theory implies an increase in diversity as time passes. The Burgess Shale may indicate that mass extinction events and chance have played a greater role in the evolution of life than was previously thought.

Although you may see researchers working at the Burgess Shale site above the trail, the area is closed to public access. Guided tours are available. Inquire at the park information centre at Field.

47. Hamilton Lake

Hamilton Lake

TRAIL THUMBNAIL

Day-hike; see map, p. 180

Route	Elev. (m)	Dist. (km)
Trailhead	1302	0
Hamilton Falls	1352	0.7
Hamilton Lake	2149	5.3

Trailhead
Follow Highway 1 to the Emerald lake Road, 2.6 km west of Field. Turn north and follow the road 8 km to its end at the Emerald Lake parking area. The trailhead is at the southwest corner of the parking area.

Maps
NTS: 82 N/7
Gem Trek: *Lake Louise and Yoho*

Best lighting: mid-morning to mid-afternoon

The Hamilton Lake trail makes an unwavering ascent to a beautiful tarn. The outing features rainforest, whitebark pine trees, and alpine meadows. A waterfall and a mountain display an ancient geological boundary. If you are fortunate, you may see moose, hoary marmots, porcupines, and golden eagles. The final approach to the lake is frequently snowbound until early July, and winter ice may linger on the lake's surface equally as long.

Trailhead to Hamilton Falls

The trailhead is located in the deep basin that surrounds Emerald Lake; a place that traps storm systems and creates abundant precipitation. Vegetation along the first 700 m contains species typical of the Western Interior Cedar-Hemlock "rainforest," normally found farther west in BC: western redcedar, western hemlock, western yew, thimbleberry, and devil's club. Queen's cup, western meadowrue, foamflower, and dwarf dogwood are common wildflowers. The white flower of queen's cup yields a striking blue-coloured berry in late summer, hence its other folk name – "bluebead." You may see black bears and moose here.

The trail draws alongside Hamilton Creek and follows it to some large Douglas-fir trees at the shaded base of Hamilton Falls. The damp environment here gives rise to brilliant yellow tree lichens. The features named "Hamilton" honour a prospector who discovered the falls while in quest of more material rewards. Hamilton Creek was formerly the water supply for Emerald Lake Lodge. You may see artifacts associated with the water intake system and pipeline. The falls are at the mouth of a hanging valley, and are being eroded into Chancellor Formation limestone.

Hamilton Falls to Hamilton Lake

You leave the damp forest as the trail switchbacks to a fenced viewpoint at the upper cascades of Hamilton Falls. Here you can see plunge pools and potholes, and where a bedrock fault has captured Hamilton Creek. Hamilton Falls is the last viewpoint for 2.5 km, during which the grade is often steep. The forest gradually changes from one dominated by lodgepole pine, to the combination of subalpine fir and Engelmann spruce typical of subalpine elevations. At km 3.9, you may rest at an opening in the forest that allows a view to Emerald Lake.

Leaving this viewpoint, the trail angles sharply northwest and the grade lessens. The whitebark pine trees at trailside indicate that you have reached the upper subalpine life zone. One of these pines has six trunks growing from a single base. Porcupines have damaged the bark of many nearby trees. These rodents strip the outer bark in culinary quest for the sweet, inner cambium layer. A tree girdled of its bark will usually die.

> *I had chosen a high conical mountain which overlooks Emerald Lake on the west side, as a (survey) station, and made the ascent to the foot of the steep broken ridge which leads to its summit; but the rumbling of the slides of the freshly fallen snow, carrying down masses of rocky débris, warned us of the imminent danger, and we abandoned the ascent.*
>
> Surveyor J.J. McArthur; *Report of the Department of the Interior 1887*

The trail crosses several avalanche slopes, with views southwest to the Van Horne Range – named for William Cornelius Van Horne, who oversaw construction of the Canadian Pacific Railway from 1881-1885, and who later served as its president. The peak with the cleft between its two summits is known locally as "Nimrod Peak," named for the Stoney guide of the Palliser Expedition. (*Nimrod* means "great hunter.") The higher peak to the north, with the prominent niche glacier, is Mt. King (2892 m). Named for a Canadian astronomer and surveyor, the mountain was first climbed in 1892 by J.J. McArthur. The peaks of the Ottertail Range, including glacier capped Mt. Vaux (VOX) (3310 m), stand out to the south. To the southeast (left) of Mt. Vaux, you can see the twin summits of Mt. Goodsir (3567 m, 3507 m), the highest mountains in Yoho National Park, and 10th- and 12th-highest in the Rockies. (Mt. Goodsir South is also the 10th-highest mountain in BC.) On the western skyline, 90 km distant, you might pick out the granite spires of the Bugaboos in the Purcell Range of the Columbia Mountains.

At a switchback you pass a massive Engelmann spruce, more than a metre thick at the base, and 35 m tall – truly a giant for this elevation. In early July, glacier lilies bloom in profusion on the final approach to Hamilton Lake. The protein-rich corm of this plant is a favourite food of grizzly bears. Two other favourite grizzly snacks – hoary marmots and Columbian ground squirrels – live nearby, so approach the lake with caution.

An upturned lip of Chancellor Formation shale impounds Hamilton Lake. This rock dam precisely marks the boundary between the eastern main ranges and the western main ranges. The Chancellor Formation dips steeply to the southwest. The eastern main range rock formations are horizontal. You can see the boundary where it bisects the southeast ridge of Mt. Carnarvon (car-NARR-von) (3046 m), the backdrop to the lake. The mountain sits atop a massive anticline – an arch-shaped fold in the bedrock. Mountain goats frequent the grassy areas on the mountain's lower slopes.

While it has been claimed that Hamilton Lake was not "discovered" until 1936, it is in plain view from the south ridge of Mt. Carnarvon, which was first occupied as a survey station in 1887. James Hector named the mountain in 1858 for the fourth Earl of Carnarvon, who later was author of the British North Act. Hector saw the peak from the Kicking Horse Valley. Mt. Carnarvon was first climbed in 1904. The blocky peak north of Hamilton Lake is known unofficially as "Top Hat." Watch for golden eagles, soaring on thermals overhead. I've seen them on almost every visit.

Hamilton Falls

AN ANCIENT BOUNDARY

The trailhead is on the boundary between two geological provinces. The eastern main ranges are to the east. They are typified by the castellated or "layer cake" mountain, whose flanks exhibit resistant cliffs of quartzite, limestone, and dolomite, separated by recessive ledges of shale. For the most part, the rock formations are in horizontal layers. The western main ranges are to the west. These mountains contain mostly weak shales and slates, which have been eroded into more rounded shapes that exhibit much folding and faulting – as you can see in the peaks of the Van Horne Range. The sediments of eastern main range mountains were deposited in relatively shallow seas, teeming with life, whereas those of western main range mountains collected at the same time in much deeper water, devoid of life. The trail follows the boundary between the two geological provinces all the way to Hamilton Lake, where you can see the transition, or facies change, in the south ridge of Mt. Carnarvon.

The Rockwall

Kootenay National Park

Established in 1920 as Canada's tenth national park, Kootenay includes 1406 km2 on the western slopes of the Rockies in BC. The park features tremendous geographical and ecological diversity. It is the only national park in Canada in which you may find a cactus and see a glacier. Kootenay is not heavily developed. It offers just under 200 km of hiking trails. The Classic Hikes in the park immerse you in rolling meadows, alpine ridges, wilderness valleys, and glacial barrens that were covered by ice less than a century ago.

The 104 km-long Kootenay Parkway (Highway 93) bisects the park. This road connects Castle Junction on Highway 1, 34 km west of Banff, with Highway 95 at the town of Radium Hot Springs, 105 km south of Golden. Access to the park is by car or by passenger bus. Park information centres are at Vermilion Crossing and in the village of Radium Hot Springs. Accommodation and limited services are available in the park at Vermilion Crossing, and near the Radium Hot Springs pools. More extensive services are available at the village of Radium Hot Springs; at Invermere, 14 km south of Radium on Highway 95; and at Banff. The park is in the Mountain time zone, the same as Banff and Jasper.

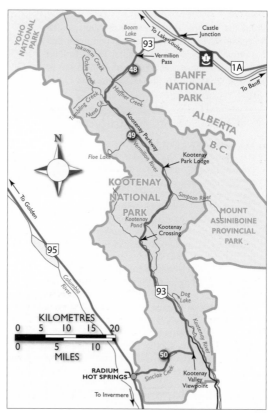

48. Stanley Glacier

Stanley Glacier

The Stanley Glacier trail explores a hanging valley and offers close-up views of three processes that have shaped the landscape of the Rockies: fire, avalanches, and glaciation. The trailside displays of wildflowers are spectacular, so if you are hiking in mid- to late-July, consider this outing even if the weather is not great. You may see moose, mountain goats, white-tailed ptarmigan, and hoary marmots.

Trailhead to Stanley Glacier Viewpoint

From the parking area, the trail descends to the Vermilion River and switchbacks up into forest that has burned twice in recent decades. The Vermilion Pass burn consumed 2360 ha of subalpine forest in July 1968. The Kootenay fires of 2003 burned 17,715

TRAIL THUMBNAIL

Day-hike

Route	Elev. (m)	Dist. (km)
Trailhead	1593	0
Stanley Glacier viewpoint	1921	4.2

Trailhead
South side of the Kootenay Parkway, 13.4 km west of Highway 1; 91.5 km east of Highway 95.

Special consideration
Due to the hazard of falling trees, avoid this hike during windy weather.

Maps
NTS: 82 N/1
Gem Trek: *Kootenay National Park* or *Banff and Mt. Assiniboine*

Best lighting: mid-morning to mid-afternoon

ha; 12.6 percent of the park's area. Lightning caused both of these fires.

The trail climbs steadily through the burned forest, gaining 220 m of elevation in the first 2.4 km. With the forest canopy removed by the fires, a profusion of sun-loving wildflowers blooms. Many are pioneering species that grow after fires – camas, fleabane, pink wintergreen, yellow columbine, yellow hedysarum, groundsel, and vibrantly coloured paintbrush. Until the forest canopy closes in again, the arnica and common fireweed displays here will likely remain unmatched in the Rockies. Damp areas feature rein-orchids and gentians. You may hear the buzzy calls of varied thrushes. After you crest a small rise, the trail descends slightly to a footbridge. The entrances to most hanging valleys in the Rockies are

Mr. Edward Whymper, another veteran of world-wide fame, spent six months in 1901 among these summits and returned to England full of enthusiasm and admiration for the immensity of the alpine area, the grandeur of the peaks, and the sublimity of the scenery throughout the entire region...

James Outram; *In the Heart of the Canadian Rockies*

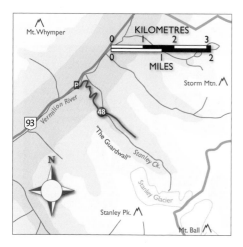

Burned forest

blocked by moraines that were pushed up alongside the larger glaciers in the main valleys. The rise just before the footbridge indicates the moraine at this location. From here on, you hike out of earshot of the highway.

The 2003 fire killed many small lodgepole pines that grew after the 1968 fire. You can now see thousands of tiny lodgepoles that date to the later burn, but note how, near the creek, some of the older saplings survived. This patchwork of tree ages will eventually result in a forest with more diversity than if most of the trees were the same age.

The colossal cliff that flanks the west side of the valley is known as "The Guardwall." The lower 300 m of cliff is Cathedral Formation limestone and dolomite. It contains a number of solution caves – caverns eroded by naturally acidic rainwater. The upper cliff is Eldon Formation limestone. Between the cliffs is a fossil-rich ledge of Stephen Formation shale. These formations date to the Middle Cambrian. The dark streaks on the cliffs are water seeps and rock lichens. In the perpetual shade of winter, the seeps freeze into sheets of ice that become a destination for waterfall ice climbers. In some years, the ice endures into July.

As you near the end of trail, note how the 2003 burn did not go as far up the valley as did the 1968 burn, and how the earlier burn reached almost to the very last tree. On the west side of the trail, there is a stand of mature forest that escaped both burns. Listen for hermit thrushes. A sign on a knoll marks the end of the maintained trail, from where you can study Stanley Glacier. Several lobes of ice terminate on cliffs. Less than two centuries ago, the glacier flowed over these cliffs to reach valley floor. You may hear the creaking and groaning of the ice as it creeps forward and, with fortune, see an ice avalanche. Meltwater that cascades over the cliffs is sometimes caught in updrafts, creating waterfalls that seem to disappear in mid-air.

Toward Stanley Glacier the valley is a barren world of boulders and screes that is home to mountain goats, hoary marmots, pikas, and white-tailed ptarmigan. The summit of Stanley Peak (3153 m) is concealed from view. James Hector originally

MOUNTAIN MAGIC

The 15 species of arnica in the Rockies span the life zones from valley bottom to near mountain top. You will most often encounter arnica blooming from early July onwards, in the understories of lodgepole pine forests on lower mountainsides. The deep yellow blooms are easy to recognize, making arnica an "easy" genus for non-botanists (like me.) However, keying out the individual species can be a problem – they hybridize.

Almost any botany guidebook will tell you that arnica is poisonous if eaten. True. But some fail to mention the plant's powerful medicinal properties if properly prepared. Tinctures and ointments made from arnica roots have well-proven capacities to reduce bruising, swelling, and inflammation. We carry arnica tincture in our first-aid kit, and apply it immediately to any harsh bruise or sprain where the skin is not open. Presto! No bruising; no pain. Some homeopathic formulations can be taken internally – I use them instead of Ibuprofen to reduce joint pain after long days on the trail. Arnica is literally magic for the inevitable tumbles and bumps that kids take on the trail and elsewhere.

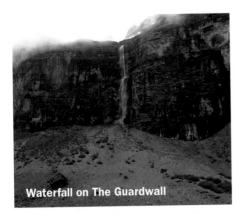

Waterfall on The Guardwall

named the mountain "Mt. Ball" in 1858. However, that name subsequently came into use for a higher mountain to the southwest. The name, Stanley Peak, was given by Edward Whymper in 1901, to honour Frederick Stanley, then Governor General of Canada. Lord Stanley's name also adorns the ultimate prize in North American hockey – the Stanley Cup.

Looking north, you can see the U-shape of this hanging valley. Valleys in the Rockies were originally V-shaped, the products of erosion by streams and rivers. As Stanley Glacier advanced through this valley – most recently during the Late Wisconsin Glaciation – it undercut the surrounding mountainsides. When the glacier receded, the mountainsides collapsed, widening the valley floor.

Among the silvery skeletons of the burned forest, common fireweed is sure to catch your eye. A pioneering plant on disturbed ground, fireweed often grows in thickets. Since the 2003 fire, the Stanley Glacier trail has been the fireweed capital of the southern Rockies. Each plant features a multitude of pink flowers, atop a stem that may reach 2 m in height. The lowest flowers open first, and it is usual for flowers, buds and purple seedpods to be present on the same plant in late summer. The flowers shed a thick, yellow pollen. Common fireweed is the territorial emblem of the Yukon. Mountain fireweed (river beauty, see p. 118) is a smaller plant that grows at higher elevations and along glacial melt streams.

EDWARD WHYMPER: GREAT EXPECTATIONS

Mt. Whymper (2844 m) is framed by the valley walls in the view north from Stanley Glacier viewpoint. The mountain was named for Edward Whymper, who was in the first party to climb the Matterhorn, in 1865. Whymper made five trips to the Rockies in the early 1900s. The first three were under arrangement with the Canadian Pacific Railway. In return for free rail passage and an outfit of mountain guides, Whymper was to pen magazine articles and to make suggestions regarding the location and construction of trails and facilities. The railway hoped to capitalize on Whymper's illustrious reputation, and to make the Rockies into a "new Switzerland."

Whymper had a dour temperament and a legendary capacity for alcohol. He rapidly alienated his mountaineering guides and packers, and accomplished few of his objectives. Perhaps the greatest disappointment for the railway was that, during his first visit, Whymper did not even attempt to climb Mt. Assiniboine, "the Canadian Matterhorn." The moguls of the railway soon tired of his scheme. Whymper's only significant Canadian mountaineering – accomplished at the prompting of his guides

– was completed during the 1901 trip, when the group made first ascents of Mt. Whymper, Stanley Peak, and a number of mountains in what is now Yoho National Park.

49. Rockwall

Rockwall Pass

TRAIL THUMBNAIL

Overnight 4-6 days

Route	Elev. (m)	Dist. (km)
Floe Lake trailhead	1338	0
Floe Lake CG	2058	10.5
Numa Pass	2337	13.2
Numa Creek CG	1530	20.0
Numa Creek jct	1530	20.4
Tumbling Pass	2256	25.3
Tumbling Creek CG	1890	27.9
Wolverine Pass jct	2188	31.0
Rockwall Pass	2214	31.7
South fork of Helmet Creek	1753	39.5
Limestone Summit	2174	36.3
Helmet Creek CG	1753	39.5
Goodsir Pass jct	1761	40.1
Helmet Creek bridge	1523	48.5
Helmet-Ochre CG and Ochre Creek jct	1520	48.7
Tumbling Creek jct	1470	53.0
Paint Pots	1464	54.0
Paint Pots trailhead	1448	55.0

Trailhead
West side of the Kootenay Parkway, 32.6 km west of Highway 1; 72.1 km east of Highway 95.

Special consideration
Due to the hazard of falling trees, use caution in the Floe Creek valley on windy days.

Maps
NTS: 82 N/1
Gem Trek: *Kootenay National Park*
The Adventure Map: The Rockwall

P eak, pass, and precipice; meadow, forest, and stream; waterfall, glacier, and tarn – the Rockwall weaves these quintessential elements into one of the more rewarding backpacking excursions in the Rockies. The roller-coaster nature of this outing will make demands on your fitness, but the five campgrounds allow you to break the hard work into short sections. The passes are usually snowbound until early July. Drinking water is scarce. Carry an extra water bottle and top up whenever you draw alongside a clear stream. The hike traverses prime grizzly bear habitat. Travel accordingly.

Trailhead to Floe Lake

The trail descends to cross the Vermilion River at a canyon eroded into Chancellor Formation slate. The river's name refers to the red stains of iron oxides found along its banks, upstream. Here, the river is often chalky gray in colour, choked with glacial sediment. The trail follows the riverbank northwest to Floe Creek, which you cross on an aluminum bridge.

Most of the forest in the Floe Creek valley burned in the Kootenay fires of 2003 (see pp. 194-95). Before the fires, this forest included some old-growth pockets with large Douglas-firs and devil's club. At km 8.0 the trail reaches the base of the headwall, where you begin

WATER-WORN AND SCOURED BY SNOW

Floe Creek occupies a steeply walled, V-shaped valley, typical of the western main ranges, where the valleys have been sculpted more by the effects of flowing water than by moving ice. The weak shales and slates of the underlying bedrock erode readily, helping to create the deeply entrenched valley. The steep slopes become natural paths for snow avalanches. Avalanche slopes comprise almost half the area along Floe Creek.

VARIATIONS

- Hike the route in reverse.
- Day-hike to Floe Lake; 21.0 km return.
- Camp at Floe Lake (10.5 km). Day-hike to Numa Pass; 5.4 km return.
- Backpack from the Paint Pots to Helmet Creek campground (15.5 km). Day-hike to Wolverine Plateau; 8.5 km. Day-hike to Goodsir Pass; 4.0 km.
- See "The Heart of the Rockwall", p. 200.
- By crossing Ball Pass and descending 9.7 km along Hawk Creek, you can add this outing to the Lakes and Larches (Classic Hike #9), making possible a trip of 88.8 km; 6-9 days.

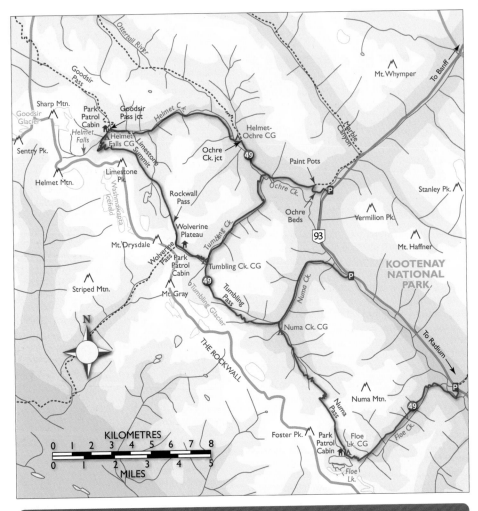

THE ROCKWALL: LARGER THAN LIFE

The Rockwall takes its name from the cliff that extends 53 km through western Kootenay and southwestern Yoho national parks, and which forms the backdrop at Floe Lake. In places, this rampart of Ottertail Formation limestone and dolomite is almost 900 m high. Up close, the rock looks like zebra stripes – alternating layers of darkish limestone and paler dolomite.

Most western main range mountains consist of weak shales and slates, created from sediments deposited in deep sea water that was largely devoid of marine life. The mountains are more eroded and gentle in appearance than the craggy peaks to the east. The Ottertail Formation is an exception. Its sediments were deposited in shallow sea water that probably supported abundant marine life. It seems incredible, but tiny crystals of lime deposited mostly by floating colonies of marine algae and cyanobacteria essentially created this monolithic cliff. It didn't happen overnight. The formation was laid down over a period of 10 million years during the Late Cambrian. It's devoid of fossils, so we don't know the specific creatures responsible; only that there were many of them. They didn't leave an impression, but, collectively they left their mark.

Floe Lake

Numa Pass meadow

a tough climb – 400 m in the next 2.5 km. The toil ends a few hundred metres before Floe Lake campground, where there is an abrupt transition to upper subalpine treeline forest, dominated by Lyall's larch.

Floe Lake occupies an inspiring setting that embodies all the classic features of the Rockwall. The lake is named for the ice floes or "growlers" that calve from the glacier at the base of the cliff. You may hear the cracking and booming of the glacier as it advances and, with fortune, you may see an iceberg calve into the lake. Sunrise here is one of the more memorable sights in the Rockies.

Floe Lake to Numa Creek

Cross the campground to a park patrol cabin, and then ascend steeply across a series of benches to Numa Pass. The hard work is on a delightful trail that winds through upper subalpine larch forest and glades that feature tremendous displays of wildflowers. Given the high elevation and heavy snows here, the blooms of these flowers are typically at their peak in early August – a few weeks later than at most other locations.

The final kilometre to Numa Pass is across shales and alpine tundra. Repeated freezing and thawing churns the soil into mounds called earth hummocks. A few scraggly larch trees in kruppelholz form have

A NATURAL SNOWFENCE

The cliffs of the Rockwall are oriented south-east-northwest, along the grain or strike of the Rockies. By coincidence, this is at a right angle to the prevailing, southwesterly air flow. The cliffs intercept moisture-laden air from the Pacific. As the air rises it cools. The moisture condenses into clouds; precipitation falls.

In the alpine life zone, more than 75 percent of the precipitation is snow. The prevailing winds scoop the snow from the southwest slopes of the Rockwall and deposit it into niches and basins on the leeward (northeast) side, where it accumulates to form and sustain drift glaciers, like the one that feeds Floe Lake. Not only does the cliff create the glacier, but the shade it casts helps to sustain the ice.

taken root on the hummocks. The black-tipped sedge, *Carex nigricans*, is common in the hollows, as are mountain heather, woolly everlasting, and white mountain-avens.

Numa Pass is the highest point on this outing. Mt. Temple (3544 m) and the "back sides" of the Wenkchemna Peaks are featured in the view north. Foster Peak (3201 m) rises west of the pass. *Numa* is Cree for "thunder." Numa Mountain (2721 m) was originally known as "Roaring Mountain."

The trail traverses west from the pass on a track beaten into the screes, and then descends north to treeline. The drop to Numa campground is among the more abrupt on any of the Classic Hikes – 807 m in 6.8 km. The basin north of Foster Peak contains a cirque glacier whose meltwater plummets over cliffs into the upper reaches of Numa Creek. The cliffs rise above avalanche paths that provide excellent habitat for bears. Travel accordingly. The lush vegetation at the edge of the avalanche paths has a rainforest ambiance. Several fallen spruce trees cut from the trail show more than 400 annual rings.

Cross the south fork of Numa Creek on a bridge. The red berries of dwarf dogwood, wild strawberry, and dwarf raspberry are common here in late summer. Tent sites at Numa Creek campground are on both sides of the tributary stream. Porcupines frequent this campground. Don't leave your boots or packs unattended.

Numa Creek to Tumbling Creek

At the junction 400 m beyond Numa Creek campground, you can make a quick exit from the Rockwall. The trail straight ahead (northeast) follows Numa Creek 6.4 km to the Kootenay Parkway. Otherwise, turn west (left) to ascend to Tumbling Pass.

Avalanche slopes flank the north fork of Numa Creek. The heavy precipitation in this area supports lush vegetation. In few places in the Rockies will you see shrubs this tall, such a variety of succulent forbs, and such an abundance of berries. Red elderberry is common. In my field notes I called this section of trail "a grizzly grocery store." Visibility is often poor. Make lots of noise to be heard over the sound of the creek.

The well-conceived trail switchbacks steadily upward through the course of a glacially fed tributary stream. The torrent can be considerable on a hot afternoon. Rock-hop or ford as required. Much of the rubble at trailside is moraine that was pushed over the cliff edge during the Little Ice Age advance of the glacier concealed above. During the climb, you can see Mt. Ball (3294 m) to the east.

After completing the climb, the trail rambles through a kilometre-long boulder meadow – a delightful upper subalpine garden. From the north end of the meadow, you climb steeply over the scree shoulder east of Tumbling Pass. The extra climb detours around a lateral moraine that blocks the true low point of the pass. Ahead is the next installment of spectacular Rockwall scenery, dominated by the convoluted, rubble-covered mass of Tumbling Glacier.

The trail descends from Tumbling Pass alongside a lateral moraine that marks the trimline of Tumbling Glacier. To the east of the trail is upper subalpine forest, to the west is a barren of rocks and ice-cored moraines. During the peak of the Little Ice Age, Tumbling Glacier advanced this far east, obliterating the forest.

After you reach the north end of the lateral moraine, angle northeast and descend steeply to Tumbling Creek. You can exit from the Rockwall at this point, 10.3 km along Tumbling Creek and Ochre Creek to the Kootenay Parkway. The Tumbling Creek

Numa Creek avalanche terrain

campground is 300 m west of the bridge. The water in Tumbling Creek is usually too silty to drink. The creek you cross just east of the campground may be dry lower down, however it should be flowing a few hundred metres to the north. It provides clear drinking water. The next water source is in 7.4 km.

Tumbling Creek to Helmet Creek

If you stay at Tumbling Creek campground, the ascent to Wolverine Plateau is a rude awakening, beginning directly from the tenting area. However, now that you are accustomed to the roller-coaster rigors of the Rockwall, this climb will seem short. The trail makes a sharp turn on a slope that overlooks the extensive moraines of Tumbling Glacier. The view northeast includes a surprising landmark – the tower of Castle Mountain in the Bow Valley. The ascent continues through ancient larch forest, leading to the extensive upper subalpine meadows of Wolverine Plateau. The displays of western anemone and paintbrush here are astounding. In 1985, a Lyall's larch with a circumference of 3.86 m was found nearby. This is the thickest Lyall's larch yet recorded in BC.

WOLVERINE PASS (2205 M), 225 M

It is only half as far to Wolverine Pass as the park trail sign indicates. The short walk takes you to the boundary of Kootenay National Park, and to the only significant break in the rampart of the Rockwall. By scrambling a short distance up the scree slopes north of the pass, you are rewarded with a view over Dainard Creek to the Beaverfoot Valley and the distant Purcell Mountains. Extensive clear-cuts scar the valley. This habitat loss affects some wildlife species within the national park, by disrupting travel routes and by concentrating animals where they compete to mutual detriment. A forestry road leads along Dainard Creek to within 2 km of Wolverine Pass. The easy access granted is at the heart of a chronic poaching problem in this part of the national park.

The peaks flanking Wolverine Pass are Mount Gray (2886 m) to the south, and Mount Drysdale (2932 m) to the north. Charles Drysdale was a geologist, and William Gray his assistant. The two drowned on the Kootenay River while conducting fieldwork in 1917. Dainard Creek was named for Manuel Dainard, an outfitter from Golden in the late 1890s.

HEART OF THE ROCKWALL; 2-4 DAYS

If you want to pick some plums on the Rockwall without going the full distance, try these variations. From the northerly terminus of the Rockwall at the Ochre Beds/Paint Pots trailhead, follow the Ochre Creek trail for 3.4 km to the Tumbling Creek junction. Hike the lush valley of Tumbling Creek for 6.6 km to Tumbling Creek campground, passing a ruined cabin and Tumbling Falls. Camp. Day-hike to Wolverine Pass and Rockwall Pass (4.3 km). The following day, you can day-hike to Tumbling Pass (2.6 km), then backpack out along Tumbling Creek; or backpack over Tumbling Pass to Numa Creek (7.5 km). Either camp at Numa Creek campground (+0.4 km) or carry on down Numa Creek, 6.4 km to the Kootenay Parkway.

Tumbling Glacier

At the first knoll on the plateau, a sidetrail branches northeast to the Wolverine park patrol cabin. With its idyllic setting, this rustic shelter epitomizes mountain heaven for many a park employee. The Rockwall trail contours the western edge of the plateau, through an outcrop of Chancellor Formation shale. You reach the Wolverine Pass junction in 3.1 km from Tumbling Creek campground. Turn west (left) for the short sidetrip to the pass; keep straight ahead to continue on the Rockwall.

Rockwall Pass is the scenic climax of this hike. The 4 km long precipice of Ottertail Formation limestone between Mt. Drysdale and Limestone Peak (2888 m) dominates the view northwest. This monolithic example of natural architecture is rarely duplicated in form or extent elsewhere in the Canadian Rockies. Another drift glacier lies at the base of the cliff. Its meltwaters drain into a substantial marginal lake. With the alpine meadows of Rockwall Pass in the foreground, the scene is unforgettable.

THE WOLVERINE: A BAD REPUTATION, A GRIM SITUATION

Wolverine Pass is named for the largest terrestrial member of the weasel family. The adult male wolverine is about 1 m long and half that high at the midpoint of the back, and weighs 14 to 21 kg. The thick fur is generally dark, with a highlight across the forehead and down each flank. Considerable colour variation occurs. Its scent glands secrete a rank smelling musk, which gives rise to one of its folk names – "skunk bear." The wolverine's range includes the upper subalpine of areas like Wolverine Plateau. It runs with a lumbering gait, and travels in arrow-straight lines. Once, on a ski mountaineering trip, I topped out on a corniced ridge. A wolverine had come up the valley from the south and – judging from the tracks – without pause, had stepped off the cornice. I peeked over. The animal had bum-slid a short distance down a steep slope and then carried on to the north, its tracks fading from sight, perhaps ten kilometres away. There are many stories of wildlife biologists following wolverines that had covered more than 60 km in a day.

The wolverine is an opportunistic scavenger, eating carrion, small birds, and mammals. The animal has a fierce reputation, hence its other folk name – "devil-beast." One wolverine was observed

protecting a kill from an approaching grizzly bear. The animal's formidable appearance has contributed to its reputation. It has the typical pointed weasel face, and sharp teeth, which it will bare at any intruder while making an array of intimidating sounds. You can imagine the smell of its breath. You won't soon forget a face to face encounter with a wolverine.

The wolverine is a species of special concern in western Canada because it is particularly sensitive to human activities. The animal requires vast terrain – 2000 km² is typical for an adult male – and most habitat has been fragmented. Wolverine fur is desired for parka hood trimmings because it resists ice build-up.

The surface of the unnamed glacier beneath Mt. Drysdale features alternating dark and light bands called ogives (OWE-jives). These result from different rates of glacial retreat and advance during summer and winter. Black exposures in the extensive moraine system on the near side of the glacier are ice-cored moraines. The melting of these features sustains a number of small ponds.

Five couloirs on the north face of Mt. Drysdale funnel snow, ice, and rock onto the glacier. The ice is dotted with talus (TAY-luss) cones – piles of this debris that the moving ice has transported away from the mountain wall. The series of lateral moraines adjacent to the trail records at least five distinct advances of glacial ice during the Little Ice Age. It is not often you will see such a sequence this well preserved. Usually, the largest of the advances obliterated evidence of the lesser ones. In this case, apparently none of the existing moraines was overridden during subsequent advances – in other words, the first advance was the greatest.

The trail descends to cross the outlet of the marginal lake, the headwaters of the south fork of Helmet Creek. There is a waterfall and canyon downstream. The number of animal trails in the area indicates that mountain goats visit the canyon to lick sulphur-bearing minerals from the shales.

The next climb, to Limestone Summit, is broken in two by a meadow. Looking south, you obtain a final, grand, close-up view of the Rockwall. Limestone Summit is not a true mountain pass, but a larch covered spur of Limestone Peak. The steady descent north brings you to the alluvial flats at Helmet Creek campground. On the way you have fine views of Helmet Falls. With a total drop estimated at 352 m, Helmet Falls is among the higher waterfalls in Canada. Surveyors argue over whether all the cascades – or just the highest – should be included in a waterfall's height. While Della Falls on Vancouver Island is unquestionably the highest in Canada, Helmet, Hunlen, and Takakkaw each have proponents that claim them to be "second highest."

The headwall that flanks Helmet Falls is a good place to look for mountain goats. This animal is the

symbol of Kootenay National Park, which is home to 200 goats. Another 400 goats live in neighbouring Yoho. To the north of Helmet Falls, an underground stream discharges from the cliff in a small waterfall.

Helmet Creek to the Paint Pots

The Rockwall concludes by following Helmet Creek east to its confluence with Ochre Creek, and then southeast along Ochre Creek to the Paint Pots and the Kootenay Parkway. It's a pleasant hike involving a gradual descent through lush subalpine forest. Red and white baneberry, and the lily, twisted stalk, are common in the undergrowth, along with the wildflowers, dwarf dogwood and queen's cup.

From the bridged crossing of Helmet Creek, you have a last, distant view west to the Rockwall, featuring Helmet Mountain and part of the Washmawapta Icefield. An icefield is a substantial body of ice that sends tributary glaciers into more than one valley. The Washmawapta is the southernmost feature in

THE RED EARTH

The last points of interest on the Rockwall trail are the Paint Pots and Ochre Beds. "Ochre" is clay that has been stained yellow and red with iron oxides. This "red earth" was a valuable trading commodity for Ktunaxa (toon-AWK-ah) (Kutenai) First Peoples from the Columbia Valley in the 1700s. The Ktunaxa collected the ochre, shaped it into cakes and baked it in fire. The resulting compound was mixed with fish grease or animal fat to create a body paint used in rituals. The Ktunaxa would stop at the Ochre Beds to gather ochre on their way to Kootenay Plains on the North Saskatchewan River. Their travel route, "The Kutenai Trail" took them north over Goodsir Pass or Ottertail Pass through what is now Yoho National Park, and across Amiskwi Pass and Howse Pass. The iron-rich water that stains the clay percolates from three cold mineral springs – the Paint Pots. The ochre has stained rocks downstream in the Vermilion River – the origin of its name. What once was considered sacred still is. Please do not disturb or remove the ochre.

THE ICE RIVER ALKALINE COMPLEX

North of Helmet Falls, Sharp Mountain (3046 m) contains an outcrop of the Ice River Alkaline Complex. The complex is the largest assemblage of igneous (once molten) rock known in the Canadian Rockies. This blob of magma intruded into older sedimentary formations approximately 245 million-years-ago. Many rare minerals occur. In total, the complex covers 19 km^2. The portion within Yoho and Kootenay national parks is a Special Preservation Area. Access and collecting are prohibited. Mining claims exist just outside the parks along Moose Creek.

Helmet Falls

the Rockies to which the term "icefield" is officially applied. *Washmawapta* is Stoney for "ice river."

Downstream from the bridge, the trail skirts a shale canyon at the mouth of Helmet Creek, then climbs through forest before descending to Ochre Creek. Many of the subalpine fir trees in this vicinity have been stricken with a needle cast that has defoliated them. As you descend to Ochre Creek, notice the V-shape of the Helmet Creek and Ochre Creek valleys.

Cross Ochre Creek to a campground and trail junction. Turn south (right) and follow signs at the subsequent junctions for "Highway 93." At the far side of the Ochre Beds, the Rockwall trail crosses the Vermilion River on a suspension bridge, to end at the Paint Pots parking area on the Kootenay Parkway, 12.9 km north of the Floe Lake trailhead.

> *From the snow-covered top the view was superb. One could see most of the great peaks of the Rockies and Selkirks, range after range fading away into the blue distance.*
>
> Katie Gardiner; *Canadian Alpine Journal 1934*

GOODSIR PASS (2195 M), 4.0-7.6 KM

Strong hikers can quick-trip Goodsir Pass from Helmet Creek campground, and still hike out the same day. But I recommend adding a day to the trip to savour this destination.

Head northeast from Helmet Creek campground for 600 m to the Goodsir Pass junction, where the trail forks. Keep north (left). You gain a solid piece of elevation on this hike – 445 m in just 4 km – but it's on a well-graded trail. The rambling entry to the pass takes you across an ancient rockslide. You might be expecting the Kootenay-Yoho boundary to be on the crest of the pass. It isn't. Yoho's boundary – set 34 years before Kootenay was established – follows an illogical path (no principal summits) from Neptuak Mountain to Sharp Mountain. The trail rambles for almost 4 km across the pass, through flower-filled meadows and glades of larch. For those adept at off-trail travel, the ridge northeast of the pass beckons.

What you probably came for is the incredible view of the north faces of Mt. Goodsir. The South Tower (3567 m) and the North Tower (3507 m) are the two highest peaks in Yoho and, respectively, are the 10th- and 12th-highest in the Rockies, and the 10th- and 15th-highest in BC. The South Tower is the highest mountain between Mt. Assiniboine and the Columbia Icefield. These mountains do not owe their stature to some tough dolomite or quartzite in their flanks. These are truly rotten

peaks, assembled from the smashed up shales and slates of the McKay Group of formations with the use of very little glue. The mountains' saving grace is that the rocks lie in horizontal layers that are not readily eroded. James Hector of the Palliser Expedition named the mountains for the Goodsir brothers – Harry and John – medical doctors from Scotland. Hector had studied under John Goodsir at Edinburgh University. Harry Goodsir, surgeon on HMS *Erebus*, disappeared on the Third Franklin Expedition. The South Tower was first climbed in 1903, and the North Tower in 1909. "The Goodsirs," as they are known, are normally climbed from the Ice River valley, but both north faces have been climbed. The stupendous elevation gain – more than 2000 m – and the awful rock, combine to turn back many hopefuls on any route. Sentry Peak (3257 m) stands guard to the southeast of the South Tower.

50. Kindersley – Sinclair

Kindersley Summit

The Kindersley–Sinclair trail packs tremendous diversity, travelling from the damp forests of Sinclair Creek to an alpine ridgecrest. The wildflower displays of early summer are superb. Although it gains 875 m in 8.4 km, the approach trail is one of the better constructed in the Rockies, and the grade is seldom steep. Kindersley Pass and Kindersley Summit are usually snowbound until late June.

Trailhead to Kindersley Pass

From the Kootenay Parkway, the trail ascends through a damp forest dominated by Douglas-fir, the climax species of forests in the montane life zone of the southern Rockies. The tree's fire-resistant bark enables it to withstand the periodic ground fires that remove competing vegetation. Western Canada violet, white geranium, western meadowrue, yellow columbine, baneberry, birchleaf spirea, and prickly wild rose are common wildflowers and shrubs in the undergrowth. Where the trail climbs away from the creek onto drier soils, lodgepole pine and massive white spruce grow, with Oregon grape in the undergrowth. This holly-like shrub has yellow flowers that produce blue-coloured berries. In autumn, the thick, waxy leaves turn purple and red.

At km 2.8, the view opens to an avalanche path across the valley. The lush vegetation on the slope includes cow parsnip and other succulents that are favourite foods of black bears and grizzly bears. The shrubs offer browse for elk and mule deer. This pocket of habitat is but one in the mosaic that sustains the diversity of wildlife in this valley. You may see mice, voles, squirrels, deer, snowshoe hares, American martens, coyotes, and – if fortunate – a cougar, a lynx or a wolf. The ancient trees offer great habitat for northern flickers and other woodpeckers.

The switchbacking soon resumes. During the next 5 km, you may see the blooms of more than 30 species of wildflowers if you are hiking early in the season. Two of these species have corms (bulbs) that are favourite foods of grizzly bears – glacier lily and western springbeauty.

TRAIL THUMBNAIL

Day-hike

Route	Elev. (m)	Dist. (km)
Kindersley trailhead	1335	0
Lookout Point ridge	1936	6.0
Kindersley Pass	2210	8.4
Kindersley Summit	2393	10.1
Sinclair Creek trailhead	1433	16.1
Kindersley trailhead	1335	17.4

Trailhead
Kootenay Parkway, 10.5 km east of the junction with Highway 95; 94.2 km west of Highway 1. The small parking area is on the south side of the highway. This is a dangerous turnoff for westbound travellers. The trailhead is across the road. Use caution crossing the highway.

Maps
NTS: 82 J/12, 82 K/9
Gem Trek: *Kootenay National Park*

> *The characteristics of the range vary largely in its long-drawn sweep from sunny south to icy north; the structure and scenery change from time to time as one passes from one section to another along its mighty length.*
>
> James Outram; *In the Heart of the Canadian Rockies*

VARIATION

- Hike to Kindersley Pass and Kindersley Summit; 20.2 km return.

THE ICE-FREE CORNER OF THE ROCKIES

The view from a steep sideslope at km 4.0 clearly reveals the V-shape of this unnamed valley, indicating that it has been eroded principally by water, not by glacial ice. If the bedrock here were resistant limestone or dolomite, the creek would have eroded a slot canyon. As the bedrock is weak shale and slate, principally of the Chancellor Group of formations, the V-shape results. The western ranges between Golden and Invermere do not contain any glaciers today.

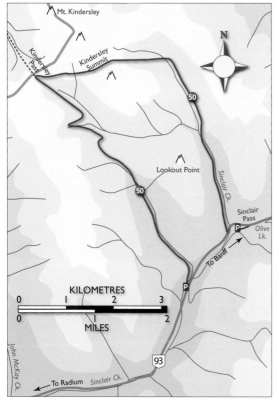

At km 6.0, the trail crests the forested ridge west of Lookout Point, and contours into an avalanche basin that contains Lyall's larches. Look for the tracks and scats of wolves. More switchbacks through avalanche terrain lead to the final approach to Kindersley Pass – a confined, snowmelt stream course, adorned with western anemone. The consolidated avalanche snow here frequently endures the summer.

Kindersley Pass to Kindersley Summit

Kindersley Pass is on the national park boundary, and offers only limited views north into the Brisco Range. Cutblocks scar upper Kindersley Creek – a reminder of the pressures that affect protected areas. Follow a steep track northeast along the park boundary to an errant sign that indicates "Kindersley Pass," perhaps erected here because the view is better than on the true pass below. The trail angles sharply southeast (right), and begins a treeline traverse across avalanche gullies to Kindersley Summit.

Kruppelholz tree islands of Engelmann spruce and subalpine fir dot the mountainside. The firs form twisted mats, from which grow the taller spruce. Bighorn sheep frequent these slopes. Kindersley Summit is the high point on this hike. It should probably be called "Sinclair Summit," as it is at the head of the Sinclair Valley, not the Kindersley Valley.

Kindersley Summit to Kootenay Parkway

The most straightforward exit from Kindersley Summit is to retrace your route to the trailhead. To make the loop, follow trail markers east into the avalanche basin at the head of Sinclair Creek. Descend a steep, sketchy path for 1 km, after which the trail becomes better defined in the vicinity of the creek, which you hop to its east bank. From here on it's smooth sailing, on a steep trail that descends through lush vegetation to the Kootenay Parkway. You cross to the west side of the creek 1.7 km before trail's end. The Kindersley trailhead is 1.3 km southwest (right) along the Kootenay Parkway. Cross the road with caution and walk facing traffic. Sinclair Creek commemorates James Sinclair, who in 1841 and 1854, led groups of settlers through the Rockies to the Oregon Territory.

AN EAGLE-EYE VIEW

Mountaineers may readily ascend the unnamed peaks southeast (2515 m) and northwest (2683 m) of Kindersley Summit. Both offer detailed views of a tremendous length of the continental divide. Mt. Joffre (3433 m) looms in the distant southeast and Mt. Goodsir (3567 m) dominates the skyline in the northeast. Directly east you have an unfamiliar view of a well known mountain – Mt. Assiniboine (3616 m) – highest point in the southern Rockies, and 8th-highest in the range. The Purcell Range of the Columbia Mountains forms the skyline to the west. Look for golden eagles on the thermals overhead, and gliders (sailplanes).

From the northerly summit, the view also includes the Columbia Valley and the complete length of the western ranges, from northeast of Golden to south of Invermere. The western ranges were the first to be thrust above sea level in the Rockies, about 100 million-years-ago. Their weak shales and slates exhibit extensive folding and faulting.

Mt. Sir Douglas

Kananaskis Country

Created by the Alberta government in 1977, Kananaskis Country is a 4200 km² parcel of provincial land that lies south of Highway 1 between Morley and Canmore. Unlike the nearby national parks, where resource extraction and most motorized recreation are prohibited, Kananaskis Country is a "multi-use recreation" area. It incorporates wildland provincial parks, forestry reserves, ecological reserves, mining and petroleum leaseholds, resorts, and recreational developments. *Kin-oh-ah-kis* was a hard-headed Cree warrior, reportedly struck by an axe but not killed. It may also be that *Kin-oh-ah-kis* is a Stoney word that means "meeting of the waters." The park information centres are on Highway 40 near Barrier Lake, 6.8 km south of Highway 1; on the Kananaskis Lakes Trail, 3.5 km south of the junction with Highway 40, 1.2 km south of the junction with Route 742; and on Highway 66, south of Bragg Creek.

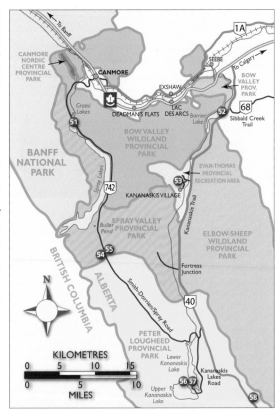

51. Ha Ling Peak

Ha Ling Peak

TRAIL THUMBNAIL

Day-hike

Route	Elev. (m)	Dist. (km)
Trailhead	1665	0
"Miner's Peak" jct	2330	2.3
Ha Ling Summit	2408	2.7

Trailhead
From the west end of Main Street in downtown Canmore (106 km west of Calgary, 22 km east of Banff), follow signs for the Canmore Nordic Centre and the Smith Dorrien-Spray Trail ("Spray Lakes Road," Route 742). Follow this road to the Goat Creek Day Use area turnoff, 5.2 km past the Nordic Centre, 8.8 km from downtown. Turn west (right) and park. The trail begins across the road. Head up the gated Trans-Alta road. Cross the canal on a bridge. Look for the trailhead in the shaded spruce forest, behind a building.

Special considerations
Although the way is well-beaten and obvious, this is an unmaintained trail, recommended to experienced mountain travellers only. On the summit, if you misplace a step and fall to the east or northeast, you will certainly die. If the day is uncommonly windy, if there is snow or ice on the upper part of the route, or if there is lightning nearby, turn back. If you take children along, keep a close watch on them near the summit. I say again: If you slip and fall the wrong way at the summit, you die.

Maps
NTS: 82 O/3
Gem Trek: *Canmore and Kananaskis Village*

Best lighting: any time

Few trails make for the mountain with such crazed purpose as does the track beaten into the screes of Ha Ling Peak. In terms of hiking experience, about all that you can reasonably expect on a trail that gains 743 m in 2.7 km (an average grade of almost 28 percent), is a solid workout. You certainly get that on the way to the summit, as do the members of Canmore's athletic crowd, for whom the trail is a training ground.

IMMORTALIZED IN ROCK

Ha Ling Peak is a striking but minor eminence on a group of mountains between Whiteman's Gap and Three Sisters Pass. Stoneys knew this massif as *Ehagay Nakoda* – which roughly translates a legend that a Stoney was transformed into rock so that he could stay on the Earth after all others had left. It is perhaps fitting that the other officially named peak in this group, Mount Lawrence Grassi (2682 m), commemorates another true man of the Earth – an Italian immigrant, railway worker, and Canmore miner who built many trails in the Rockies in the 1920s and 1930s. (See Lake Merlin p. 82; Lake McArthur pp. 176-77.) Grassi knew the mountains so well, he became a defacto mountain guide. He made the first solo ascent of Mt. Assiniboine, and climbed Banff's Mt. Louis 32 times. In a 1938 tribute to Grassi, it was said: "The world needs Grassis... men who will seek new paths; make the rough places smooth; bridge the chasms that now prevent human progress; point the way to higher levels and loftier achievements." Grassi died in Canmore in 1980 at age 90.

Trailhead to Miner's Peak Junction

Ha Ling Peak is a classic dipslope mountain. In the Rockies, these feature steep, southwest-facing slopes that end on northeast-facing cliffs. Today's trail was built in the 1990s by the Trailminders of the Bow Valley – a Canmore-based volunteer group. Their handiwork attempted to cooperate with the geology rather than taking a headlong run at it, as was the case with the original scree bash in a gully to the south.

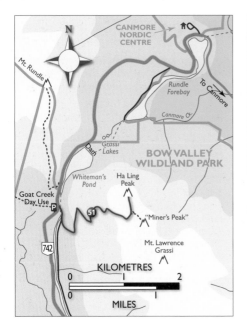

Upper slopes of Ha Ling Peak

STOP PINCHING!

For the first half of the distance to the summit, the trail makes a series of broad switchbacks in the forest on the lower west face of the peak. Most of the trees here are lodgepole pines. Note that many of them have twisted and curved trunks. This is either a local genetic anomaly, or is a compensation by individual trees for the steep slope on which they grow. During an ascent in this forest we heard four hermit thrushes calling and responding to each other in an ethereal chorus.

As you break through treeline, views open up over the Spray Valley and toward the Goat Range, and north into the valley of Goat Creek. If the day is clear, the skyline view north will include Mt. Temple (3544 m) and some of the Wenkchemna Peaks, and the cliff-like, east face of Pilot Mountain (2954 m). Whitebark pines grow here. I found a tiny spruce growing out of a crack in a limestone slab. Leaving most of the trees behind, the track scrapes over shales and small ledges to a junction of sorts, about 2.3 km from the trailhead. The route to Ha Ling Peak swings northeast (left). Straight ahead to the southeast, a track leads to "Miner's Peak".

Summit Slopes

You are most of the way there, now. The final 400 m is a steep, diagonal grind along the summit ridge. To your right, the world falls away into the Bow Valley, of which you can see a 40 km length – from Lac des Arcs in the southeast, to near Cascade Mountain in the north. Also to the north, the principal summit of Mt. Rundle (2980 m) rises above the minor summits on its south ridge. The Fairholme Range forms the

The view of Canmore from the summit ridge is a bit like being in an airplane. If vertigo strikes, have a seat. To a conservation biologist, the view is more likely to produce a spinning head and nausea for other reasons. When the Canmore Mine closed in 1979, the town's population was scarcely 3000. Thirty years later, it topped 16,000. Promoters want to see it max out at 20,000. When those developers tire of the bustle and decide to move on, others will probably want to increase that number. The valley-wall to valley-wall sprawl in view is a perfect example of a pinch-point. Wildlife travel routes along and across the Bow Valley have been severed by this ill-conceived development. Farther east in the Bow Valley, mining, and development at the mouth of the Wind Valley add to the squeeze. Pinch points such as Canmore inevitably bring large mammals into conflict and competition with people. Grizzly bears, black bears, cougars, wolves, coyotes, and elk are the species most affected in this instance. At some other locations in the Rockies, pinch points have been alleviated by creating "set asides" that maintain habitat connectivity and permit passage for wildlife. But in the Canmore area, this opportunity has been lost. Housing, hotels, new roads, and golf courses cram the terraces along the valley sides. Fore!

Mt. Lawrence Grassi (left) and Ha Ling Peak

How strangely the world has been built, bed after bed of limestone or slate or quartzite, pale gray or pale green or dark red or purple, built into cathedrals or castles, or crumpled like coloured cloths from the rag-bag, squeezed together into arches and troughs, into V's and S's and M's ten miles long and two miles high; or else sheets of rock twenty thousand feet thick have been sliced into blocks and tilted up to play leap-frog with each other.

A.P. Coleman; *The Canadian Rockies, New and Old Trails*

eastern wall of the Bow Valley. On the southwest skyline, you can see some peaks of the Royal Group.

Alpine cinquefoil and purple mountain saxifrage brighten the gray limestones of the summit area. Least chipmunks will make raids on your lunch. Please do not feed them. K-Country rescue specialists keep an equipment cache on the summit. Please leave it alone. Do not throw anything over the east face. Rock climbers are often below. If you are comfortable in high places and if the day is fair, you might want to tag the summit of "Miner's Peak" (0.6 km round-trip from the junction, and 50 m elevation gain) before taking the plunge back to the trailhead.

A SURE BET

Ha Ling was a CPR restaurant cook who, in 1896, had accepted a 50-dollar bet that he could not climb this mountain in less than ten hours and plant a flag on its summit. It is reported that, on his next day off, Ha Ling began his climb at 7:00 a.m. and was back in town for a late lunch. The flag was too small to be visible from town, so the next day, Ha Ling led a party of skeptics to the summit, where he planted a more stout pennant beside its predecessor, and collected on the bet.

A century later, Ha Ling Peak was at the centre of a controversy. Locals had long known the mountain by the unofficial name, Chinaman's Peak. In 1977, the late Jon Whyte of Banff pointed out that the mountain bore no official name. To honour Ha Ling's remarkable achievement, he suggested

that the name Chinaman's Peak be made official. In 1980, Alberta's Historic Sites Board consulted Canmore-ites about the proposed name. No complaints were registered, so the Board approved the name. However, beginning in 1989, Canadians of Chinese heritage began to voice offence. They were countered by a petition signed by 1500 residents of Canmore who asked that the name not be changed. The issue simmered for eight years until May 1, 1997, when the Alberta Historic Resources Board held two public meetings – one in Calgary, one in Canmore – to hear submissions concerning the name. The overwhelming response was that Chinaman's Peak was derogatory to Chinese Canadians. The Board rescinded the name and a year later made the name Ha Ling Peak official.

52. Prairie View

Barrier Lake from Prairie View

TRAIL THUMBNAIL

Day-hike

Route	Elev. (m)	Dist. (km)
Trailhead	1385	0
1st jct	1415	1.1
East Stoney trail jct	1450	1.6
McConnell Ridge	1700	3.6
Old fire lookout site	1835	4.2
Prairie View and jct	1910	4.6
Jewell Pass	1620	6.3
Jewell Falls	1485	7.6
West Stoney trail jct	1390	9.0
Lakeshore trail jct	1430	10.4
1st jct	1415	11.8
Trailhead	1385	12.9

Trailhead
Follow Highway 40 (Kananaskis Trail), 8.6 km south from Highway 1 to the Barrier Dam Day Use area. Turn right (west) and follow the sideroad 300 m to the parking area.

Maps
NTS: 82 O/3
Gem Trek: *Canmore and Kananaskis Village*

Best lighting: any time

It's been a sentinel position for centuries. The Stoneys called it *Tokyapebi ipa*: "lookout point for the Blackfeet." From the upper slopes and summit of this front range outlier, in the clearer air of pre-industrial times, Stoneys would keep watch over the prairies for the approach of their enemies. Since 1960, from two locations on this hike, employees of the Alberta government have looked more intently into the mountains than away from them – watching for lightning strikes and scanning for the telltale smokes of forest fires. In any direction and for any reason that you look from the high points on this hike, the mountain and prairie views are fantastic. And considering that you gain a fair amount of elevation, the trail is seldom steep. This outing goes by a few other names: Yates Mountain, McConnell Ridge, and Barrier Lake Lookout.

Trailhead to Prairie View

From the parking area, keep left and head west to pick up the gravel road that crosses the Barrier Dam. If it's a windy day, you may have to hang on to more than your hat as you cross. Not a lake but a reservoir, Barrier Lake came into being in 1947 following construction of this dam. Prisoners of war had cleared the reservoir site in 1945. The power generated by the 13MW installation is added to the Alberta grid during peak periods. The reservoir has an area of 3.08 km^2.

VARIATIONS

- Hike to Prairie View and return the same way; 9.2 km.
- Add a visit to Barrier Lake Lookout; 1.4 km return.
- Hike the loop in reverse.

Across the dam, follow either the road or a trail just to its right; each climbs and veers north (right) across a small meadow. There are wonderful displays of paintbrush here. Keep straight ahead (north) at the first junction at km 1.1. You enter an ancient aspen forest with a few scattered lodgepole

The pageant of the Rockies began to solidify and take shape once more, and the foot-hills became foot-hills again, when the real mountains occupied the stage... The mountains visibly lifted themselves into the sky as we rattled westwards past Kananaskis Falls, past higher foot-hills, and through the portal of the "Gap," where two bare, gray sentinels rose sharply three or four thousand feet above the Bow [Valley].

A.P. Coleman; *The Canadian Rockies, New and Old Trails*

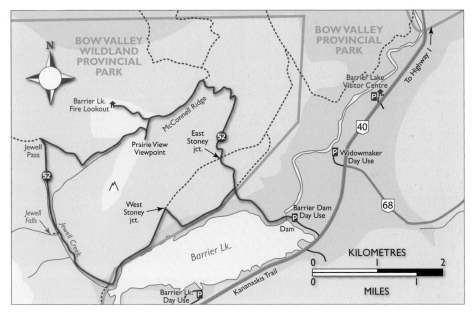

pines and white spruce, and many wildflowers in the understory, including clematis and calypso orchids. After 500 m, you reach the east Stoney Trail junction. Jog right (northeast) a short distance and then left (north) into forest, still on a road-width trail. You will see where shortcut trails circumvent some of the 11 switchbacks on the ensuing climb. You won't save

BARRIER LAKE LOOKOUT (1995 M), 0.7 KM

The trail follows the northern rampart of Yates Mountain, climbing steeply to the trés deluxe lookout installation on the highpoint. Along the way, you have grand views of the foothills and prairies to the east (the real "prairie view" on this hike), and the mountain/foothills contact to the north. The fencing along the cliff edge is not to keep you from falling to a certain death, but to protect the nests of peregrine falcons from anything that you might knock over the cliff. We once spooked a golden eagle here. Continue a short distance past the lookout, losing a bit of elevation to obtain another great view – this one of the Bow Valley toward Lac des Arcs. Barrier Lake is the only staffed fire lookout reached on a Classic Hike. Alberta still has about 130 active fire lookouts. Each is located to take in a view of about 5000 km². Lookout staff are the first to spot about 40 percent of the forest fires in the province. Please respect the lookout keeper's privacy, and do not tamper with equipment or buildings.

much distance by taking them, and the walking is easier on the main trail.

About 3.6 km from the trailhead, you gain the northeast end of McConnell Ridge, which you ascend, heading southwest. After about 600 m the trail levels at the former site of Pigeon Mountain fire lookout. The building is now gone, but the vista remains – a wonderful panorama over Barrier Lake, with Mt. Baldy (2192 m) to the south. A Stoney sacred site is nearby. The trail turns northwest (right) and climbs steeply toward Yates Mountain. No, a few prairie wildflower species have not climbed with you to this point – you are looking at subalpine variations of two common grassland species: showy yellow locoweed and elliptical-leaved penstemon – both are abundant here.

Prairie View to Jewell Pass

The climb ends at a junction atop a cliff. Although this vantage point is called Prairie View, Barrier Lake is the centrepiece. Vague trails branch off in two directions. If you would like to visit Barrier Lake Lookout (1995 m), head northwest (right). The trails in that direction eventually converge. To carry on for Jewell Pass, head south from the junction. The trail soon swings westerly along a cliff edge. Use care here. After a few hundred metres, the trail cuts northwesterly (right) to drop off the ridge and across a scree slope, into the trees. A steady descent brings you to a junction on forested Jewell Pass. Turn south (left).

Soon, the tiny gatherings of Jewell Creek are your companion. You cross the stream on a bridge and enter the beginnings of a canyon-like valley. About 1.3 km from the pass, you reach the forks of Jewell

The prairies from the lookout trail.

Creek and a short sidetrail west (right) to Jewell Falls. Carrying on downvalley, the trail crosses to the east bank, and then descends steeply before turning north (left) to cut over the south end of McConnell Ridge to drop to the shore of Barrier Lake.

For the next 1.4 km, head northeast along a powerline right of way, sometimes on road, sometimes on trail. If you are hiking in early summer, great wildflower displays will compensate for the somewhat unappealing trail. After 1.4 km you reach the west Stoney trail junction. Turn south (right). In about 400 m, where the trail draws alongside the reservoir, turn east (left) to carry on and complete the loop at the 1st junction on the hike, from where it is 1.1 km to the parking area. If the reservoir level is low, you may be able to walk the shoreline as far as the dam.

IT'S ALL MCCONNELL'S FAULT

In this part of the Rockies, the McConnell Thrust is responsible for the mountain front – the dramatic wall of front range peaks – where ancient limestone has been thrust up and over not-quite-so ancient sandstones and shales of the foothills. This fault runs for almost 400 km, from the Highwood River to near the Athabasca River. Just as you can't miss the effect of the McConnell Thrust, you also can't miss the fault itself. On this hike, you stand atop the leading edge of the thrust, with the foothills and prairies falling away to the northeast, and the front ranges stacking up to the southwest. If you bashed your way to the base of McConnell Ridge from the northeast, you could literally put a fingertip on the trace line of the fault – the contact surface between rock formations that are 445 million years difference in age. Your feet would be in the foothills geological province, your head and shoulders in the front ranges. The McConnell Thrust commemorates Richard George McConnell, surveyor and geologist of the Canadian wilds between 1880 and 1914, and later Canada's Deputy Minster of Mines. He travelled in this area with George Dawson between 1883-86, and made the first description of the fault that was named for him more than 60 years later.

53. Centennial Ridge

Centennial Ridge

TRAIL THUMBNAIL

Day-hike

Route	Elev. (m)	Dist. (km)
Trailhead	1506	0
1st jct	1526	0.4
2nd jct	1566	1.1
Mine Scar viewpoint	1760	2.2
Rock step	2200	3.3
"Olympic Summit"	2457	4.3
Rock Garden	2480	5.5
Mt. Allan summit	2819	7.8

Trailhead
Follow Highway 40 (Kananaskis Trail), 22.8 km south from Highway 1 to the Kananaskis Village junction. Turn west (right) onto Mt. Allan Drive. Follow the road 1.6 km, across the Kananaskis River. Take the first left (southwest) onto Centennial Drive. In 300 m, turn northwest (right) onto Ribbon Creek Road. Follow this 500 m to the Ribbon Creek parking area at road's end. The trailhead is at the northeast (closest) corner of the parking area.

Special considerations
The trail is closed each year from April 1 to June 21, inclusive, to protect bighorn sheep lambing habitat. When the rock step below "Olympic Summit" is snow covered, you may require an ice axe. The weather station on "Olympic Summit" consistently records some of the strongest winds in western North America – greater than 200 km/hour a few times a year; greater than 100 km/ hour monthly. When the wind is blowing hard enough to knock you down, you will hear it in the parking area – a low moan sweeping the ridge above. Even if it is only breezy at the trailhead, choose another outing.

Maps
NTS: 82 J/14
Gem Trek: *Canmore and Kananaskis Village*

Best lighting: any time

After a gentle warm-up in forest, the Centennial Ridge trail rockets skyward like no other. By the time you stop climbing at Mt. Allan's summit, you will be more than 75 m higher than the highpoint of any other Classic Hike. Save this outing for fair weather in July and August, when the views will be stellar and the wildflower displays on the lower part of the ridge will be a marvel. We owe this remarkable trail to the Rocky Mountain Ramblers of Calgary, who constructed it between 1966 and 1968 to commemorate Canada's centennial. Although this is not a particularly long outing, its up-and-down nature and its overall ascent (1313 m – an average grade of almost 17 percent) make it a solid workout.

Trailhead to Mine Scar Viewpoint

You need to tag a few junctions in the early going to stay on track. In 2010, these were all clearly marked with the ubiquitous, metal K-Country trail-map signs. The initial routing is north for 400 m on the road-width, Hidden Lake trail. At the first junction, turn west (left). Follow this trail, still road-width, for 700 m to another junction. Keep straight ahead. The tread narrows and the grade steepens. Lodgepole pines dominate the forest. Arnica is common in the understory.

> *The original tilted blocks and symmetrical or overturned folds were, of course, only the raw material out of which the present mountains have been carved, and the file and chisel are still busy in the shaping process, which will never be compete till the ranges are worn down to hills or a plain.*
>
> A.P. Coleman; *The Canadian Rockies, New and Old Trails*

You will note that a wider track switchbacks across the trail in places. This is an old mining road, now used for cross-country skiing. Follow the marked hiking trail. Eventually, you hook up with the road, where the trail angles southwest. At the Mine Scar viewpoint, the trail forks. Walk south (left) a short distance onto a grassy slope that provides a

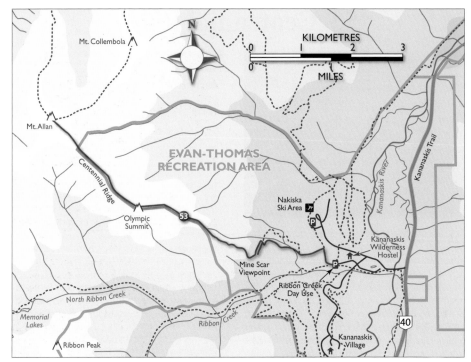

great overview of the Kananaskis Valley. Between 1947 and 1952, this slope was the site of coal mining – both a strip mine and an underground operation. A town called Kovach developed on the north bank of Ribbon Creek; at one time it numbered 200 residents. Downslope, you can see some debris from the mining operations. You will see coal in the tread, higher up on the ridge.

Mine Scar Viewpoint to "Olympic Summit"

Back on the main trail, you reach the beginning of Centennial Ridge proper in 40 m. Turn right (northwest) into the trees. For the next 500 m, you switchback through pine forest, to emerge in a wind-blasted aspen grove. As these trees thin, the climb begins in earnest on the grassy spine of the southeast ridge of Mt. Allan.

The array of wildflowers on this ridge is tremendous. You will find common species that prefer dry soils in the alpine – showy yellow locoweed, Jacob's ladder, showy fleabane, sawwort, and scorpionweed; along with some surprises – alpine forget-me-not, and stunted shooting stars. During this climb, your eyes will shift between the flowered foreground and the distant views, as great vistas open up to the two summits of Mt. Kidd (north, 2958 m; south, 2893 m) to the south, and Mt. Bogart (3144 m) to the southwest. Stuart Kidd was an Alberta rancher who,

between 1907 and 1911, managed a trading post at Morley, the Stoney settlement near the mountain front. Dr. D. Bogart Dowling was a geologist who mapped coal seams in K-Country in the early 1900s. You will have ample time to appreciate the panorama, as the precipitous ascent will slow even the most athletic hikers.

The trail levels for a short distance with views northeast to the Nakiska ski area. (*Nakiska* means "to meet." This was the site of the alpine skiing events of the 1988 Winter Olympic Games.) Larch forest cloaks the ridge in that direction, adding to the appeal of late season hiking. You have probably been eyeing the quartzite step ahead, and perhaps have been wondering how you are going to get past it. The trail works its way along a series of broad ledges and up easy gullies on the northeast (right) side of the rocks. It is only really steep for a few short sections and, unless snow clings in the gullies, should pose no great difficulty. You may have to use your hands for a couple of moves. If you find yourself doing some sustained rock climbing, you are off route. This climb delivers you onto the shale dome of "Olympic Summit" – the taking off point for the Olympic men's downhill. Follow the beaten path past two remote weather stations.

The trail cuts under the leeward side of the ridge, with fine views ahead to Mt. Sparrowhawk (3121 m), the triangular prow of Wind Mountain (3153 m), Mt. Allan, and the cliffs of Mt. Lougheed (3107 m). HMS *Sparrowhawk* was a Royal Navy destroyer, accidentally

Mt. Kidd and Mt. Bogart

Rock Garden

rammed by a crippled British ship in the Battle of Jutland in 1916. As the *Sparrowhawk* foundered, another British ship collided with her stern. When another cruiser attempted to tow the *Sparrowhawk*, the lines broke and the ship was scuttled.

In 1858, Eugene Bourgeau of the Palliser Expedition gave the name, Wind Mountain, to the mountain now known as Mt. Lougheed. Bourgeau named it from the Bow Valley, because clouds were blowing around its summit. In 1926, the family of the recently deceased Calgary lawyer, senator, and cabinet minister, James Lougheed, who had practiced law with the future prime minister, R.B. Bennett, objected when a mountain along Healy Creek was named for Lougheed. Bennett saw to it that Bourgeau's Wind Mountain – certainly a more high profile choice to commemorate a Calgarian – was renamed Mt. Lougheed. The name Wind blew around for a while and finally became officially lodged in 1983 on the highest peak seen from this hike. Mt. Allan commemorates the first professor of geology at the University of Alberta, and later founder of the Alberta Geological Survey. In the 1910s, J.A. Allan appraised and mapped most of Alberta's coal seams, including the one eventually responsible for the Mine Scar.

"Olympic Summit" to Mt. Allan Summit

After a brief climb over the apex of "Olympic Summit", the trail descends past some shattered limestone outcrops onto a shale saddle. The following climb into the Rock Garden is gradual, as the trail threads its way past fantastic shapes of Gog Formation conglomerate which has been eroded from vertically-thrust fins of the bedrock. The one that grabs the most attention is, fittingly, The Claw. From here, you can look west into North Ribbon Creek valley and the Memorial Lakes.

Just beyond the Rock Garden is a spot that could offer the most trouble on the hike. The trail cuts over the spine of the ridge from east to west. Although markers indicate the best way to get down the resulting step, you could lose the way. If you are actually downclimbing, you are off route. After cresting

another minor rise, you again lose a bit of ground before the final pull to the summit. Near the peak, there are paths on either side of the ridge – choose the route with the least snow, if that is a concern. Avoid being lured west (left) on a horizontal-ish track just before the top. It's a sheep track. Baah.

Mt. Allan's apex provides a bomber view of the limestone ramparts of Mt. Lougheed, which pretty much obscure everything else to the northwest. Looking northeast, a scree ridge connects to Mt. Collembola (2758 m) (with a tarn in the valley beneath). *Collembola*, also known as springtails or snow fleas, have 16 eyes and are the most abundant insects on Earth. Flip over just about any rock and you will find some. The mountain was named because a doctorate student did just that on its slopes. Beyond is Pigeon Mountain (2394 m) and the Bow Valley, with Grotto Mountain (2707 m) an obvious landmark. You can see much of Canmore. Perhaps, after your hike, you will be in town gazing back to this spot – once you know where to look; it is easy to pick out.

I hope that you have saved a bit of energy for the return. Looking back (southeast) along your undulating route of ascent, you might initially despair. But like all hardships in the mountains and in life, the route goes easily if taken one step at a time. Which is not to say that by the time you reach the parking area, your body will not know that you have climbed a mountain. And a half.

WITHERING HEIGHTS

According to archived data on Environment Canada's website, on our first visit here the whirly-gigs on "Olympic Summit" clocked maximum gusts of 115 km/hour. The day's high temperature was 8.6°C. With all our gear on, we froze. Just after crossing "Olympic Summit" we had to turn back because the wind literally threatened to blow us off the ridge. I returned four days later for another attempt in mediocre weather. The wind was trifling – with maximum gusts of 78 km/hour. I topped the summit in a snow squall.

54. Burstall Pass

Below Burstall Pass

TRAIL THUMBNAIL

Day-hike

Route	Elev. (m)	Dist. (km)
Trailhead	1910	0
Robertson Glacier floodplain	1985	3.7
Burstall Pass	2362	7.6

Trailhead
From the west end of Main Street in downtown Canmore, follow signs for the Nordic Centre and the Smith Dorrien-Spray Trail (Route 742). Follow this road 44 km south to the Burstall Day Use area turnoff. Turn west (right). The trailhead is on the west edge of the parking area.

Special considerations
Carry river shoes to use when fording the outflow from Robertson Glacier. You share the first 2.9 km with mountain bikers.

Maps
NTS: 82 J/14
Gem Trek: *Kananaskis Lakes* or *Banff and Mt. Assiniboine*

Best lighting: any time

The lofty break of Burstall Pass provides stunning views that encompass three provincial parks and one national park. The Spray Mountains are close at hand, with distant Mt. Assiniboine a prize for the eye on fair days. Wildflower displays are superb; they peak a bit later than average – early August. The environs of the pass are a wonderful place to ramble.

Trailhead to Burstall Pass

You are already on a mountain pass when you begin this hike. Smith-Dorrien Summit separates Smuts Creek, to the north, from Smith-Dorrien Creek, to the south. All of the waters eventually reach the Bow River, but because of hydro-electric installations on both tributary systems – the Spray and the Kananaskis – Mud Lake, at the trailhead, is dammed to ensure that all of its water drains north. Osprey frequent the lake. Jan Smuts was a South African statesman. Horace Smith-Dorrien was a British general in WWI.

Walk across the earthen dam. Turn west (right) at the first junction. The trail here is an old logging road – you'll see stumps. The logs were hauled to a now-abandoned sawmill site near the lower Burstall Lake. Arnica, buffaloberry, false-azalea, and white rhododendron grow at trailside. The forest here is great habitat for birding. I have heard boreal chickadees, hermit thrust, warbling vireo, and the drumming of a three-toed woodpecker. In the Rockies, if a woodpecker's drumming speeds up as it trails off, it's probably a three-toed that's making the racket. At about km 1.7 you pass a huge limestone erratic, dropped here when the Burstall valley glacier receded. Sidetrails lead down to each of the three Burstall Lakes, which make nice places to linger if you've packed your bug dope. Henry Burstall was a commander of Canadian forces during and after WWI.

The trail narrows and becomes rocky and rooted beyond the bike lock-up. The surrounding forest is damp, with foamflower, twinflower, wintergreen, bronze bells, cow parsnip, arnica, yellow columbine, and horsetails in the understory. You pass a limestone bluff covered in feathermosses. The trail crosses the forested, less active part of the Robertson Glacier floodplain, where the tributary streams usually behave themselves, flowing in box culverts. You emerge from the forest at km 3.7. Now the fun begins.

VARIATIONS

- Extend the hike to the Leman Lake viewpoint; 1.4 km return.
- Ramble over the intervening ridge to South Burstall Pass to make a 19.0 km loop.

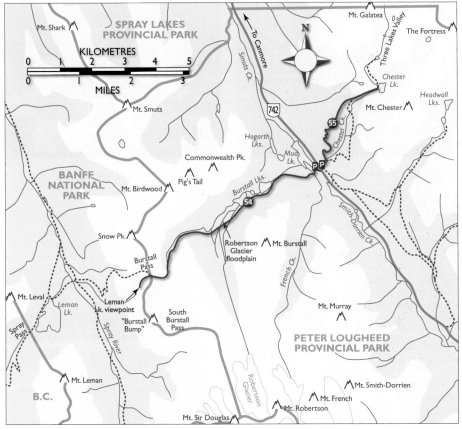

It's only about 550 m across the Robertson Glacier floodplain, but, depending on the volume of the numerous streams, it might take you a bit of time. Water levels rise in early summer during peak snow melt, and in August during peak glacier melt. The water will typically be higher in the afternoon. If you time this hike for low water, you'll get across with the assistance of various logs that have been tossed into the streams, and the odd awkward hop. If the water is high, you'll be putting on river shoes and splashing through ankle-deep to shin-deep channels.

> *Part of the sensation of a pass is the effort required to attain it. Part of the sensation is the concealment and the revelation which are so closely enjambed. A pass is not a single point of view, but it is a temporal translation. The photograph or the painting cannot disclose what the view was like a moment before the new vista was unveiled.*
>
> Jon Whyte; *Mountain Chronicles*

Follow the markers across. William Robertson was a British Army general during WWI. You can see his rapidly receding, namesake glacier – responsible for your wet socks – to the south. The horseshoe traverse of Robertson, Haig, and French glaciers is popular with ski-mountaineers.

Vegetation on the floodplain includes elephant-head, yellow hedysarum, yellow paintbrush, yellow mountain saxifrage, yellow mountain avens, and beautiful patches of bog orchids and rein orchids. Please spare them when you step. Downstream, cotton-grass grows profusely near the upper Burstall Lake. White-crowned sparrows sing from within the clumps of willow. These birds, and those I have heard on the west side of Burstall Pass, give unique variations on the typical song.

Leaving the floodplain, you enter ancient spruce-fir forest and begin a climb of 100 m over the next kilometre. Where the trail draws alongside Burstall Creek, note the transition to upper subalpine groundcover. The view downvalley includes the upper Burstall Lake. The trail levels as it swings southwest. Larches dot classic glades of upper subalpine meadows. You may detect a reddish tinge on snowpatches in the views ahead to Burstall Pass. This

217

Burstall Pass

White mountain avens

is "watermelon snow," coloured by the pigment of one-celled algae.

The climb resumes over ancient limestone benches – natural terraced gardens where western anemone, yellow mountain heather, white mountain avens, alpine buttercup, cinquefoil, golden fleabane, dwarf hawksbeard, moss campion, alpine forget-me-not, and glacier lilies grow. Look back during the climb for fine views of the procession of dogtooth mountains on the north side of the valley, and to the limestone slabs of Whistling Ridge to the east. But the vista that tops them all is the bomber view to the south – the glaciated north face of Mt. Sir Douglas (3411 m). The mountain was named for – you guessed it – a British army commander in WWI. I've seen wolf scat and bear scat on the trail here. Burstall Pass is a key wildlife corridor in this part of the Rockies. Keep left at the junction where the path to "South Burstall Pass" departs. (You can descend later on that path if you choose to traverse along the ridge from Burstall Pass.)

The trail swings northwest to gain the pass and the Banff National Park boundary, where another spectacular mountain vista is added – the east face of distant Mt. Assiniboine (3616 m), 8th-highest peak in the Rockies. Look for golden eagles overhead.

DOGTOOTH MOUNTAINS

Banff's Mt. Louis (see Classic Hike #4) is the most celebrated dogtooth mountain in the Rockies. But at least half a dozen other peaks, including two visible from this hike, rank as equals. The sedimentary formations in dogtooth mountains thrust up toward the vertical. Mt. Birdwood (3097 m), a classic example, dominates the north side of the Burstall valley. The mountain's resistant slabs are limestone and dolomite of the Palliser Formation. Mountaineers often climb routes on the southwest-facing slabs of dogtooth mountains, or, in some cases, on the steep, mini-ridges created by the south-facing edges of the slabs. First climbed in 1922, Mt. Birdwood was named for William Birdwood, a military commander in WWI.

Burstall Pass to Leman Lake Viewpoint

The trail crosses the pass and skirts the south edge of a 100-m-deep sinkhole – a depression eroded into the underlying Palliser Formation limestone. Mountain sorrel, roseroot, and red-stemmed saxifrage grow on the screes. Were you not in a protected area, you could make a vitamin-rich salad from the leaves of the first two plants. Keep left where the trail

CAPTAIN JOHN AND COMPANY

In the 1850s, much of western British North America (now Canada) was unmapped beyond the standard fur trade routes. A young Irishman, John Palliser, stimulated by a hunting trip on the upper Missouri River in 1847-48, dreamed of charting that ground. He took his idea to The Royal Geographical Society as something of a one-man show. The Society liked his idea, but suggested that some men of science accompany him on what they called the "North West America Exploring Expedition." Eugene Bourgeau, the "prince of botanical collectors," was named to the team, along with meteorologist, Thomas Blakiston; geologist and medical doctor, James Hector; and mathematician and secretary, John Sullivan. After a frenzied year of preparation, the Palliser Expedition departed in 1857. Over the next two years – including forays made in the dead of winter – the Expedition trooped through the southern and central Rockies, assessing passes, and collecting natural specimens.

The two reports of the Palliser Expedition are matter of fact and make for dry reading – the titles alone each occupy half a page. Stories are told in outline. But if you know something of the country in which the expedition travelled, you soon sense that it is in the unrecorded details that the real adventure is described. We are fortunate that Palliser and his colleagues were such observant people. They left us a legacy of place names and travel routes, some now the paths of highways, others sketchy trails to seldom-seen places in the back of beyond.

forks after 525 m – the right-hand fork descends to the Spray Valley. The left-hand trail climbs gently for 175 m to a knot of spruce and fir on a knoll that overlooks the broad sweep of the upper Spray Valley and the environs of Palliser Pass, with Leman Lake featured in the view. The Interprovincial Boundary Survey of 1923-25 renamed some of the features in this area that had originally been named by the Palliser Expedition. At least the name of Palliser Pass has endured as a tribute to the monumental journeys of that expedition.

"Burstall Bump"

Experienced ridge ramblers won't be able to resist the climb onto "Burstall Bump" (2575 m), the minor summit south of Burstall Pass. The views go up a notch or two, particularly that of Mt. Sir Douglas. From the highpoint you can backtrack, or head south

Leman Lake

toward South Burstall Pass, from where you descend east over limestone benches (no trail) to pick up the path that rejoins the main trail about 1 km below Burstall Pass. Carry an ice axe if you attempt this route in early summer.

55. Chester Lake

Chester Lake

S hort and sweet – and perhaps, crowded – sums up the outing to Chester Lake. The trail to this beautiful tarn is justifiably popular, summer and winter. The meadows near the lake are flush with wildflowers, the afternoon light seems to animate the slabby cliffs of Mt. Chester, and the sidetrail to Three Lake Valley provides a delightful ramble through larch forest to lake-dotted, limestone barrens. This is a great hike for birding. Although I don't normally advocate beginning a hike in the evening, when the forecast is fair, experienced hikers might consider packing a dinner instead of a lunch, and striking off about 6:00 p.m. I imagine that sunset at Chester Lake would be a magical experience. The first 1.6 km is open to mountain bikes. Don't let the crowdedness of this hike fool you; grizzly bears like these meadows, too.

TRAIL THUMBNAIL

Day-hike; see map, p. 217

Route	Elev. (m)	Dist. (km)
Trailhead	1920	0
Chester Lake	2220	4.0

Trailhead
From the west end of Main Street in downtown Canmore, follow signs for the Nordic Centre and the Smith Dorrien-Spray Trail (Route 742). Follow this road 44 km south to the Chester Day Use area turnoff. Turn east (left). The trailhead is at the northeast corner of the parking area.

Maps
NTS: 82 J/14
Gem Trek: *Kananaskis Lakes*

Best lighting: afternoon and evening

Trailhead to Chester Lake

The trail begins as a gravelled path through spruce-fir forest. Look and listen for gray jays and hermit thrushes. The path soon reverts to old logging road. You cross Chester Creek after about 150 m. By keeping left at all the upcoming forks and junctions, you won't end up on a winter ski trail or on an abandoned skidder track. Labrador tea, fireweed, paintbrush,

VARIATION

- Extend the hike to Three Lakes Valley. The first lake is 2.4 km return.

EARTH HUMMOCKS

Hike enough trails in the Rockies, and certain landscape themes become familiar. One of these is the subalpine frost meadow. A trail levels at the crest of a climb, emerging from forest onto the floor of a tributary valley. A tiny stream meanders through the valley, bordered by meadows. Willows grow near the stream. Small mounds called earth hummocks dot the grassy alp that surrounds the willows. Most people who live in northern climes know about frost heaves on roadways – bumps in the pavement that emerge in autumn and spring. The same sort of process was at work in these meadows when they were underlain by permafrost. The Mazama ash – a layer of volcanic fallout from the eruption of Mt. Mazama (in present day Oregon), 6850 years ago – is where many earth hummocks in the Rockies took purchase. Most earth hummocks are now relict features. The soil is marginally warmer atop them than in the surrounding hollows, so many support shrubs and small trees.

DROP THOSE NAMES

The Alberta-British Columbia Boundary Commission of 1913-25 faced an enormous job. While delineating the boundary between the two provinces, the surveyors trooped up and down the slopes of hundreds of mountains, packing their survey gear and cameras. The enterprise seemed not to exhaust them physically, but when it came to naming features – many of which they were the first ones to closely inspect – their imaginations emptied. Rather than appending names that described an aspect of the landscape, in some locations the surveyors – led principally by A.O. Wheeler – resorted to naming groups of mountains after Italian, French, and British politicians, military commanders, and battleships. Of the 44 named mountains in Peter Lougheed Provincial Park, Wheeler named 38. So prominent was his naval vessel motif in this area, locals formerly knew the peaks as the "Battleship Mountains."

Although the patriotism of the era is understandable, virtually all of the military names have no legitimate connection with the Rockies. Some, such as Pétain, are now viewed as embarrassments. The sentiment of most contemporary mountain lovers is that the names of mountains – places to which we make peaceful, restorative quests – should not be inspired by acts of war. It is now uncommon for the names of persons, living or dead, to be accepted as placenames in Canada. Descriptive words are preferred. New submissions are often rejected with the explanation that the feature might best remain unnamed. Here's an instance where I side with the bureaucrats: In some cases, anonymity helps to protect wilderness.

IT'S BEEN A SLICE

The view from the last meadow just before the lake provides insight into the local and regional geology. The steeply tilted slabs of Mt. Chester are characteristic of dip-slope mountains in the front ranges. The formations in the mountain are part of the Sulphur Mountain Thrust, an assemblage of rocks that was pushed northeastward during mountain building. Between the trailhead and the summit of The Fortress (3000 m), northeast of Chester Lake, the entirety of this thrust sheet – spanning 12 sedimentary formations – is visible, with the formations in sequence. The trailhead is among the shales and siltstones of the 135-million-year-old, Fernie Formation. The summit of The Fortress is 366-million-year-old, Palliser Formation limestone. It's not often that such a large slice of the crumbly sedimentary sandwich is so well preserved at the surface in the Rockies. You can see the division between two rock types on the scree slopes above the southeast shore of Chester Lake. Tan coloured sandstone is to the west; gray limestone is to the east. Both rocks belong to the Etherington Formation.

Elephant Rocks

wild strawberry, buffaloberry, and arnica grow in the forest understory. The road makes a series of wide switchbacks with the grade at times moderately steep. Views back include the environs of Burstall Pass, Mt. Smith Dorrien (3151 m), and up French Creek to Mt. Robertson (3177 m) and Mt. Sir Douglas (3411 m).

Beyond the bike lock-up, the trail narrows and becomes rooted. It levels and then descends to a frost meadow whose earth hummocks are topped with yellow mountain heather. The east edge of this clearing features a fantastic larch tree snag – chewed on by porcupines, and riddled with woodpecker holes. After a short forested section, you emerge into a second meadow; this one larger, with fine views ahead to Mt. Chester (3054 m). HMS *Chester* was a British battle cruiser, severely damaged in the Battle of Jutland in 1916 but back at sea a few months later.

When the trail re-enters the forest, you might notice that the character of the tread is different. The trail here has been capped with gravel, delivered in barrel buckets slung under a helicopter, and placed over soil blanket. The blanket prevented the gravel from quickly being punched down into the muck. It's an expensive fix for a muddy trail, but the only worthwhile method on a route this popular. Further on you'll see where trees have been

THREE LAKES VALLEY (2310 M), 1.2 KM

Follow the trail around the west shore of Chester Lake. About 80 m beyond a footbridge over a tributary stream, you come to a small stand of subalpine fir. Turn north (left) onto any of several paths that soon converge. The initial climb away from the lake is steep. The trail swings west to the edge of a sandstone canyon that harbours a lively stream. I have watched dippers fly through here, too. This canyon marks the seam between the same sandstone and limestone formations that you saw in Mt. Chester. The trail soon levels at a meadow that contains the Elephant Rocks – huge, shattered and beautifully eroded, limestone blocks of the Livingstone Formation that have tumbled from the slopes above. Some of the rocks feature *rillenkarren* – grooves eroded into the limestone by water. The best route is to keep to the east (right).

Delightful larch forest borders the trail as it works north, descends slightly, and then angles northeast into the Three Lakes Valley. (The pond to the west (left) does not rank as one of the Three Lakes.) Alpine speedwell, western anemone, Drummond's anemone, western springbeauty, grouseberry, yellow columbine, alpine forget-me-not, and Sitka valerian grow at trailside. The outlying slopes of Mt. Galatea (3185 m), ahead, are a favourite haunt of mountain goats. HMS *Galatea* was yet another British naval vessel involved in the Battle of Jutland in 1916.

The trail alternately cuts over and parallels low, gray bluffs – limestone of the fossil-rich, Mount Head Formation. Finally, it takes one of these mini-headwalls head on, delivering you in 150 m to the first of the Three Lakes. Those accustomed to travelling off-trail can pick their way farther up-valley, beginning with a rough route around the west shore of the first lake. The second lake is an attractive spot, the third lake, less so. The views southwest from all are superb, but I like the first lake the best for its cotton-grass fringe and pleasing greenery.

transplanted into trail braids to encourage you to keep on track.

The last meadow bisected by the trail is the largest of the three. Although the lake is close by, the wildflower displays will probably slow your pace. Western anemone, yellow paintbrush, Sitka valerian, fleabanes, and – in early summer – superb displays of glacier lilies, colour the meadows. Just before the lake, you pass an outhouse that appears to be on stilts. The explanations: This is a popular skiing destination; if you elevate the outhouse, you don't have to shovel the door as much. Also, if you elevate the waste barrel (which is flown out when full), you don't have to dig holes in the ground.

The trail forks at the lakeshore. The right-hand path crosses the outlet to a grove of spruce, larch, and subalpine fir – a good place to take in the view. Across the lake, a seasonal stream tumbles from a slot canyon. The songbirds I have seen and heard here did not surprise me – hermit thrush, pine siskin, Tennessee warbler, boreal chickadee, yellow-rumped warbler, robin, white-winged crossbill, and dipper – but the behaviour of two of the species amazed me. While I waited for the light, I watched two pairs of dippers come and go. They fed at the outlet of the

Contorted beds, of unknown age,
My weary limbs shall bear,
Perhaps a neat synclinal fold
At night shall be my lair.

Poem penned by geologist, George Mercer Dawson, who surveyed the Kananaskis area in 1884

lake, diving underwater and hauling out onto rocks. Two robins joined them, hopped into the stream and foraged underwater. They, too, hauled out on rocks, mid-stream. The robins did everything to emulate the dippers but sing their songs and bob their tails. I have also seen yellow-rumped warblers here, foraging on foot for bugs at creekside.

DIP, DIP, DIPPER

The dipper is the only aquatic songbird in North America, and is a marvel of adaptation. It is a year-round resident of the mountains, protected from the chill of glacial water and winter by thick, soot-coloured, down that is impregnated with oil. The dipper feeds on insects, snails, and fish fry in turbulent streams. It has flaps that cover its nostrils during dives – allowing it to remain submerged for more than a minute – and an extra set of transparent eyelids that allow it to see underwater. Its call is a metallic, staccato trill, made on the wing. Dippers also have a fine repertoire of songs – warbler-like, buzzy, and whistling. K-Country is dipper country. The Christmas bird counts here consistently yield North American highs for the species.

South Kananskis Pass

56. South Kananaskis Pass

Upper Kananaskis Lake

TRAIL THUMBNAIL

Day-hike or overnight

Route	Elev. (m)	Dist. (km)
Trailhead	1722	0
Upper Kananaskis Lake jct	1746	0.8
Point CG jct	1760	2.2
Invincible Creek	1775	3.8
Kananaskis River canyon	1740	5.7
Forks CG	1785	7.2
Base of headwall	1950	9.2
Top of headwall	2190	10.6
Three Isle Lake CG	2180	10.8
Three Isle Creek CG	2185	11.2
South Kananaskis Pass	2301	13.5

Trailhead

From the west end of Main Street in downtown Canmore, follow signs for the Nordic Centre and the Smith Dorrien-Spray Trail (Route 742). Follow this road 64 km south to the junction with the Kananaskis Lakes Trail. Turn south (right), and drive 13 km to road's end at the North Interlakes Day Use Area. From Highway 1, follow Kananaskis Trail (Highway 40), 50 km south to the Kananaskis Lakes Trail junction. Turn south (right) and follow the Kananaskis Lakes Trail, 15 km to road's end at the North Interlakes Day Use Area. The trailhead is at the north end of the parking area.

Maps

NTS: 82 J/11
Gem Trek: *Kananaskis Lakes*

The outing to South Kananaskis Pass shares a trait common to only two other Classic Hikes – Fryatt Valley and Berg Lake. For most of the considerable distance to the destination, the grade is relatively gentle. But a headwall intervenes, offering a solid piece of exercise. The climb deters many backpackers from camping at Three Isle Lake; they opt instead to base themselves at Forks campground. But this headwall, as with any other steep climb, goes easily enough if you take it one step at a time.

Although the upper Kananaskis Valley is rich in human history, details connected with this trail are unclear. Some have argued that South Kananaskis Pass was "first" crossed in 1854 by a party of Red River settlers under the direction of James Sinclair, led by a Cree guide named Mas-ke-pe-toon. The guide had a shortcut across the Rockies in mind, but finally had to admit that he was lost. Accounts of what followed are vague, but it seems unlikely – as you will see – that a hundred people with cattle, kit, and caboodle would have made it up the headwall.

Trailhead to Invincible Creek

The trail begins by crossing the earth-filled Interlakes dam between Upper Kananaskis Lake and Lower Kananaskis Lake. Calgary Power built the dam in 1955 as part of the hydro-electric development on the Kananaskis River. Cliff swallows nest on the spillway gate, and anglers inevitably dot the bouldery shore of Upper Kananaskis Lake. Across the spillway, the trail (formerly a fire road) curves west through subalpine forest along the north shore of the lake. Sun-exposed bark on some of the lodgepole pines is remarkably orange in colour. Red squirrels and dark-eyed juncos are common. I once saw a snowshoe hare, here.

Buffaloberry, dwarf dogwood, wild strawberry, yellow hedysarum, cow parsnip, paintbrush, white geranium, Hooker's thistle, and thimbleberry are among the flowers and shrubs at trailside. You can see Lower Kananaskis Falls at the west end of the

lake, and Hawke Island. HMS *Hawke* was among the early British naval casualties of WWI. The island seen today is also a casualty of sorts – the remains of a much larger landform, inundated by the reservoir. Three other named islands in the upper lake were completely submerged. Keep right (west) at

VARIATIONS

- Day-hike to Three Isle Lake; 21.6 km return.
- Day-hike to the pass; 27.0 km return.
- Backpack to Forks campground (7.2 km). Day-hike to Three Isle Lake and the pass. Day-hike to North Kananaskis Pass. (See Classic Hike #57.)
- Backpack to Three Isle Lake (10.8 km) or Three Isle Creek (11.2 km).

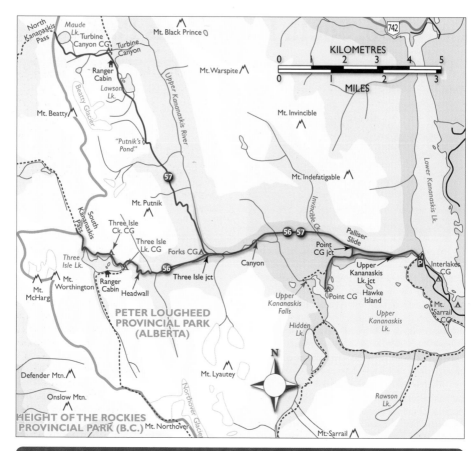

BEDS AND DIPS

The Palliser Slide from Mt. Indefatigable consists not of Palliser Formation limestone, but mostly of limestone and dolomite of the Rundle Group of formations, which were deposited in ancient seas approximately 350 million-years-ago. (The name, "Palliser," comes from the site's connection with the Palliser Expedition.) John Palliser's party clambered over the rockslide deposits in 1858.) It is true in the Rockies that what went up during mountain building must, eventually, come down. This is mostly accomplished through the chip-chipping of erosion but, occasionally, calamitous events such as rockslides tear the mountains down.

The front ranges of the Rockies are rockslide country. If you look at the slopes above the trail, you can see why. The rock of Mt. Indefatigable is layered and dips steeply to the southwest – at angles as great as 50°. The sedimentary layers are known as beds. When deposited they were horizontal; their orientation to each other known as the bedding. Although the layers are no longer horizontal, you can see that they are still parallel. The angle at which the formations now rest is called the dip of the bedding. When the ice of the Late Wisconsin Glaciation flowed through this valley, it widened it, cutting into the lower valley walls, removing some of the support for the rocks above. Enter gravity. With such a steep dip, it was only a matter of time before rock layers broke free along their beds and slid to the valley floor. The process was expedited by the freezing and thawing of water that had percolated into fissures between the beds, pushing them apart and providing lubricant. The volume that let go here is estimated at 90 million cubic metres. Other rockslides will happen in the front ranges; perhaps here, perhaps there. Kind of makes you want to pick up the pace, doesn't it?

the next two trail junctions, which provide access, respectively, to the shore of the lake and to Point Campground.

Small stands of trembling aspen mark a transition where the trail begins to cross a series of avalanche slopes and rockslide paths on the south flank of Mt. Indefatigable (2667 m). The aspens grow near snow-melt streams. The well-drained soils support common juniper, blue penstemon, yarrow, stonecrop, fireweed, paintbrush, and a few Douglas-firs. Avalanches have snapped off some of the trees. The standing dead trees now serve as dens for woodpeckers and squirrels. One Douglas-fir has rocks piled into a split, high up its trunk. The debris probably melted out of avalanche deposit and never made it to the ground. Wolf lichen graces many of the tree trunks.

For almost 1.5 km, the trail cuts across the path of the Palliser Slide – the largest rockslide in Peter Lougheed Provincial Park. Looking south, you can see the path of the slide and the boulderfield that resulted. Ponds fill depressions in the debris. Across the lake, the view includes the valley of Aster Creek. The prominent mountain with an armchair-like cirque in its north slopes is Mt. Lyautey (3045 m), named for a French Minister of War in WWI. The cirque sits in the base of a U-shaped fold known as the Lyautey Syncline.

Look for spotted saxifrage along the trail. The centres of some of these plants have died as the plants grow outward in a circular fashion. The low profile allows the mats to survive avalanches. The name, saxifrage, comes from the Latin words, *saxum* – "rock," and *frangere* – "to break." The name was given because some saxifrage species grow from within cracks in rocks. This led to belief in a folk medicine cure – saxifrage powder was fed to patients suffering from gallstones. A massive Engelmann spruce – almost a metre thick – stands on the far side of the rockslide where the trail re-enters the forest. The trail descends to the flash-flood stream course of Invincible Creek – the end of the mountain bike trail. You may have to pick your way if the trail has been recently washed out.

> *For about a mile from this lake our course was difficult to the horses, on account of the broken rocky character of the country. In some places large blocks of the limestone, which composes the mountains in this part, were lying all broken and heaped in a singularly artificial manner.*
>
> John Palliser; August 21, 1858, *Papers Relative to the Exploration of British North America*

Three Isle Lake headwall

Invincible Creek to Forks Campground

Across the creek, the trail narrows, heralding a marked transition in hiking experience. Gone is the rocky tread underfoot, replaced by soft earth covered with spruce and fir needles. For the next 1.7 km you walk through a quiet, damp forest dominated by sub-alpine fir. Many of the trees are afflicted with a rust – probably *Pucciniastrum epilobii*. Although hard on the trees, it is not necessarily a fatal affliction. Feathermosses, dwarf dogwood, arnica, twinflower, pink wintergreen, yellow columbine, grouseberry, and false-azalea are common at trailside. Although a firestorm affected parts of the Kananaskis Valley in 1936, pockets in the upper valley escaped. A stand of Engelmann spruce nearby has been dated to 1586.

The trail crests a low, rocky rise and descends to the Upper Kananaskis River at a canyon cut into blocky dolomite of the Banff Formation. It is interesting to contrast the wild nature of the upper river with the timid nature of the river below the Kananaskis Lakes. Here, the fluctuations are responses to rainfall, runoff, snowmelt, and glacier melt. Down in the main valley, the river's fluctuations are dictated by the manipulations of spillways and the demand for electricity.

Cross the bridge and turn west (right) to head upstream. For the next 1.5 km, the trail follows the river through a narrow breach in the limestone ramparts to Forks Campground. Log jams and gravel bars dot the river's meandering course. Moose frequent this area; look for their tracks and droppings. Horsetails grow in wet margins. The trail crosses a talus slope where you can look and listen for pikas. Upvalley, you get your first view of the headwall. Mt. Putnik (2924 m) – with graceful limestone slabs – is on the north, named for a Serbian commander in WWI. An unnamed peak on the north ridge of Mt. Northover is to the south of the headwall. Downvalley, the view includes Mt. Indefatigable. The spar trees from a forest fire cloak its upper slopes.

You cross an alluvial fan and the braids of the tributary stream that drains from the north face of Mt. Lyautey. Use the footbridges or rock-hop, as required. Yellow mountain avens grows on the gravels between the streams. I have watched a dipper here, diving into the clear pool of a spring in quest for bugs and invertebrates. Forks campground is located in the angle between the Upper Kananaskis River, which comes in from the north, and Three Isle Creek, which comes in from the west. To carry on for Three Isle Lake, keep left (southwest) at the trail junction just before the campground.

Forks Campground to Three Isle Lake

Three Isle Lake

The trail skirts the south edge of the campground. Blue clematis, false Solomon's seal, dwarf dogwood, arnica, twisted stalk, fairybells, and foamflower grow in this tranquil, ancient, tumble-down forest. Listen for the haunting, flute-like songs of hermit thrushes. For about 1 km, the trail is rough where it is sandwiched between Three Isle Creek and the south slopes of Mt. Putnik. You walk a 40 m section of flash-flood creekbed where you might lose the way. The trail cuts upslope to the northwest (right) and crosses avalanche slopes, where cow parsnip, water hemlock, harebell, yarrow, yellow columbine, groundsel, bracted honeysuckle, and bristly, black currant grow. As is often the case, a massive tree towers on the second slope – an Engelmann spruce more than 1 m thick at its base. Although dead, it has escaped destruction by avalanches for centuries. From the third avalanche slope you have your first clear view of the headwall.

Many people take a break before the upcoming climb, pausing near a cataract on Three Isle Creek. The waterfall is the emergence of the underground drainage from Three Isle Lake. The resting place is in a pocket of good bear habitat. Make lots of noise. When you leave the stopping place, the trail switchbacks away through lush vegetation. The final leg crosses screes to the base of the headwall.

The Three Isle Lake headwall features limestone and dolomite of the Palliser Formation, the classic front range, cliff-builder. Although cliffs often surround you as you hike in the Rockies, it is a rare trail that tackles one head-on. The route ahead appears formidable but is only occasionally steep. The worst is at the corner just above the initial staircase. But for most of the way, the well-conceived trail switchbacks and takes advantage of natural contours. The hanging gardens on this cliff are a flower-fest of those that prefer drier soils: showy Jacob's ladder, orange-flowered false dandelion, golden fleabane, scorpionweed, creeping beardtongue, low larkspur, white geranium, and Canada violet. One flower grows with a riotous profusion I haven't seen elsewhere – yellow columbine, sometimes in hybrid form. Note how it prefers sheltered spots.

I have heard red-breasted nuthatches, pine siskins, robins, and Wilson's warblers in the forested draw near the top of the climb. This dry gully is the ancestral drainage from Three Isle Lake, occupied before the lake's water eroded its subterranean outlet. From the crest of the headwall, you can clearly see the U-shaped form of the valley in the view east. The trail drops into the old streamcourse, where glacier lilies and mountain heather grow. After a gradual descent, you reach Three Isle Lake campground in 200 m. To carry on to South Kananaskis Pass, follow the trail through the campground. To visit the lakeshore, keep straight ahead. Take care with your pack and boots, and don't go barefoot at the campground; it is notorious for its monster porcupines.

Three Isle Lake to South Kananaskis Pass

From the east shore, Mt. Worthington (2915 m) – named for a BC soldier who died in WWII – is central in the view across Three Isle Lake. Because it drains underground, the lake's level fluctuates. The Interprovincial Boundary Survey named the lake "on account of the fact that there are three little islands in it." Really? Nobody of late seems to have seen the third island. The fluctuating water level also affects the trail to South Kananaskis Pass, which skirts the north shore of the lake. When the lake level is high, parts of the trail will be submerged.

You reach Three Isle Creek campground in 400 m. Rather than follow the convoluted lakeshore, with its mini-peninsulas, the trail now keeps its distance. You cross a rocky avalanche path off the westerly outlier of Mt. Putnik before entering cool forest where snow lingers. Arnica, western springbeauty, and a marvelous display of globeflowers – the match of any in the Rockies – brighten trailside. The trail descends to shoreline near the west end of the lake, with fine views south, including the glaciated, northwest ridge of Mt. Northover (2999 m). The mountain was named posthumously for a Canadian Victoria Cross recipient of WWI. I have seen solitary sandpipers here on the beach.

Hybrid columbine

alongside an ancient reef. The first larches appear near treeline. The trail makes a sharp turn to deliver you suddenly to the crest of South Kananaskis Pass, with its tremendous view north. A narrow alp, dotted with earth hummocks and bordered by larches, stretches away to the slopes of Mt. Beatty (3004 m), named for David Beatty, a British naval commander in WWI. The pass marks the boundary between Alberta's K-Country and BC's Height of the Rockies Provincial Park. For those with the time to explore and who are capable at travelling off-trail, the ridges that flank either side of the pass beckon. Or you could ramble 2 km north across the pass, to where a view of Beatty Lake awaits. But if you've day-hiked from the trailhead, you'll probably want to park it and drink your fill of the marvelous view.

From the west shore of the lake, the trail heads north, winding and climbing steadily through spruce-fir forest. Bedrock here is 378 million-year-old mud-stone and siltstone of the Yahatinda Formation, which was deposited on the shore of a bay that formed

Maude Lake

57. North Kananaskis Pass

This is an outing packed with wonders. If you take it on as a day-hike on a fair day, you will marathon your way into backcountry bliss; your mind and body drenched in all the best that a limestone world can bring: turbulent streams, dark forests, bright meadows, tranquil ponds, gem-stone lakes, larch forest, and a wildflower festival which – when at its prime – is rarely matched elsewhere in the Rockies. When you finally get to bed, you will surely sleep soundly, with mountains avalanching your dreams. Take a more traditional approach, using either or both of the campgrounds as basecamps, and the dream-time may endure for days on the trail.

VARIATIONS

- Day-hike to the pass; 34.4 km return.
- Backpack to Forks campground (7.2 km). Day-hike to the pass. Day-hike to Three Isle Lake and South Kananaskis Pass. (See Classic Hike #56.)
- Backpack. Camp at Forks CG and/or Turbine Canyon CG, and explore.

TRAIL THUMBNAIL

Day-hike or overnight; see map, p. 224

Route	Elev. (m)	Dist. (km)
Trailhead	1722	0
Upper Kananaskis Lake jct	1746	0.8
Point CG jct	1760	2.2
Invincible Creek	1775	3.8
Kananaskis River canyon	1740	5.7
Forks CG	1785	7.2
Putnik Pond	2205	12.0
Lawson Lake	2220	13.5
Turbine Canyon CG	2225	15.0
Trail highpoint	2370	16.5
Maude Lake	2350	16.8
North Kananaskis Pass	2362	17.2

Trailhead
From the west end of Main Street in downtown Canmore, follow signs for the Nordic Centre and the Smith Dorrien-Spray Trail (Route 742). Follow this road 64 km south to the junction with the Kananaskis Lakes Trail. Turn south (right), and drive 13 km to road's end at the North Interlakes Day Use Area. From Highway 1, follow Kananaskis Trail (Highway 40), 50 km south to the Kananaskis Lakes Trail junction. Turn south (right) and follow the Kananaskis Lakes Trail, 15 km to road's end at the North Interlakes Day Use Area. The trailhead is at the north end of the parking area.

Maps
NTS: 82 J/11 (trail shown incorrectly)
Gem Trek: *Kananaskis Lakes*

"Putnik's Pond"

Lawson Lake

The description for the first 7.2 km of this outing is the same as for South Kananaskis Pass. Please refer to pages 223-26.

Forks Campground to "Putnik's Pond"

From the junction just east of Forks campground, head northwest through the campground. The trail works is way up and down on the west bank of the Upper Kananaskis River before beginning a sustained ascent on the east slopes of Mt. Putnik (2924 m). In winter and spring, avalanches sweep these slopes. Much of the forest cover is stunted spruce-fir, hammered by the snow. With tree growth suppressed, a complex understory of vegetation proliferates. You will find a magnificent array of wildflowers, including low larkspur, clematis, stickseed, Sitka valerian, twisted stalk, evergreen violet, and glacier lily. Keep your head up, here – this is excellent bear habitat. When we were descending this section late in the day, I saw a large, brown animal move off the slope below the trail, heading for the river – could have been a moose; could have been a bear.

After about 3 km the grade relents and you head back into spruce-fir forest. The trail crosses the unnamed, glacier-fed stream that flows from the valley north of Mt. Putnik. Relish this short distance through glades, decked with white globeflowers and alpine buttercup, before the climb resumes in ancient spruce forest. The last switchbacks deliver you to a notch on a rocky spur; a spot often choked with snow. Here, you shift gears from uphill grind to long-distance cruise. The remaining 5.3 km to the pass involve comparatively little climbing. You have earned the vistas that now parade into view from the north. The first of these is "Putnik's Pond" – a meltwater puddle that sits in an ancient rockslide hollow, with the distant, limestone fangs of Mt. Maude (3043 m), Mt. Jellicoe (3075 m), and Mt. French (3244 m) rising beyond.

"Putnik's Pond" to Turbine Canyon

The trail drops into the hollow, follows the east shore of the pond, then climbs over another spur to descend to Lawson Lake. Although the atmosphere is nowhere near as "walled-in" as on the Rockwall, those who have had the pleasure of hiking that trail may sense a similarity in the setting, here.

A classic limestone pocket harbours Lawson Lake. Judging by the "pavement" shoreline, much of its water probably drains underground, although some does flow north above ground to Maude Brook. The shells of common pond snails are abundant. Looking north, from this perspective it appears that Mt. Maude has twin summits. The right-hand elevation is, in reality a bump on the southeast ridge, almost 300 m lower than the true summit. The features on this hike named "Maude" commemorate Lieutenant General Frederick Stanley Maude, who commanded Allied forces during WW1. To the east (right) of Mt. Maude, you may be able to pick out the terminus of Haig Glacier, a summer training site for Canadian, Olympic-class cross-country skiers.

The trail hugs the west shore of Lawson Lake before ducking back into forest for the last kilometre to Turbine Canyon, passing a park patrol cabin en route. If you are packing overnight gear this far, you will be happy to gain Turbine Canyon campground.

> The streams from the glaciers on the north and south sides of the pass summit meet close by the trail and drop perpendicularly into a rock-well at the head of a very remarkable box-canyon; this well and the force of the falling water have suggested the name Turbine Canyon...
>
> *Report of the Commission Appointed to Delimit the Boundary Between Alberta and British Columbia, Part I, From 1913 to 1916*

But if you have arrived early enough in the day and with gas still in the tank, you might want to consider pitching camp quickly and carrying on to the pass, even if that was your plan for tomorrow. Why not do a great thing twice?

Turbine Canyon to North Kananaskis Pass

Cross Maude Brook on a bridge and turn west (left) at the Turbine Canyon campground junction. Although the upper reaches of Maude Brook are a relative trickle, over the eons they have worn a considerable valley. It's a beautiful place, perhaps more so because of how quickly you make the transition from subalpine forest to treeline glades as you climb along the stream course. Looking south, you have a fine view of Mt. Beatty (3004 m) and Beatty Glacier. These features were named for David Beatty, a British naval commander in WWI.

The climb tops out on a knoll from which explodes another prize view – Maude Lake, with the tiny alpine saddle of North Kananaskis Pass just beyond. It's an unusual view, too, because it seems as if it's downhill to the pass. Actually, it is. You drop from here to the lakeshore and don't quite regain this elevation on the pass. The trail contours around the west shore of the lake, cutting across boulderfields and snow patches to

TURBINE CANYON

After witnessing the travesties in the lower valley, you might be thinking that the name of Turbine Canyon comes from some failed attempt to install a hydro-electric generating facility. Not so. The Interprovincial Boundary Survey applied the name more than three decades before that dam-building business came to K-Country. The roar of the water deep within the limestone slot inspired the name. Note how the canyon changes course, often making right-angle turns – the water has eroded a feature known as a joint set. Turbine Canyon has five natural bridges and is exceedingly narrow in places. Don't think of it! Keep well back from the edges.

the final, meadowed approach to the pass – a narrow breach on the continental divide. Carry on a short distance to where the valley of Le Roy Creek begins to fall away. Gawk at the limestone cathedrals that rake the sky in every direction. If the day is fair, your eyes will invariably be drawn to the impossible-looking architecture of the northern peaks of the Royal Group to the west. Another stellar vista is the pointed, ice-draped summit of Mt. Sir Douglas (3411 m), to the north, framed in the notch between Mt. Le Roy (2970 m) and Mt. Monro (3094 m).

Far be it from all-said-and-done when you turn your back on this stunning place to begin the trip home. The view south across Maude Lake is better than the view north toward the pass. The vista-parade resumes in reverse, and if you are returning to Forks campground or beyond, the late afternoon or evening light will play on the limestone slabs and ridges of mountains that may have been shaded earlier in the day. You will descend from sun-drenched rock, now cooling, into the shade world of mountain dreams. Savour every step; the journey is a marvel.

PASS THIS WAY?

***Kin-oh-ah-kis* was a Cree** – something of a legend in his time for surviving an axe blow to his head. In 1858, John Palliser gave a corrupted version of the hard-headed warrior's name, Kananaskis, to the river and to the pass that his party crossed in their first traverse of the Rockies. As is often the case, the name, Kananaskis, migrated to other features in the vicinity, including the destination of this hike. But in that migration the name has also created a lingering headache for historians: Which pass did Palliser cross? Palliser's account mentions little difficulty. He also described a lake on the crest of the pass, from which waters flow to the Pacific Ocean. Maude Lake is not on the crest of the pass, and its waters drain to the Atlantic slope. Many think that Palliser crossed the Rockies by way of Elk Pass – a much easier route – but one which also lacks a double-drainage lake.

In 1901, American explorer, Walter Wilcox, took a hopeless stab at finding North Kananaskis Pass from the Palliser River. Undeterred by that failure, he made a second approach from the Kananaskis Lakes, accompanied partway by the expedition's packer, Jim Wood. In an epic day, Wilcox, after ditching Wood and thinking at first that Lawson Lake marked the pass, carried on to his desired destination, finally reaching it at 4:00 p.m. In July 1916, surveyor R.W. Cautley made a crossing of the pass – on snowshoes. The Interprovincial Boundary Survey considered the route useless for developed transportation, and so did not install permanent boundary markers.

58. Ptarmigan Cirque

Ptarmigan Cirque

TRAIL THUMBNAIL

Day-hike

Route	Elev. (m)	Dist. (km)
Trailhead	2200	0
Ptarmigan Cirque jct	2200	0.4
Cross Highway 40	2205	0.5
Loop trail jct	2347	1.2
Trail high point	2408	2.2
Loop trail jct	2347	3.2
Trailhead	2200	4.4

Trailhead
From Highway 1, 31 km east of Canmore, follow Kananaskis Trail (Highway 40), 67 km south to Highwood Pass. The parking area is on the west side of the road, just south of the pass. An interpretive brochure may be available at the kiosk. Highway 40 is closed to motor vehicles south of the Kananaskis Lakes Trail junction, from December 1 to June 14.

Maps
NTS: 82 J/10
Gem Trek: *Kananaskis Lakes*

Best lighting: afternoon

The valley that leads to Ptarmigan Cirque is a miniature version of hundreds of other recently deglaciated valleys in the Rockies. Plants and animals cling tenaciously to life; the hallmark of ice is everywhere. The bedrock reveals the fossilized remains of lifeforms that lived in ancient seas. Although the trail is popular – often crowded – grizzly bears frequent the area. The trail may be closed from time to time to prevent encounters. If it is closed, please hike elsewhere.

Trailhead to Loop Junction

Walk north from the parking area on a wide, gravelled path through the Highwood Meadows. Look for bighorn sheep nearby. The chemistry of bedrock influences the plants that grow on the resulting soils. In many places in the Rockies, the bedrock is mostly limestone, which creates alkaline, calcium-rich soils that limit the growth of many plants. The bedrock in Highwood Pass is shale, coal, and sandstone, which foster a relative abundance of plant species. Permafrost in the meadows churns the soil and creates sinkholes. When, over a period of centuries, a series of sinkholes connects, a new stream is created.

The Highwood River, a major tributary of the Bow River, has its westerly sources in Storm and Mist creeks, south of Highwood Pass. The Stoneys called the Highwood River, "Tall Trees River," in reference to the height of aspen trees along its banks much farther downstream. It is a curious coincidence that, despite the high elevation of the pass, it is not above treeline. So this also makes it a "high, wooded pass," a feature noted by Thomas Blakiston of the Palliser Expedition when he trooped by in 1858.

The Canadian Rockies contain relatively few rock arches – natural features eroded from ridge crests. So it is unusual that from Highwood Pass you can, weather and lighting permitting, see two arches. To the southeast, look for the handle-shaped arch on Storm Mountain (3095 m), south of Highwood Pass. To the southwest, look for a much more delicate arch on the east ridge of Mount Tyrwhitt (2876 m).

You reach the Ptarmigan Cirque junction in 400 m. Turn northeast (right), and ascend to the west shoulder of Highway 40. Look and listen for traffic (and sheep!); cross the road when it is safe to do so, and pick up the trail on the other side.

The climb begins through an upper subalpine, spruce-fir forest. Yellow hedysarum, blue pentemon, wild strawberry, grouseberry, daisy fleabane, western anemone, paintbrush, common fireweed, alpine springbeauty, bracted lousewort, yellow

> *If one halts by chance anywhere on a mountain pass, all sorts of thrilling things are going on around. Lovely flowers are opening eagerly to the sun and wind of Spring – in mid-August, with September's snows just at hand, a whole year's work of blossom and seed to be accomplished before the ten months' winter sleep begins.*
>
> A.P. Coleman; *The Canadian Rockies, New and Old Trails*

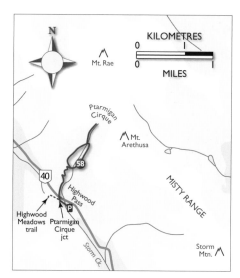

mountain heather, arnica, glacier lily, low larkspur, and stickseed all grow at trailside. The trail switchbacks steeply in a pocket of subalpine fir as it heads southeast toward the drainage from the cirque. You have fine views down to Highwood Pass. Listen for hermit thrushes.

ROCK SANDWICH

The southwest ridge of Mt. Arethusa (2912 m) is a classic signature of front range geology. The Rundle Group of formations that comprise the mountain was tipped toward the vertical during mountain-building, 85 million-years-ago, when great sheets of rock were being driven northeastward. The rock fractured along thrust faults, the sheet behind each fracture being driven upward and over rocks ahead, to the northeast, creating what are now called dip-slope mountains. Alternating resistant (limestone-dolomite) and recessive (shale) layers create what appears to be a multi-layered sandwich, dropped on end. The mountain was not named for the nymph of Greek mythology, but for an ill-fated British battle cruiser, sunk in the 1916 Battle of Jutland, just two days after the craft was put to sea.

Loop Trail

The trail angles back to the northwest. The first larches appear at trailside just before the loop trail junction. Trail signs encourage you to keep straight ahead so that your hike will match the numbered interpretive stops, but feel free to be unfettered in your choice of route. Keeping straight ahead, the trail soon breaks through treeline into a heath meadow. Look for Columbian ground squirrels. Listen for white-crowned sparrows. You've done most of the climbing now; the trail ahead sidehills and undulates on its approach to the limestone benches at the apex of the loop. Complex lichen colonies cover the screes.

As everywhere in the Rockies, snowcover, wind, and temperature groom the vegetation in this valley, dictating what can grow, and where. Gullies offer shelter from the drying effects of wind, promoting growth; depressions collect cold air, stunting growth. Taller, more supple plants – able to withstand moving snow – grow on avalanche paths, offering browse for large mammals. Mat-like plants hug the ground in the open, a survival strategy to thwart the full blast of the wind. Many of the wildflowers have fuzzy stems and leaves – natural insulation to buffet the cold and to reduce moisture loss. Some of the trees flag the wind, others are wind-trained – a few branches curl around the trunk from the windward side to the leeward side. Except for the wet meadow in the base of the valley, much of the landscape is virtually desert. Water is frozen for much of the year; the poor, rocky soils drain rapidly. Wind and harsh sunlight quickly evaporate much of what water is available.

The outbound leg of the loop ends where the trail swings southeast (right) at a low headwall. The rock is limestone of the fossil-rich Mt. Head Formation. If you examine the boulders nearby, you may see bumps – the fossilized remains of horn corals that

TOO COOL

One of the creatures that lives in the Highwood Meadows is the rock crawler, a slender, wingless insect. The name "ice crawler" might be more appropriate, for these bugs of the genus *Grylloblatta* live in caves, under rocks, or on snow and ice, thriving at temperatures that cause most lifeforms to shut down. Only 10 species are known. They are thought to be related to cockroaches, mantids, and locusts. Rock crawlers eat other insects that become torpid on the snow. Because of where and how they live, rock crawlers probably survived glaciations that killed-off many contemporaries. So cold-adapted is this insect, if you were to place one in the palm of your hand (please don't), it would die from the effects of your body heat.

date to 350 million-years-ago. Looking downvalley, you can see Mt. Tyrwhitt (2876 m) on the west side of Highwood Pass. Reginald Tyrwhitt was a British naval commander in WWI.

When the valley is clear of snow, you can follow a rough track northeast from the apex of the loop for 700 m to a second headwall at the mouth of the cirque. But please keep to the trail. The route ascends beside a stream that bisects a meadow. The blooms of moss campion, sawwort, and alpine forget-me-not brighten the rocks. True to the name of the trail, I have seen a ptarmigan hen (the one in the photo) with four chicks here. Seeps on the second headwall feature travertine deposits. Travertine is thin limestone, deposited by algae as a byproduct of photosynthesis. From the top of the headwall, the view north reveals the upper part of the cirque on the slopes of Mt. Rae (3364 m) – the most recent "addition" to the list of 11,000-foot peaks in the Rockies. John Rae was a surgeon with the Hudson's Bay Company, and later participated in the search for the "lost" Franklin Expedition. It was Rae who brought back to England the unwelcome (but true) news that at least some of Franklin's men had resorted to cannibalism. For this, he was vilified. James Hector, however, thought highly of Rae, and named the peak for him. The valley contains a rock glacier. Travel beyond this point is on a sketchy trail exposed to rockfall – not recommended.

Leaving the loop trail's high point, you rock-hop the stream and descend the south flank of the valley. The trail is atop the crest of a ridge of rocks – a combination of glacial moraine and a rockslide debris from Mt. Arethusa. Pikas and hoary marmots inhabit the boulderfields nearby. Hop the stream again at treeline. A sidetrail leads south (left) to a bench and a viewpoint that overlooks a cascade. The rock exposed is sandy dolomite of the Kananaskis Formation. This waterfall marks the true mouth of the hanging valley that contains Ptarmigan Cirque. It was near here that, during the Late Wisconsin Glaciation, the Ptarmigan Cirque glacier merged with the main valley glacier that once filled Highwood Pass. This point is known as the "break in slope." The slope beneath – as you know from the approach – is steeper than the slope above.

Tree islands

Return

After a short descent through forest, you meet the approach trail at the loop junction. Turn southwest (left) to return to the trailhead. If you have the time, detour north (right) at the Highwood Meadows trail junction, 400 m from the parking area. Interpretive signs along this short trail describe the tough life of plants and animals in the upper subalpine life zone.

SNOW-BIRD, ROCK-BIRD

The white-tailed ptarmigan (TAR-mih-gan) is a ground-dwelling grouse-like bird of the high country. Its feathers change colour from white in winter, to a mottled brown, gray, and black in summer. The tail is always white. Males have a reddish-orange comb over each eye during mating season. In winter, feathers grow on all surfaces of the feet, and the toes grow longer, creating natural, insulated snowshoes that decrease the bird's penetration into snow. Ptarmigan are well-camouflaged but unwary, advertising their presence with clucking and soft cooing. The clutch of up to ten chicks typically dwindles drastically through predation. Ptarmigan are non-migratory, foraging for berries, buds, flowers, and bugs. They gather into small flocks in winter. Skiers in the high country occasionally encounter snowbanks with many sets of blinking, black eyes – ptarmigan bedded down. When alarmed, these birds make explosive bursts of flight.

Lineham Ridge, Tamarack Trail

Waterton Lakes National Park

Established in 1895 as Canada's fourth national park, Waterton Lakes includes 505 km² of the front ranges in the extreme south-western corner of Alberta. The park's theme is "where the mountains meet the prairie." Many viewpoints along the park's 200 km of trails reveal remarkable vistas of the front ranges rising from the plains.

Waterton Lakes National Park is 264 km south of Calgary via highways 22 and 6; and 130 km south-west of Lethbridge via Highway 5. There is passenger bus service to Lethbridge, Pincher Creek, and Fort Macleod. Shuttle service may be available from those places to the park. Otherwise, access is by car. The village of Waterton Park offers supplies, services, and accommodation. The nearby towns of Cardston and Pincher Creek also cater to travellers. The park information centre is just north of Waterton Park village, on Highway 5.

The Waterton Classic Hikes include the Forum Lake – Wall Lake outing in neighbouring Akamina-Kishinena Provincial Park, BC. Access is the same as for Waterton. There is one backcountry campground in the BC park. To reserve a campsite, phone 800-689-9025. The park has no other developed facilities.

233

59. Bertha Lake

Bertha Lake

TRAIL THUMBNAIL

Day-hike or overnight

Route	Elev. (m)	Dist. (km)
Trailhead	1295	0
Upper Waterton Lake viewpoint	1410	1.4
Lakeshore jct	1400	1.5
Lower Bertha Falls	1475	2.9
Trail summit	1767	5.4
Bertha Lake CG	1755	5.7

Trailhead
In Waterton Park village on Evergreen Avenue,
500 m south of Cameron Falls

Maps
NTS: 82 H/4
Gem Trek: *Waterton Lakes National Park*

Best lighting: early morning at the east shore,
afternoon at the west shore

The Bertha Lake trail climbs steeply to Waterton's most accessible backcountry lake, a charming body of water, surrounded by lush forest. The hike is a delight for botanists.

Trailhead to Lower Bertha Falls

The initial climb is gradual, through a mixed montane forest on the lakeshore trail toward Bertha Creek. Fleabane, false hellebore, white geranium, bear grass, harebell, yarrow, paintbrush, fireweed, and pearly everlasting line the trail. Trembling aspen, mountain ash, cottonwood poplar, white birch, Douglas maple, and lodgepole pine are the common trees. Many of the pines are standing-dead. A mountain pine beetle infestation between 1976 and 1983 killed 50 percent of the lodgepole pines in Waterton, and as many as 75 percent of the trees in some stands. The beetles are at work again; all of Waterton's pines are now in jeopardy.

Severe winds have toppled other trees in this forest. Beetle infestations and blowdowns open the forest canopy and allow new growth. The sunlit areas that result support shrubs and wildflowers, and are important feeding areas for many large mammals. One of the common shrubs here is buffaloberry, whose red and amber berries are a staple food of black bears.

At km 1.4, a short path leads straight ahead to a viewpoint that overlooks Upper Waterton Lake. Across the lake to the southeast is Mt. Cleveland (3190 m), highest mountain in Glacier National Park. Conservationist George Bird Grinnell named the peak in 1898 for Grover Cleveland, then U.S. president. Cleveland had established the Lewis and Clark Forest Reserve the year before. The reserve included the area that became Glacier National Park in 1910. The limber pines that formerly grew at this viewpoint have been killed by white pine blister rust. Look for brown-eyed Susans here.

In August 1935, a fire consumed the forest between Boundary Creek and Bertha Creek along the west shore of Upper Waterton Lake. The conflagration, which threatened the village, was extinguished by the efforts of 533 firefighters, aided considerably by wet weather and a change of wind. The young pine forest that you see along the lakeshore is a legacy of this burn.

Backtrack to the main trail and descend to the west. Keep straight ahead at the junction in 40 m to approach Bertha Creek. The trail contours around a limestone bluff of the Altyn Formation, whose layers plunge toward the southwest. This is the dip of the underlying rock formations in Waterton. Whether you look at a small cliff or a mountainside, you will see this orientation consistently exposed. Wild bergamot, Jacob's ladder, creeping beardtongue, stonecrop, yellow false dandelion, and bearberry grow on the dry, gritty soils at the base of the bluff.

Along Bertha Creek the vegetation quickly changes to species characteristic of damp subalpine forests. A prominent storm track along the 49th parallel brings significant moisture into the southern part of the park, creating damp micro-habitats that support 100 vegetation species more typically found in BC. Waterton has the most diverse vegetation of any Rocky Mountain park. It is home to more than 1000 native vascular plant species – 55 percent of the total

VARIATION

• You can add a 4.6 km loop around the lake.

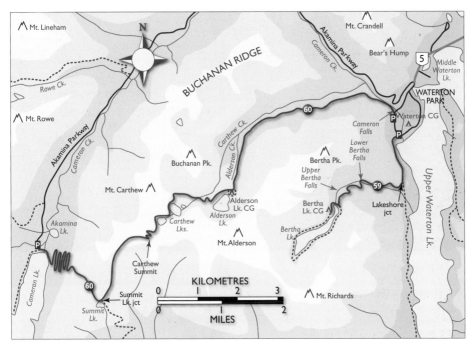

BEAR GRASS

The showy, white bloom of bear grass is the floral emblem of Waterton Lakes National Park – the only national park in Canada in which it is found. Growing from a stem that is 50 cm to 120 cm tall, bear grass blooms grace meadows throughout Waterton from mid-June to August. Some bear grass plants exhibit a peculiar crook in the upper stem. It is thought these bends occur when the flower head matures during wet periods. Individual bear grass plants bloom sporadically, averaging one to three times in every ten years. Adjacent plants often bloom together, so the local "intensity" of the displays varies greatly from year to year.

Bighorn sheep, deer, and elk eat bear grass flowers. Mountain goats eat the mature leaves, and bears eat the younger leaves in spring. First Peoples wove the leaves into baskets and items of clothing. Although the leaves appear grass-like, the plant is a member of the lily family. Bear grass does not grow north of Crowsnest Pass.

found in Alberta. Of these, 400 species are mosses and lichens. Of all the species, 179 are rare in Alberta, 22 are unrecorded in the province outside the park, and two are found nowhere else in Canada. Western yew and devil's club formerly grew along lower Bertha Creek, but have not been seen for many years.

Lower Bertha Falls cascades over another outcrop of the Altyn Formation. At the base of the falls, the water is eroding into the seam between two upturned edges of rock. This creates a natural gutter that captures the flow, channelling the water away to the southeast, along a right-angle turn in the stream course. When bedrock dictates the flow of a stream in this fashion, it is said to have structural control. The step-like cascades downstream are also caused by upturned edges of rock in the creek bed.

Lower Bertha Falls to Bertha Lake

Cross the bridge at the falls and begin a switchback ascent on the lower slopes of Mt. Richards. This is excellent bear habitat. Make lots of noise. After about 2 km, you have views through the trees to Upper Bertha Falls, which are 75 m high. The trail angles away from the falls. From openings in the trees you can look east to Upper Waterton Lake and Vimy Peak (2385 m). The trail makes one final switchback along the base of a cliff before descending to the mouth of the hanging valley that contains Bertha Lake. The campground is 110 m beyond the outlet stream bridge.

Lower Bertha Falls

With an area of 30.2 ha and a depth of 50.3 m, Bertha Lake is the second largest and second deepest of Waterton's high country lakes. The lake is dammed by upturned rock strata, and occupies a hollow eroded in the shattered shales of the Grayson Formation. A tremendous cliff of Siyeh (SIGH-yuh) Formation limestone and dolomite, 500 m high, forms the backdrop to the lake. This cliff extends from Mount Alderson (2692 m) on the northwest, to Mt. Richards (2377 m) on the south. Bertha Peak (2454 m) stands to the north of the outlet. A waterfall tumbles down its south slopes.

It is thought that the name "Bertha" was originally applied to the lake that we know today as Alderson Lake. Bertha Ekelund was an early Waterton resident, reportedly jailed for issuing counterfeit "prescriptions" for alcohol during Prohibition. This made her into a folk hero. She was also a sometime companion of Joe Cosley. A true mountain man, Cosley was, at various times between 1890 and 1930, a prospector, a trapper, and a Glacier park ranger and guide. He probably knew the landscape of Waterton-Glacier better than anyone else in his day. Cosley named many features for himself, his friends, and – in the case of Bertha and other lakes – for his occasional female companions. The lake had formerly been known as "Spirit Lake."

Colour in the rocks, colour in the flowers, colour in the skies! Colour indeed seems to be the principal attribute of Waterton Lakes National Park; even its history is marked by that quality.

Donald Buchanan; *Canadian Geographic Journal*, February 1933

CIRCUIT OF BERTHA LAKE, 4.6 KM

To fully appreciate Bertha Lake and its valley, allow time for a circuit of the lake. However, use caution; the upper valley is excellent bear habitat. You may also see a cougar or wolverine here. From the outlet bridge, follow a good trail along the north shore of the lake, alternating between meadows and stands of ancient subalpine forest. In early to mid-July, there are tremendous displays of bear grass here.

The trail crosses two red bluffs of Grinnell Formation argillite that dip toward the lake. The bluffs feature mariposa lily, stonecrop, umbrella plant, creeping beardtongue, meadowsweet, and spotted saxifrage. Together with shrubby cinquefoil and juniper, these plants give the illusion of montane meadow at a subalpine elevation. Between the two bluffs the trail follows the lakeshore with a gravelly beach of red argillite underfoot. In wetter areas, you may see red monkey flowers.

Rock-hop the principal inlet stream. The trail climbs over a bluff, crosses two more inlet streams, and descends to a small pond beyond the western shore of the lake. An abandoned stream course tells of days-gone-by when this pond fed directly into the larger lake. The stupendous cliffs above are home to mountain goats.

The return trail follows the south shore and cuts through several argillite gullies. From the open scree slope near the lake's east end, you obtain fine views of the lake, which is only 50 m wide at this spot. The circuit concludes at the stand of dead trees near the lake's outlet. Climb up to the approach trail to hike out, or cross the outlet bridge to return to the campground.

60. Carthew – Alderson

Carthew Lakes

The Carthew-Alderson trail traces a spectacular route from Cameron Lake to Waterton Park village. It immerses you in ancient forests, takes you across an alpine ridgecrest, and visits five backcountry lakes. The vistas span everything from mountain top to prairie. The trail is usually passable by mid-June, however the slopes north of Carthew Summit can be snowbound into July. Avoid this outing during poor weather and when thunderstorms are forecast. You share the trail with horses.

Trailhead to Summit Lake

The trail begins at the outlet of Cameron Lake in the heart of a dense subalpine forest. Engelmann spruce, subalpine fir, false hellebore, cow parsnip, foam-flower, water birch, bear grass, arnica, queen's cup, thimbleberry, feathermosses, grouseberry, and ferns grow at trailside. In a few places, you may see red monkey flowers, whose attractive blooms are frequented by hummingbirds. As you climb toward Summit Lake you pass some of the oldest trees in the park, aged 250-300 years. As elsewhere in Waterton, there are many standing-dead trees. Tree lichens, notably *Bryoria* species and wolf lichen, cling to their branches.

Constructed in 1910, the trail to Summit Lake illustrates how trailbuilders can tackle a formidable slope, yet create a walking surface that is seldom steep. Long switchbacks across this 50-degree side-slope produce a gentle, well-graded ascent. Through breaks in the trees you enjoy views of Cameron Lake, Akamina Lake, and Akamina Pass. *Akamina* (ah-kah-MEE-nah) is a Ktunaxa (toon-AWK-ah) word that means either: "high bench land," "watershed," "mountain pass," or "valley."

TRAIL THUMBNAIL

Day-hike or overnight; see map, p. 235

Route	Elev.	Dist.
	(m)	(km)
Trailhead	1661	0
Summit Lake jct	1931	4.3
Carthew Summit	2311	7.9
Upper Carthew Lake	2195	9.3
Lower Carthew Lake	2159	9.9
Alderson Lake jct	1811	13.1
Alderson Lake CG	1811	+0.2
Cameron Falls trailhead	1295	19.9

Trailhead
Follow the Akamina Parkway for 16 km from Waterton Park village to the parking area at Cameron Lake. The trailhead is across the footbridge at the outlet of Cameron Lake. Daily shuttle service (fee charged) is available to Cameron Lake. Inquire at the park information centre.

Maps
NTS: 82 G/1, 82 H/4
Gem Trek: *Waterton Lakes National Park*

At km 3.7 the trail levels and traverses through treeline forest toward the Summit Lake junction. Open meadows here are filled almost entirely with bear grass. The meadows are frost hollows that stunt the growth, hence most plants do not support stalks and blooms. You will see some fine examples of ripple rock at trailside.

At km 4.3 you reach the Summit Lake junction. Summit Lake is nearby; a shallow kettle pond, often

CAMERON LAKE

Early morning is a great time to appreciate Cameron Lake. The lake is 39 m deep and has an area of 17.2 ha. It occupies a hollow excavated by glacial ice, and is dammed by a glacial moraine. The lake commemorates Donald Cameron, who led the British party that surveyed the international boundary in 1874. The summit of Mt. Custer (2707 m) at the south end of the lake lies entirely within Glacier National Park, Montana. The mountain was not named for the famous general, but for Henry Custer, a topographer with the U.S. Boundary Survey who worked in this area in 1860 or 1861. Grizzly bears frequent the avalanche paths at the south end of the lake.

VARIATION

• Day-hike to Carthew Summit; 15.8 km return.

teeming with bugs. You may see mule deer, licking at the mineral-rich mud. Mt. Custer and Chapman Peak (2867 m) are reflected in the lake on calm days. Robert Chapman was a superintendent of Glacier National Park in 1912. Some glaciologists believe that Summit Lake once drained northwest into the Akamina Valley. Glacial overdeepening of the Cameron Lake basin altered drainage patterns. Today, Summit Lake drains south into Boundary Creek, in Montana.

Summit Lake to Carthew Summit

At the Summit Lake junction, turn northeast (left). After a gradual climb of about 500 m, the trail traverses beneath a rock bluff decorated with bear grass, creeping beardtongue, fleabane, and white draba. The surrounding forest contains Lyall's larch trees. The north fork of Boundary Creek drains the basin south of the trail. The surrounding slopes support a ghostly forest of ancient standing-dead trees.

The trail breaks through treeline and contours across a steep, avalanche-swept slope, climbing gradually toward Carthew Summit. From the open scree slopes you have pleasing views southwest over lush, wet meadows. This foreground contrasts with the forbidding north face of Chapman Peak beyond. Lake Wurdeman – a textbook example of a cirque lake – lies at the base of the peak. The lake's name commemorates yet another topographer with the U.S. Boundary Survey, J.V. Wurdeman. Piikani (Peigan) First Peoples knew the lake as "Bird Rattle Lake," after one of their warriors.

The red rock underfoot is argillite (ARE-jill-ite) of the 1.3 to 1.5 billion-year-old Kintla Formation. Argillite was created from muddy sediments that were deposited on a river delta. The sediments in this rock were exposed to air after deposition, and the iron "rusted." In cases where the iron did not oxidize, the resulting argillite is green. Kintla Formation argillite is thinly layered and easily eroded. It comprises the many colourful scree ridges in the western part of Waterton Lakes National Park.

The final climb to Carthew Summit is on a series of long switchbacks. Scorpionweed, sky pilot, yellow draba, and alpine forget-me-not dot the red screes. Please follow the orange painted markers and keep to the beaten path. You can see Summit Lake and Lake Nooney, to the west and south, respectively.

The scenic climax of this hike bursts into view as you crest Carthew Summit. Framed between

the ridges of Mount Carthew (2420 m) and Mount Alderson (2692 m), the Carthew Lakes lead your eye through a rugged hanging valley to the distant prairie. Although glaciers are now absent from Waterton, their legacy in creating this exceptional landscape is everywhere. By their arrangement, the Carthew Lakes are known to glaciologists as a glacial cirque staircase, or *paternoster lakes*. The lakes occupy basins eroded by glacial ice as it flowed down the valley. Each basin is at a progressively lower elevation.

The screes that flank Carthew Summit feature roseroot, Sandberg's wild parsley, and sky pilot. The pygmy (dwarf) poppy also grows here. This yellow-flowered plant is rare in Canada. Most of the places that it grows are in Waterton. Lt. William Carthew was a Canadian land surveyor who worked with the Interprovincial Boundary Survey when it delineated the Alberta-BC boundary between 1913 and 1925. As part of his duties, he climbed Mt. Carthew in 1914.

Many hikers ramble south a short distance from Carthew Summit and scamper onto the bluff that affords views south over Boundary Creek. Avoid this high point if poor weather is approaching.

Carthew Summit to Alderson Lake

Snow patches may initially complicate your descent from Carthew Summit to Upper Carthew Lake. At first, the trail angles slightly northeast. Then it switchbacks to the southeast to skirt the largest of the snow patches above the west shore of Upper Carthew Lake. Please keep to the beaten path. For your safety, stay off large snow patches.

The trail follows the north shore of Upper Carthew Lake to an ancient kruppelholz forest at the outlet. Compressive forces during mountain building thrust rock layers upward to the northeast. The resistant leading edges of some thrusts have endured as the natural dams that impound many of Waterton's backcountry lakes, as is the case here.

The trail switchbacks down alongside cascades between the upper and lower lakes. Rock-hop the outlet stream to its south side. As you descend to the west shore of Lower Carthew Lake, you will probably encounter more snow. The trail makes a hairpin turn to the north (left) to follow the west and north shores of the lake. Rock-hop the inlet stream. When the lake level is high, you may have to traverse some rocks just above the water. Two bodies of water comprise Lower Carthew Lake. The largest is 7.3 ha in area and 11 m deep. A dam of rockslide debris separates it from the much smaller Carthew Pond.

The trail gains the crest of the cliff that separates the Carthew Lakes from Alderson Lake. Wildflowers that prefer dry habitats cling to the thin soils here – stonecrop, rocky mountain goldenrod, spotted

> *This is what I have seen in my dreams, this is the country for me.*
>
> Kootenai Brown; 1865

Alderson Lake

MULE DEER

The mule deer is the more numerous of the two species of deer in the Canadian Rockies, and is abundant in Waterton. To distinguish a mulie from a white-tailed deer, look first at the tail. The mule deer's tail is narrow and white with a black tip. The white-tailed deer's tail is broad, and is the colour of the coat above, and white underneath. The antlers of mule deer bucks are equally forked, whereas those of white-tailed bucks branch upward from a forward reaching beam. The coats of both species are reddish-brown in summer, changing to gray in winter. The rumps are white.

Deer graze on grasses and wildflowers in summer. In autumn and winter, they browse on twigs and buds. In late winter, mule deer may resort to stripping tree bark to get at the sugary cambium layer beneath. The cougar is their principal predator.

Waterton's mule deer are not shy. Accustomed to humans and to handouts, many have lost their wildness. But please remember that these animals can inflict serious injury by kicking with their front hooves. Do not approach a doe with fawns, or any deer during the autumn rut. If a deer approaches you, scare it away by shouting, by waving your arms, and, if necessary, by throwing things at it.

saxifrage, and scorpionweed. The trail angles north and then east, descending steeply into the basin between Mt. Carthew and Buchanan Peak (2606 m). The cliff is limestone and dolomite of the Siyeh (SIGH-yuh) Formation, which contains an intrusion of igneous rock called the Purcell Sill. You may see eroded fragments of this dark, crystalline, lava-like rock on the trail.

The outflow from the Carthew Lakes cascades in a fine waterfall. Rock-hop its stream. Continue the steep descent through a ragged kruppelholz forest and across scree slopes, with views of Alderson Lake ahead.

If you look carefully at the west shore of Alderson Lake, you will see a series of remnant terminal moraines. These moraines were probably formed during the Little Ice Age, which ended in the mid-1800s. The glaciers responsible have since disappeared. Glaciers in other localities in the Rockies advanced as much as 3 km during the Little Ice Age, and often extended beyond the cirques that housed them. Evidence shows that no glaciers in Waterton have advanced beyond their cirque basins in the last 10,000 years. The cliffs above Alderson Lake are a good place to look for mountain goats.

The trail turns northeast above the north shore of Alderson Lake. The slopes below the trail are festooned with bear grass. You might expect that Carthew Creek, flowing through the meadows to the north of the trail, would empty into Alderson Lake. Alderson Lake has been impounded by a moraine. The trail travels along its crest. This moraine keeps Carthew Creek away from the lakeshore.

With a maximum depth of 60 m, Alderson Lake is the deepest of Waterton's high country lakes. It has an area of 10.2 ha. The lake was probably the original "Bertha Lake." Its name was changed in 1915 to honour Lt. General E.A.H. Alderson, who commanded Canadian Forces in France during WWI.

At km 13.1 you reach the Alderson Lake junction. You have the option of staying overnight at the campground on the lakeshore. However, most hikers do not want to haul a heavy pack over Carthew Summit to camp here, when Waterton Park village is only a few hours away. The campground is 250 m east (right) of the junction. It can be a buggy place in mid-summer.

Alderson Lake to Cameron Falls

A few hundred metres beyond the campground junction, an alternate route to the campground branches east (right). Keep left. The lush upper subalpine forest along Alderson Creek is similar to the one at the trailhead near Cameron Lake, except most of the trees are not as old. The trail bisects numerous avalanche paths that are excellent bear habitat. Make lots of noise here as visibility is limited. If you look up the valley from open slopes, you can see the waterfall on the headwall below the Carthew Lakes. Rock-hop tributary streams as required.

The descent of this valley may seem interminable if you expended all your energy earlier in the day. However, it is hardly a "boring walk in the woods." As you lose elevation, notice the change from species of the damp subalpine forest to dry montane forest species, including Douglas-fir and lodgepole pine. About halfway along the valley, just to the north of the trail, look for a massive Engelmann spruce tree, 1.4 m in diameter at its base.

At long last, the trail switchbacks down and you can see Waterton Park village through open forest. The trail parallels a fence at the brink of Cameron Creek canyon. In the creek bed you can see structures built for flood control, and the former water supply for the village. In one 12-month period, the temperamental creek exhibited a 1000-fold increase in volume of flow between November and the following July. In June 1964, runoff from Cameron Creek and other tributaries raised the level of Upper Waterton Lake 2.8 m above its previous record high, inundating Waterton Park village. The most recent serious flood was in 1995. Sediments deposited by Cameron Creek have built the alluvial fan on which the village is situated.

At an unmarked junction, turn sharply north (left), and descend into a cottonwood grove at trail's end, Cameron Falls. The 10 m high falls are being eroded into an outcrop of 1.5 billion-year-old Waterton Formation limestone, the oldest sedimentary rock known in Alberta.

LIGHTNING!

Waterton experiences more electrical storms than other areas in the Rockies. You should avoid the park's passes and high ridges when the weather forecast calls for thunderstorms. Time your outings so that you are on your way down from summits and high points by 1:00 pm, after which time thunderstorms are more common. However, any time that you see a thunderstorm approaching, or hear a buzzing sound emanating from metallic objects or your hair, it is time to descend quickly.

What do you do if you are caught in a high place during a thunderstorm? First, descend at least 100 m vertically from a summit or ridgecrest, avoiding open meadows, lakes, glaciers, and snow patches. Do not seek shelter under isolated rock pinnacles or trees. Crouch at the base of a cliff or in a depression that does not have tall trees or large boulders nearby. Keep 1 m away from the cliff or depression walls, as these channel the current of a local strike. Stay out of shallow caves. The metallic objects you carry will not attract a lightning strike. However, they may cause burns if there is a strike within 30 m. Remove these items from your pack and your pockets.

LATE-LYING SNOW

The novelty of encountering snow patches in July and August lures many unwary hikers into trouble in places like the basin above Upper Carthew Lake. Because these snow patches have been through many freeze and thaw cycles since the previous winter – and perhaps even the winter before that – they contain ice. This ice sometimes appears snow-like – especially near the edges – where footing can be treacherous.

If you fall on the granular snow and ice, you may cut yourself badly. In addition, you may begin to slide downslope, out of control toward boulderfields. If you are wearing shorts and short sleeves, you will be, at best a mess, at worst a stretcher case. Unless you have an ice axe in hand, are competent at using it for self-arrest, and are dressed appropriately, stay off late-lying snow. The reddish tinge in these snow patches is called watermelon snow, and is caused by algae with a red pigment.

61. Crypt Lake

Crypt Lake

No other outing in the Rockies can top Crypt Lake for its variety of experiences. You begin by crossing Upper Waterton Lake by boat. Then you follow a steep trail from montane shoreline to treeline through a valley of waterfalls. The diversity of the approach culminates with a 25 m crawl through a limestone tunnel, and an airy traverse on an imposing cliff. As if all this isn't enough, you can follow a rough track around Crypt Lake and cross the international border into the U.S..

Crypt Landing to Crypt Lake Headwall

From Crypt Landing, head south and begin a switch-back ascent toward the drainage of Hell Roaring Creek. The forest near the trailhead is extremely damp and diverse, with a mixture of montane and subalpine tree species – Douglas-fir, white spruce, white birch, Douglas maple, and subalpine fir. Note the large Douglas-firs with bark cloaked in tree lichens. You would not normally expect to see a damp forest at a low elevation in Waterton. However, the bay of Crypt Landing is sheltered from the ever-present winds that would otherwise dry the soils and foliage. Thimbleberry, false Solomon's seal, fairybells, arnica, and western meadowrue are common in the undergrowth.

At km 0.4 you reach the lower Hell Roaring Falls junction. This sidetrip is best left until your return, when the falls and their canyon may be sunlit. At approximately km 1.5, the main trail switchbacks across an open, west-facing slope, surrounded by a more typical low-elevation Waterton forest – one dominated by lodgepole pine with sun-loving flowers in the undergrowth. This slope provides open views of Upper Waterton Lake and the valley of Bertha Creek. Please do not shortcut the switchbacks.

VARIATIONS

- Make a circuit of Crypt Lake; 1.8 km.
- Visit Hell Roaring Falls; add 500 m to the outing.

The trail traverses southeast into the drainage of Hell Roaring Creek to contour above the creek through open pine forest. Buffaloberry is common here. Black bears and grizzly bears frequent this south-facing slope. Use caution. "Hell Roaring" is a most appropriate name for the turbulent creek. The name was probably connected with a mining claim in this area in the late 1800s. Keep straight ahead at the upper Hell Roaring Falls junction. The grade eases and the trail contours in and out of drainage gullies. Rock-hop as necessary. Across Hell Roaring Creek, Twin Falls cascades from a hanging valley on the north slope of Mt. Boswell (2454 m).

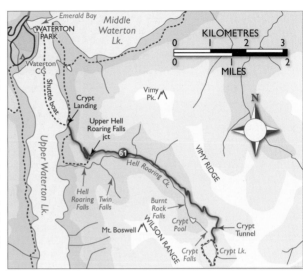

The trail swings south, following Hell Roaring Creek to its sources. You cross more avalanche slopes and pass through another pocket of damp subalpine forest. The shales underfoot have been washed down in flash-floods from the mountainside to the east, creating an alluvial fan that has spread through the forest. When you reach the stream that has created the fan, you get your first view of Burnt Rock Falls.

In the next 3 km the trail climbs approximately 300 m and is often rocky. As you switchback away from the creek, you get several close views of Burnt Rock Falls. The red or "burnt" rock at the base of the falls is iron-rich, Grinnell Formation argillite. Above it is older, pale, Altyn Formation limestone. Why is older rock above younger rock? The Mt. Crandell Thrust separates the two formations. During mountain building, the bedrock underlying this area fractured, and the Altyn Formation slid upward and northeastward over younger layers along the fault. Note the massive hollow eroded into the weak Grinnell Formation at the base of the falls. The Altyn Formation resists the flow of water and endures as the brink of the waterfall.

As you draw equal with Burnt Rock Falls, use care as you rock-hop the tributary stream that crosses the trail on a bare rock slab. Now Crypt Falls comes into view, tumbling 175 m down the Crypt Lake headwall. Crypt Pool lies at the base. The remainder

WINDY WATERTON

More often than not, it is windy on Upper Waterton Lake. The average daily wind speed at Waterton Park town is 32.5 km per hour, and gusts of 180 km per hour have been recorded in winter. At such times, spray from the lake collects on the windows of the Prince of Wales Hotel 150 m away, and 40 m above the lakeshore. Chinooks cause many of the windy days in winter and spring. A chinook (shih-NOOK) occurs when a Pacific storm system sheds its moisture on the western slopes of the Rockies. The air is forced high to clear the crest of the range. As the dry air sweeps down the eastern slopes and its pressure increases, its temperature rises 1.5°C for each decrease in elevation of 100 m. Chinooks are heralded by a cloud known as a chinook arch, which often spans the length of the southern mountain front. At the same time, lenticular clouds may form over the mountains to the west.

Chinook means "snow eater." The wind can raise local temperatures dramatically. The most precipitous rise recorded in Canada was 40°C in 20 minutes at Lethbridge. Calgary's record is 30°C in four hours. If a chinook weather event terminates with the arrival of an Arctic front, an abrupt *drop* in temperature can take place. The U.S. all-time record for this occurred at Browning, Montana in January 1916, when the temperature fell from +7°C to -49°C in 24 hours. There is no corresponding Canadian record available.

In a typical winter there will be 30 Chinook days at the mountain front. Chinooks that last several days can warm the air as far away as Medicine Hat in southeastern Alberta. During a Chinook the weather in the mountains is usually unsettled. Chinooks reduce snow accumulation at the mountain front and in the front ranges, and are a key element in the development of montane vegetation communities. Elk, bighorn sheep, and deer depend on grasslands here to survive the winter. The winds also prevent the formation of ice on the Waterton Lakes in some years.

of the steep climb to the headwall is across avalanche gullies. Bear grass, and cottonwood poplar trees in kruppelholz form, grow at trailside.

Crypt Lake Headwall to Crypt Lake

Rock-hop or ford the creek below the headwall, and follow the trail that angles southwest through the boulderfield. Look and listen for pikas. You may also hear the shrill whistle of hoary marmots, and with luck see these large rodents, the self-appointed guardians of the Crypt Tunnel.

Near the eastern portal of the tunnel, a sign warns you to stay on the trail – not that you have much choice. The Crypt Tunnel is a natural, water worn fissure that extends laterally for 25 m through the limestone of the Crypt Lake headwall. The tunnel has been slightly enlarged to ease passage. Gain the eastern portal by climbing a 2 m metal ladder. The tunnel narrows and angles down toward the west. When at its narrowest point, you will be obliged to crawl on your hands and knees. Two cautions: watch for ice on the tunnel floor, and do not enter the tunnel wearing a bulky pack – particularly one with an external frame. If your pack gets caught, take it off and push it ahead of you. Exit the western portal over an awkward 1.3 m rock step.

The section just beyond the western portal of the Crypt Tunnel gives this hike its notorious reputation. For 50 m, you traverse and ascend an exposed cliff, which may intimidate those afraid of heights. Use the handy steel cable. Take care not to bump your pack against the cable or its anchor posts, especially during descent. This could throw you off balance.

The airy traverse beyond the tunnel delivers you to the crest of the Crypt Lake headwall. Tufts of pink mountain heather grace the clearings in the upper subalpine forest. Looking north along Hell Roaring Creek, you can see Vimy Ridge and Vimy Peak (2385 m), named for the ridge in France taken by Canadian forces in WWI.

Crypt Falls

The final section of trail traverses beneath a low limestone bluff. At an unmarked junction, you may follow a sidetrail west to the underground outflow of the lake and the brink of Crypt Falls. Use caution. The main trail angles south, ascending an old watercourse that may have been Crypt Lake's outlet before the karst system developed. Descend gradually to the north shore of the lake.

Crypt Lake has an area of 13.5 ha and a maximum depth of 44 m. It occupies a cirque eroded into shales of the Grayson Formation. Ice lingers on the lake well into summer. The word "crypt" is derived from the Greek *kryptos*, which means "hidden." Mount Boswell, to the west, commemorates W.G. Boswell, a veterinary surgeon with the British Boundary Commission of 1872-76. The name was officially applied in 1917. Before that time, the mountain had been called Street Mountain, after Jack Street, a Mountie who died in an avalanche on its slopes. The cliffs of Mount Boswell are a good place to look for mountain goats.

SINKS AND SOLUTIONS

A series of upturned, glaciated limestone bluffs impounds Crypt Lake. Limestone is readily eroded by naturally acidic rainwater in a process called solution. Over time, cracks in limestone bedrock are deepened by rain and meltwater into fissures. The fissures connect into systems that create underground drainage channels called karst. Crypt Lake has no surface outlet. It drains through a karst system, and is known as a sink lake. The rock at trailside just before the lake contains *rillenkarren*, miniature grooves eroded by water.

This corner of the mountains appeared to be a very windy spot, and when it was not blowing much on the plain a strong breeze came from the south down the gorge in which is Upper Waterton Lake.

Thomas Blakiston; *Papers Relative to the Exploration of British North America*

A rough track, about 1.8 km long, leads around Crypt Lake, although during times of high runoff some of the route will be underwater. At its most southerly point, the track takes you into Glacier National Park, Montana. A portion of the circuit crosses the rubble-covered surface of a drift glacier at the water's edge. Use care. The southeast shore of the lake contains an ancient alluvial fan, now partially vegetated. Atop this, streams are depositing a newer alluvial fan. Subalpine meadows fringe the east shore.

The "undefended border" at the south end of Crypt Lake typifies the spirit of the Waterton-Glacier International Peace Park. Established in 1932 as a gesture of friendship between Canada and the United States, the two existing national parks were combined into the world's first peace park. Today, the parks work together on resource conservation issues and to serve visitors.

On a pleasant day, and after the exertions of the approach, you will be tempted to wile away the hours at Crypt Lake. But be sure to leave yourself enough time to catch your return boat from Crypt Landing.

Crypt Lake headwall

Hell Roaring Falls

On your return to the trailhead you may visit Hell Roaring Falls. From the upper junction, approximately 3 km from Crypt Landing, take the left-hand trail. This descends steeply to the canyon and falls, which have been eroded through colourful, vertically tilted rock. Bears frequent this area. As it angles away from the canyon, the trail offers a view over the alluvial fan at the mouth of Hell Roaring Creek. The trail then contours west above the lakeshore for 1 km, before joining the Crypt Lake trail, 400 m from the trailhead. This sidetrip will add about 500 m to the overall length of the outing.

62. Tamarack

Crown of the Continent

Although not as strenuous an outing as the Rockwall in Kootenay National Park, the Tamarack trail is cut from the same undulating cloth. This energetic excursion parallels the eastern slope of the continental divide, traversing the heads of three valleys, and crossing a mountain ridgecrest that provides a panoramic vista of the southern Rockies. It travels through excellent habitat for mountain goats, bighorn sheep, mule deer, cougars, and grizzly bears. The two campgrounds are located at backcountry lakes; sidetrails lead to other lakes. You share the

Tamarack trail with horses. Lineham Ridge, the apex of the trail, is the 7th-highest point reached on the Classic Hikes. It will be snow-plugged until mid-July in most years.

> ... In that portion of the Rocky Mountains comprised between the parallels of 45° and 54° north latitude, rise the four great rivers of the continent, namely, the Mackenzie, running north to the Arctic Ocean, the Saskatchewan east to Hudson's Bay, the Columbia west to the Pacific, and the Missouri to the Gulf of Mexico; thus we may say, that in a certain sense that portion of the mountains is the culminating point of North America, and I now, on the Kootanie Pass, stood as nearly as possible to the centre of it.
>
> Thomas Blakiston; August 21, 1858,
> *Papers Relative to the Exploration of British North America*

TRAIL THUMBNAIL

Overnight, 3-4 days

Route	Elev. (m)	Dist. (km)
Rowe-Tamarack trailhead	1600	0
Lower Rowe Lake jct	1940	3.9
Lower Rowe Lake	1950	+0.3
Rowe Meadow	2010	5.2
Upper Rowe Lakes jct	2015	5.5
Lineham Ridge Summit	2560	8.5
South fork of Blakiston Creek	1870	13.6
Lone Lake Summit	2250	15.7
Lone Lake and CG	1990	17.7
South Kootenay Pass jct	1940	21.5
Blakiston Creek jct	1935	21.6
Twin Lake Summit	2150	23.5
Lower Twin Lake jct	1975	24.7
Upper Twin Lake and CG	1970	24.9
Sage Pass jct	1970	25.0
Snowshoe CG, Lost Lake jct	1740	27.9
Lost Lake	1875	+1.9
Goat Lake jct	1569	31.7
Goat Lake and CG	2025	+2.6
Red Rock Canyon	1495	36.1

Trailhead
Follow the Akamina Parkway for 10.5 km from Waterton Park town to the Rowe-Tamarack trailhead.

Maps
NTS: 82 G/1
Gem Trek: *Waterton Lakes National Park*

Trailhead to Upper Rowe Lakes Junction

The trail begins on the alluvial fan that Rowe Creek has built at its confluence with Cameron Creek. The broad path leads uphill into a doghair pine forest. At the prominent corner at 0.3 km, you can see where Rowe Creek is eroding into the red argillite of the Grinnell Formation. The trail climbs away from the creek onto an open slope, where stonecrop, yarrow, umbrella plant, yellow beardtongue, low larkspur, and pearly everlasting grow. After re-entering subalpine forest, look for bear grass, thimbleberry, cow parsnip, queen's cup, and mariposa lily.

At approximately km 2.4, the trail emerges from forest onto avalanche slopes beneath the cliffs of Mt. Lineham. These slopes provide excellent food sources for bears and for mule deer. Views back down the valley include Buchanan Ridge (2400 m) and Mount Crandell (2381 m). At km 3.9, the sidetrail to Lower Rowe Lake branches south (left). It is 300 m to the lake's outlet. Walled by the east ridge of Mt. Rowe, and dammed by a rockslide, the lake beckons as a

rest stop. The inlet stream is a waterfall that drains the Upper Rowe Lakes. Hoary marmots and pikas whistle and eeeep from the talus slopes to the west.

Beyond this junction, the trail re-enters forest and crosses Rowe Creek several times before Rowe Meadow at km 5.2. Surrounded by the amphitheatre-like cliffs that connect Mt. Rowe to the south, with outliers of Mt. Lineham to the north, the meadow is home to a boisterous colony of Columbian ground squirrels and to swarms of horse flies. The trail leads southwest across the meadow to a bridge over Rowe Creek. The Upper Rowe Lakes junction is 20 m south of the bridge.

Upper Rowe Lakes Junction to Lone Lake

Rowe Meadow marks the end of smooth sailing for the next day and a half. There are no water sources in the next 8 km. Turn west (right) at the Upper Rowe Lakes junction, and begin a steep climb for 500 m onto a bench beneath the cliffs of the continental divide. The cliffs contain the two elements of the Siyeh (SIGH-yuh) Formation. The lower, more weathered part of the cliff is siltstone and sandstone. The upper, more blocky part is limestone and dolomite. Geologists in the U.S. have subdivided the Siyeh accordingly, calling the lower part the Empire Formation, and the upper part the Helena Formation. The Purcell Lava Sill – an injection of igneous rock – occurs in the Helena Formation as a thin, dark green or black layer. The Siyeh Formation is the backbone of the continental divide in Waterton. It flanks the Tamarack trail between here and Twin Lakes.

The grade moderates and the trail undulates through some depressions. Blazed as a horse route, the Tamarack trail makes many such superfluous climbs and descents in the next 20 km. The hard work created for hikers would be unnoticed by someone on horseback, although probably not by the horse. There are fine examples of ripple rock at

VARIATIONS

- Day-hike to the Upper Rowe Lakes; 15.4 km return.
- Exit along Blakiston Creek, 2 days; 31.7 km.
- Hike the route in reverse.
- Backpack the northern leg of the outing, camping at Goat Lake and Upper Twin Lake; 3 days, 27.6 km return.
- Make a shorter loop beginning and ending at Red Rock Canyon. Hike the Snowshoe trail to camp at Upper Twin Lake. Follow the Tamarack trail south to Blakiston Creek. Exit to Red Rock Canyon; 2 days, 24.7 km

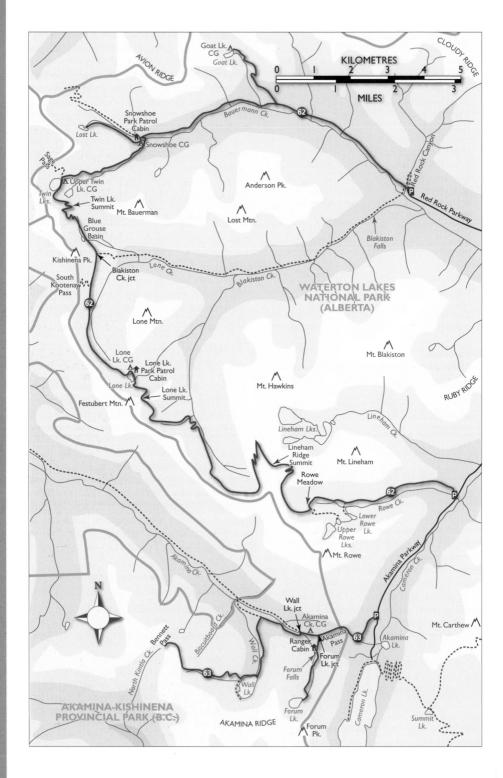

KILOMETRES

0 1 2 3 4 5

0 1 2 3

MILES

Goat Lk. CG
Goat Lk.

CLOUDY RIDGE

AVION RIDGE

Bauermann Ck.

62

Snowshoe Park Patrol Cabin

Lost Lk.

Snowshoe CG

Red Rock Canyon

Sage Pass

Upper Twin Lk. CG

Twin Lks.

Twin Lk. Summit

Mt. Bauerman

Anderson Pk.

Lost Mtn.

P

Red Rock Parkway

Blakiston Falls

Blue Grouse Basin

Kishinena Pk.

South Kootenay Pass

Blakiston Ck. jct

Lone Ck.

Blakiston Ck.

WATERTON LAKES NATIONAL PARK (ALBERTA)

62

Lone Mtn.

Mt. Blakiston

RUBY RIDGE

Lone Lk. CG

Lone Lk. Park Patrol Cabin

Lone Lk.

Lone Lk. Summit

Festubert Mtn.

Mt. Hawkins

Lineham Ck.

Lineham Lks.

Lineham Ridge Summit

Mt. Lineham

Rowe Meadow

62

P

Rowe Ck.

Lower Rowe Lk.

Upper Rowe Lks.

Mt. Rowe

Akamina Ck.

Cameron Ck.

Akamina Parkway

N

Bennett Pass

Biscuitboard Ck.

Wall Ck.

Wall Lk. jct

Akamina Ck. CG

Ranger Cabin

Akamina Pass

Forum Lk. jct

63

P

Akamina Lk.

Mt. Carthew

North Kintla Ck.

63

Wall Lk.

Forum Falls

Forum Lk.

Forum Pk.

Cameron Lk.

Summit Lk.

AKAMINA-KISHINENA PROVINCIAL PARK (B.C.)

AKAMINA RIDGE

trailside. The pockets of avalanche meadow contain glacier lilies and western anemone. From treeline, the trail begins a sweeping rise toward the west ridge of Mount Lineham, on a path beaten into red screes of the Kintla Formation. Use caution if you must cross late-lying snow patches. Scan the slopes above for bighorn sheep.

As you gain elevation, views open to the south, including Mount Custer (2707 m) and Chapman Peak (2867 m) south of Cameron Lake; and Mt. Cleveland (3190 m), the highest mountain in Glacier National Park. Soon, the three Rowe Lakes are visible, along with the spectacular peaks in western Glacier. Treeline is high on the northern slopes of Rowe basin, and the trail skirts a kruppelholz forest that features lifeless, silvery spars of wind-blasted, sun-bleached whitebark pine. Centuries old, these skeleton trees serve an important purpose – they anchor the screes, stabilizing thin soils and allowing other vegetation to take root.

Follow the painted orange markers as the trail switchbacks westward to Lineham Ridge Summit – the apex of the Tamarack trail. A remarkable 360° panorama takes in most of Waterton and Glacier national parks, BC's Akamina-Kishinena Provincial Park, and the Rockies north to Crowsnest Pass. The Lineham Lakes nestle in the basin to the northeast. The lakes are known individually as Water Cudgel, Hourglass, Ptarmigan, Channel, and Larch. John

Lineham was an Alberta businessman of the 1880s, with interests in oil, lumber, and ranching. Mt. Blakiston (2932 m), highest in Waterton, rises northeast of Lineham Basin. Thomas Blakiston explored here in 1858, with the Palliser Expedition.

After traversing north for 1 km, the trail switchbacks to the south and begins a steep descent on scree into the south fork valley of Blakiston Creek. Follow the orange trail markers. The pale mauve blooms of sky pilot dot the slopes. The grade moderates when you reach the larch forest in the valley bottom. The trail curves northwest and parallels the continental divide, heading north toward Lone Lake Summit. For the most part it is pleasant hiking through upper subalpine woods, with only a few muddy spots. You will appreciate the shade of the cliff on a hot day, and the fact that your toes are no longer being jammed into the fronts of your boots. Springs issue from the cliffs and may offer water. Soak your hat here if you need help to cool off.

The next climb is the most trying of this long, first day. The trail climbs 380 m in 2.1 km. Your first steady descent is *not* to Lone Lake campground. There is more uphill to come. Rock-hop streams as required. A section of trail is routed along a rocky, seasonal stream course. It will be a torrent during heavy rains.

From Lone Lake Summit on the east ridge of Festubert Mountain (2520 m), the nearby campground at Lone Lake beckons. The mountain

UPPER ROWE LAKES (2168 M), 1.2 KM

Keep straight ahead at the junction on the south side of Rowe Meadow. The trail switchbacks on an open slope and then ascends east into a treeline forest of Lyall's larch. After rounding the spur north of the valley that harbours the Upper Rowe Lakes, the trail descends to the southwest and delivers you to the shore of the upper lake. Its east shore features a kruppelholz larch forest. Kruppelholz means "crippled wood" in German. Another translation sometimes given is "elfin timber." These gnarled and ragged trees do suggest a fairytale forest.

As with most of Waterton's backcountry lakes, the two Upper Rowe Lakes are situated in a cirque at the head of a hanging valley. They occupy bedrock hollows scooped by a glacier. Although glacial ice is no longer present, perennial snow drifts cling to shady recesses along the south shores of the lakes. A natural dam of resistant rock separates the two lakes, which are connected by waterfalls. The outflow of the smaller lake cascades more than 150 m to Lower Rowe Lake. The abundance of larch trees and bear grass, and the opportunity to see bighorn sheep and mountain goats add to the charm of this destination. If you don't want to lug overnight packs here, consider day-hiking from the trailhead on a separate trip.

commemorates a village in France where Canadian troops fought in WWI. The view northeast features the whaleback scree peaks of northern Waterton.

You will probably cross a snow patch as you leave Lone Lake Summit. The descent switchbacks through a remarkable Lyall's larch forest. It is not often that you see this tree species in such a uniformly aged and widely spaced stand. Lyall's larch grows at high elevation on rocky soils, and consequently is seldom consumed by fire. Several of the trees here are more than a metre in diameter at their bases, indicating ages of perhaps 300 years or more.

The descent ends at an avalanche path that contains a conical mound of landslide debris. As you gain the southeast shore of Lone Lake, pause to admire the view northeast over the U-shaped valley of Blakiston Creek. Rock-hop the outlet of the lake, and follow the trail along the cliff edge, north to the campground.

Lone Lake is 13 m deep and has an area of 2.5 ha. Glaciologists speculate that it once drained entirely north into Lone Creek. A moraine subsequently blocked the drainage, forcing most of the outflow to spill northeast over the cliff into the upper reaches of Blakiston Creek. Don't forget your insect repellent. Lone Lake is bug heaven. A park patrol cabin is northeast of the lake.

Lone Lake

BIGHORN SHEEP

Rowe Basin is one of the better places to see bighorn sheep in the backcountry of the Rockies. A sheep's coat is tawny brown with a white rump patch and a dark brown tail. The bighorn ram stands about a metre tall at the shoulder and, when mature, has a set of thick brown horns that spiral forward. These horns are never shed. Together with the skull, they can account for 16 kg percent of a typical animal's 125 kg weight. It is possible to determine the approximate age of a ram by counting the annuli, or rings, on one of its horns. Each annulus contains a dark and light band, together representing one year of growth. The female sheep (ewe) grows horns too, however these are less spectacular, and curve backwards.

The rams flock together in high places during summer and early autumn. The dominant ram must constantly defend his place. Usually, this is done without battle in what is called the "present" (pree-ZENT) – when two rams turn their heads sideways, to allow each to inspect the horns of the other. As the autumn rut approaches and the issue of who will breed with a harem of ewes becomes more crucial, diplomacy wanes. The rams duel, charging headlong at each other and meeting with a mighty crash. Thick armour bones beneath the horns usually prevent serious injury. However, duels to the death do take place.

Grasses are the most important foods for bighorn sheep. The animal cannot tolerate snow depths of more than 0.3 m that limit its travel and access to food. Hence, wind-scoured slopes in the front ranges offer the best winter habitat for bighorns. Waterton's sheep periodically suffer die-offs caused by parasites or by hard winters. Grizzly bears, wolves, and cougars are the animal's principal predators. They often achieve success by forcing a sheep to run over a cliff. Poaching along the western boundary of Waterton also takes a toll on these animals.

Bighorn sheep are generally accustomed to people, and will often allow hikers to approach closely. This puts you and the sheep in peril. With their horns and sharp hooves, sheep can inflict serious injury. Accustomed to nutrition-poor handouts, sheep may not be able to endure a hard winter. If a sheep approaches you, scare it away.

THE CROWN OF THE CONTINENT

George Bird Grinnell, the conservationist who was the strongest proponent for the establishment of Glacier National Park, Montana, first coined the phrase, "Crown of the Continent." Grinnell later founded the Audubon Society.

Grinnell envisioned a series of protected areas that would preserve the backbone of the southern Rockies. Today, environmentalists still push for recognition and protection of the Crown of the Continent Ecosystem – extending from central Montana to Crowsnest Pass. In the face of the habitat disruption and fragmentation that has accompanied ranching, logging, mining and petroleum drilling, protection of this ecosystem has become as crucial as it is elusive. If wide-ranging carnivores and natural processes are to survive in the southern Rockies and elsewhere, existing national parks must be connected with other reserves, to offer more than small pockets of protected habitat.

Lone Lake to Twin Lake

After the rigors of the first day, your second day on the Tamarack trail brings two options, both of which are much less energetic. You can hike to Twin Lake campground in 7.2 km, or to Snowshoe campground in 10.2 km. You can add short sidetrails to South Kootenay Pass and Sage Pass.

The trail north from Lone Lake alternates between delightful upper subalpine meadows and ancient forest as it descends gradually to the Blakiston Creek junction. This is excellent habitat for grizzly bears. You cross two wet meadows from which you can study the cliffs of the Siyeh Formation, immediately west.

Fifty metres north of the South Kootenay Pass junction, you reach the Blakiston Creek junction. You may exit the Tamarack trail at this point, by turning east (right), 10.1 km to Red Rock Canyon. Otherwise, keep straight ahead.

Hop the outlet stream of the pond in Blue Grouse Basin. From appearances, the pond formerly

SOUTH KOOTENAY PASS (2106 M), 1.7 KM

The South Kootenay Pass trail was part of an historic route used by Ktunaxa (toon-AWK-ah) First Peoples and the first European explorers in this region. Known as the Buffalo Trail, this route connected Ktunaxa territory west of the continental divide with seasonal hunting and fishing grounds on the prairies. Hostile Stoneys and tribes of the Blackfoot Confederacy had displaced the Ktunaxa to the western side of the divide by the early 1700s. The Ktunaxa used this trail until bison were eliminated from the wild in the 1880s.

The Ktunaxa traded with the Salish, Nez Percé, and Flathead peoples west of the continental divide, from whom they obtained obsidian for making arrowheads and tools. This material has been found at some of the 358 known archaeological sites in Waterton. The Buffalo Trail followed Blakiston Creek to Lower Waterton Lake. Fifty-six of the park's archaeological sites are in the Blakiston Valley. The ruts made by travois – sleds that were pulled by dogs, and later by horses – scar the Blakiston Creek alluvial fan. Evidence of five ancient camps, along with scattered artifacts and rock cairns, has been found on South Kootenay Pass.

The first crossing of the pass by Europeans was from west to east in 1858, by a group led by Thomas Blakiston, an officer of the Palliser Expedition. Blakiston applied the name Pass Creek to the stream now known as Blakiston Creek. It is not likely that today's trail to the pass follows the precise route of The Buffalo Trail. In places

you can see where a much older, windfallen trail cuts across, taking a steeper grade to the pass. Ancient trees in the area carry blazes that may mark the original route.

For all its history, South Kootenay Pass is not particularly scenic. The sparsely forested saddle offers limited views west into the logged valleys now included in BC's Akamina-Kishinena Provincial Park, and east over Lone and Blakiston creeks. You will be obliged to carry your packs on this sidetrip, as there is no safe place to cache them.

occupied a much larger area. Now it is filling with vegetation. The blue grouse is one of three grouse species in the Rockies. It prefers upper subalpine habitats like this, where it feeds on berries and insects. The cliffs of Kishinena Peak (2434 m) are to the west. The mountain's name is a Ktunaxa word that means "balsam fir" or "white fir."

After the tiring climbs on day one, you will hardly notice the modest ascent to Twin Lake Summit. From the crest of the climb, you have glimpses through larch forest to the Twin Lakes, to the north. After a steep descent, the trail contours across a scree slope at the head of the cirque that contains Lower Twin Lake. At the Twin Lakes junction, the sidetrail to the east (right) leads to Lower Twin Lake. The campground at Upper Twin Lake is 200 m straight ahead. It is something of a disappointment, set amid seeps, out of view of the lake.

Twin Lake to Red Rock Canyon

Hop the outlet stream of Upper Twin Lake. The trail turns east and begins a steady descent along upper Bauerman Creek, named for H.B. Bauerman, a geologist with the British Boundary Commission. After about 1.5 km the trail draws alongside the creek. The meadow here contains many wildflowers and shrubs typical of the montane life zone – a strip of prairie in the heart of a subalpine valley.

You cross Bauerman Creek to the Snowshoe campground and park patrol cabin, 3.0 km after leaving Upper Twin Lake. From here, it is an easy 8.2 km walk along the undulating fireroad to Red Rock Canyon. You share the fireroad with mountain bikers. You pass the sidetrail to Goat Lake en route. The steep (455 m in 2.6 km) hike to the lake is not recommended to those with heavy packs unless you plan to spend the night at the campground there.

Some of the rocks along the fireroad feature star-shaped crystals of feldspar known as phenocrysts. As you approach Red Rock Canyon, note the change in the character of the forest. Cottonwood poplar becomes common. The rustle of its leaves on the ever-present wind heralds your arrival at trail's end. Red Rock Canyon is 23 m deep and is being eroded into red and green argillite of the Grinnell Formation. The circuit of the canyon is only 700 m, and is highly recommended.

SAGE PASS (2134 M), 1.4 KM

 Head north from the campground and hop the outlet stream of Upper Twin Lake. The trail turns east. In 100 m, the Sage Pass trail branches north (left) and climbs steadily to the treed pass, from where mountaineers can pick their way northeast or southwest onto ridges for better views. Sagebrush, a shrub of the montane life zone, is common just across the pass, in southeastern BC.

TAMARACKS OR LARCHES?

"Tamarack" is a common name applied throughout North America to three species of coniferous trees that shed their needles annually – tamarack, Lyall's larch, and western larch. The tamarack is the most common of these three trees in Canada, found in every province and territory. However, it is not widespread in the Rockies, occurring only in low-elevation wetlands on the eastern slopes, north of the North Saskatchewan River. The western larch is found principally in southeastern BC, with a few stands in southwestern Alberta.

The deciduous conifers along the Tamarack trail are Lyall's larch (see photo, p. 74), also called subalpine larch. This tree species often forms treeline forests. Clearwater Pass in Banff National Park is its northern limit. The tree was catalogued by Eugene Bourgeau of the Palliser Expedition. He named it for David Lyall, a naturalist and surgeon of the Royal Navy, who, in the 1840s and 1850s, made botanical collections in the Arctic, Antarctic, New Zealand, and the territory of British Columbia.

LOST LAKE (1875 M), 1.9 KM

 Head north from Snowshoe campground. At the junction in 0.9 km turn northwest (left). The trail ascends gradually through a damp forest to the lush shore of the jade-coloured lake. Cow parsnip and bear grass grow in abundance along the trail and at the lake. It's an excellent pocket of bear habitat. Travel accordingly. Lost Lake was stocked with fish in the past, but avalanche deposits in the lake have killed them.

Akamina-Kishinena Provincial Park

63. Forum Lake – Wall Lake

Forum Lake

TRAIL THUMBNAIL

Day-hike or overnight; see map, p. 246

Route	Elev. (m)	Dist. (km)
Trailhead	1670	0
Akamina Pass	1783	1.5
Forum Lake jct	1770	2.2
Ranger Station	1775	2.4
Forum Falls jct	1780	2.7
Forum Falls	1785	+0.1
Forum Lake	2020	4.4
Forum Lake jct	1770	6.6
Akamina Creek CG	1765	6.8
Wall Lake jct	1755	6.9
Wall Lake	1750	9.6
Bennett Pass jct	1780	10.0
Bennett Pass	2220	13.2

Trailhead
Follow the Akamina Parkway 15 km from Waterton Park village to the Akamina Pass parking area on the east side of the road. The trailhead is across the road. Daily shuttle service is available (fee charged). Inquire at the park information centre.

Maps
NTS: 82 G/1 (trail shown incorrectly)
Gem Trek: *Waterton Lakes National Park*

Best lighting: morning and evening are best at the lakes

Long a favourite haunt of backcountry skiers, the hike to Forum Lake and Wall Lake became a popular summer outing with the establishment of Akamina-Kishinena Provincial Park in 1995. The lakes – one higher and lesser, one lower and greater – lie buried in glacial cirque pockets beneath stupendous cliffs. If you extend the outing by making the grind to Bennett Pass, you are treated to a wild view south over the headwaters of North Kintla Creek, and into Glacier National Park, Montana. In a good year, the bear grass blooms are stunning. You share the trail with horses and mountain bikers.

Trailhead to Forum Lake Junction

Waterton's Cameron Lake region is the snowfall capital of southern Alberta. The forest at the trailhead is wet in character, more like what you would expect in British Columbia, which is but a 20 minute walk away. As testimony to the wetness, thimbleberry, queen's cup, false hellebore, cow parsnip, western meadowrue, water hemlock, birch-leaved spirea, and bear grass provide much of the ground cover at the trailhead.

The trail to Akamina Pass was cut as an exploratory tote road following the discovery of oil on Cameron Creek in 1901. In 1927, there was a proposal to extend the recently-constructed Akamina Parkway over Akamina Pass, to allow a "triangle tour" from Waterton to the Flathead Valley, returning through Glacier National Park, Montana. The BC section of the road was never built, but the tote road into Akamina-Kishinena Provincial Park remains. In places, you'll see sections of corduroy – logs laid

251

Wall Lake

across the width of the tread. *Corduroy* is a French expression that means "road of the king." To keep the king's carriage out of the muck of feudal France, the peasants would lay logs across the tread. A bumpy ride resulted, but at least the king got to his palace without sullying his boots and gown. Hike on; regal wonders await.

You climb steadily through an old pine forest, crossing a small stream in 400 m. Note the red rock in the stream bed. This is 1.5 billion-year-old argillite of the Grinnell Formation. You catch glimpses of Cameron Lake through the trees. White rein orchids, hooded ladies'-tresses, meadow parsnip, dwarf false asphodel, groundsel, horsetails, and fleabane line a wet section of trail on the final approach to the forested pass.

There's not much to look at on the pass but a typical mass of signs that welcomes you to BC and the entry to Akamina-Kishinena Provincial Park. Bear warnings will be posted here, and you have the opportunity to sign the register. But please note – this is not a safety register; your information is used for statistics only. The trail descends gradually from the pass to the Forum Lake junction in 700 m. The registration box for the campground is beside the trail. To hike to Forum Lake, turn south (left).

VARIATIONS

- Day-hike to Forum Lake; 8.8 km return.
- Day-hike to Wall Lake; 10.4 km return.
- Day-hike to Wall Lake and Bennett Pass; 17.6 km return.
- Day-hike to both lakes and Bennett Pass; 26.4 km return.
- Camp at Akamina Creek (2.4 km) and explore.

Forum Lake

The park ranger cabin is 175 m along the trail. Branch left just beyond. This is the end of the bike trail. Just 50 m into the trees you come to a junction. Forum Falls is a short distance to the west (right) – it's a pleasant sidetrip to the base of the small cascade. Dippers nest here and frequent the stream. Keep south (left) for Forum Lake.

The rambling trail alternates between steep grades and level sections, now at creekside, now away. In one section, you hike in an abandoned creek bed. Three shrubs – false-azalea, grouseberry, and blueberry – are common along the trail. Subalpine fir is prevalent in the forest, but more than 30 percent of the trees are standing dead. As you ascend, the regular complement of subalpine flowers appears.

Far away in northwestern Montana, hidden from view by clustering mountain-peaks, lies an unnamed corner – the Crown of the Continent. The water from the crusted snow-drift which caps the peak of a lofty mountain there trickles into tiny rills, which hurry along north, south, east and west, and growing into three rivers, at last pour their contents into three seas. From this mountain-peak the Pacific and the Arctic Oceans and the Gulf of Mexico each receive its tribute.

George Bird Grinnell; "The Crown of the Continent," *Century* magazine, September 1901

Red-tailed hawk

On this north-facing slope and with the heavy snow-fall here, they bloom late. I have seen shooting stars and glacier lilies, freshly in bloom on August 1. The trail crosses a wet meadow on a split log boardwalk. A patch of perennial avalanche snow lies just beyond. You hike through larches. A short distance later you arrive at a bay on the northeast shore of Forum Lake. This spot, in all my experience of the backcountry of the Rockies, was the quietest place I have ever been. It must have been a rare day. Waterton's windiness usually stirs these waters, too.

The colourful cliffs of Akamina Ridge rise almost 500 m above the lake, blocking the sun for much of the day. Look for mountain goats and bears on the terraces. *Forum* comes from the Latin word for "outside." The British Boundary Commission named the lake. The forum of Roman times was an outdoor market or meeting place. Forum Peak (2415 m) was later named for the lake. It's an appropriate name because the mountain is the meeting place for many borders. Seven jurisdictions criss-cross its slopes: two national parks, one provincial park, two provinces, and two countries.

Golden-mantled ground squirrels and Columbian ground squirrels will probably attend your arrival at the lake. Robins, red breasted nut-hatches, and white-winged crossbills are common. A

A COUPLET FULL OF DEFINITIONS

The name of Akamina-Kishinena Provincial Park incorporates two Ktunaxa (toon-AWK-ah) (Kutenai) words, the precise meanings of which elude toponymers. *Akamina* might mean "high bench land," "mountain pass," "valley," or "watershed." All of these are appropriate for the features so named by the British Boundary Commission. Some people pronounce the name, ah-kah-MY-nah, but most say ah-kah-MEE-nah. The meanings given for *Kishinena* (kish-ih-NEE-nah) that I like best are "balsam" and "white fir." Akamina-Kishinena: It's an exotic sound-ing couplet that has a down-to-earth meaning – rocks and trees.

pure stand of larches grows on the steep slope above the rocky east shore.

Forum Lake drains underground (the emergence is just above the wet meadow), so its level fluctuates. If the water level is high, you might be confined to the bay on the northeast shore, from where a shin-tangle of spruce and fir impedes westerly progress. When the water level is lower, you can follow a path west along the shore. But if the bear grass is in its prime, as it has been for me, you won't feel obliged to go anywhere. You'll probably just gawk in amaze-ment at the blooms and at the tremendous setting of the lake.

Forum Lake Junction to Wall Lake

It is only 200 m from the Forum Lake junction to Akamina Creek campground, and another 50 m to the three bridges that span the outflow from Forum Lake. Across the creek, turn southwest (left) for Wall Lake.

The trail to the lake initially makes a gradual descent through an old forest of lodgepole pine, Engelmann spruce, and subalpine fir. Arnica, queen's cup, and foamflower are among the wildflowers. After about 1.9 km, the trail swings south to enter the Wall Creek valley where it begins a gradual ascent. The trail runs along the base of avalanche slopes off the spur that separates Forum Lake from Wall Lake. Huge spruce grow here – some are more than 1 m in diameter at the base and 45 m tall. These avalanche slopes – with their glacier lilies, bear grass, cow parsnip, and berry bushes – are deluxe bear habitat. Fireweed, ragwort, wild onion, and bracted honey-suckle grow on the trail margins.

Wall Lake

The setting at Wall Lake is similar to that at Forum Lake, but the arrangement of the pieces differs. Wall Lake is two-and-a-half times the size of its neigh-bour. Akamina Ridge rises half as high again – some 750 m from the south shore of Wall Lake – shutting out the sky. An ancient forest, with a lush understory, rings the north shore. Look for red monkey flowers at trailside. Cutthroat trout abound in the lake. If you packed a fishing rod, make sure that you also packed a BC Fishing Licence.

A good trail leads around the north and west shores of the lake to two bays on the southwest shore, passing the Bennett Pass junction in 400 m. The first of the bays was the former site of a popular back-country campground, closed in 1997 on the advice of a bear biologist. Don't camp here. I saw sandpipers and five redhead ducks near shore. The trail ends 150 m later on a scree fan above the second bay. Here, a

Western wakerobin

perennial snow patch – the product of innumerable avalanches – melts into the lake. Keep off the snow. It has been the site of mishaps and close calls over the years. You may see gray-crowned rosy finches feeding on torpid insects on the snow. On my visit a bear had recently flipped over a great number of the argillite shale slabs here, looking for grubs beneath. Arnica and Sitka valerian carpet the peninsula that juts into the lake. Mt. Rowe (2469 m) rises across the Akamina Valley. It was named for V.F. Rowe, a surveyor and officer with the International Boundary Commission of 1872-76.

Bennett Pass

The Bennett Pass junction is about 400 m west of the outlet of Wall Lake. It's an honest 3 km to the pass; the ascent took me an hour and fifteen minutes with a light pack. The trail makes a couple of tight switchbacks away from the lakeshore before rambling through lush forest on the initial ascent, twice drawing alongside the creek that drains the sidevalley. Look for twisted stalk and red monkey flowers along the trail. After about 1 km, you pop out onto an avalanche slope with views ahead to a cliff that spans the valley. I could have raved over the bear grass displays at any number of points on this hike, but I've saved the superlatives for the view west from the top of this cliff. Some locals will tell you that the blooms of bear grass peak every seven years; some say every five. The truth is that each plant blooms every 3-10 years. Neighbouring plants often bloom at the same time. So each year, the locations of the blooms and their relative intensity will be different. I hope that, at some point on your travels in the Waterton area, you will see displays to match what I have seen in this hanging valley above Wall Lake. On one visit, the blooms numbered in the tens of thousands, and each, it seemed, was at its prime.

The trail sidehills along the dry north slope of the valley where sawwort and scorpionweed grow. Look back for views of Wall Lake. Red argillite is common

THE SIYEH FORMATION

The front range mountains of the Rockies south of Crowsnest Pass lack the massive, blocky, limestone and dolomite cliffs of the front ranges farther north. Except for one thick limestone layer, the rock is shaly and weak. However, because the layers are usually not steeply tilted, they resist erosion and form cliffs as impressive as those farther north. The main cliff-builder of Akamina Ridge – as elsewhere in the Waterton area – is the 1.35 billion-year-old Siyeh (SIGH-yuh) Formation. The formation takes its name from *saiyi*, a Siksika (Blackfoot) word that means "mad" or "rabid."

The Siyeh has three principal elements, visible at Forum Lake and Wall Lake. The lower two, known to U.S. geologists as the Empire Formation and the Helena Formation, typically create a cliff. The Empire (lower part of the cliff) contains siltstone, sandstone, and greenish argillite rocks formed, respectively, from silt, sand, and mud. The argillite is green here rather than the usual red, because the iron in its clays was reduced (lost attached oxygen molecules) after deposition. The Helena Formation (upper part of the cliff) is a thick, pale-weathering limestone layer. Above that is the lower Snowslip Formation, another U.S. name applied to the upper part of the Canadian Siyeh Formation and layers above that. These are reddish argillite and siltstone, the red color coming from rusted iron that has retained its attached oxygen molecules. Forming an obvious dark band in the Helena Formation limestone is the Purcell Sill, an intrusion of igneous (once-molten) rock that squeezed between the layers. The Purcell Lava, which poured out of a volcano, sits atop that. The lava covered the seabed, then was itself buried under younger layers of sediment.

Southwest from Bennett Pass

on this slope. Argillite is shale that formed in shallow seas and was subsequently altered by heat or by pressure. Look for proof of its marine origin – ripple rock that records the lapping of wavelets on an ancient shore. Just before the second step in the valley, the trail may be buried under avalanche deposit. If the way ahead looks uncertain, aim to ascend the step along the north (right) side of the stream. Stickseed, yellow columbine, and wild chives grow on the outcrop. I saw tiger swallowtails and veined white butterflies on the trail. Nearby, I found the large, delicate bloom of a western wakerobin. This member of the lily family is a rarity on the Classic Hikes.

You get a brief reprieve from the climb where the trail passes through the saddle between Akamina Ridge and its outlier to the north. Many of the trees

are now Lyall's larches, some of them half a metre in diameter – big trees for this aspect and elevation. You'll see something else unusual on the climb ahead – larches in kruppelholz form. Looking north, you can see the continental divide ridge, from Mt. Rowe (with the provincial boundary cutline) to Kishinena Peak (2434 m). Biscuitboard Creek rises on the slopes beneath the trail, to drain into Akamina Creek. The origin of the name is unrecorded, but likely had something to do with a sourdough who staked a claim or two nearby.

The last 1.5 km to Bennett Pass is as single-minded a piece of trail as you will find anywhere. It ascends about 240 m, and does this on a sidehill without a hint of a switchback. Fine displays of upper subalpine wildflowers provide distraction from the toil. Golden-crowned kinglets buzzed from tree to tree on my visit, and for a few minutes, a red-tailed hawk soared overhead. You'll be glad when the grade kicks back and the trail begins to turn west around the north end of Akamina Ridge, with the true saddle of Bennett Pass about 50 m below and 250 m west of the trail. Watch your step – the trail is exposed to a tremendous drop for a short section. The trail forks. Straight ahead is the route into North Kintla Creek. Keep left to climb onto the screes of Akamina Ridge. Pick a spot to collapse, catch your breath, and take in the stupendous view into the northwest corner of Glacier National Park, Montana.

Return

Retrace your route to Wall Lake. If you've visited all the destinations as a day-hike, don't be ashamed at the pull in your calves on the modest climb back over Akamina Pass.

PEACE PARK PLUS

BC established the Akamina-Kishinena Provincial Recreation Area in 1986 when logging threatened to gut the forests along Akamina Creek. Much of the clear-cutting then taking place was "salvage logging" – the cutting of standing dead trees killed by mountain pine beetles. When provincial park status was conveyed in 1995, the logging stopped in the upper watersheds. More recently, there has been a proposal to add the provincial park – along with 40,500 ha of BC's upper Flathead Valley – to the Waterton-Glacier International Peace Park. The Canadian government supports the idea and, remarkably, the BC government has set aside logging and mining plans for the Flathead Valley. Help nudge the Peace Park Plus process along.

💻 www.thebigwild.org

Wildflower Guide

Here are thumbnail images of 109 plants that bloom in the Rockies, and one that doesn't bloom (horsetail.) Most of these are wildflowers, some are shrubs, one is a sedge, and one (surprise) is a horsetail. Most are common to abundant; a few are gems not seen often. With the exception of ox-eye daisy, all are native to the Canadian Rockies. The page numbers indicate where a plant is described in detail or where you will find a larger image. Look under "wildflower hot spots" in the index for the best places to see wildflowers. Please remember: when out on the trail, pick only with your eyes.

Common fireweed (p. 196)

Mountain fireweed (p. 118)

Arctic raspberry

Pink mountain heather (p. 146)

Pink paintbrush

Nodding onion

Bearberry (p. 105)

Pink wintergreen

Prickly wild rose

Twinflower

Red monkey flower

Western meadowrue

Hybrid columbine

Red paintbrush

Mountain sorrel

Western wood lily

Western columbine

Roseroot

False azalea

Brown-eyed Susan

Alpine hawksbeard

Rocky mountain goldenrod

Rocky mountain groundsel

Yellow lady's slipper

Yellow mountain avens

Goatsbeard

Alpine buttercup

Arnica (p. 195)

Stonecrop

Yellow-flowered false dandelion

Double bladder pod

Golden fleabane

Bracted honeysuckle

Alpine cinquefoil

Butter and eggs

Evergreen violet

Glacier lily

Mountain meadow cinquefoil (p. 156)

Northern dandelion

Yellow columbine

Yellow draba

Yellow mountain saxifrage (p. 84)

Yellow mountain heather (p. 146)

Yellow hedysarum

Showy locoweed

Yellow paintbrush

One-sided wintergreen

False hellebore

Bracted lousewort

Bracted orchid

Horsetail

Drummond's anemone

Stickseed

Alpine forget-me-not

Alpine harebell

Alpine speedwell (p. 128)

Butterwort (p. 66)

Clematis

Harebell

Sky pilot

Aster

Fleabane

Four-parted gentian

Western wake robin (p. 254)

Alpine lousewort (p. 144)

Calypso orchid (p. 166)

Creeping beardtongue

Elephant-head

Inflated oxotrype

Mackenzie's hedysarum

Moss campion (p. 139)

Northern blue columbine

Purple saxifrage

Scorpionweed (p. 31)

Bear Grass (p. 235)

Coltsfoot

Cow parsnip

Daisy fleabane

Dwarf dogwood

False Solomon's seal

Foam flower

Fringed grass-of-Parnassus

Hooded ladies'-tresses

Labrador tea

Mountain marsh marigold (p. 84)

Northern green rein-orchid

Ox-eye daisy

Pearly everlasting

Queen's cup

Red and white baneberry

Red elderberry

Red osier dogwood

Red-stemmed saxifrage

Twisted stalk

Rock jasmine

Silver rockcress

Sitka valerian

Spotted orchid

Western anemone (p. 77)

Western anemone seedpod (p. 77)

White camas

White geranium

White globeflower

White mountain avens

White mountain heather (p. 146)

White rhododendron

Wild strawberry

Woolly everlasting

Western Canada violet

Cotton grass

Nuts and Bolts

Park Regulations

The following are the principal rules that govern backcountry travel in the Rockies. Please note that some of these are enforceable laws which, if broken, can result in criminal charges.

- Drivers of vehicles stopping in national parks must pay the appropriate fee at a park gate or at a park information centre. Call 800-748-7275 for details.
- Firearms are not permitted unless securely locked or dismantled.
- Hunting and trapping of wildlife is not permitted.
- Anglers must obtain a national park fishing permit or a provincial fishing licence, and be aware of relevant restrictions and catch limits.
- It is illegal to disturb, remove or deface any natural, cultural or historic object or artifact.
- It is illegal to approach, feed, entice or harass wildlife.
- It is illegal to enter a closed area.
- Fees apply to overnight backcountry use.
- Mountain biking is permitted only on certain trails. Check at a park information centre.
- There are restrictions on taking dogs into the backcountry in most parks. Check at a park information centre.

WILDLIFE WATCH

Poaching – hunting out of season, and the illegal hunting of protected animals – is a significant threat to wildlife in the Rockies. Elk, bighorn sheep, and mountain goats are the species particularly affected.

If you see someone committing what you consider to be an illegal act – poaching, illegal fishing, harassing wildlife, arson, polluting, theft or destruction of natural objects – you can gather information and make a report at the end of your hike. Don't confront the individuals. Observe the act. Write down the details – descriptions of those involved, the time, the location, any vehicle involved and its licence plate number, and any conversation overheard. In the national parks, dial 9-1-1 and ask for Banff park dispatch. In Kananaskis Country or on Alberta provincial lands, call 800-642-3800. Outside the national parks in BC, call 877-952-7277.

Backcountry Fees

You require a "wilderness pass" for overnight backcountry trips in the national parks. You may purchase a wilderness pass for an individual outing, or a season pass for a twelve-month period. If you will be camping seven nights or more in the coming year, purchase the season pass. If you are not sure how much camping you will be doing, save your permits. Tally seven nights and you can turn the permits in at a park information centre for a season pass at no charge. You must still obtain a camping permit (free) for each outing after you have purchased the season pass. Refunds are not given for inclement weather. Parks Canada has not instituted a fee for day-hikes, but has considered the possibility. Sigh.

Purchase your wilderness pass immediately prior to your hike, at a park information centre in the park where your hike is located. Groups of more than six persons are discouraged. Larger groups require the permission of the park superintendent.

Camping in provincial parks is also subject to fees. You may reserve campsites on the South Kananaskis Pass and North Kananaskis Pass trails by phoning the Peter Lougheed Provincial Park information centre, 403-591-6322. Pick up your permit on the way to the trailhead. For Berg Lake, purchase your trail permit at the visitor centre at Mt. Robson Junction on Highway 16. A portion of the trail quota can be reserved in advance. Phone 250-566-4325 or 800-689-9025 for details. To reserve space and find out about fees at Og Lake and Lake Magog campgrounds, and at Naiset Cabins, phone Mt. Assiniboine Lodge, 403-678-2883. A fee applies to camping in Akamina-Kishinena Provincial Park. Phone BC Parks at 250-422-4200 for details; phone 800-689-9025 to make a reservation. Place your fee in the drop box at the Forum Lake junction. To enquire about staying at the Alpine Club of Canada huts at Lake O'Hara, the Little Yoho Valley, Outpost Lake, and the Fryatt Valley, phone 403-678-3200, or email info@AlpineClubofCanada.ca

Staying in a hut offers some conveniences, obviously, but these come at the cost of a more peopled experience. I have done both, and recommend sleeping in a tent.

Quotas

All backcountry campgrounds have quotas. When they are filled, wilderness passes and camping permits will not be issued. The national parks accept reservations for a portion of backcountry campground quotas up to three months in advance. The Lake O'Hara campground is usually booked solidly three months ahead. If you plan to visit in July, make your reservation in April. A portion of any quota is also set aside for issue on the day of use, so early risers can *usually* get onto their desired trail on the desired day.

However, be flexible when scheduling a hike on a popular trail – particularly Berg Lake, Skyline, Tonquin Valley, Brazeau, and those in Yoho.

Parks Canada and provincial park agencies will close some trails and campgrounds seasonally to protect wildlife such as grizzly bears, wolves, and caribou. Some trails are closed during snowmelt to protect vegetation and to reduce trail damage. I have excluded trails from this edition that have been, or that may soon be subject to outright closure. However, please abide by any new regulations that supercede the information here.

Equipment

Boots

Hiking boots are your most important equipment. Lightweight boots are suitable for day-hikes on well-maintained trails. Leather boots with a Vibram or similar sole are the best choice when you will be carrying a heavy pack or plowing through horse muck. Most experienced hikers have a selection of footwear, matching the boot to the proposed trip and the expected hiking conditions. If you find a pair of boots that you really like and can afford it, buy two pairs. Styles change like the wind. Two or three years from now, chances are that you won't be able to find the same model.

Take your hiking socks and orthotics, if you use them, with you when you try on boots. There should be enough room at the rear of the boot for you to slip your index finger between the boot cuff and your achilles tendon, without the boot slipping there as it flexes. Ensure that your toes do not feel crowded, especially while walking down a flight of stairs or a ramp. Bring a loaded backpack with you to see how the boots feel when you are carrying weight. Spend half an hour in the pair of boots that feel best, to be sure that you (and your feet) like them. Although boots are better designed than in years past, it is still a good idea to get your feet used to them by wearing them around home for a day or two before heading out on the trail.

Leather Boots

Leather boots have a reputation as being stiff, heavy, and expensive. On the last two counts this is true when compared to synthetic boots, but bootmakers have introduced innovations to leather boots – articulated uppers, for instance – that make them more supple, providing support without inhibiting gait. Well-made leather boots last longer than lightweight boots. They offer more ankle and arch support, they are more waterproof, they are warmer, and they cause less trail damage by allowing you to walk through muck on the trail.

Look for deep lugs on the sole, and for a lacing system that allows you to vary the lace tension between the toes and the ankle. A gusseted tongue helps to keep out dirt and water. A rubber rand that encircles the sole and midsole seams helps to keep feet dry. Fewer seams on the uppers means less likelihood that a boot will blow out. A half-shank of nylon, fibreglass or steel gives extra support.

Lightweight Boots

Lightweight hiking boots are those with hybrid uppers – canvas, leather, and synthetic. Many come with Vibram or similar soles. They are usually cut lower at the ankle. They cost slightly less than good leather boots, they cause less damage to dry trails, and they require less energy. (Every kilogram carried on your feet is equivalent to 6 kilograms carried on your back.) However, lightweight boots have drawbacks:

- They are less durable and less waterproof than leather boots.
- You are more likely to step off the trail to avoid wet spots or snow patches, causing more damage off-trail than heavier boots cause on-trail.
- They cannot be edged effectively into the tread when descending steep or slippery trails, scree or snow slopes.
- They do not offer much ankle or arch support – something you may notice when you carry a heavy pack.
- They are not as warm as leather boots, wet or dry.

ARE YOU HAVING A FIT?

No matter how much attention you paid to sizing your boots in the store, you will notice that they fit differently on different days. On hot, dry days the leather will shrink and your feet will swell. Presto! Tight boots. Vice versa for the soggy days. Try different sock combinations to help compensate.

TEN STEPS TO HAPPY HIKING

If you've got these covered, you are well on the way to avoiding problems in the backcountry.

- Strive to carry less than one-quarter of your body weight.
- When hiking in a group, share equipment to collectively reduce pack weights.
- Plan for worst-case-scenarios. Carry essential equipment together: stove, fuel, pots and hot food in the same pack; tent, pegs, fly, and cold food in the same pack.
- Never let someone else carry your sleeping bag.
- Carry snacks and water; drink often. On overnight hikes, pack a treat.
- Test all equipment at home; inspect your boots.
- Line the inside of your pack with a durable plastic bag.
- Hike with partners of like mind and like fitness.
- Keep to your planned route. When the weather is truly foul, turn around and go home.
- Take bear safety seriously.

UNDER THE HOOD

The hood is the part of your pack that you will use most. The best packs have an externally accessible, large pocket, and a smaller, zippered pocket on the underside of the hood. You want to keep things that you need often, or that you will need in a hurry, in the outer pocket. Put your permits, vehicle keys, identification, and money in a reclosable bag in the inner pocket.

Boot Care

Clean your boots after each hike with a stiff brush and warm water. Treat them when they are dry to enhance their ability to repel water, using synthetic or natural compounds. (Don't use leather softeners.) Silicone compounds may attract dirt. Even properly treated boots will eventually soak through. To help dry a pair of waterlogged boots, stuff them with newspaper; changing the newspaper as it becomes wet. Do not attempt to dry boots with direct heat or in an oven. A pair of soggy boots will usually dry during a sunny day on the trail. If you hike often and can afford it, buy two pairs of boots and alternate their use. This will allow each pair to air dry between trips, and will prolong the life of the stitching.

Dry and treat your boots before storage. When stored, ensure that the boots maintain their proper shape by using a boot tree. Check boots before storage to see if they require resoling, patching, new laces or stitching in the uppers. These repairs are more convenient during the off-season.

Socks

Wool and wool-blend are the warmest and most durable choice for outer socks. Calf length socks are suitable most of the time. Carry two pairs of socks on overnight trips and wear them on alternate days, or exchange them as they become wet. Thin polypropylene or nylon inner socks help reduce the chance of blisters, and wick moisture away from your feet into the outer sock. Some hikers swear by Gore-Tex socks. Give them a try if you are having trouble keeping your feet dry.

Gaiters

Gaiters should cover your lower leg from the boot laces to just below the knee. The most durable gaiters are those made from coated Cordura. Gore-Tex uppers help reduce sweat build-up. To prevent the gaiters from riding too high at the heel, they should have a strap or cable that passes under the sole of the boot. Besides keeping rain, snow, and mud out of your boots, gaiters also keep out scree. They help keep your feet and legs warm on cold, windy days. When the weather clears, you can tie wet gaiters to the outside of your pack to dry as you hike.

Blister Prone?

A blister is a painful, localized inflammation of the skin, caused by friction. If left unattended, it may become infected. Blisters are a chronic condition for some hikers. The cause is almost always boots that do not fit well. With a correctly sized pair of boots on your feet, there is a simple trick to reduce the

likelihood of blisters: wear a thin, inner sock and a thicker, outer sock. Much of the friction that could create blisters now takes place between the socks. You can try wearing the inner socks inside out. This places smoother material against your skin, especially across the toes. Experiment with different socks and insoles until you find a combination that works.

Stop immediately (that means, now!) when you detect a "hot spot" on your feet. Take off your boots and socks. Clean the offending area, dry it, and apply a blister dressing, such as Moleskin or Second Skin. In a pinch, use a piece of duct tape lined with first-aid dressing. If the cause was a piece of grit or a crumpled sock, your problem is solved. If a boot is too tight across the toes, jam a clean rock into the boot for a while to stretch the leather, or skip the front lacing rings. If your boot is too loose, put on thicker socks, change insoles, or pad the offending part of the boot with a blister dressing. If you blister at the heel while wearing heavier leather boots, the boots may be too long, causing the heel to lift with each stride. You may have to purchase a pair of boots that fit better. The key is prompt action to help prevent many kilometres of misery. Do not burst blisters while out on the trail, as infection may result.

Tips for Foot Comfort

Trim your toenails before each hike. When hiking, change your socks at lunchtime; if it's a nice day, air your socks, boots, and feet. When you make camp, pick grit and twigs out of your socks. If the weather is favourable, rinse your socks in a stream and hang them to dry. Wet boots or wet socks can cause blisters. Remove your boots to ford streams when the water is ankle deep. Wear river shoes. Use a bandana or handkerchief to dry your feet after fords. A wet pair of feet will quickly make you cold at camp. Wear river shoes or old sneakers. Change into these and dry socks before you pitch your tent. You will be less likely to become chilled. Don't go barefoot at camp in porcupine country. At the end of a long, hot day on the trail, soak your feet in a stream or lake. The cold water will reduce swelling. Despite the initial shock, your feet will be refreshed.

Packs

Backpacks, like backpackers, come in all shapes and sizes. If you will be hiking a variety of trails, you will probably require a day pack and an overnight pack. Pack bodies made from coated fabrics are lightweight and relatively waterproof. Those made from coated packcloth are more durable. Some packs combine both fabrics to create a waterproof body with a durable base. Mesh panels on the back, shoulder, and hips – if well designed – help keep you drier. Ensure that a pack has durable zippers, and buckles that you can

All this gear goes into two packs

operate while wearing mitts or gloves. If you never carry crampons, ice axe, snowboard or skis on your pack, save weight; don't buy a pack with attachment points for those items. Avoid lots of extras – the zippers, buckles, and stitching add unnecessary weight, and are usually the first things to fail on an otherwise serviceable pack.

Overnight Packs

For overnight trips, most people require a pack with a capacity in the 75-80 litre range. Although a large volume pack tempts you to take more gear than you need, a smaller pack with odds and ends strapped all over is the makings of backcountry disaster, and is more uncomfortable and inefficient to carry.

Most backpackers use internal frame packs. Look for an adjustable shoulder yoke, a comfortable hip belt, a sternum strap, compression straps, one or two easily accessible outer compartments, and adequate padding. Some models of overnight packs come in tall, regular, and small sizes. You may be of "average" height, but what is more important for pack fit is the length of your back. Have the pack fitted to your torso by a knowledgeable salesperson. With the pack fully loaded, the hip belt should take two-thirds to three-quarters of the weight.

If your pack does not have zipper pulls, add short loops of 3 mm cord or bootlace to create your own. Zipper pulls make access to your pack easier while

YOUR EMPTY PACK

What should you do with your pack when camped in the backcountry? Some people choose to hang their pack with their food at night. This is the safest thing to do, as it minimizes the chance that scents on the pack will attract a bear to your tent. However, if it rains the pack will be soaked. Worse, squirrels and jays may damage it while you snooze. Porcupines may chew a pack left on the ground or low in a tree. I put a pack cover over my empty pack and tuck it under the tent fly or vestibule.

you are wearing gloves or mitts, and also lengthen the life of the zippers. Line the inside of your pack with a durable, light-coloured plastic bag. Besides the additional waterproofing, it will make it easier to find items. Purchase a coated pack cover that will fit your pack with any lashed on gear, to use on inclement days.

Day Packs

A pack with a volume of 35 litres is adequate for day-hikes. A zippered hood compartment and a single storage compartment are all that you need. For the day-hiking options on overnight trips, carry a nylon teardrop pack (15-20 litre capacity) to stow in the bottom of your backpack, or compress your main pack using its compression straps.

Tents and Accessories

Many backpackers have two tents – a three-season model for use at any time, and a lighter, summer tent for use during fair weather spells. If most of the body of the tent is mesh and it has only two poles, it is a summer tent no matter how it may be marketed. Keep the following in mind when you go tent shopping.

TENT PEGS

Carry a variety of tent pegs – metal and plastic. Believe it or not, the aluminum noodles provided by tent manufacturers sometimes actually work – such as when you have to force a peg between rocks. If the ground is so hard that you can't peg your tent, weigh down the corners by putting rocks inside. Tie the fly to rocks or nearby trees. Do this anyway if it is windy. I once had a tent blow into a creek, sleeping bags and all.

YOUR DOG

Your dog is perfectly obedient and is always on a leash. It never pees in a stream or poops on the trail, and if it does, you always pick up after it and pack out the wreckage. Your dog does not jump up on strangers or wrap its leash around their legs, knock over children and bark in their faces, or chase ground squirrels. It always steps to the side of the trail when you meet other hikers. No bear would ever come near your dog, and your dog would never approach a bear. Your dog does not so much as whimper when at camp. In fact, your dog is so well trained and well behaved, nobody except you realizes that it is in the backcountry. Because this sounds like everybody's dog... and nobody's dog, I recommend leaving your hound at home.

- Choose a tent that will comfortably accommodate your party; 3.5-4 m2 of floorspace for two people; 4-5.5 m2 of floorspace for three people. Consider how much room the door allows for entry and exit beside your slumbering partner(s). Your sleeping bag will brush against the walls of a narrow or short tent. In wet weather, this means a soggy bag.
- Choose a tent that is light enough to carry without complaint.
- Choose a tent that has a large fly that nearly reaches the ground. If the fly clips to the poles, it will allow better ventilation, reducing condensation inside.
- Choose a free-standing tent. They are easier to set up, and can be dried quickly by hanging them from a tree on a windy day. Some of the tent pads at campgrounds on popular trails have been "hardened" and are almost impossible to peg.
- Choose a light coloured tent. They are more cheerful when it's pouring outside and you are stuck inside. They dry more quickly and it is easier to read and to spot bugs inside them.
- Choose a tent with a vestibule for storing gear and boots out of the weather.
- If the tent has poles of different lengths, colour-coding helps to eliminate confusion during set-up.
- Taped seams are not necessary and make the tent heavier. But you should goop the seams of the fly and the floor before each season.
- A good tent is expensive. Spend as much as you can afford. The poles and zippers on a cheap tent may only last a season.
- Get inside the tent and stretch out before you buy it. Most stores have display models set-up.

Nylons and tent materials decay and shrink in sunlight, so don't leave your tent pitched when you won't be using it. Spray-on sunscreens for fabrics are available; the manufacturers claim that these minimize damage from UV radiation. Tent fabrics are highly flammable. Do not cook, smoke or use a candle in a tent. Follow the manufacturer's care recommendations. Some people put a thin "footprint" tarp under the tent when they pitch it. I find this unnecessary. To pack a wet tent, carry a plastic bag in the bottom of your pack. Carry tent poles in a sack, secured beneath the side compression straps of your pack. Tie the sack to one of the straps so that it doesn't go for a hike of its own. To maximize the life of your tent, take off your boots before you get in. Unfold and fold shock-corded tent poles carefully. Pick your freestanding tent up and shake it out before packing – grit will abrade the fabric. Dry the tent fly by draping it, inside out, over a shrub. Tip the tent body up so that the floor faces the sun or wind.

Completely air-dry all components of your tent after each trip – including shock-corded tent poles. Store the tent and fly loosely in a plastic tub.

You may be accustomed to going without a tent, and sleeping on the ground in a bivvy sac. In drier, warmer, less buggy, and more predictable climates, this is a viable option – which means, not in the Rockies. The same goes for sleeping in a hammock.

An overhead tarp is a great addition for camp comfort in inclement or scorching weather. Strung between trees (practice beforehand!), it can provide additional shelter for cooking and eating. You can buy lightweight backpacking tarps or fashion your own from hardware store poly and a grommet kit.

Sleeping Bags

Even in mid-summer, nights in the Rockies are cool. Most backpackers opt for a three-season, mummy-style, synthetic bag, or a summer-weight, down-filled bag. Early and late in the hiking season, some people will be more comfortable in a winter bag. As a rule, carry a sleeping bag rated 5°C colder than the lowest temperature that you expect. A bag with a durable water repellent (DWR) fabric shell will help keep dampness at bay. Down bags are lighter and more compressible but are more difficult to wash. If you use your sleeping bag often, a cotton liner will help keep it clean.

In any sleeping bag, a hood with a drawstring, a draft collar, a foot box large enough to allow your feet to stick straight up, and a snag-free, full-length zipper backed by a draft tube are essential features. Stuff (don't roll) your sleeping bag and carry it inside your pack. Line the inside of its stuff sack with a large plastic bag for extra protection against rain and sweat. (Some people use a paddling dry bag.) If the morning is fine, air your sleeping bag in the sun while you make breakfast and pack.

Completely air-dry your sleeping bag before storing it after a trip – a blast of full sunshine is best. Place it loosely in a cloth bag. Store it, your tent, and your pack where they will not be permeated by food odours. Wash your sleeping bag only when it really needs it, by hand or in a front-loading washer. Use the soap and the drying technique recommended by the manufacturer. Don't dry-clean a down bag.

Sleeping Pads

Whatever sleeping bag you choose, a sleeping pad is essential. The most comfortable and most expensive pads are inflatable. Carry a repair kit. Less expensive and less effective (but lighter) are closed-cell foams. Carry your sleeping pad in a stuff sack to keep it dry and to protect it from scuffing and punctures. If there is room, stow it inside your pack. For a backcountry pillow, fill a stuff sack with extra clothing. Use an old piece of closed-cell foam as a bum pad to sit on at camp.

Clothing

A versatile backcountry clothing system incorporates a series of layers that you can put on or take off quickly, as required. The expression, "cotton kills" is true. Avoid cotton, denim, and leather, as they soak easily, become clammy, and take a long time to dry. Choose wool, pile, fleece, and other synthetic fabrics.

Always carry a set of long underwear – tops and bottoms – liner gloves, and a pair of heavier outer gloves or wool mitts. Fingerless wool gloves are useful. A pair of knee length socks and a down vest make camp life more comfortable early and late in the season. Top off your cool weather gear with a warm winter-style hat, such as a toque with ear flaps, or a balaclava. If you loose a glove or mitt, use a spare sock to cover your hand.

Rains in the Rockies can be extremely cold. Although your backpack helps keep you warm and dry, you should invest in a full suit of coated raingear with adjustable cuffs, and a snug hood. Full or partial zippers on the legs assist with ventilation and getting the pants on over boots. Choose a rain jacket a size larger than normal to allow extra clothing to be worn underneath, and to compensate for the fact that a full backpack will make your jacket bunch at the shoulders. No fabric is completely waterproof. Your rainsuit can double as a windsuit when required.

TOO COOL FOR COMFORT?

Your sleeping bag is rated to -10°C. There was no frost last night but you froze. Why? You're not sleeping in a laboratory. Everyone's metabolism is different. Most people know whether they sleep warmly (few blankets) or coldly (lots of blankets.) The same will be true in the backcountry. Purchase a bag that is rated accordingly. If your sleeping bag is not keeping you warm, try the following.

- Eat more food. Have a hot drink before going to bed.
- Exercise vigorously for a few minutes before you get in the bag.
- Use a beefier, inflatable sleeping pad.
- Un-stuff your sleeping bag hours before you go to bed. Fluff up the bag just before you get into it.
- Draw the mummy hood closed.
- Sleep wearing long underwear or dry clothes, including light gloves, socks, and hat.
- When possible, air your bag in the morning to help dry it.

What about the sunny days? Shorts, T-shirts, and a sun hat should be part of your layered system. Skin burns more rapidly at higher elevations. Carry an effective sunscreen (at least SPF 30), and apply it liberally. Zinc ointment is the best for fair-skinned people. Don't forget to apply it to noses, lips, cheek bones, and ear lobes. Light coloured fabrics have two advantages: they keep you cooler and tend to dry more quickly than darker fabrics. You can use a large cotton handkerchief or bandana as a scarf, a head cover, a towel, a sling, and a pressure dressing.

Leave a change of dry clothes, including shoes, in your vehicle at the trailhead. You'll appreciate the comfort if you spent the hike in a monsoon or if ended it in a blizzard.

Trekking Poles

Many hikers (not just the older ones) appreciate the support of trekking poles, especially on downhills. Walking with poles also helps you keep a rhythmic stride, which can save as much as 20 percent of your energy over the course of a day. The extra support can be crucial when crossing streams. Don't trust all your weight to these devices. If they shift when weighted, you could take a nasty tumble. If you hike with collapsed poles strapped to your pack, make sure that they don't protrude where they can jab other hikers.

Sunglasses

Your sunglasses should block all but 0.1% of UVA and UVB light, and pass not more than 10% of visible light. Glass lenses are more scratch-resistant than plastic. Don't forget to bring a hard case to protect them when they are in the hood of your pack.

Binoculars

Compact, lightweight binoculars in the 8 x 20 to 8 x 30 range are the one "luxury" item I would recommend above any other. They are great for birding and for studying other wildlife from a distance. They can also help you to tell if that dark blob on the slidepath ahead, above where you plan to camp, is a bear or a tree stump. Many respectable binos cost less than a pair of good sunglasses.

Nightlight

Twilight lasts a long time during summer in the Rockies. You won't often need a nightlight but you should have one available for emergencies or for hiking early and late in the season. A headlamp is the best choice as it keeps your hands free. LED bulbs greatly increase battery life. Always carry spare batteries and bulb. Pack your light carefully so that it doesn't light up the inside of your pack all day.

Stoves and the Camp Kitchen

A camp stove is a backcountry necessity in the Rockies. Fires are not allowed at many campgrounds. Even if allowed, cooking with a wood fire can be time-consuming – a fact that you will not appreciate during inclement weather, when a quick, hot cup of tea or soup might save the day.

Carry one stove for every 2-3 people. Take care not to scorch or burn picnic tables at campgrounds. Place

---

CHILL-OUT

These tips will make cold weather camping more enjoyable.

- Before you pitch camp, change out of wet clothing (including socks) right away. Put on extra layers (including shells/raingear), winter hat, and hood.
- Split the camp set-up chores – one person pitches the tent and unpacks the sleeping gear, the other makes hot drinks and gets a start on dinner.
- Cold air collects in hollows. Avoid camping in them.
- Knock falling snow off your tent before it does damage.
- Don't let your boots freeze. Put them in a plastic bag and sleep with them if you have to.
- Leave the door or vent partially open to allow air to circulate in the tent. This reduces frost build-up.
- Keep lighters and fuel bottles warm.
- Although they sound cozy, zip-together sleeping bags are a bust in cold weather. Too much air escapes from around your shoulders. Go it alone and wear clothing and a hat to bed.
- Carry extra clothing – down vest, knee length socks, and scarf.
- The sun's first rays often function as a natural alarm clock. If you plan an early start, choose a tent site that will not be shaded in the morning. If there was frost, rain or snow overnight, a sunny tent site will also aid greatly in drying out before you repack.

COUNT YOUR STARS

A clear night in the backcountry provides many people with a rare opportunity for star-gazing. Bring a small star chart to help you identify constellations. The Perseid meteor shower peaks during the second week of August.

your stove on bare ground, on a flat rock or on top of a metal fire-box.

Backpacking liquid-fuel stoves made by MSR, Optimus, and Coleman are the most popular. These stoves are lightweight, dependable, stable, and have built-in pressure pumps that allow for easy priming. This compensates for pressure losses due to cold weather and altitude. The stoves burn white gas (naptha, Coleman fuel) – a fuel that is readily available at outdoor stores, hardware stores, and most service stations. Stoves with the adjustment knob on the burner, rather than on the fuel bottle, have less lag time for adjustments and generally simmer better. But ensure that you can use the little knob without burning your fingers or knocking over the pot.

Backcountry cooking

Buy a field-maintainable stove and carry a repair kit. Test and clean your stove before each trip, and learn how to troubleshoot. The 22 ounce (US) MSR bottle is usually sufficient to cook breakfasts, dinners, and hot drinks for two people during an outing that lasts three days and two nights. You will use more fuel if you treat your drinking water by boiling it. Carry extra fuel in a combination of one-litre and half-litre bottle sizes to allow you to most efficiently use the space in your pack. Remember to leave an airspace when filling the stove fuel bottle.

Fuel cartridges are usually available locally for the backpacking versions of butane and propane stoves. If you bring a cannister stove to the Rockies, be sure that it takes a generic cannister, as proprietary cannisters might not be available. The new generation of cannister stoves – especially those with a propane-butane mix – perform better than their ancestors, but are still a notch below white gas stoves in cold and windy weather. They are expensive to operate – a single cannister can cost as much as 4 litres of white gas. Their other disadvantages are that – apart from a slight drop in the level of the flame – you don't know that you are low on fuel until you run out; and you are tossing a metal cylinder when it's empty. On the plus side, cannister stoves don't need to be primed. Test fit each cannister to the stove before your trip to make sure that it seals, as manufacturing flaws do happen.

Lighters and Matches

Carry two lighters as well as waterproof, strike-any-where matches. Seal the matches in doubled plastic bags. Check the lighters before each trip and pack them in different places. A wet lighter can be dried in a pocket. Wet matches may take days to dry, and often disintegrate. You can dip match heads in melted paraffin to waterproof them.

Pots and Utensils

Stainless steel cooking pots are more durable than aluminum pots. Carry two cooking pots for every 2-3 people. Use one pot for boiling water, the other for cooking foods. This simplifies clean-ups and prevents the experience of drinking tea that tastes like spaghetti sauce. Carry your stove and pots in stuff sacks. Hang them with your food at night. Don't forget the potholder and a scrubbing pad. Each person should carry a pocket knife, a plastic bowl, a plastic mug, and a spoon – don't bother with a fork. If you are hiking solo, skip the bowl and eat out of a pot.

Food

You can take three approaches to backcountry food: freeze-dried; low budget noodle-ectomy; and dehydrate your own. Each has its advantages. The first is the most convenient but you pay a premium price for it. The second is hit-and-miss but is great for trips thrown together at the last minute. For those who backpack often, the investment in a food dehydrator will pay back in a season or two, allowing you to create your own backcountry cuisine with more flavour and higher nutritional value. Choose foods that are less likely to attract bears – avoid meats, fish, and mint. Use reclosable plastic bags to carry meal-sized portions. Write instructions in ink, directly on the bag. Use a straw to suck air out of bags as you fill and seal them. You'll be amazed at how much smaller your food bag will be.

Ensure that your diet includes fresh vegetables and fruits. These will keep for two or three days if you pack them carefully. A daily vitamin-mineral supplement will help compensate for a lack of fresh foods, especially if you are backpacking for an entire summer. Salt tablets are hard on your digestive system. Add extra salt to your food instead, to help maintain your electrolyte balance.

Many people find that they eat more food and more often than normal while hiking. Keep mixtures of nuts, raisins, seeds, and candies handy, and eat on the move, especially during foul weather. If you feel yourself becoming lethargic or cranky, eat! Low blood sugar is often the culprit. Snacking will usually improve your energy and your outlook. Snacks may become your survival food in an emergency.

Always pack a few extra soups and hot drink mixes. Use them for a hot lunch during inclement weather or as emergency rations if your trip takes one night longer than planned.

Hang your food, stove, and cooking kit at night or when you are away from camp. The risks to your properly stored food are, in order of magnitude: weather, other campers, squirrels and birds, and bears. A see-through dry-bag will weatherproof your food. It's a bit more of a setback than a nylon stuffsack if a critter chews it, but the convenience outweighs that concern. To prevent squirrels and birds from eating your trail mix and cereals (their favourites), store these foods in reclosable bags inside your cooking pots.

Drinking Water: Boil It, Blast It or Filter It?

Hikers in the Rockies often reach meltwater streams within a stone's throw of their glacial sources. This should be some of the purest water on earth. But is it?

Not always. If your habit is to drink straight from streams, you will eventually get sick. The hazards are protozoa, bacteria, and, to a much lesser extent, viruses. The protozoan parasite *Giardia lamblia* gets the most attention. *Giardia* (zjee-ARE-dee-ah) gets into water in contaminated feces. The complaint it produces when ingested by humans, giardiasis, is commonly called "beaver fever." But beavers get a bad rap; all mammals can host this parasite.

Giardiasis, and the ailment created by its more recently introduced protozoan cousin, *Cryptosporidium parvum*, produce general weakness and gastro-intestinal upset. Diarrhea, abdominal cramps, foul-smelling gas and feces, and lack of appetite are typical symptoms, occurring 1-2 weeks after ingestion of the cysts. Lower abdominal pain while walking downhill is a classic giardiasis indicator. Giardiasis is sometimes – but not always – diagnosed through a stool sample, and is controlled by the drug Flagyl. By the time you are done with the disease and the treatment, your innards will indeed feel flagellated. Untreated, giardiasis runs its course in 2-6 weeks, but many who have been afflicted say that they never feel right again. *Cryptosporidium* runs its course in 2-10 days and is untreatable.

Bacteria are the next greatest threat. They may cause gastro-intestinal upset and other illnesses. The most widespread bacteria is *Campylobacter jejuni*, which has on onset of 2-5 days and a duration of 1 week. Viral threats in Rockies water are generally not a concern, but may include strains of hepatitis.

Responsible attitudes toward human waste in the backcountry will help reduce the contamination of water. As dogs carry protozoa and may also track the feces of people and other animals into watercourses, it is a good idea not to take Fido on the trail.

Filters

Portable, pump-action, water filters are the environmental choice for treating water. They do not require fossil fuel or chemicals, and allow you to treat water relatively quickly on the spot by pumping water through one or more filter elements. Protozoan cysts are larger than 1.0 micron in diameter, whereas bacteria are generally smaller than 0.5 micron. (A micron is one one-millionth of a metre.) A filter pore size of 0.3 micron or less should be considered standard, but no matter how small the pores, some bacteria (if present) will get through, as will all viruses. If this concerns you, use a water purifying system (see below) or add iodine and let the water stand before filtering.

The most convenient filters are those that will screw onto Nalgene widemouth (63 mm) bottles. Health Canada has declared Bisphenol-A, a component of many food grade plastics, to be poisonous. Check that your water bottles are BPA-free. Choose a filter that has a durable and easily cleaned element. Buy a spare. Silt harbors pathogens and bacteria, and will clog a filter quickly. If you must pump silty water, scoop it first into a pot and let the silt settle, or strain it through a bandana. (Boil water in the pot afterward to purify the pot.) Use the float and screen to keep the intake line off the bottom of the watercourse. Pay special attention to the mechanical action of the filter pump. Choose a model that fits your hand and that is not tiring to use. Allow time in the day for the job of filtering water, but remember that you don't have to filter water that will be boiled before consumption. A squeeze-bottle filter processes one bottle at a time, but slowly. It's an extra piece of gear to carry but may be a worthwhile choice for solo day-hikers.

COMPARISON OF WATER TREATMENT METHODS

	Eliminates Giardia?	Eliminates Crypto?	Eliminates Bacteria?	Eliminates Viruses?	Environmental Rating
Boiling	Yes	Yes	Yes	Yes	2nd
Iodine	Yes	No	Yes	Yes	3rd
Chlorine	Yes	No	Yes	Yes	4th
Chlorine Dioxide	Yes	Yes	Yes	Yes	4th
Filter ≤ 0.3 micron pore size	Yes	No	Partially	No	1st
Purifier	Yes	No	Yes	Yes	3rd
Ultraviolet	Yes	Yes	Yes	Yes	2nd

Boiling

The US Centres For Disease Control states that, at sea level, three minutes of boiling kills every type of pathogen. The boiling point of water decreases 1°C for each 300 m above sea level, so boil longer at higher elevations. Carry extra fuel, and budget time for boiling and cooling the water before you put it into bottles. When it has cooled, boiled water tastes flat. Add a drop or three of lemon juice.

Chemicals, Chemicals, Chemicals

Chemical treatment of drinking water can be effective, but has limitations, risks, and environmental costs that might exceed those of boiling water. All manufacturers of chemical water treatments recommend that you filter the water first. The drawbacks to using chlorine dioxide are that it involves premixing chemicals, and it takes time – up to 4 hours for the chemical to do its work. Straight chlorine (i.e., bleach) quickly takes care of protozoa other than *Cryptosporidium*, and all bacteria and viruses, but when dissolved in water, chlorine will kill friendly bacteria in your gut and will form compounds that are suspected carcinogens. Iodine – in liquid, crystal, or tablet form – kills bacteria, viruses, and the cysts of *Giardia*. In the Rockies, you will need to use more of it or let it stand longer, because water colder than 10°C reduces iodine's potency. Don't let chemically-treated water stand in your tent – iodine and chlorine fumes in an enclosed space are toxic. All chemicals have a shelf life, so record when you open the container. Discard the contents appropriately when the time is up.

Add a few drops of lemon juice to chemically treated water to mask the flavour. Pregnant women and those with thyroid disorders should avoid more than occasional iodine use. If you use iodine and then filter the water, allow time for the iodine to work

before filtering. Most filters include a carbon stage that removes the chemical from the water. If you add iodine after filtering, you will taste it.

Purifiers

A water purifier combines a water filter with a chemical treatment, usually iodine, which is removed by a secondary element. These gadgets are more expensive in the initial outlay, and require more maintenance than simple filters, but they are the most effective. If you will be processing large volumes of water, they will be the most cost-effective in the long run.

Ultraviolet Light

Battery operated, pen-like devices that zap water with shortwave ultraviolet radiation are one of the newer water purification technologies. The devices work, and more quickly than pumping water through a filter. However, they tend to gobble batteries. Silt and cold temperatures reduce their effectiveness. In the Rockies, you will probably have to pre-filter the water to remove silt.

Dehydration

Now that you have treated the water, how much should you drink each day? Lots. Dehydration affects your body's ability to digest food, to circulate nutrients, and to eliminate toxins, to stay warm in cold weather, and to stay cool in hot weather. A loss of just 5 percent of body fluids may result in a 25-30 percent loss of physical energy. Dehydration also contributes to altitude sickness – the symptoms of which may occur at elevations as low as 2450 m – and to the build-up of lactic acid, which causes stiff muscles and fatigue.

The best gauges of adequate hydration are to check how often you pee, and the colour of your urine. You should pee at least three times in a 24 hour period. If your urine is clear or pale yellow, you are drinking enough fluids. If your pee is dark, drink at least a litre of water. Any time that you feel thirsty, you are probably down at least a litre. Avoid beverages that contain alcohol or caffeine, as they contribute to dehydration.

The trick is to drink often. Drink a litre of water in the morning before you break camp. Drink every time you stop. Many backpacks now come with a water bottle holster on the waist strap. Use durable, one-litre plastic water bottles. Those manufactured by Nalgene are the best. Most water filters and purifiers screw onto the Nalgene wide-mouth bottles, but there are some oddballs, so check.

Water is not always close at backcountry campgrounds, especially during hot summers when small streams dry up. Carry a "water billy" to reduce the number of trips you make to the water source, thereby reducing trampling of vegetation. Commercial water billies come in 2-litre to 10-litre capacities. You can also use a refillable liner from a 4-litre wine or juice box.

A litre of water weighs 1 kg (2.2 lbs). A large hydration system (Platypus, Camelbak, etc.) adds a lot of weight. If you are day-hiking in hot weather, a small hydration system may help check your thirst. Don't forget to clean your water bottles and hydration system components regularly. Left unattended, they are wonderful grunge factories.

Camping and Trail Etiquette

On all but a few of the Classic Hikes, camping is allowed at designated campgrounds only. Please do not camp elsewhere. The standards for campgrounds differ. In Banff, all sites are equipped with outhouses, a food storage system, and rustic picnic tables, although some of these are in disrepair. In Jasper, all campgrounds have food storage systems and some kind of privy. Some of the popular campgrounds in Yoho and Kootenay have been "hardened" with gravelled tent pads and trails, and picnic tables built from pressure-treated wood. Four of the campgrounds along the Berg Lake trail have shelters.

In designated campgrounds, camp on an established site. Do not dig drainage trenches around your tent. Share picnic tables, campfires, and food storage cables and lockers with other parties when a campground is crowded. Observe quiet hours between 10:00 pm and 7:00 am, and please, do not use portable music devices or make or receive non-emergency cell-phone calls. Groups larger than six persons are discouraged.

At night or when you will be away from camp, hang your food, stove, cooking kit, and garbage on the storage cables or stow it in lockers. Be sure to clip the cables to the eye hooks after use. Unattached cables are a hazard to antlered animals. If an elk, moose or deer snags an antler in a cable late in the autumn, it may die a slow death from starvation.

Random Camping

Only three of the Classic Hikes contain areas where random camping is permitted – Glacier Lake and Dolomite Pass in Banff, and the non-core area of Mt. Assiniboine Provincial Park. A park use permit is required for random camping in Banff. The campsite must be at least 5 km from the nearest trailhead and 50 m from the closest trail and water source. Choose a site that hasn't been used before – one that has no vegetation or has durable vegetation cover; or choose a site that is already heavily impacted. In this case, confine your movements to areas that are already trampled to avoid enlarging the disturbed area. Do

not camp on or near wildlife trails. If you pitch more than one tent, keep the tents well apart. Tent sites should be moved every three days. The maximum group size is 10.

You will need to carry a "bear barrel," or a 30 m piece of nylon rope or 5 mm cord and a carabiner to hang your food at night. String food, pots, and stove so that they are suspended at least 5 m off the ground, halfway between two trees at least 5 m apart. You want this to be at least 50 m downwind from your campsite. Rigging the system is much more easily said than done; practice at home. In my experience, the process takes 45 minutes to an hour. Set up your system before you cook. You don't want to be falling out of trees in the dark.

Campfires

A campfire is an irresistible aspect of trail life. If campfires are permitted at your campground, ask yourself: Do I really need one? If fires are allowed, it will say so on your park use permit. As a general rule, if a metal firebox is not provided or if the wildfire hazard is high, campfires are not allowed.

Cooking over a campfire can be time consuming and undependable. Use a lightweight camping stove instead. For emergency or wet weather situations where a fire is absolutely necessary for warmth or safety, carry a small piece of candle to use as firestarter. To reduce air pollution and the effects of firewood gathering, share your campfire with fellow campers.

At heavily impacted sites, build your campfire in an existing fire ring or in the metal fireboxes provided. In pristine areas, it is best to build your fire in a stream bed, on a gravel bar below the high water level. Otherwise, carefully create a fire ring from rocks. Keep your fire on mineral soil, not in the organic layer. Dismantle the ring afterward.

Keep potential firewood in its natural lengths until ready to burn. Scatter unused wood. Remember that nationwide, improperly tended or unextinguished campfires are the leading cause of forest fires. (Cigarette smoking is the second leading cause.) To extinguish your fire, pour water on the coals and mix the slurry thoroughly with a stick. Douse the coals again.

Most fire pits in the backcountry are tarnished with garbage left behind by inconsiderate backpackers. Don't attempt to burn tin cans, other metals and aluminum foil, plastics, multi-laminate soup and sauce packages, Tetra-paks, and twist ties. Make the effort to pack out all recyclable items.

Answering Nature's Call

At campgrounds and trailheads, please use the outhouses provided. The facilities that you will encounter vary. Some backcountry campgrounds now have plastic, open-air thrones that, during inclement weather, guarantee a soaking. Think of them as a view without a room. Toilet paper is not provided. Put the lid down and secure the outhouse door (if it has one) after use.

When an outhouse is damaged or not available, do your business well off trail, away from tenting areas, and at least 100 m from all watercourses. Human urine contains three percent sodium on average. Mule deer, bighorn sheep, porcupines, and marmots are attracted by the salt, and will eat urine-soaked turf. If you pee near your tent, you may find one of these animals chomping on your front lawn soon after.

When you defecate, dig a small "cat hole," maximum 10 cm deep, in the dark, biologically active layer of the soil. Cover your business, including toilet paper, with the excavations. Alternately, you may pack your used toilet paper to the next outhouse, or toss it in a burning campfire.

Feminine Hygiene

Be prepared for your period even if you don't expect it until after the hike. Stresses – even healthy ones such as hiking – can alter your menstrual cycle. Use unscented tampons or pads. Carry extra supplies for clean-up. Keep sanitary materials handy, double sealed in reclosable plastic bags. Seal soiled materials inside a small reclosable bag. Seal this inside a larger, clean reclosable bag, and hang it while at camp. Never bury used sanitary materials in the backcountry, and don't try to burn them; complete incineration is impossible in a responsible campfire.

Backcountry Cleanliness

You need a few basics to stay respectable during an overnight trip in the backcountry. Carry a toothbrush, a brush or comb, toilet paper, some baking soda (in a small cannister), any essential medications, and a thin nylon rope to use as a clothesline. If you wear contact lenses, carry a travel kit with your required solutions, and don't forget your eyeglasses in a hard case.

Leave your cosmetics at home. The only mousse you want to see in the backcountry is the kind that eats swamp salad. Soap, deodorant, toothpaste, gel, cologne, and perfume are potential pollutants, and contain scents that may attract bears. Your pack will be lighter and safer.

As a backpacker, you have a right to smell like old socks – up to a point. On hot days, rinse your head, underarms, legs, and feet in a creek or lake. If you are brave, go for a dip. The cleaner your body, the cleaner your sleeping bag and the less often you will have to wash it. If you are gassing out your companions, tea tree oil is an effective natural deodorizer.

HIGH TECH – HOW HIGH?

The proliferation of micro-electronic technology has risen to the summits and flooded the valleys worldwide – handy-cams and satellite phones on the summit of Mt. Everest, pagers and cell-phones at Healy Pass. The blatant intrusion of superfluous technology into backcountry settings threatens to erode the very being of wilderness and our ability to enjoy it.

On some outings in this book, you will be more than twelve hours away from the closest outside help. Rather than perceiving this as a threat that requires mitigation through technology, let's celebrate it for the reality – rare, sobering, and enlivening – that it represents. It is only our possible vulnerability in the backcountry that maintains a collective healthy respect for it; that prevents wilderness from being denigrated by increments until it is, at least figuratively, paved.

If you cannot venture onto these trails without carrying gadgets to make emergency contact, it is probably safe to say that wilderness travel, of the character found on these hikes, is not for you. Global positioning system (GPS) devices are not necessary to navigate the trails as described in this book. Personal locator beacons (such as SPOT), which, when activated, may lead to a search and rescue response, are a non-intrusive means of back-up. Cell-phone calls placed during emergencies have greatly benefited both the rescued and the rescuers in the Canadian Rockies. If you feel that you must carry a cell-phone, please restrict your use of it to emergencies only. Be aware that cell-coverage is not uniform in the mountains and that cold temperatures reduce battery power.

Large groups might find two-way VHF radios useful in coordinating their movements, but for most of us they will just be more dead weight in our packs and noise in our ears. If you find that you must send and receive e-mails while in the backcountry, perhaps you should consider doing something else, somewhere else, on your days off.

Brush your teeth with warm water. Once a day, add some baking soda to the toothbrush.

Rinse dirty T-shirts, underwear, and socks in creeks without using soap. Hang them on a clothesline, on bushes, in the tent, or on your pack while on the trail. The clothes won't be squeaky clean, but they will be tolerable for another day.

Use a water-billy to bring washwater to your dishes. Do the washing on well-drained ground, 100 m away from watercourses and tent sites. If food is burned onto a pot, fill it with hot water and let it stand, then use a small amount of sand as an abrasive. Scatter the wastewater over a wide area or use it to douse campfire coals. If the wastewater contains many food particles, you may strain it first through a porous cloth. Pack out the strainings or burn them. This simple method will keep dishes suitably clean throughout a five day trip – assuming that your cooked food does not include excessive fats or oils.

When possible, rinse your hands in a stream or creek after washing dishes and eating. This will help prevent the spread of food odours over your pack and clothing.

First-Aid

Your first-aid kit should include blister dressings, adhesive dressings, closure strips, adhesive tape, sterile gauze, pain-killer, tensor bandage, tweezers, disposable medical gloves, pencil, and paper. You can improvise splints from branches, packs or tent poles. You can improvise slings and dressings from extra clothing. Carry required medications and inform your hiking partners of your allergies and conditions. People with chronic conditions should wear a Medic-Alert bracelet or necklace. Insulin-dependent diabetics should be aware that vigorous exercise may affect their response to medication. Anyone with a pre-existing heart or lung condition should be cautious in their approach to hiking.

When someone is ill or injured, make a quick assessment to gauge the seriousness. Cuts, abrasions, bruises, sprains, and minor burns usually can be patched-up sufficient to allow the party to carry on or retreat. Simple fractures – those with no bone protrusion – usually can be field-stabilized, but evacuation may be required. Unresponsiveness, compound (bone protrusion) or multiple fractures, choking, difficulty breathing, non-traumatic abdominal pain or chest pain, vaginal bleeding in pregnancy, diabetic and anaphylactic reactions, hypothermia, heat induced collapse (heat stroke), and severe hemorrhage are the true emergencies of the backcountry and elsewhere. In these cases:

- Do not move the person unless the local environment is life-threatening and shelter is nearby.

- Gently open the airway and assist with rescue breathing, if required.
- Control all deadly bleeding using direct pressure and sterile dressings.
- Assist with medications, if required.
- Cool the heat stroke patient rapidly. Move them to shade.
- Warm the mildly hypothermic patient. Handle all hypothermic patients extremely gently, especially if unconscious.
- Immobilize fractures.
- Treat the person for shock. Most injured patients should be kept on their backs unless this compromises their breathing. Keep the person warm and comfortable. Be reassuring. For medical complaints or compromised breathing, allow the patient to choose the position of greatest comfort. Most will probably want to be propped-up.
- Patients who are semi-conscious or who are otherwise unable to protect their airway should be placed in the "recovery position."
- Give no food or drink unless the patient is diabetic or rescue is more than a day away.
- At least one person should stay with the injured.
- If your group is large enough, one or two people should seek help, taking a written description of the injury and the patient's location with them. Take note of possible helicopter landing sites close to the patient. Remember that helicopters can only fly in daylight and in reasonable visibility. If you have a cell-phone, now is the time to use it.
- In cases of cardiac arrest, limit cardio-pulmonary resuscitation to 30 minutes. The chances of resuscitation in the field beyond that are effectively nil.

Too Cold, Too Hot

Hypothermia (commonly called "exposure") is the lowering of the body's core temperature. It is one of the greater risks in the backcountry because its onset can be insidious. If allowed to progress from mild (37°C to 35°C), to moderate (35°C to 30°C), to severe (<29°C), hypothermia kills.

You lose heat while hiking in four ways, even on a sunny day:

- convection (wind)
- conduction (sitting on a cold rock or a wet stump)
- radiation (ambient heat loss into the air)
- evaporation (sweat, breath vapour).

The initial symptom of hypothermia is shivering – the body's attempt to produce heat. Soon, blood is shunted from the extremities toward the vital organs.

Pulse and breathing rate go up. This is mild hypothermia, reversible by seeking shelter and by putting on warm, dry clothing. If cooling progresses, muscular rigidity develops. The person stumbles and slurs words. Thinking becomes muddled. Pulse and breathing rate decrease. At this point, the moderately hypothermic hiker is unable to salvage the situation without the clear thinking and help of a hiking partner who is not affected. The progression of symptoms can take place over a period of days of inclement weather or in a few hours.

Your ability to resist hypothermia is determined by age, body mass, fitness, underlying medical conditions, diet, and effectiveness of clothing, but most of all by common sense. You are (or should be) carrying extra clothing; wear it! As much as 55 percent of body heat goes out through the top of your head. Wear a winter hat and gloves. Layer-up on inclement days; try to do this before you reach a high-point raked by the wind. Take shelter when resting on lousy days. Watch your companions carefully for the onset of symptoms. Insist that they wear more clothing if you think that they are at risk. Take their advice if they offer the same to you. Eat and drink adequately. Turn back or descend if conditions are truly foul.

Actively rewarm a mildly hypothermic patient. Get them into dry clothing. Help them to exercise to restore circulation. Give them warm drinks. Rewarming of moderately and severely hypothermic patients cannot be accomplished in the field. Help them into dry clothing and zip them up tightly, alone, in a dry sleeping bag. Send for, or go for help. Unconscious hypothermic patients are at risk of cardiac arrest. Handle them very gently.

On some days, you can overheat while hiking. If the forecast for Banff or Jasper towns is 26°C or above, protect yourself from exposure to the sun and the risk of dehydration. Wear light-coloured clothing and a sun hat. Use sunscreen. Drink lots and often. Begin your hike early and end it by early afternoon. Seek shade while taking breaks. Watch your companions for early symptoms of heat exhaustion – flushed faces, fatigue, and irritability – and take action to cool them. You may need to be assertive. Any person who has ceased to sweat in extreme heat is suffering from severe hyperthermia, a dire medical emergency. Get help right away.

Bugs

Although biting bugs in the Rockies are nowhere near as numerous as in the far north or in the lake country of the Canadian Shield, you will undoubtedly become acquainted with black flies, horse flies, deer flies, no-see-ums, and the 28 species of mosquitoes that call these mountains home. Biting bugs are attracted by body warmth and by exhaled carbon dioxide. From the bugs' points of view, some people are more attractive than others. Dark coloured clothing attracts mosquitoes, as do some cosmetics.

Biting bugs generally become noticeable in late June or early July, and are gone most years by mid-August. Warm, damp weather helps them to proliferate. Cool weather kills them off. Breezes keep them away. Campsites near lakes are often bug heaven. Some of the buggier backcountry campgrounds are Luellen Lake, Baker Lake, Amethyst Lake, Lone Lake, Surprise Point, Three Isle Lake, and Lake Magog.

Insect Repellents

Controversy over DEET – the principal active ingredient in most synthetic insect repellents – has raged since the substance was introduced in 1957. DEET dissolves plastics, and removes paints from metal surfaces. It will foul your sunglasses, camera, and Gore-Tex. Nonetheless, the US Food and Drug Administration insists that DEET is safe. Health Canada implemented a ban of certain DEET products in 2002. Health Canada is also requiring stricter labelling. The gist of the rulings:

- Do not use DEET on infants less than 6 months old.
- For children aged 6 months-2 years in areas with a risk of mosquito-borne disease, one application per day of a product containing DEET at maximum 10 percent concentration may be used.
- For children 2-12 years, three applications per day of a product containing DEET at maximum 10 percent concentration may be used. Avoid contact with the face and hands. Avoid prolonged use.
- For people over 12 years old, products with greater than 30 percent concentration of DEET will no longer be acceptable.

If you use DEET, apply the product to non-synthetic clothing, not to your skin. Wash your hands after application. Wash yourself thoroughly when you are clear of the bugs. Be mindful that DEET-covered hands dipped into backcountry watercourses introduce pollution. Keep DEET formulas out of cuts and scratches. Avoid products that combine DEET with sunscreen as, over the course of a sunny day, you will apply far more DEET than is necessary.

Bug repellents made from natural substances (principally oil of eucalyptus, and oil of citronella)

MIRACLE TREATMENT

Zinc oxide ointment works great as a sunscreen and also takes away the sting of heat rashes and friction rashes. You can re-use an empty lip balm container to carry a backcountry supply.

are not as effective; meaning that you need to apply them more often – perhaps as often as every 20 minutes. But they are easier on you, and, by way of the manufacturing process, they are also easier on the environment. What about those citronella-impregnated wristbands, cosmetic cures, and garlic and vitamin deterrents? The studies that I looked at have shown them all to be useless.

If bugs really have it in for you, a head net is an inexpensive, lightweight, and effective way to keep bugs off your face and neck. If you have intense reactions to the bites of mosquitoes, you may want to carry topical or oral antihistamines to help alleviate the swelling. Cool compresses, using stream or lake water, will provide temporary relief from itching. Many people experience strong reactions to early season bites, but suffer less as they develop a seasonal immunity with continued exposure.

West Nile Fever and malaria – two mosquito-borne diseases – are spreading in North America but, as of 2010, were unreported from the Rockies.

Ticks

Whereas the bites of flying bugs are usually only a nuisance, the bite of the Rocky Mountain wood tick can be a more serious matter. Ticks resemble tiny, flattened spiders. They are usually encountered in the montane life zone (low elevation valley bottoms) from early April until mid-June. Areas frequented by bighorn sheep, elk, and deer are havens for these parasites. The tick life cycle has four stages, three of which require the tick to ingest a blood meal. It is the adult stage that preys upon larger mammals.

Adult ticks climb grasses and low shrubs to await their prey. Once lodged in the fur or clothing of a potential victim, the tick seeks out fleshy areas to inflict its bite and draw its meal of blood. When it bites, the tick injects an anti-coagulant to accelerate bleeding. The mouth parts penetrate the skin and the tick's body balloons with the fluid of its host.

The dangers to humans from tick bites are Rocky Mountain spotted fever – characterized by a headache and fever that develop 3-10 days after the tick bite; and tick paralysis – a reaction to tick induced toxins that can impair functions of the central nervous system. It develops 5-6 days after the tick bite. Both afflictions can be fatal but, as yet, there has not been a confirmed fatality in the Canadian Rockies. Lyme disease, a multi-system bacterial infection that causes encephalitis, is carried by western black-legged ticks. It has been reported from Waterton and from the Cranbrook area in the southern Rockies.

What can you do to protect yourself? Wear long pants and long sleeves. Apply insect repellent to socks and pant cuffs. Tuck your pant cuffs into your socks. Tuck your shirt into your pants. Wear light coloured clothing so that you can spot ticks easily. Avoid grassy meadows during May and June. After any outing in tick terrain, search your clothing, equipment, skin, and hair thoroughly. Have a friend check your scalp, neck, and back, and the places where the elastic straps of underwear press against your skin. A tick will usually roam the skin of a potential host for several hours before biting. Ideally, you are trying to find it before it bites. If you find a tick after it has bitten, or if you detect a red circle around a bite, see a physician promptly. Change your clothes and boots, and empty your pack outside after your hike. Go through all your gear to ensure that you don't inadvertently transport a tick or three into your tent, vehicle or home.

BACKCOUNTRY BIRDING

Three hundred and thirty-six species of birds occur in the Canadian Rockies, of which about two-thirds are seen frequently. The typical backcountry hike takes you through a variety of habitats – forest, riparian, and alpine – enriching the potential for sightings. Carry lightweight binoculars to enhance your birding experience.

Two species of songbirds vie for being the most abundant in the Rockies: black-capped chickadee, a year-round resident; and dark-eyed junco, which arrives in late March. The ubiquitous American robin is a close third. Other common songbirds of the subalpine forest are: ruby-crowned kinglet, golden-crowned kinglet, gray jay, common raven,

Clark's nutcracker, mountain chickadee, boreal chickadee, varied thrush, yellow-rumped warbler (photo), and warbling vireo. Look for ruffed grouse, spruce grouse, and blue grouse along trail edges. The white-tailed ptarmigan inhabits boulderfields at and above treeline. Look for dippers and harlequin ducks along fast-flowing streams. When you are camped in subalpine forest, listen at night for barred owls, boreal owls, and great horned owls. Backcountry lakes will yield sightings of osprey, common loons, mallards, teals, mergansers, goldeneyes, and perhaps, bald eagles. Golden eagles are more commonly observed soaring over the high country. They nest on cliffs.

Family camping

Hiking as a Family

by Marnie

In the hundreds of kilometres that we have back-packed with our children, we have discovered that they, like their parents, are happiest when on the trail or part way up a mountain. Here are a few tips that we've learned along the way.

When hiking with babies and toddlers, ensure that the child carrier fits both baby and adult well. We prefer a self-standing model. The carrier needs a hood, and some form of pack cover that totally encloses your little one, pack, and gear. I designed our own from coated nylon, with a clear vinyl face shield. Don't forget to incorporate air vents. When the sun reappears after a storm, be mindful of overheating. A fleece sleeve over the baby's harness will prevent neck chaffing.

LOCATION, LOCATION, LOCATION

The idyllic campsite: flat, sheltered, well-drained, easy to peg, close to water, far from neighbours, with no bugs, and a view of mountains, glaciers, and waterfalls. If you find it at a campground on the Classic Hikes, please let me know. The truth is, you've probably spent the day walking through paradise; you can settle for something a bit less at night. But to ensure that you make the best choice of the available sites, take off your pack and leave it with a companion before you look around. Without that beast on your back, you will be less likely to flop onto the first, "I guess this will do," site.

Remember that a little one in a child cover is sitting while you are hiking, so layer them well from head to toe. Carry a sunhat, UV sunglasses, and a one-piece rainsuit. A down vest inverted with the neck and arm holes sewn shut makes a perfect sleeping bag. Foldable, cotton gauze, birds-eye diapers (5 pairs of doubles on multi-day trips) work great in combination with breathable diaper pants. Employ a large Zip-loc bag and a few drop of biodegradable soap for washing, and a few alligator clips lashed to the backs of packs to secure diapers for drying. A piece of plastic works well for a change/play mat.

Use a hiking stick or hiking poles when on tricky terrain and fording creeks. Be careful when leaping; the baby won't be prepared for the jolt. Pare down your equipment as much as possible; bring the essentials only.

Children should hike between parents, carrying their own outer clothing, water, snacks, whistle, and an orange garbage bag to use as a emergency shelter. The most important thing, as with adults, won't fit in a pack – the knowledge of how to take care of themselves in the backcountry. Searching for the gnomes and fairies along the way, and for treats when in gummy bear habitat, keeps everyone happy. Children are wonderful and capable hikers. Enjoy your experience on the trail as a family

Bears

Grizzly bear

Bears are synonymous with the Canadian Rockies. They are the stuff of fear and fascination and everyone wants to see one – that is, until a bear walks into their backcountry campground. Perhaps 150-200 grizzlies range through these parks. Even fewer black bears occupy the same area. You are more likely to see a bear while you are driving to a trailhead than you are on a trail.

Most backcountry bears are wary of people. With its keener senses, a bear will usually detect you and leave before you become aware of it. As a result, in the backcountry, most times that you are close to a bear, you will not know it.

Bears are both a possible peril and a dwindling promise for the perpetuation of wilderness. In the Rockies, wildlife biologists refer to the grizzly bear as an "umbrella species." Because it is near the apex of the food web and has tremendous spatial requirements, if the grizzly bear is protected and stable, so are 90 percent of other species that share its habitat. The Bow Valley of Banff National Park is the most disturbed habitat in North America where grizzly bears still exist. If we were to lose the grizzly bear from this landscape, its wilderness would crumble.

IS THERE SAFETY IN NUMBERS?

At time of publication, there was no record of a person hiking in a group of four to six people being killed by a bear, and no record of a bear attacking any person in a group of six or more people. Nonetheless, for aesthetic and logistical reasons, most people prefer to hike in smaller groups, and some prefer to hike alone. I suggest grouping together when you are certain that there is a bear about. If you travel in a large group, remember, you have gained nothing if your group is strung out over a kilometre of trail.

A grizzly bear cub enjoys a lengthy apprenticeship with its mother – two summers, sometimes three. This training enables the cub to become familiar with the diverse and seasonally varied sources of food that comprise bear diet. The mother bear (sow) will vigorously protect her young in order to ensure their continuation. Coming between a grizzly sow and her cubs is the ultimate backcountry blunder, and should be avoided at all costs.

Possible Causes of a Bear Attack

- You are between a sow and her cubs or have presented a perceived threat to the cubs.
- You have encroached on a buried kill or are passing through an area that offers a secure food source – a lush berry patch, a field of glacier lilies, a marmot colony.
- You surprise a bear on the trail.
- A heavy snowfall in late summer or early autumn has driven bears to lower elevations where they are in greater competition for food, and are less tolerant of people.
- You have encountered a predatory bear.

Avoiding Close Encounters

Nothing can guarantee that you will not encounter a bear. By heeding the following do's and don'ts, you will minimize the chances of being in the wrong place at the wrong time.

Do:

- Learn how to identify the two species of bears in the Rockies. (See p. 11.)
- Enquire at a park information centre regarding recent bear activity on your chosen hike. Choose to hike elsewhere if bear activity is reported.
- Travel with a partner or two. Stay close together.
- Make noise while hiking. Use your voice.
- Make noise more often when travelling alongside streams, through tall shrubs, and across avalanche slopes.
- Continue to make noise at intervals during rest stops and while fording streams.
- Observe avalanche slopes and berry patches keenly before you cross them – use binoculars. Be cautious on trails lined with buffaloberry bushes in fruit.
- Pay attention to bear sign on the trail. Look for tracks and scrapes in muddy areas, and for scats. Note the direction of travel. Are they the tracks of a sow and cubs? Make more noise if the sign is fresh.

- Stop every once in a while when hiking through good bear habitat. Look and listen.
- Leave the area immediately if you discover an animal carcass.
- If you see a bear before it sees you, give it a wide berth.
- Be especially observant on trails marked with a bear caution sign.
- Cook at least 50 m downwind of your tentsite. Eat all you cook.
- At night or when away from camp, hang all food, snacks, garbage, pots, stove and strongly scented non-food items from the food storage cables provided, or by rigging your own food storage system if random camping. Double-check your pack and pockets for bits of gorp, etc.
- Pack out all your garbage.
- Report any bear sighting or encounter at a park information centre for the safety of those who follow.

Do not:
- Enter an area that is closed due to bear activity.
- Cook or eat in or near your tent.
- Store your food in your tent or at your campsite.
- Leave your pack unattended.
- Stop or camp in areas where there is fresh bear sign.
- Dispose of food or food wastes in tenting areas.
- Take fresh meat, fish or seafood into the backcountry.
- Catch and retain fish.
- Expect that a bear will hear you coming.
- Hike at night.

What to Do in a Bear Encounter

Consider yourself fortunate on three counts if you see a bear from a good distance away. First, you are paying attention. Second, you have seen a bear. Third, you have a chance to leave before things develop into an encounter. Continue on the trail if you will not come any closer to the bear, but note the wind direction. Don't turn your back on the bear until you are well clear of the area. If continuing on the trail means that you will approach the bear, choose another route or turn back.

If the bear has seen you and is far enough away that you feel you can safely leave, do so by "quartering" away, either to the left or to the right of the trail, giving the bear a wide berth. Do not run and do not turn your back on the bear. When you first see a bear, assume that it is a sow with cubs until you know otherwise. If you see a small bear, assume that it is a cub until you know otherwise. Start looking for its mom and its siblings.

In a close encounter on the trail, a bear will probably be as startled at seeing you, as you are at seeing it. If a stand-off develops in this scenario or in any of the "what if" scenarios below: stay calm, form into a group, stand your ground, talk quietly to the bear, take out your bear spray, do not run, do not climb a tree, and keep your pack on

Running away or climbing a tree may provoke a predatory response. You may need your pack later for protection. Dropping it may entice a bear to hang around and investigate. A bear may not be interested in you, but may simply want to continue along the trail in the direction it was going. Form into a group; keep children behind adults. Talk quietly to the bear – let it know that you are not a food source. Look for cubs. Ideally, you want the sow to be between you and her cubs. You also want the wind to be blowing from you to the bear, so that it can smell you.

Drop your pack and climb a tree only as a last resort. If the bear has not made contact, climbing a tree is unnecessary and may provoke the bear to follow you. A black bear can climb up to 30 m. A grizzly bear can easily climb to 10 m, sometimes higher – and can do this much more quickly than you. If the tree is small, a grizzly bear might be able to just push it over. But if the situation dictates that you must, climb quickly and carefully. Bears have hauled people out of the lower branches of trees by grabbing their legs. In other cases people have fallen out of trees to their deaths, only to be left alone by the bears involved. If the bear climbs toward you, climb as high as you can. Kneel or squat on the uppermost sturdy branch. Do not leave your legs dangling.

BEARS, BEARS, EVERYWHERE

One time on the Brazeau loop we hiked in the presence of at least three different grizzly bears. On the third day of the hike we had a head-on encounter and standoff with a bear in Poboktan Pass. At the conclusion of that episode we met two approaching hikers. They told us of their recent standoff with a bear – a different bear that they had met just over a knoll.

A day later, an upslope snowstorm hit the front ranges. We hiked from Brazeau Lake to the highway in a very long day. As we crossed Nigel Pass at dusk, we met two hikers, tromping through the slop, inbound to Four Point camp. About ten minutes later, just before I got out the headlamp, I chanced to look down on the trail. There, atop the bootprints of the two hikers we had just met, were the tracks of a large grizzly, heading the same direction as us. We followed that bear in the dark more than 6 km to the highway – the headlamp naturally quitting on the way.

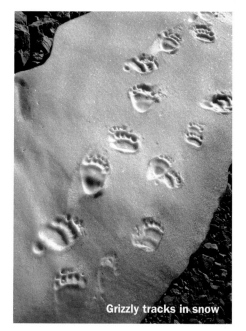

Grizzly tracks in snow

What If?

The bear appears to be nonchalantly eating, but stops often to raise its head and look at you.

You are disturbing the bear. Some bears have attacked with no apparent warning other than this simple disruption of the eating routine. If the bear is a good distance away, leave slowly by giving it a wide berth.

The bear is standing on its hind legs, looking at you.

The bear is scenting you. Talk quietly to the bear – let it know that you are not a food source.

The bear is huffing, woofing, slapping the ground, clacking its teeth, rising and falling.

Yes, the bear is agitated, but it isn't necessarily going to attack.

The bear charges and pulls up short.

This is common. No matter the species, the bear perceives you as a threat and is testing you. It may be trying to run you off. If it succeeds, it may begin to think of you as prey. Stand your ground. Have your bear spray ready. Hold up the other hand to indicate "stop." Keep talking to the bear. If the bear does not back off and is within 6 m and conditions are favourable, spray it. If it is farther away, set off a bear banger.

The bear does not appear to be agitated but has been hanging around.

Danger! A bear that hangs around the perimeter of a camp may be predatory, waiting for what it perceives to be an opportunity to attack. Leave if you can. If you cannot, go on the offensive: make a stockpile of weapons – rocks and sticks – then set off a bear banger. Get out your bear spray and be prepared to fight.

A bear is approaching closely and you are weaponless – no bear spray, no bear bangers, no rocks .

At least one bear researcher recommends that you should turn the tables – that *you should charge the bear.* Sometimes, apparently, it works. But if it doesn't.... Yikes!

Deterrents have not worked or you were unable to use them. The bear charges and makes contact.

If it is a black bear, fight for your life. People have killed black bears with pocket knives, driven them off with sticks, stones, and hiking boots. If it is a grizzly bear, "play dead." Roll face down. Clasp your hands behind your neck, elbows on the ground, legs together. (If your legs are splayed the bear has more leverage to roll you if it grabs one.) If the bear flips you over, roll back. If a grizzly bear stays over you for more than two minutes, inflicts wounds after the initial contact, or drags you away, you are dealing with a predatory bear. The rules have changed; fight for your life.

The bear is attacking you in your tent.

No matter the species, it is predatory. Shine a light into its eyes. Shout at it. Fight for your life. Don't use bear spray or launch a bear banger from within a tent.

You are witnessing an attack on your partner or another hiker.

The usual outcome when someone intervenes in a bear attack is that the bear switches focus and attacks the would-be rescuer. This person is often severely injured or killed. If you dare, set off a bear banger and try stoning the bear. Have your bear spray and other weapons ready.

Bear Deterrent: Sound

Three things are proven bear deterrents – sound, bear spray, and force. Making noise is your first defense. Your voice – whether a shout as you move along the trail, or a gentle "hello" at the beginning of an encounter – is the best sonic deterrent. Bear bells are ineffective. Clap your hands now and then as an along-the-trail alternative.

Bear-bangers are miniature fireworks that you launch from a spring-activated, pen-launcher. They typically travel 20-30 m in just under a second before exploding. The sound is generally sufficient to startle or to scare away a bear, if the animal is unaccustomed to the treatment. If the banger explodes beyond the bear, the animal may run toward you. Banger shells are a hazardous material and should be treated with care and kept dry. The shells have a life of two years. Inspect them frequently. If the plastic housing has a grayish colour, propellant may have leaked from the shell. If you launch such a shell, it may travel only a few metres before exploding, subjecting you to risk of burns, deafness, and shrapnel. Banger shells come as rim-fire or centre-fire. Make sure that your launcher is configured to match.

Bear Deterrent: Bear Spray

Bear sprays are pressurized aerosols that contain *Oleoresin capsicum* (capsaisin) – the oil from pulverized hot peppers. The spray comes in a cannister about 20 cm tall and 3 cm in diameter, weighing about 225 gm. (Smaller, "purse" sizes are illegal in Canada.) You activate the spray by removing a safety and depressing a tab near the nozzle. The spray severely irritates the eyes and respiratory tract of any critter that breathes it (including you), and will temporarily incapacitate most threatening bears, allowing you to escape. The spray lasts from three to six seconds and forms a cloud with a maximum initial dispersion of 5-9 m. The truly effective range of the spray is 3-6 m, in other words – when considering its use against a bear – face to face. If you spray into the wind or crosswind, the spray will be less effective and may also affect you or others in your party. In rain or at temperatures less than 5°C, the spray may not disperse well. And although it sounds too stupid to be true, some people have intentionally sprayed themselves before heading out on the trail, thinking the potion akin to mosquito repellent. Dial 9-1-1.

Aim the spray no more than a metre off the ground, so that if the bear comes closer, it is most likely to get the spray in its face. Hold your breath. If spraying the bear stops its approach, take your cue and leave. But don't turn your back on the bear.

Do bear sprays work? Yes, used properly under ideal conditions, bear sprays have saved hikers and campers from serious bear-inflicted injury. They may also prevent eventual injury to the bear – a bear that has been scared off may not become a "problem bear," one that is subject to being trapped and destroyed. Generally, the spray – or the noise of it being discharged – stops the bear from doing what it was doing immediately prior to the spray's release. This might buy you the time to leave. Although there are many variations as to what the bear does next, research is conclusive that spraying a bear does not turn a curious bear into an aggressive one. It also does not harm the bear in any lasting way. Some bears are only briefly deterred by the first spray; they continue to approach. This seems especially true of black bears. Some bears return after fleeing from the first spray and are not deterred by a subsequent spray.

Some bears are attracted to the residue of the spray, hours or days after it was used. So don't camp where you have discharged a spray.

Everyone in your group should carry a spray. Practice using it. Buy two cannisters. Discharge one on a calm day in a remote, unpeopled place to see how it works. Test fire the one that you will carry for half a second each year. Buy a new spray every third year.

Remember, if you choose to carry bear bangers or bear spray, they do not replace the care, common sense, and sound judgement required of you when you travel in bear country. As one researcher has stated, bear spray "ain't brains in a can."

CONVERSIONS

SI (metric)	Imperial
1 millimetre (mm)	0.0394 inches
1 centimetre (cm)	0.394 inches
1 metre (m)	3.28 feet
1 kilometre (km)	0.62 miles
1 hectare (ha)	2.47 acres
1 square kilometre (km²)	0.386 square miles
1 kilogram (kg)	2.205 pounds
1 tonne (t)	0.9842 UK tons (1.102 US tons)
1 litre (L)	0.22 UK gallons (0.264 US gallons)
1° Celsius (C)	1.8° Fahrenheit

Imperial	SI (metric)
1 inch	2.54 centimetres (cm)
1 foot	0.305 metres (m)
1 mile	1.61 kilometres (km)
1 acre	0.405 hectares (ha)
1 square mile)	2.59 square kilometres (km²)
1 pound	0.4536 kilograms (kg)
1 UK ton	1.016 tonnes (t)
1 US ton	0.9072 tonnes (t)
1 UK gallon	4.55 litres (L)
1 US gallon	3.78 litres (L)
1° Fahrenheit	0.55° Celsius (C)

- The freezing point is 0°C.
- One hectare = 100 m by 100 m.
- A rough formula for converting distances and heights from metric to Imperial, is to multiply by 3 and add 10 percent of the product. Example: 30 m x 3 = 90, plus 9 = 99. So 30 m = approximately 99 feet.

CLASSIC CHECKLIST FOR OVERNIGHT HIKES
(copy and use for each outing)

CAMP

- ☐ backcountry permit/ wilderness pass
- ☐ bowl, mug, spoon
- ☐ food and storage bags
- ☐ fuel
- ☐ pots, potholder, scouring pad, stuff sack
- ☐ sleeping bag
- ☐ sleeping pad
- ☐ stove, repair kit, stuff sack
- ☐ tarp and lines
- ☐ tent, poles, fly, pegs
- ☐ toilet kit and meds
- ☐ toilet paper
- ☐ water billy
- ☐ water bottle
- ☐ water filter
- ☐ waterproof matches

CLOTHING

- ☐ bandana
- ☐ boots
- ☐ bug hat
- ☐ fleece or pile jacket
- ☐ gaiters
- ☐ gloves or mitts, liner gloves
- ☐ rainsuit
- ☐ river shoes (optional)
- ☐ shorts/pants
- ☐ socks (2 sets)
- ☐ sun hat
- ☐ T-shirt
- ☐ thermal underwear (2 tops, 1 bottom)
- ☐ winter hat

GEAR

- ☐ backpack
- ☐ bear spray, bear bangers
- ☐ binoculars (optional)
- ☐ day pack for day-hiking
- ☐ camera
- ☐ compass
- ☐ first-aid and repair kits
- ☐ headlamp or flashlight
- ☐ insect repellent
- ☐ large garbage bag
- ☐ lighters (2)
- ☐ maps and route info
- ☐ pack cover
- ☐ paper and pencil
- ☐ piece of candle
- ☐ plastic bags
- ☐ pocket knife
- ☐ rope (30 m) and carabiner for hanging food
- ☐ space blanket
- ☐ star chart (optional)
- ☐ sunglasses
- ☐ sunscreen, lip balm, zinc
- ☐ trail snacks
- ☐ trekking poles
- ☐ whistle

Contacts

To contact the Minister responsible for national parks, contact Reference Canada:
- ✆ 800-622-6232
- 💻 www.canada.gc.ca

To e-mail the Superintendent of a national park, use this formula:
- ✉ Banff.Superintendent@pc.gc.ca

Change the park name accordingly.

For assistance contacting Alberta provincial parks while in Alberta:
- ✆ 310-0000.

For assistance contacting BC provincial parks while in BC:
- ✆ 800-663-7867.

Banff National Park
Box 900, Banff, AB, T1L 1K2
- 💻 www.pc.gc.ca/eng/pn-np/ab/banff
- ✉ banff.vrc@pc.gc.ca
- ✆ 403-762-1550
- ✉ lakelouise.vrc@pc.gc.ca
- ✆ 403-522-3833
- ✆ Road report: 403-762-1450
- ✆ Trail conditions: 403-760-1305
- ✆ Weather: 403-762-2088 (24 hr. recording)
- ✆ Highway conditions (for the four national parks): 403-762-1450
- ✆ Emergency: 911 (ask for Banff park dispatch)

Jasper National Park
Box 10, Jasper, AB, T0E 1E0
- 💻 www.pc.gc.ca/eng/pn-np/ab/jasper
- ✉ pnj.jnp@pc.gc.ca
- ✆ 780-852-6176
- ✆ Backcountry trail reservations: 780-852-6177
- ✆ Columbia Icefield Centre: 780-852-6560
- ✆ Weather: 780-852-3185 (24 hr. recording)
- ✆ Road report: 780-852-3311
- ✆ Emergency: 911

Yoho National Park
Box 99, Field, BC, V0A 1G0
- 💻 www.pc.gc.ca/eng/pn-np/bc/yoho
- ✉ yoho.info@pc.gc.ca, 250-343-6783
- ✆ Lake O'Hara Reservations: 250-343-6433
- ✆ Emergency: 911

Kootenay National Park
Box 220, Radium Hot Springs, BC, V0A 1M0
- 💻 www.pc.gc.ca/eng/pn-np/bc/kootenay
- ✉ Kootenay.info@pc.gc.ca
- ✆ 250-347-9505
- ✆ Emergency: 911

Waterton Lakes National Park
Box 22, Waterton Park, AB, T0K 2M0
- 💻 www.pc.gc.ca/eng/pn-np/ab/waterton
- ✉ Waterton.info@pc.gc.ca
- ✆ 403-859-5133
- ✆ Emergency: 403-859-2636

- ✆ **Parks Canada backcountry trail reservations:** 403-292-4401
- ✆ **Parks Canada frontcountry campgrounds:** 877-737-3783,
- 💻 www.pccamping.ca

Peter Lougheed Provincial Park
Suite 201, 800 Railway Ave.
Canmore, AB, T1W 1P1
- ✉ PLH.InfoCenter@gov.ab.ca
- ✆ Information Centre: 403-591-6322
- ✆ Emergency: 911

Mt. Robson Provincial Park
Box 579, Valemount, BC, V0E 2Z0
- ✆ Information Centre: 250-566-4325
- ✆ Berg Lake trail reservations: 800-689-9025
- ✆ Emergency: 911

Mt. Assiniboine Provincial Park
Akamina-Kishinena Provincial Park
Box 118, Wasa, BC, V0B 2S0
- ✆ 250-422-3212
- ✆ Naiset Hut and Lake Magog campground reservations: 403-678-2883
- ✆ Akamina Creek campground reservations: 800-689-9025

There is no telephone system or road access in either park.
- ✆ Mt. Assiniboine emergency: 911 (ask for Banff park dispatch)
- ✆ Akamina-Kishinena emergency: 403-859-2636 (Waterton)

Transportation Contacts

Banff Airporter
- 💻 www.banffairporter.com
- ✉ info@banffairporter.com
- ✆ 888-449-2901, 403-762-3330

Brewster Airport and Resort Connector
- ✆ 800-760-6934, 403-760-6934

Calgary Airport Authority
- 💻 www.calgaryairport.com
- ✉ calgaryairport@yyc.com
- ✆ 403-735-1200

Edmonton International Airport
🖥 http://flyeia.com
✉ info@flyeia.com
☎ 800-268-7134, 780-890-8900

Greyhound Canada
🖥 http://greyhound.ca
☎ 800-661-8747

Sundog Tours
🖥 http://sundogtours.com/
✉ res@sundogtours.com
☎ 888-786-3641, 403-762-4343, 780-852-4056

Via Rail
🖥 www.viarail.ca
☎ 888-842-7245

Tourism Contacts

At the park information centres at Canmore, Banff, Lake Louise, Columbia Icefield, Jasper, Mt. Robson, Field, Golden, Radium, K-Country, and Waterton Park, you will find publications that provide detailed descriptions of where to dine and where to shop in the Rockies. Use the following websites and phone numbers to help find accommodation and information about local businesses and services.

Banff Lake Louise Tourism
🖥 www.banfflakelouise.com
☎ 403-762-8421

Field
🖥 www.field.ca

Jasper Tourism and Commerce
🖥 www.jaspercanadianrockies.com
✉ info@jaspercanadianrockies.com
☎ 780-852-3858, 800-473-8155

Radium
🖥 www.radiumhotsprings.com
✉ info@radiumhotsprings.com
☎ 250-347-9331, 888-347-9331

Tourism BC
🖥 www.hellobc.com
☎ 800-435-5622

Tourism Canmore Kananaskis
🖥 www.tourismcanmore.com
☎ 866-CANMORE, 403-678-1295
✉ info@tourismcanmore.com

Tourism Golden
🖥 www.tourismgolden.com
✉ info@tourismgolden.com
☎ 250-439-1111, 800-622-4653

Travel Alberta
🖥 www1.travelalberta.com
✉ travelinfo@TravelAlberta.com
☎ 800-252-3782

Alpine Club of Canada hut system
🖥 www.alpineclubofcanada.ca/
✉ info@AlpineClubofCanada.ca
☎ 403-678-3200

Hostelling International
🖥 http://www.hihostels.ca/
✉ info@hihostels.ca
☎ 800-663-5777

Recommended Reading

Mountain Equipment Co-op's website is the best reference for information on backpacking equipment, tips, and how-to:
🖥 www.mec.ca

Gadd, Ben. *Handbook of the Canadian Rockies.* Jasper: Corax Press, 2008.

---*Canadian Rockies Geology Road Tours.* Jasper: Corax Press, 2009.

Kershaw, Linda, Andy MacKinnon and Jim Pojar. *Plants of the Rocky Mountains.* Edmonton: Lone Pine Publishing, 1998.

Pole, Graeme. *Canadian Rockies Explorer.* Hazelton: Mountain Vision Publishing, 2010.

Sibley, David. *Field Guide to the Birds of Western North America.* New York: Knopf, 2003.

Index

Hike names are in bold. Entries with bold page numbers include an explanation or a photo.

The Photographs

With the exceptions noted below, colour photography is © Graeme Pole/Mountain Vision. Other photographers are credited where known.

GMA: Glenbow Museum Archives, Calgary
WMCR: Whyte Museum of the Canadian Rockies, Banff

5: © Marnie Pole; 7: photo © Birgit Freybe Bateman; artwork "Heritage – Bald Eagle," © Robert Bateman 2008; used with permission of the artist's representative; 23: GMA NA 1363-5; 48: Ron Duke, WMCR V90/278 (PA); 49: © Marnie Pole; 50 left: WMCR NA 66-262; 51: © Marnie Pole; 57 lower: collection of Graeme Pole; 65: W.M. Notman, GMA NA 293-3; 69 left: © Marnie Pole; 69 right: W.D. Wilcox, WMCR NA 66-2251; 81: WMCR V544/NA 66-1108; 92 left: J.N. Collie, WMCR V14/AC-OP/772; 109 upper: © Dan Smith, Department of Geography, University of Victoria; 109 lower left: B.W. Mitchell, collection of Graeme Pole; 112: James Monroe Thorington, collection of Graeme Pole; 118 right: WMCR V14/AC00P/82; 145: WMCR V527-NG-17; 151: Mary Schäffer, WMCR V527-PS-1-129; 163 upper right: © Marnie Pole; 167: John McGregor, Alexander Turnbull Library, Wellington, NZ; PA1-q-264-17-4; 173: J.E.H. MacDonald, "Lake McArthur," 1925; National Gallery of Canada; 177: Library and Archives Canada PA 23141; 184: WMCR V622 NA-3; 196 lower: GMA NA 699-1; 201 lower: © Kurt Hahn/iStockphoto; 239 lower: © Marnie Pole; 262: © Marnie Pole; 266: © Marnie Pole; 288: © Marnie Pole; Back cover, glacier lily: © Marnie Pole

For 26 years (1982-2008) I used a series of Pentax K-1000 camera bodies and Pentax manual zoom lenses, recording the images on Kodachrome films until 1996, and subsequently on Provia 100. Having thus been a technological dinosaur and not wanting to become an outright technological footnote, I went digital in 2008, choosing the learning curve offered by a Nikon P-80. For this book I scanned the 35 mm films for pre-production using a Nikon film scanner and Vue Scan, with adjustments made to these scans and to digital originals using two programs: Graphic Converter and Aperture. I can attest that the film and digital photographs have been tweaked only to improve their characteristics to the point necessary for printing. None of the photographs was taken from a helicopter or an airplane. All wildlife photographs were taken in the wild.

Graeme Pole

Graeme Pole has written eleven books that describe the human history and the natural history of western Canada. He lives with his family near Hazelton in northwestern BC, where he serves as a paramedic.

⌨ www.mountainvision.ca
✉ graeme@mountainvision.ca

Look for these **Canadian Rockies Companion Guides:**

Canadian Rockies Explorer
Walks and Easy Hikes in the Canadian Rockies

Check the Mountain Vision website for *Classic Extras* and updates.